CREATING VALUE

Strategic Management Society Book Series

The Strategic Management Society Book Series is a cooperative effort between the Strategic Management Society and Blackwell Publishers. The purpose of the series is to present information on cutting-edge concepts and topics in strategic management theory and practice. The books emphasize building and maintaining bridges between strategic management theory and practice. The work published in these books generates and tests new theories of strategic management. Additionally, work published in this series demonstrates how to learn, understand, and apply these theories in practice. The content of the series represents the newest critical thinking in the field of strategic management. As a result, these books provide valuable knowledge for strategic management scholars, consultants, and executives.

This new book contains essays on the strategies businesses are using in the new millennium to create value. The chapters cover such emerging issues in strategic management and entrepreneurship as value drivers for new business models, the use of real options and knowledge creation in high velocity environments. There has been an unanticipated increase in "new winners" operating in the new millennium competitive landscape. These "new winners" have built their businesses on unique business models by operating in an entrepreneurial, discovery-driven mode to identify opportunities in the turbulent environment. This book describes the various strategies employed by the "new winners" to succeed in the current competitive environment. Thus, it is an exciting new book with cutting-edge ideas valuable to academics and executives alike.

Michael A. Hitt
Series Editor

Creating Value

Winners in the New Business Environment

Edited by

Michael A. Hitt
Raphael Amit
Charles E. Lucier
Robert D. Nixon

Blackwell Publishers

© 2002 by Blackwell Publishers Ltd
a Blackwell Publishing company
except for editorial arrangement and introduction © 2002 by Michael A. Hitt, Raphael Amir,
Charles E. Lucier, and Robert D. Nixon

Editorial Offices:
108 Cowley Road, Oxford OX4 1JF, UK
  Tel: +44 (0)1865 791100
350 Main Street, Malden, MA 02148-5018, USA
  Tel: +1 781 388 8250

First published 2002 by Blackwell Publishers Ltd

Library of Congress Cataloging-in-Publication Data has been applied for.

ISBN 0–631–23511–6 (hardback)

A catalogue record for this title is available from the British Library.

Typeset in 10 on 12 pt Galliard
by Ace Filmsetting Ltd, Frome, Somerset
Printed in Great Britain by TJ International, Padstow, Cornwall

For further information on
Blackwell Publishers, visit our website:
www.blackwellpublishers.co.uk

Contents

Contributors

Amit, Raphael
University of Pennsylvania
e-mail: *amit@wharton.upenn.edu*

Beekman, Amy
George Mason University
e-mail: *abeekman@som.gmu.edu*

Choi, Young Rok
Rensselaer Polytech Institute
e-mail: *Choiy3@rpi.edu*

Clark, Kevin
Villanova University
e-mail: *Kevin.clark@villanova.edu*

Collins, Chris
Cornell University
e-mail: *Ccollins@rhsmith.umd.edu*

Deeds, David L.
Case Western Reserve University
e-mail: *Dsd52@po.cwru.edu*

Garbi, Esmeralda
Florida State University
e-mail: *egarbi@fau.edu*

Golden, Peggy
Florida Atlantic University
e-mail: *peggygolden@attglobal. net*

Hitt, Michael A.
Arizona State University
e-mail: *Michael.Hitt@asu.edu*

Lévesque, Moren
Rensselaer Polytech Institute
e-mail: *levesm@rip.edu*

Lucier, Charles E.
Booz, Allen & Hamilton
e-mail: *Lucier_Charles@bah.com*

Maula, Marrku
Helsinki University of Technology
e-mail: *Markku.maula@hut.fi*

McNamara, Gerry
Michigan State University
e-mail: *Mcnama39@pilot.msu.edu*

Murray, Gordon
London Business School
e-mail: *gmurray@london.edu*

Nixon, Robert D.
University of Louisville
e-mail: *Robert.Nixon@louisville.edu*

Nonaka, Ikujiro
Hitotsubashi University

Peng, Mike W.
Ohio State University
e-mail: *Peng.51@osu.edu*

Reinmoeller, Patrick
Erasmus University
e-mail: *preinmoeller@fbk.eur.nl*

Reuer, Jeffrey
Ohio State University
e-mail: *Reuer_1@cob.osu.edu*

Richey, Brenda
Florida Atlantic University
e-mail: *brichey@fau.edu*

Robinson, Richard
University of South Carolina
e-mail: *robinson@sc.edu*

Rothaermel, Frank T.
Michigan State University
e-mail: *ftr@msu.edu*

Shepherd, Dean
University of Colorado at Boulder
e-mail: *Dean.shepherd@colorado.edu*

Vaaler, Paul
Tufts University
e-mail: *Paul.vaaler@tufts.edu*

Wang, Heli
Ohio State University
e-mail: *Wang.504@osu.edu*

Zott, Christoph
INSEAD
e-mail: *Christoph.zott@insead.fr*

CHAPTER ONE

Strategies for the Entrepreneurial Millennium[1]

Raphael Amit, Charles E. Lucier, Michael A. Hitt, and Robert D. Nixon

Introduction

The most striking features of business life at the turn of the millennium are volatility, turbulence, and unpredictability. New winners emerge quickly and unexpectedly; established leaders decline or disappear. Foster and Kaplan (2001), for example, found that turnover in the S&P 90 increased from about 1.5 percent per year during the 1920s and 1930s to nearly 10 percent in 1998. Economy-wide tsunamis occur like the six-year "New Economy:" from the IPO of Netscape through John Chamber's lament about the "hundred-year flood" that washed out Cisco's consistent earnings increases (Anders, 2001). Decisions by courts and regulators redirect the path of industry evolution such as repelling Napster's attack on the music industry, slowing the application of biotechnology to agriculture, blocking General Electric's dominance of the aerospace industry, and the two-year (unsuccessful) battle by the government to break up Microsoft. Other examples include disruptive technologies like the Internet that produce not only hype and uncertainty in the short term but also lasting changes like dominant new competitors (AOL–Time Warner) and new business models (e.g., auctions and exchanges) and new hybrid organizational structures designed to capture the benefits of integrating traditional off-line business operations with on-line operations while leveraging the deep interconnectivity (enabled by the Internet).

Stakeholders demand increasingly higher levels of performance. Shareholders expect all companies – not only high technology firms – to increase revenues more quickly than the overall economy and to increase earnings even faster than revenues. George David, CEO of United Technologies, calls it the "5/15 problem:" how can a company sustain annual growth in earnings of 15 percent when business units are in industries growing at only 5 percent? The reality of the 5/15 problem is demonstrated by table 1.1, which summarizes the performance during the 1990s of each quintile of the S&P 500 (sorted by total returns to shareholders, including stock price appreciation and dividends). Among the above-average performers, the median company gener-

Table 1.1 Performance of S&P 500, 1990–9

Quintile of performance for shareholders	Annual returns to shareholders (%)	Annual growth in earnings (%)	Annual growth in revenue (%)
Top	34.0	29.3	20.6
Above average	21.8	14.6	8.3
Average	14.7	9.8	5.2
Below average	10.0	4.7	4.9
Bottom	3.2	1.1	5.2

ated annual revenue increases of 12.9 percent and average annual earnings increases of 19.3 percent.

The "war for talent" in employees has not only increased compensation for the highest performers, but also increased the expectation that work will be interesting and personally fulfilling. When large companies are unable to meet these expectations, the free agent economy of part-time or self-employed workers is an increasingly available option, especially in the United States.

The expectations of citizens and governments are even higher than for others. For example, rising standards for safety (both legal standards and public expectations) are apparent in the mad cow disease and genetically-modified organism regulations and reaction in Europe, in the asbestos litigation-related bankruptcies at *Fortune* 500 companies like Owens-Corning, Johns Manville, Eagle Picher, Armstrong, and USG, in the tobacco industry reshaping settlements in the United States, and in the termination of the long-standing relationship between Ford and Bridgestone/Firestone over responsibility for accidents of Ford Explorers caused by tread separation. Of course, the public's expectations are high in many areas other than safety, including: environmental responsibility, accessibility for the economically or physically disadvantaged, privacy, and loss of control because of globalization.

While this new landscape is highly turbulent and uncertain (Hitt et al., 1998; Hitt, 2000), it also presents entrepreneurial opportunities (McGrath and MacMillan, 2000; Shane and Venkataraman, 2000). For example, there are opportunities to take market share from less innovative competitors by offering new and better goods and services to the market. Entrepreneurial firms may capture existing markets with innovative goods and services but also may create new markets (Hamel, 2000).

Entrepreneurs who seize the opportunity in volatile environments to create successful new businesses or to revitalize existing businesses are the central figures in the new economic landscape. In fact, the number of new business start-ups reached record levels in the USA in 1998–9, especially in the high technology sector. Also, the number of companies funded and the amounts provided by venture capital firms reached unprecedented levels ($15.59 billion in 1997, $27.73 billion in 1998 and $46.1 billion in 1999). Those firms that accessed public markets for capital (growing from 119 companies in 1997 to 246 in 1999) represent only the tip of the entrepreneurial iceberg. A better indication of the pervasive impact of entrepreneurs is the study of

1,335 large companies publicly traded in the United States from 1965 to 1995 by Lucier et al. (1997). They found that more than 90 percent of the companies that provided long-term returns ranked in the top decile for shareholders had pioneered the successful application of a disruptive technology or a fundamentally new business model in an industry – the hallmarks of the most successful entrepreneurs.

The Entrepreneurial Millennium

The bursting of the Internet bubble and the decline of the IPO market in 2000 and 2001 do not mean that the importance of entrepreneurs is decreasing. In fact, we argue that the impact and ubiquity of entrepreneurs will increase, driven by the positive feedback cycle of today's entrepreneurial success, thereby creating even more opportunities for future entrepreneurs. In turn, this will attract more entrepreneurs and serve as a catalyst for a greater amount of entrepreneurial activity.

Successful entrepreneurs represent the new winners who change the economic landscape and cause much of the turbulence. They create new-to-the-world industries, shift the boundaries of existing industries, and cause industries to converge. They challenge legislators and regulators to address new questions (e.g., is cloning legal for humans, other animals, or plants?) and to redefine "intellectual property" in new settings. Their successful commercialization of disruptive technologies (e.g., microprocessors) accelerates the development of additional technologies (e.g., genomics) that, in turn, disrupt additional industries. The new business models they develop in one industry stimulate the development of analogous business models in other industries, such as the propagation of power retailing format created by Toys "Я" Us across 16 other retailing industries. Thus, opportunities for entrepreneurs continue to increase exponentially.

Past success and current opportunities are expanding the supply of potential entrepreneurs. Well-publicized extraordinary rewards for successful entrepreneurs like Bill Gates, Richard Branson, and Larry Ellison attract additional entrepreneurs. Increasingly effective support infrastructures – incubators, angel investors, venture capitalists, and networks of experienced entrepreneurs – are evolving not only in Silicon Valley but globally (Reynolds et al., 2000). Established companies are trying to enhance entrepreneurship as well, for example, through corporate venturing groups (sometimes in partnership with venture capitalists) or new business pilot ventures.

This spiral of entrepreneurial success, greater opportunities, and increasing numbers of entrepreneurs shapes the new millennium. Large companies are likely to become more entrepreneurial but with the turbulent landscape and increasing entrepreneurial activity, we can also expect greater turnover among *Fortune* 500 companies.

Strategy for the Millennium

Twenty years ago, strategists shared a paradigm: a consistent set of concepts, processes and tools grounded in Marshallian microeconomics and industrial organization economics. However, the traditional paradigm is not effective in explaining behavior in a volatile, discontinuous environment where increasing stakeholder expectations demand innovation more than optimization. Although an effective and widely accepted strategy paradigm for the entrepreneurial millennium has not yet emerged, some new concepts, processes, and tools are available.

One example is the concept of *strategic entrepreneurship* explained in a recent special issue of the *Strategic Management Journal* (Hitt et al., 2001) and a forthcoming book (Hitt et al., 2002). Essentially, this concept suggests entrepreneurial actions be taken using a strategic framework. In other words, entrepreneurial ventures develop and implement new business models within which entrepreneurial opportunities are identified and exploited through the application of strategic discipline to create wealth (Hitt et al., 2001). Thus, opportunity-seeking and advantage-seeking behaviors are integrated (Hitt et al., 2002).

In the emerging world of continuous structural change, competitive advantage may be defined by the extent and duration of abnormal profits during disequilbrium conditions as compared to a defensible position in equilibrium. Linear industry value chains are disappearing, replaced by webs of complex relationships where a firm can simultaneously serve as an alliance partner, competitor, customer, and supplier. A company's competitive cost position is determined less by structural factors like scale than by its business model. Furthermore, competition is based on knowledge and capabilities derived from a firm's resources.

An integrated entrepreneurial and strategic process balances commitment to a strategic intent with the ability to sense and seize opportunities as they arise: neither an inflexible plan nor pure opportunism. Coherence and coordination across the enterprise are provided less by formal strategic plans than by sharing the vision, priorities, and assumptions about the competitive landscape and environment and information. Adaptation and innovation are stimulated by an organization's culture and the provision of *ba* (loosely translated as "space"). The result is a true learning organization involving scanning, adapting, learning, and launching new businesses.

Applied game theory and dynamic modeling tools such as complex adaptive systems are in transition from research tools to use in the strategic management and operations of a business. Options are a powerful metaphor for the future potential of current business positions and possible moves. Options may prove to be a more powerful tool than net present value in evaluating decisions.

A strategy paradigm for the new millennium (integrating these concepts, processes, and tools) should logically center on entrepreneurs. Such a paradigm should help new entrepreneurs emulate other successful entrepreneurs. However, it should also be for entrepreneurs, thereby enhancing their success. Entrepreneurs have made little use of the traditional strategy paradigm, utilizing neither the concepts, the strategic planning process, nor the strategic management analytical tools. A powerful paradigm that increases the success of entrepreneurs can accelerate the dynamic environment and economic development by creating more opportunities, expanding the supply of entrepreneurs, intensifying volatility, and increasing the performance of the businesses for shareholders, employees, and society.

Wealth-Creating Business Models and Identifying Opportunities

Several scholars, including Hitt and Ireland (2000) and McGrath and MacMillan (2000), have argued that e-commerce presents an opportunity to integrate entrepreneurship and strategic management research streams. However, academic research on e-commerce is sparse, with little articulation regarding the central issues related to this new phenomenon or with insufficiently developed theory that captures the unique features of virtual markets. In particular, there has been little research on the new business models needed to create wealth in the new economic landscape. Chapter 2 by Amit and Zott begins to address this need. First, they derive a relatively new business-model construct by building on the value chain framework (Porter, 1985), strategic network theory (Dyer and Singh, 1998), and the transaction cost perspective (Williamson, 1975). A business model refers to the structure, content, and governance of transactions that are enabled by a network of firms, suppliers, complementors, and customers. Amit and Zott argue that this new construct, the business model, provides a deeper understanding of value creation than is possible with other units of analysis (e.g., firm or industry) and is especially useful in analyzing interactive, rapid growth electronic markets. Second, the authors develop a model to describe the value drivers (i.e., factors that enhance the total value created by a business model) of e-commerce business models. They argue that the total value created is the sum of all the values that can be appropriated by the participants in a business model – the firm, its partners, and its customers (Brandenburger and Stuart, 1996). Amit and Zott examined the business models of 59 European and American e-firms and found the major value drivers of novelty, lock-in, complementarities, and efficiency to be critical for value creation in an e-commerce environment.

Chapter 3 by Peng and Wang introduces an intermediation-based view of entrepreneurship to explain why entrepreneurs act to take advantage of market opportunities, and why some entrepreneurs outperform others. Integrating transaction cost theory and resource-based theory, they argue that many entrepreneurial activities can be appropriately conceptualized as intermediations which are, in essence, *market makers* by connecting complicated sets of suppliers and customers. The authors present examples of entrepreneurial activities in financial, labor, distribution, and technology markets showing that the information asymmetries (and thus high transaction costs) between transaction parties create opportunities for entrepreneurial intermediation. Those entrepreneurs who can reduce transaction costs for both sides can carve out new market niches. Thus, the large amounts of intermediation needs in the new economy create entrepreneurial opportunities. From a resource-based perspective, Peng and Wang suggest that entrepreneurs who possess and bundle resources to help buyers/sellers reduce search, negotiation, and monitoring costs provide an important service to the markets and have a high probability of creating wealth.

As noted earlier, a strategic options approach can be useful to entrepreneurs when assessing future opportunities and the value of potential entrepreneurial actions. Chapter 4 by Reuer presents a real options-based perspective that allows entrepreneurs to gain access to upside opportunities in the future while at the same time limiting downside risk in entrepreneurial activities such as investing in a new technology or exploring new markets. Reuer examines the application of real options in international joint ventures. He suggests that through discretionary investments, corporate entrepreneurs can enhance value by embracing, rather than avoiding, uncertainties; that multinational networks are distinctive in enabling shifts in multinational firms' value-chain activities across borders in response to changes in product, factor, and currency markets; and that using a real options logic allows entrepreneurship to overcome an anti-failure bias. In addition, Reuer argues that joint ventures can be helpful in entrepreneurial undertakings intended to test new products, technologies, or foreign markets as part of a sequential investment approach. While firms also use joint ventures to leverage existing assets, from a corporate entrepreneurship perspective, joint ventures can be useful in implementing exploratory initiatives by taking on partners with different and needed resources. With data from 121 international joint ventures, Reuer explores the likelihood that a call opportunity (to buy out a partner) is present and how cultural differences, relevance to the firm's core business, and the host environment affect that likelihood. Therefore, Reuer's chapter provides a useful introduction to the application of real options thinking to entrepreneurial opportunities.

Along with the creation of new ventures and the emergence of new industries, new organizational forms (intentional and unintentional) have appeared. One of these is the strategic network that involves the development of strategic alliances. Chapter 5 by Rothaermel and Deeds focuses on three types of strategic alliances in the biotechnology industry: (1) *vertical-upstream* alliances with universities, research institutions, government labs, hospitals, and industry associations; (2) *horizontal* alliances with other biotechnology firms; and (3) *vertical-downstream* alliances with pharmaceutical and chemical firms. The authors argue that previously hybrid forms of organization such as alliances were generally limited to non-critical projects with relatively low levels of complexity and uncertainty. Projects that were critically important or had high levels of uncertainty and complexity were internalized because of fear that partner firms would be opportunistic. However, while many new high technology ventures have the knowledge resources and creativity to create valuable new products, they often lack other important resources to fully develop and commercialize them. As such, the young technology ventures have turned to strategic alliances for access to the complementary resources necessary for complex, uncertain, and costly research and development projects. However, this argument is not unique to the literature. Other research has suggested and found a relationship between strategic alliances and innovative activity (e.g., Stuart, 2000). Alternatively, all firms have limited managerial and financial resources and, eventually, the costs of simultaneously managing a large number of alliances exceed the gains obtained from the alliances. Rothaermel and Deeds hypothesize that the number of strategic alliances into which a firm enters and its new product development will be related in a curvilinear (inverted-U) manner; that the type of alliance will affect the inflection point of the relationship, and that the firm's experience will influence the number of alliances it can manage. Rothaermel and Deeds use data from 2,226 strategic alliances entered between 1975 and 1997 by 325 new biotechnology firms. Finding general support for their hypotheses, they conclude that there are limits to a firm's ability to manage alliances. Past a certain point, one more vertical-upstream, horizontal or vertical-downstream alliance may reduce new product development. In addition, they argue that different types of alliances pose different types and amounts of challenges to managers and, for different types of alliances, declining returns occur at different levels of alliance intensity. Rothaermel and Deeds also conclude that there exists an experience curve in alliance management; more experienced firms can successfully manage a larger number of alliances than less experienced firms.

In their chapter on knowledge creation and utilization, Nonaka and Reinmoeller suggest that creative renewal in industries, organizations, and teams is critical for effective strategic actions in the entrepreneurial millennium. Routines of creative renewal involve the processes that create and exploit knowledge within large organizations. When new ventures and start-ups threaten incumbents, the management of knowledge, its creation and use, increase in importance. They argue, however, that explicit knowledge and best practices often diffuse quickly and personal knowledge of employees can be lost with unplanned turnover, if this is not embedded in patterns of interaction. To embed such knowledge, Nonaka and Reinmoeller develop the concept of creative routines that emphasize dialogue and improvising. Creative routines make complex idiosyncratic relationships in dynamic business systems visible, trigger pragmatic action and contribute to competitive advantage because they drive knowledge conversions, even of authentic, hidden and difficult-to-imitate tacit knowledge. Using three case studies, the authors illustrate how dynamic business systems and creative routines affect information technology, organizational systems, and procedural systems through dialogue, improvising, and distributed leadership. They conclude that the concept of creative routines is a pragmatic way to introduce entrepreneurial processes to organizations, to leverage deep tacit knowledge, and to harness the creative forces in dynamic contexts.

While developing effective business models, identifying, and creating entrepreneurial opportunities are important, the next section examines means of exploiting opportunities for creating wealth.

Exploiting Opportunities for Wealth Creation

After entrepreneurs identify new business opportunities, they must successfully exploit them to obtain entrepreneurial rents. Successful entrepreneurs shift from exploration (a focus on activities and/or investments to reduce technological and market uncertainties surrounding the potential opportunity) to exploitation (activities and/or investments committed to building efficient business operational systems to generate profits). Moving an innovation to market quickly can realize benefits earlier while delaying its introduction may allow further development and cost reductions in production. Likewise, Choi, Levesque, and Shepherd, in chapter 7, argue that a similar trade-off exists for an entrepreneur in deciding when to shift from exploring a new opportunity to its exploitation. They suggest that, on the one hand, entrepreneurs can increase profit potential by exploiting the opportunity earlier and capitalizing on first mover advantages, but, on the other hand, entrepreneurs can reduce a new venture's mortality risk by delaying exploitation, further exploring the opportunity, and thereby reducing its liabilities of newness. The authors construct an analytical optimization model to identify the optimal time for an entrepreneur to shift from exploration to exploitation and thus maximize performance (i.e., optimize the trade-off between profit potential and mortality risk). Their optimization model results in several important propositions. First, the optimal time to exploit a new opportunity occurs when the entrepreneur's uncertainty level reaches a specific threshold that corresponds to the net expected performance of additional exploration activity, adjusted by the marginal performance of mortality risk reduction. Second, entrepreneurs should exploit new opportunities sooner when there is an increase in the unit exploration cost or the uncertainty gap (lead time). Third, entrepreneurs should exploit new opportunities later when there is an increase in mortality risk or in irreducible uncertainty. In summary, the dynamic decision rules presented by Choi et al. should assist entrepreneurs in deciding when to end exploration or when to begin to exploit opportunities.

During the last decade, information technologies have reshaped most aspects of business operations, increasing the importance of information-intensive activities. This transformation is exemplified by the proliferation of electronic entrepreneurial endeavors (both corporate and individual) and the effect these entrepreneurial ventures have had on their more traditional competitors. For example, these ventures have forced industry incumbents to modify their operations and structures, many of them creating electronic counterparts of their own. Electronic diversification through the creation of Internet-based businesses is the focus of chapter 8 by Garbi, Golden, and Richey. They examine whether traditional diversification concepts in strategic management are adequate to understand the world of e-commerce. They argue that the core competence for firms involved in electronic commerce is often the ability to share information, rather than a functional expertise in manufacturing or new product technology. As a consequence, the ability to classify these businesses into different industries, to define the reach of multiple markets, and to establish the interrelationships among the Internet-based businesses is increasingly difficult. Garbi et al. argue that in an Internet environment, differences in firm diversification are not adequately explained by product or geographic diversification or strategic groups theory. They propose that e-commerce, especially for traditional companies venturing into the electronic world, represents a different type of diversification, the logic of which is not based on products or markets but on the channel of communication and distribution. Therefore, the authors argue that channel diversification should supplement traditional product diversification concepts in the field of strategic management.

The role of large corporations as financiers of technology-based new ventures has increased dramatically in recent years to $18 billion in 2000. Despite this investment and publicized success stories, the true benefits and limitations for entrepreneurs in accepting corporate investors as co-owners of their businesses are less clear. In chapter 9, Maula and Murray report the results of an empirical investigation on the influence of corporate investors on the performance of technology-based start-up companies. Using a sample of 325 initial public offerings in information and communications industries during 1998–9, they found that start-up enterprises co-financed by highly capitalized corporations received higher valuations than comparable firms supported by venture capitalists alone. They also found that corporate-financed start-ups outperformed firms co-financed by venture capitalists. The authors argue the superior performance of co-financed new ventures is explained by three conditions: complementary certification (i.e., increased legitimacy), the realization of operational synergies, and better investment selection. They also argue that the superior performance of start-up enterprises with multiple corporate investors is the result of incremental certification, validation of emerging dominant designs, and the reduced incidence of potential conflicts of interest between the new venture and its investors. Maula and Murray suggest several implications for corporate investors, portfolio companies, and the traditional venture capitalist investors. First, corporations are not "second best" investors; they make successful equity investments into new technology-based firms. Second, traditional venture capitalists and corporate venture capitalists may be viewed as *complementary*, rather than *alternative*, sources of financial capital. Potential complementary benefits are derived from the corporate investor's depth of commercialization experience and/or technological abilities and the traditional venture capitalist's wealth of tacit experience in nurturing and development of the managerial capabilities of nascent, and often highly vulnerable, young firms. They conclude that teaming industry-leading firms with new ventures can produce superior results, and that corporate investors are attractive partners for independent venture capitalists as well as new start-up ventures.

The focus of McNamara and Vaaler's chapter is on strategic decision-making by expert organizations in a setting characterized by increasing entrepreneurial competitiveness and environmental turbulence. Decision-making in the economic landscape in the new millennium assumes inherent instability, frequent change, and constant scanning for threats from rivals. The authors integrate several perspectives to appraise how decision-making is affected by this environment. These perspectives include upper echelon theory (assessing decision-making tendencies based on the demographic background of top managers), a decision-aids perspective (decision-making heuristics used by strategic actors and the consequent behavior to which they lead), and the dynamic capabilities viewpoint (the speed of internal decision-making processes linked to the inherent volatility of the business environment in which a firm operates). While all three perspectives are of increasing relevance in the new economic landscape, McNamara and Vaaler argue that these perspectives and others suffer from a common shortcoming. They all generally assume that the decision-making individuals and processes are *internal* to the firm. Many of the key decision-making individuals and decision-making processes may be external (e.g., outside experts in law, accounting, finance, business, and various technical fields) and firms seek disinterested, objective advice regarding major strategic decisions such as acquisitions, new product and business expansions, and foreign ventures. McNamara and Vaaler investigate how the effects of crisis and competition inherent in an increasingly diverse and volatile environment might skew external expert decision-making. Using data from credit agency risk assessments of emerging-market sovereign borrowers, McNamara and Vaaler compare the turbulent 1997–8 period (beginning with the financial crisis in Thailand in mid-1997) to the more growth/stability-oriented 1987–96 period. Testing six hypotheses, they found that crisis conditions were linked to negative (and thus costly) deviations from objective risk assessment models used by the agencies. In addition, they found that the negative deviations were related to competitive factors (e.g., incumbent versus insurgent, and global versus regional specialization). The authors conclude that their study provides insights and managerial prescriptions regarding the use of external expert organizations in an entrepreneurial environment where the stresses of crisis and competition interact.

The strategic decision-making processes of top executives are important in identifying and exploiting entrepreneurial opportunities for gaining competitive advantage in a turbulent and uncertain environment. Top management teams capable of making rapid decisions can enable their firms to be the entrepreneurial first movers in their markets. Eisenhardt (1989) proposed a model of strategic decision-making speed for firms operating in high-velocity environments. This model has become highly relevant to firms in the entrepreneurial millennium. In chapter 11, Clark and Collins test this model in a sample of 66 high technology public and private firms competing in the information technology, telecommunications, and engineering services industries. Five "tactics' can be used to speed up the decision-making process. First, fast decision-makers use real-time information to continuously update their understanding of the company's competitive position. Second, they examine multiple alternatives simultaneously rather than in a serial fashion. Third, fast decision-makers screen their decisions and integrate them into an overall pattern or plan. The fourth tactic is a two-tiered advice process that uses an experienced executive "counselor" to apply speedy heuristics to the decision. The final tactic, termed "consensus with qualification", allows the CEO to use fiat if the group does not reach consensus within a specified time. Clark and Collins' results indicate that three of the tactics (real-time information, simultaneous alternatives, and decision integration) affect decision speed, providing some support for the validity of the model. They also found that two intervening processes affect the decision-making speed of top executives in volatile environments, namely, confidence to act on decisions and an ability to accelerate cognitive processing. They conclude that top executives who are able to quickly assess the competitive landscape and make good quality decisions in a timely fashion will provide their organizations with the best chance of success in the entrepreneurial millennium.

Although the issue of how to manage growth is important to all firms, it is particularly important in entrepreneurial ventures. With growth come challenges as well as opportunities. Although past research has focused on the internal problems created by a firm's growth (e.g., rapid sales growth resulting in the need for capital and trained employees), chapter 12 by Beekman and Robinson concentrates on the effects of growth on relationships external to the firm, specifically, supplier relationships. They argue that high-growth firms increasingly engage in long-term collaborative strategies with suppliers (ranging from value-chain partnerships to equity joint ventures) to improve their competitive position. Furthermore, they often retain and expand these long-term relationships with key suppliers in periods of growth. Beekman and Robinson present two contrasting theoretical perspectives on why new, high-growth firms remain with their suppliers. The first is an economic exchange perspective that draws on transaction cost and resource-based theory. This perspective is based primarily on the effectiveness of the supplier relationship. Performance factors, such as reducing costs, improving product quality, and increasing efficiency, are critical, along with the extent to which the relationship allows the focal firm to concentrate more on its core business. The second perspective is based on social exchange where strong interpersonal ties create stability and facilitate cooperation between organizations. Additionally, trust and open communication are emphasized and detailed and timely information is shared. To test these two perspectives, the authors gathered survey data from high-growth firms in the pharmaceutical industry between 1994 and 1997. The results suggest that rapid-growth companies' partnerships follow a contingency model. A strong relationship between a focal firm and a supply partner is important, but it is likely to explain the continuation or expansion of business between firms only when the firm's top purchasing criteria like price, quality or availability are satisfied. After a supplier meets the competitive criteria critical to a focal firm, a strong relationship can lead the focal firm to expand its business with the supplier.

Conclusion

Businesses now operate in a new economic landscape in the entrepreneurial millennium. New ventures and large corporations must be entrepreneurial to survive, much less produce positive abnormal returns for shareholders. The economic landscape in the latter half of the 1990s showed the potential but the new millennium was ushered in with a vision of the challenges faced by firms to survive and succeed in the new competitive landscape (Hitt, 2000).

Firms must identify and exploit valuable opportunities in existing markets or create new ones. However, in the entrepreneurial millennium, they must do more. They must also be strategic. Thus, firms must integrate opportunity-seeking and advantage-seeking behaviors, what others have referred to as strategic entrepreneurship (Hitt et al., 2001, 2002). As explained in the chapters in this book, firms must develop and use new and effective business models. They can employ tools from other business disciplines such as real options to evaluate future opportunities. Because of a need for greater and complementary resources, firms are likely to engage in alliances and strategic networks. Alliances may thus enhance firms' entrepreneurial capabilities. These networks even present opportunities for entrepreneurial intermediation. The most successful firms in the entrepreneurial millennium will effectively manage knowledge creation, diffusion and application.

To exploit entrepreneurial opportunities, managers/entrepreneurs must balance the need for exploration and the need for exploitation of opportunities. They must seek and obtain the most effective forms of venture capital and balance risk and expert knowledge in making critical strategic decisions. Additionally, decisions must be made quickly because of the rapidity of change in the dynamic economic landscape. Finally, because of the importance of alliances for access to resources, firms must effectively manage external relationships (e.g., relationships with suppliers) (Ireland et al., 2002).

The twenty-first century is an exciting economic time, full of entrepreneurial opportunities. However, it will face complex and difficult challenges as well. Only the fittest will survive. This book provides information on how to prepare for and meet these challenges with effective strategies that will create value in the new millennium.

Note

1   Parts of this chapter draw on the work of Bertrand Shelton of Booz, Allen & Hamilton.

References

Anders, G. 2001: John Chambers, after the deluge. *Fast Company*, July, 100–11.

Brandenburger, A. M. and Stuart, H. 1996: Value-based business strategy. *Journal of Economics and Management Strategy*, 5, 5–25.

Dyer, J. and Singh, H. 1998: The relational view: cooperative strategy and sources of interorganizational competitive advantage. *Academy of Management Review*, 23, 660–79.

Eisenhardt, K. 1989: Making fast strategic decisions in high-velocity environments. *Academy of Management Journal*, 32, 543–76.

Foster, R. and Kaplan, S. 2001: *Creative Destruction*. New York: Doubleday.

Hamel, G. 2000: *Leading the Revolution*. Boston: Harvard Business School Press.

Hitt, M. A. 2000: The new frontier: transformation of management for the new millennium. *Organizational Dynamics*, 28, 6-17.

Hitt, M. A. and Ireland, R. D. 2000: The intersection of entrepreneurship and strategic management research. In D. L. Sexton and H. A. Landstrom (eds), *Handbook of Entrepreneurship*. Oxford: Blackwell Publishers, 45–63.

Hitt, M. A., Ireland, R. D., Camp, S. M., and Sexton, D. L. 2001: Strategic entrepreneurship: entrepreneurial strategies for wealth creation. *Strategic Management Journal*, 22 (special issue), 479–91.

Hitt, M. A., Ireland, R. D., Camp, S. M., and Sexton, D. L. 2002: Strategic entrepreneurship: integrating entrepreneurial and strategic management perspectives. In M. A. Hitt, R. D. Ireland, S. M. Camp and D. L. Sexton (eds), *Strategic Entrepreneurship: Creating a New Integrated Mindset*, Oxford: Blackwell Publishers, in press.

Hitt, M. A., Keats, B. W., and DeMarie, S. 1998: Navigating in the new competitive landscape: building strategic flexibility and competitive advantage in the 21st century. *Academy of Management Executive*, 12 (4), 22–42.

Ireland. R. D., Hitt, M. A., and Vaidyanath, D. 2002: Managing strategic alliances to achieve a competitive advantage. *Journal of Management*, in press.

Lucier, C. E., Moeller, L. H., and Held, R. 1997: 10X value: the engine powering long-term shareholder returns. *Strategy and Business*, 8, 21–8.

McGrath, R. G. and MacMillan, I. 2000: *The Entrepreneurial Mindset*. Boston: Harvard Business School Press.

Porter, M. E. 1985: *Competitive Advantage: Creating and Sustaining Superior Performance*. New York: Free Press.

Reynolds, P. D., Hay, M., Bygrave, W. D., Camp, S. M., and Autio, E. 2000: *Global Entrepreneurship Monitor 2000 Executive Report*. Kansas City, MO: Kauffman Center for Entrepreneurial Leadership.

Shane, S. and Venkataraman, S. 2000: The promise of entrepreneurship as a field of research. *Academy of Management Review*, 25, 217–26.

Stuart, T. E. 2000: Interorganizational alliances and the performance of firms: a study of growth and innovation rates in a high-technology industry. *Strategic Management Journal*, 21, 791–811.

Williamson, O. E. 1975: *Markets and Hierarchies, Analysis and Antitrust Implications*. New York: Free Press.

PART I

Wealth-Creating Business Models and Identifying Opportunities

CHAPTER TWO

Value Drivers of e-Commerce Business Models

Raphael Amit and Christoph Zott

Introduction

As the twenty-first century begins to unfold, e-commerce, with its dynamic, rapidly growing and highly competitive characteristics, promises new avenues for the creation of wealth. Many established firms are creating new on-line businesses, while new ventures are exploiting the opportunities the Internet provides. These developments generated more than $500 billion in revenues in 1999, representing about 6 percent of the US GDP, and a growth rate of over 100 percent per year since 1993. The sale of goods by US firms over the Internet was estimated to be $170 billion in 1999. This figure is predicted to reach $1.3 trillion by 2003.[1] Although US firms are considered world leaders in e-commerce, the rapid growth of businesses that use the Internet as a medium is a global phenomenon. Europe is expected to bridge the e-commerce gap with the USA by experiencing triple-digit growth in this area over the next three years. By 2004, European enterprises are expected to have online sales of $1.6 trillion,[2] which represents about 6.3 percent of total expected European trade. The increase in the number of e-commerce transactions at major web sites (60,000 per day in 1999 compared to 29,000 per day in 1998)[3] highlights the extraordinary growth and transformation taking place in this new business landscape.

e-commerce is clearly generating tremendous new wealth, mostly through entrepreneurial start-ups and corporate ventures. It is also transforming the rules of competition for established businesses in unprecedented ways. One would thus expect the subject of e-commerce to have attracted the attention of scholars in the fields of entrepreneurship and strategic management. Indeed, the advent of e-commerce presents a strong case for the confluence of the entrepreneurship and strategy research streams, as advocated by Hitt and Ireland (2000) and by McGrath and MacMillan (2000). However, academic research on e-commerce is sparse. As a result, the literature has neither articulated the central issues related to this new phenomenon, nor developed a theory that captures the unique features of virtual markets.

This chapter begins to fill this theoretical gap. In the first part of the chapter we derive the business-model construct by building on the value chain framework (Porter, 1985), strategic network theory (Dyer and Singh, 1998), and the transaction perspective (Williamson, 1975). A business model refers to the structure, content, and governance of transactions that are enabled by a network of firms, suppliers, complementors, and customers. We suggest that this relatively new construct in the academic literature fosters a deeper understanding of value creation in this emerging arena than is possible with other units of analysis, such as the firm or the industry. While the business-model construct applies to both on-line and off-line businesses, the rapid growth of electronic markets highlights the need to rethink the unit of analysis in entrepreneurship and strategy research.

In the second part of the chapter, we develop a model to describe the value drivers of e-commerce business models. The term "value driver" refers to any factor that enhances the total value created by a business model. Total value created is the sum of all the values that can be appropriated by the participants in a business model – the firm, its partners, and its customers (Brandenburger and Stuart, 1996). Our theory development is grounded in observations that emerge from data on e-commerce business. In order to identify the major value drivers of e-commerce firms, we study the business models of 59 European and American e-commerce firms that have recently become publicly traded corporations. The value-driver model enables an evaluation of the value-creation potential of different e-commerce business models along four identified dimensions, namely, novelty, lock-in, complementarities, and efficiency. These are explored in more detail below.

Our central proposition is that a firm's business model is an important locus of innovation and a crucial source of value creation. It goes beyond the value that can be realized through the configuration of the value chain (Porter, 1985), the formation of strategic networks among firms (Dyer and Singh, 1998), or the exploitation of firm-specific core competencies (Barney, 1991). By addressing the central issues in e-commerce that emerge at the intersection of strategic management and entrepreneurship, we hope to contribute to theory development in both fields.

The rest of this chapter is organized as follows. In the next section we develop and discuss the business-model construct and its elements. This is followed by a description of the data set and the research method used for grounding the value driver model in the data. We then introduce the value-driver model and discuss the four value drivers of business models mentioned earlier. The final section presents the conclusions of this study and draws some implications for future research.

Theory

In this section, we derive the business-model construct by drawing on value chain analysis, network theory, and transaction cost economics. We begin the section with a review of the characteristics of virtual markets and propose that the received theories of how value is created do not fully explain the value-creation potential enabled by virtual markets. We develop the business-model construct, which builds on the aforementioned theoretical perspectives, as a new unit of analysis that captures the unique opportunities for value creation present in virtual markets. Finally, we examine how the business model differs from other units of analysis, such as the firm or an industry.

Virtual markets

Virtual markets refer to settings in which business transactions are conducted via open networks based on the fixed and wireless Internet infrastructure. These markets are characterized by high connectivity (Dutta and Segev, 1999), a focus on transactions (Balakrishnan et al., 1999), the importance of information goods and networks (Shapiro and Varian, 1999), and high reach and richness of information (Evans and Wurster, 1999). Reach refers to the number of people and products that are accessible quickly and cheaply in virtual markets; richness refers to the depth and detail of information that can be accumulated, offered, and exchanged between market participants. Virtual markets have unprecedented reach because they are characterized by the near lack of geographical boundaries. Any discussion of national markets and regional barriers to entry (Bartlett and Ghoshal, 1989) is thus less relevant in the case of businesses that allow instant access to customers and suppliers across regional and national borders.[4]

As an electronic network with open standards, the Internet supports the emergence of virtual communities (Hagel and Armstrong, 1997) and commercial arrangements that disregard traditional boundaries between firms along the value chain. Business processes can be shared among firms from different industries, even without the awareness of the end customers. As more information about products and services becomes instantly available to customers, and as information goods (Shapiro and Varian, 1999) are transmitted over the Internet, integrated value chains are deconstructed (Bresser et al., 2000), traditional intermediary businesses and information brokers are circumvented, and the guiding logic behind traditional industries (e.g., travel agencies) begins to disintegrate.

There are several other characteristics of virtual markets that challenge the conventional structure of industries. These include the ease of extending one's product range to include complementary products, the potential reduction of asymmetry of information among economic agents through the Internet medium, and the proliferation of innovative market exchange mechanisms (such as on-line auctions). Industry boundaries are thus easily crossed as value chains are being redefined (Sampler, 1998). As shown below, taken together, these characteristics of virtual markets challenge conventional theories of how value is created, and hence call for a careful definition of the unit of analysis for investigating wealth creation.

Value chain analysis

Porter's (1985) value chain framework analyzes value creation at the firm level. Value chain analysis decomposes the firm into its activities and then studies the economic implications of those activities. It involves four steps: (1) defining the strategic business unit; (2) identifying critical activities; (3) defining products; and (4) determining the value of an activity. The main questions the value chain framework addresses are as follows: (1) What activities should a firm perform, and how?; and (2) What configuration of the firm's activities would enable it to add value to the product and to compete in its industry? Value chain configuration includes primary activities that have a direct impact on value creation, while support activities affect value only through their impact on the performance of the primary activities. Primary activities involve physical products and include inbound logistics, operations, outbound logistics, marketing and sales, and service.

Value chain analysis can be helpful in analyzing value creation in virtual markets. For example, Amazon.com decided to build its own warehouses in order to increase the speed and reliability of the delivery of products ordered on-line. By doing this, it was able to add value to sales and fulfillment activities. Although Amazon.com can be considered a member of the virtual market, and this decision could have been made through value chain analysis, this type of analysis may have only limited applicability for virtual markets. Stabell and Fjeldstad (1998) found the value chain model more suitable for the analysis of production and manufacturing firms than for service firms where the resulting chain does not fully capture the essence of the value creation mechanisms of the firm. Citing the example of an insurance company, they ask: "What is received, what is produced, what is shipped?" (ibid.: 414). Similar questions can be asked regarding the activities of e-commerce firms such as Amazon.com. One could argue that the main good that flows through an e-commerce firm is information. Building on this insight, Rayport and Sviokla (1995) propose a "virtual" value chain that includes a sequence of gathering, organizing, selecting, synthesizing, and distributing information. While this modification of the value chain concept corresponds better to the realities of virtual markets, and in particular to the importance of information goods (Shapiro and Varian, 1999), it still falls short of fully describing e-commerce activity. First, it may not fully capture the value-creation opportunities that result from new combinations of information, physical products and services (the realization of which, according to Schumpeter (1934) is the distinguishing hallmark of the entrepreneur), innovative configurations of transactions, and the reconfiguration and integration of resources, capabilities, roles and relationships among suppliers, partners, and customers. This last characteristic offered by e-commerce firms highlights the importance of networks in virtual markets. Second, even though a firm's value chain may be embedded in a system of inter-linked value chains, such as those of suppliers and distribution channels (Porter, 1985), value chain analysis still focuses on the firm as unit of analysis.

Strategic networks

Strategic networks are "stable interorganizational ties which are strategically important to participating firms. They may take the form of strategic alliances, joint-ventures, long-term buyer-supplier partnerships, and other ties" (Gulati et al., 2000: 203). The main questions that strategic network theorists seek to answer are as follows: (1) Why and how are strategic networks of firms formed?; (2) What is the set of inter-firm relationships that allows firms to compete in the marketplace?; and (3) How is value created through inter-firm asset co-specialization? The appearance of networks of firms in which market and hierarchical governance mechanisms coexist has significantly enhanced the range of possible organizational arrangements for value creation (Doz and Hamel, 1998; Gulati, 1998). The exploitation of relational rents would be one example (Dyer and Singh, 1998).

Strategic networks offer several sources of value creation. As Gulati et al. (2000) point out, these structures for collaboration may enable a firm to gain access to information, markets, and technologies. In addition, they offer the potential for the sharing of risk, economies of scale and scope, learning benefits (Anand and Khanna, 2000), and benefits that accrue from interdependent activities such as workflow systems (Blankenburg Holm et al., 1999). Some of these value drivers are explored in Baum et al. (2000). These authors perform an empirical analysis of a set of Canadian biotech start-up firms to study the effect of alliance network composition on performance. They find that start-ups can improve performance by establishing alliances and by configuring them into networks that enable them to tap into the capabilities and information of their alliance partners.

Burt (1992) also emphasizes the importance of network configurations, or structure, for value creation. According to Burt, networks can provide parties with informational advantages such as access, timing, and referral benefits. The configuration of the network in terms of density and centrality (Freeman, 1979) plays an important role in determining these network advantages. Moreover, the size of the network and the heterogeneity of its ties may also have an effect on the availability of valuable information sources to participants in the network (Granovetter, 1973). Other sources of value in strategic networks include improved access to valuable resources and capabilities that reside outside the firm (Gulati, 1999), shortened time to market (Kogut, 2000), enhanced transaction efficiency, reduced asymmetries of information, and improved coordination between the firms involved in an alliance (Gulati et al., 2000).

The strategic network perspective is relevant for understanding wealth creation in virtual markets because the emergence of networks is fostered by the characteristics (e.g., the high interconnectivity) of this business space. Of particular importance is the insight that there is a link between network configuration and value creation (e.g., Burt, 1992), and the idea that the spectrum of potential alliance partners encompasses suppliers, complementors, customers, and other partners with which the firm must cooperate or compete. Brandenburger and Nalebuff (1996) refer to the latter idea as a "value net;" in the context of alliance formation within the strategic management literature it is commonly referred to as the "relational view" (e.g., Dyer and Singh, 1998). It is worth emphasizing that customers can play a critical role in value creation (as lead users, for example). They may work with the firm to better assess customer needs, acting as beta sites before the product is released to a larger customer base (von Hippel, 1986; Prahalad and Ramaswamy, 2000).

We conclude that it is important to take network components (e.g., partners) and their configurations (e.g., the ties between them) into account when analyzing value creation in virtual markets. However, the strategic network perspective may not fully explain the value-creation potential of organizations that operate in virtual markets and that enable transactions in new and unique ways within network structures. For example, it may be difficult to use strategic network theory, or the tools provided by network analysis, to explain the value-creation potential of Priceline.com's business model. This business model centers on the concept of reverse markets for airline ticket purchasing, whereby a customer posts his or her desired prices and ticket providers respond. As this example indicates, virtual markets, with their unprecedented reach, connectivity, and information processing speed, open entirely new possibilities for value creation through the novel structuring of transactions.

Our understanding of value creation through networks of firms and customers in virtual markets can be augmented by arguments central to the value chain framework (Porter, 1985), in particular, the idea that processes matter. However, because of the conceptual difficulties that arise in the context of virtual markets with processes *centered on product flows* (e.g., Rayport and Sviokla, 1995; Stabell and Fjeldstad, 1998), we propose to complement this perspective by concentrating on processes that are *focused on enabling transactions*.

Transaction perspective

One of the main effects of doing business over the Internet, or in any highly net-worked environment, is the net reduction in transaction costs it may engender (Dyer, 1997). In addition to decreasing the direct costs associated with economic transactions (such as customer search costs), e-commerce also has the potential to alter several other types of transaction costs. These include a reduction in agency costs, such as the costs of opportunism, that results from the increased frequency of transactions (because of open standards, anyone can interact with anyone else), a reduction in transaction uncertainty (by providing a wealth of transaction-specific information), and a reduction in asset specificity (for example, through lower site specificity – the next site is only "one click away").[5] Under these circumstances, the implication of transaction cost economics is that transactions are more efficiently governed by market-type institutional arrangements, and less efficiently governed within fixed firm boundaries (Williamson, 1975).

Williamson suggests that "a transaction occurs when a good or service is transferred across a technologically separable interface. One stage of processing or assembly activity terminates, and another begins" (1983: 104). He thereby implies that a transaction is a discrete event. We also build on Williamson's (1975) focus on the efficiency of alternative governance structures that mediate transactions, to suggest that in addition to efficiency enhancements, there are other factors that contribute to value creation (namely, novelty, lock-in of customers, and complementarities). Also, value can be created through any combination of exchanges within a firm and through the market. In fact, by electronically supplying information in real time, the customer can "co-create value" (Prahalad and Ramaswamy, 2000), as vendors can better tailor their offerings to the customer.

Business model

We propose to use a transactions focus to synthesize insights from Porter's (1985) value chain framework with strategic network theory. From this synthesis we derive the business-model construct.

Definition: A *business model* depicts the content, structure, and governance of transactions designed so as to create value through the exploitation of business opportunities.

Transaction content refers to the goods or information that are being exchanged, and to the resources and capabilities that are required to enable the exchange. *Transaction structure* refers to the parties that participate in the exchange and the ways in which these parties are linked. Transaction structure also includes the order in which exchanges take place (i.e., their sequencing), and the adopted exchange mechanism for enabling transactions. The choice of transaction structure influences the flexibility, adaptability, and scalability of the actual transactions. Finally, *transaction governance* refers to the ways in which flows of information, resources, and goods are controlled by the relevant parties. It also refers to the legal form of organization, and to the incentives for the participants in transactions. This definition of a business model suggests that in addition to articulating what is being transacted, the business model depicts the manner in which a firm coordinates and combines the flow of information, products, and services among parties (e.g., customers, suppliers, partners) to enable transactions. The business-model concept draws on arguments that are central to the value chain framework (Porter, 1985), in particular on the ideas that processes (e.g., activity chains) and multiple sources of value (e.g., cost leadership and differentiation) matter. From strategic network theory we adopt the central ideas that there is a link between network configuration and value creation (e.g., Burt, 1992) and that the locus of value creation may be the network rather than the firm. Indeed, business models, while anchored on a particular firm that exploits a business opportunity, are often customer-centric in their design. Such business models can be hypothesized to create more value for customers (often with their help) than do other units of analysis. Further, the customer-centric view of a business model helps sharpen the boundaries of the network. Within the Gulati et al. (2000) view of a network, the strategically important ties are those that contribute in some way to satisfying customers' needs.

Our definition of a business model is applicable to firms doing business in virtual markets as well as to more conventional businesses. A business model describes the way in which the elements of market exchanges are combined and structured, that is, the way in which the flow of goods (products, services, and information) among participants is coordinated to enable transactions. Each business model is centered on a particular firm. In other words, a particular firm is the business model's main reference point. This is why one can refer to a particular business model as "firm X's business model." However, the business model as a unit of analysis has a wider scope than does the firm, since it encompasses the capabilities of multiple firms in multiple industries. A business-model perspective on value creation in virtual markets seeks to answer the following questions: (1) How do the participants to a transaction, especially the firm, which is the reference point of a business model, enable transactions? and (2) How is value created in the process of enabling transactions?

As an illustration of the concept outlined above, we use the example of eBay, which pioneered person-to-person on-line trading and currently hosts the most popular auction site on the Internet. Formed in September 1995, the company runs an Internet version of the flea market where individuals can sell and purchase virtually anything from Pezz dispensers to electronics, accessories and art. eBay users worldwide are estimated at 17 million people, which corresponds to 17 percent of all active US Internet users.[6]

Transaction structure on eBay

As depicted in figure 2.1, eBay is a person-to-person auction site, bringing together buyers and sellers of low-ticket items by providing a common online trading platform. eBay matches buyers and sellers by providing a listing service and an auctioning facility. All auctions are run electronically in English format (ascending bid) and last between three to seven days. To participate in an auction, a trader registers on-line by providing personal information and a credit card number, and by accepting the disclaimer and the rules set up by eBay. For a small fee, sellers have the right to auction and are granted space on the eBay site to display and describe their merchandise, set a number of individual parameters such as auction closing date and time, minimum bid level, and an optional secret reserved price. Buyers desiring the right to bid provide eBay with personal information and sometimes with a credit card number (if using an anonymous email address). The "bidding" button is used by a buyer to send eBay information about the amount he or she is willing to pay for an item. At auctions close, the highest bidder receives an email notification about winning, while an eBay partner, a credit card processing company, charges the seller a success fee with a benefit to eBay, ranging from 1.25 percent to 5 percent of the transaction value.

The eBay automatic notification agent provides the seller with the buyer's email address, thereby enabling a discussion of shipment and payment details. In order to improve the reliability of transactions, eBay has partnered with i-Escrow (a subsidiary of tradenable) – a third party that ensures that the buyer receives an item and that the

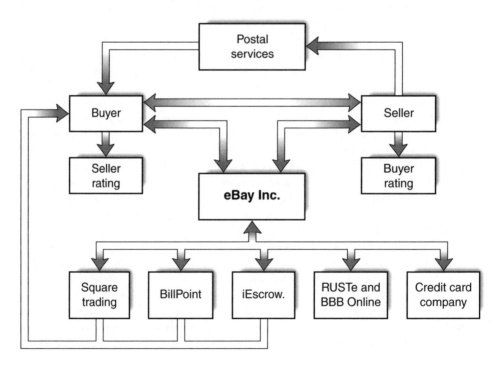

Figure 2.1   eBay's business model

seller receives the payment. Using such a service is optional, but many traders agree to register with an on-line escrow. The buyer then transmits the payment via credit card or check to an escrow service, which sends a confirmation to the seller. The seller then sends the merchandise to the buyer for inspection. If the item is acceptable to the buyer, escrow transmits payment to the seller, charging both parties the previously agreed transaction fee.

Affiliate programs increase eBay visibility and bring profits to affiliates. Each person with a web page is eligible to become an affiliate by filling-out an on-line form and by displaying the eBay logo or banner on the page. Whenever a visitor to this page clicks on the eBay logo and registers as a new member, the affiliate receives $3. eBay's business model enables important indirect network externalities: sellers benefit from an increased number of bidders, while buyers benefit from an increased numbers of sellers. A Beanie Baby collector searching for a Red Elephant on eBay has no immediate advantage from the presence of additional buyers. On the contrary, other buyers interested in purchasing a Red Elephant may outbid him. However, the presence of many buyers is a signal of current and future market liquidity, thus making it more attractive for potential Beanie Baby sellers to put their Red Elephants up for sale. This, in return, enhances the site's attractiveness to potential Beanie Babies buyers.

Transaction content on eBay

eBay auctions offer a large new combination of products, which are mostly lower-ticket items: collectibles, electronics, stamps, old newspapers, furniture, used toys, CDs, music tapes, films. In order to enable the exchange of goods a fair amount of information and pictures of offerings are made available for decision-making, along with traders' ratings that have been introduced in the form of a feedback forum.

A large amount of information on eBay is publicly available. Anyone may view listings of items for sale, and these listings remain publicly available for the few days after the auction closing. Such information on previously auctioned items is helpful to buyers when making decisions about bidding for similar items in the future.

Additionally, potential buyers are provided with a fair amount of information about goods (photo, description, gradation, or eventual certification details), and they can contact sellers on-line if they have additional questions. Information about traders is displayed in the form of ratings and certifications (such as Verified user) reducing the asymmetry of information about transaction participants. Also, access to various complementary products originating from various traders is offered (e.g., laptop and DVD drive). The company itself provides a set of complementary products such as a place to auction (bidding platform) and the place to discuss auctioning (the community), tutorials for new users, the library for collectors (containing various articles and reviews, tips and hints, such as how to estimate the value of a book). Partners offer complementary services as well. These include dispute resolution, escrow services, and insurance and grading by third parties. Vertical product offerings exist in the sense of a one-stop auction – it is possible to auction almost anything, anytime. An auction on eBay thus simulates a typical yard sale.

eBay also offers various personalized and customizable features to members. Personal Shopper, for example, is a customizable feature that remembers a member's preferences and sends an automatic email message informing buyers about new auctions of interest, while AboutMe is a personalized section, where members are able to create a personal storefront.

Transaction governance on eBay

The eBay web site resembles an entertainment park more than a serious market place: members often sell or buy products to socialize and build their reputation as good traders, making friendships through a very active on-line community forum. While transactions on the eBay site are self-governed by participants, seller and buyer ratings are maintained by eBay and provide strong incentives for buyers and sellers to "behave themselves." The third party escrow service (iEscrow) provides an additional means of securing the self-governing auction mechanism.

With the theoretical foundations of the business-model construct anchored in the transaction perspective and value chain and strategic network theories, we now turn to the definition of the value created through a business model. In doing so, we generalize Brandenburger and Stuart (1996) who define total value created (in a simplified supply chain with one supplier, one firm, and one customer) as the customer's willingness-to-pay minus the supplier's opportunity costs. Total value created can be expressed as the sum of the values appropriated by each party. We extend their approach by positing that total value created equals the sum of the values appropriated by all the participants in a business model, over all transactions that the business model enables.

Discussion of the Business-Model Construct

The perspective of the business model is nearly absent from the academic literature. There are, however, a few exceptions. Venkatraman and Henderson (1998) define a business model as a coordinated plan to design strategy along three vectors: customer interaction, asset configuration, and knowledge leverage. Hamel (1999) relates the high capitalization of Silicon Valley firms to a certain business model rather than to the talents of the entrepreneurs. Prahalad and Ramaswamy (2000: 81) state that "the unit of strategic analysis has moved from the single company to . . . an enhanced network of traditional suppliers, manufacturers, partners, investors *and* customers" and Timmers (1998: 4) defines a business model as an "architecture for the product, service and information flows, including a description of the various business actors and their roles; a description of the potential benefits for the various business actors; and a description of the sources of revenues."

These authors offer interesting insights into business models, which broadly support our conceptualization of the term. However, the theory of the "business model" is not well developed in these pieces. The same can be said about the non-academic literature, where ambiguity, contradiction, and misconception about the concept prevail. For example, a business model is often conflated with a model for generating revenues (e.g., Green 1999). In order to avoid further confusion, we offer the following definition of "revenue model."

Definition: A *revenue model* refers to the specific modes in which a business model enables revenue generation.

e-commerce firms generate revenues through subscription fees, advertising fees, and transactional income (including fixed transaction fees, referral fees, fixed or variable sales commissions, and mark-ups on direct sales of goods). They sometimes use variants of these basic revenue-generating modes, and they often use them in combination. As our definitions show, the business model and the revenue model are complementary yet distinct concepts. A business model refers primarily to value creation whereas a revenue model is primarily concerned with value appropriation.

The business model differs from its theoretical antecedents in several important ways. First, the value chain concept is a flow concept that centers on the flow of products through an organization. It describes the processes by which value is added through activities that are performed on certain inputs to produce a desired output. In contrast, the business model is centered on transactions. That is, a business model does not follow the flow of a product from creation to sale, but describes the steps that are performed in order to complete a transaction (i.e., a set of economic exchanges). Another distinction between the value chain concept and the business-model concept is that the value chain perspective is mainly concerned with how a particular firm adds value in the production of a product (Porter, 1985) while the business-model perspective includes all the participants to a transaction, including final consumers.

Second, the notion of a business model draws on network theory by building on the insight that unique combinations of inter-firm, cooperative arrangements such as strategic alliances and joint ventures can create value (Doz and Hamel, 1998; Dyer and Singh, 1998). However, while the strategic alliance and joint venture perspectives suggest that these are usually strategic choices made as extensions to a firm's core competencies, the business model perspective views inter-firm cooperative arrangements as necessary elements to the firm's ability to carry out transactions.

We believe that the business model concept enables us to address a unique set of questions that cannot be sufficiently addressed by either the value chain construct or by strategic network theory alone. We also suggest that as a firm's scope and its boundaries become less clear through the advent of virtual markets and through the impact of sophisticated information technology, strategic analyses of e-commerce ventures will have to move beyond the traditional conception of the "firm" as the unit of analysis. Scholars of strategic management increasingly recognize that the source of value creation may lie in networks of firms (Bettis, 1998; Dyer and Nobeoka, 2000; Gulati et al., 2000). We build on this line of reasoning to suggest that value is created by the way in which business transactions are enabled. In e-commerce in particular, enabling such transactions requires a network of capabilities drawn from multiple stakeholders including customers, suppliers, and complementors. Business models may thus span industry and firm boundaries.

The business model perspective offered here also builds on the resource-based view (RBV) of the firm (Wernerfelt, 1984; Barney, 1991; Peteraf, 1993; Amit and Schoemaker, 1993). Clearly, the value embedded in the business model increases as the bundle of resources and capabilities it encompasses becomes more difficult to imitate, less transferable, less substitutable, more complementary, and more productive with use (rather than less productive with use, as is the case with capital assets which depreciate). The business model perspective therefore takes into consideration the ways in which resources can be valuable, and is consistent with the VRIO framework offered by Barney (1997).

In the next sections, we adopt the business model perspective to explore the value drivers of several e-commerce business models.

Data and Method

Research strategy

A lack of prior theorizing about a topic makes the inductive case study approach an appropriate choice of methodology for developing theory (Eisenhardt, 1989). To develop a new theory that describes the value-creation potential of e-commerce business models, we thus conducted in-depth inquiries into the business models of 59 e-commerce firms. Field researchers took information from various publicly available documents (described below) for each firm, using a questionnaire with about 50 mainly open-ended questions to guide their inquiry. The fieldworkers then wrote up the answers to the questions by integrating evidence from multiple data sources, writing up to several paragraphs in response to each question.

Our research design was based on multiple cases and multiple investigators, thereby allowing for a replication logic (Yin, 1989). That is, we treated a series of cases as a series of experiments. Each case served to test theoretical insights gained from the examination of previous cases, and to modify or refine them accordingly. Such a replication logic fosters the emergence of testable theory that is free of researcher bias (Eisenhardt, 1989), and allows for a close correspondence between theory and data (Glaser and Strauss, 1967). Such a grounding of the emerging theory in the data can provide a fresh, frame-breaking perspective on a previously researched topic (e.g., Hitt et al., 1998). However, it is especially useful in the early stages of research on a topic, when it is not yet clear to what extent the research question is informed by existing theories (for a recent example of such an inductive study, see Galunic and Eisenhardt, 2000).

Using case studies is a good research strategy for examining "a contemporary phenomenon in its real-life context, especially when the boundaries between phenomenon and context are not clearly evident " (Yin, 1981: 59). In the present case, the phenomenon of interest is the value creation of e-commerce business models and its drivers, which may be closely linked with the characteristics of virtual markets. It may thus be difficult to establish the boundaries between the two. This difficulty is highlighted by the frequent treatment of value drivers and market characteristics as synonyms (e.g., Evans and Wurster, 1999).

Population of e-commerce firms

We define e-commerce companies as firms that derive a significant proportion of their revenues by participating in transactions over the Internet. This definition of e-commerce companies is quite broad. It includes, for example, Internet Service Providers (e.g., European ISP Freeserve), and companies that have not aligned all their internal business processes with the Internet but that use the Internet solely as a sales channel (e.g., companies such as the speech-recognition software provider Lernout and Hauspie). On the other hand, it excludes providers of Internet-related hardware or software, that is, firms that facilitate e-commerce but do not engage in the business activity themselves (e.g., a backbone switch manufacturer, such as Packet Engines Inc.).

Companies that derive all their revenues from e-commerce (so-called "pure plays") are relatively easy to identify using publicly available descriptions of their major lines of business (e.g., barnesandnoble.com). In other instances, however, it is more difficult to establish whether a firm derives significant revenues from e-commerce. This is the case for many incumbents (e.g., the British retailer, Iceland). We consider a significant revenue stream to be at least 10 percent of total revenues. It is often impossible to assert if this criterion has been met since companies seldom report their e-commerce revenues as a separate category. In these cases, we used other information to determine the company's fit with our target population. For example, we checked whether trade publications were referring to the company as an e-commerce firm, or whether publications such as *The Wall Street Journal* and *The Financial Times* considered the company an e-commerce pioneer or early innovator in the virtual market space.

Sample

For the USA, we created a list of e-commerce firms that went public between April 2, 1996 (Lycos) and October 15, 1999 (Women.com Networks) using information available on www.hoovers.com. This list includes about 150 firms, most of which are "pure plays." Our initial sub-sample of 30 US e-commerce companies was then taken at random from this list. It represents a broad cross-section of businesses (see Appendix). By contrast, the challenge in creating the European sub-sample was identifying public e-commerce firms in the first place. Indicators of Internet usage and e-commerce activity in Europe, as well as the number of European firms engaged in e-commerce, have lagged behind the corresponding figures in the USA in recent years (Morgan Stanley Dean Witter, 1999). Despite these difficulties, we managed to establish a sample of 29 public European e-commerce companies (also listed in the Appendix). Companies were found on all major European exchanges, as well as on new venture markets (such as Germany's *Neuer Markt*).

To be eligible for inclusion in our sample, an e-commerce firm had to (1) be based either in the USA or in Europe; (2) be publicly quoted on a stock exchange; and (3) involve individual consumers in some of the e-commerce transactions it enables. The international scope of our study not only reflects the decreasing importance of geographic boundaries in virtual markets, it also strengthens our theory development. Theory building on e-commerce value drivers from inductive case studies is less idiosyncratic if one allows for cases from different economic environments.[7]

We chose to include only public companies in our sample to ensure the availability and accuracy of information. We are aware that this limits the scope of our analysis somewhat, as there are many private firms with interesting business models. However, unlike private firms, publicly traded companies provide a wealth of data that can be collected, organized, and analyzed. At this point, it is unclear whether or not this choice introduces a large-company bias into our sample, and hence into our conceptual development, because there are many large, private e-commerce operations, and several large, public firms not included in our sample (e.g., AOL and Yahoo).

Including only public companies in our sample may bias it towards surviving companies. All companies chosen were reasonably successful, as all were listed on a public exchange. While limitations on the availability of data prevent us from broadening the sample to firms that "failed" (according to some definition of failure), we do not believe that the survival bias affects the theoretical development. First, some of the firms we studied will likely fail eventually. Second, the argument can be made for theoretical rather than random sampling of cases, and for studying "extreme situations and polar types in which the process of interest is transparently observable" (Eisenhardt, 1989: 537).

As stated in criterion (3), we focused our study on e-commerce companies that enabled transactions in which individual consumers were involved. These companies are hereafter collectively referred to as "with-C" companies. For example, our sample included so-called "B-to-C" (business-to-consumer) companies, which are companies that directly and exclusively engage in transactions with individual customers, as well as companies that deal with both other companies and consumers. We did not sample businesses that solely engaged in commercial activities with other businesses (so-called "B-to-B," pure plays, or "business-to-business" companies). We made this choice primarily because the quality of data available for "with-C" firms was higher than that available for "B-to-B" firms at the time this research project was launched.[8]

Data collection

We gathered detailed data on our sample companies mainly from publicly available sources: IPO prospectuses (our major source), annual reports, investment analysts' reports, and companies' web sites. A structured questionnaire was used to collect information about (1) the company (e.g., founding date, size, lines of business, products and services provided, and some financial data); (2) the nature and sequence of transactions that the firm enables (e.g., questions included: "What is the company's role in consummating each transaction?" and "Who are the other players involved?"); (3) potential sources of value creation (e.g., questions included: "How important are complementary products or services?" and "Are they part of the transaction offering?"); and (4) the firm's strategy (e.g., questions included: "How does the company position itself *vis-à-vis* competitors?"). Most of the approximately 50 questions enumerated in the questionnaire were open-ended, which was consistent with our primary objective of developing a conceptual framework that was informed by empirical evidence.

Much high-quality data about US firms was obtained from the SEC's EDGAR database, which is available to the public on-line. Data on companies included in the database adheres to a single, US standard set by the SEC. In Europe, however, there is no central data depository. In addition, company reporting requirements vary across European countries, ranging from strict (e.g., the UK) to relatively lax (e.g., Italy). European firms also vary widely in their accounting and disclosure practices, making comparisons between firms difficult. This made the use of multiple sources of information particularly important.

Data analysis

In inductive case studies, it is often difficult to distinguish data analysis from data collection because building theory that is grounded in the data is an iterative process in which the emergent frame is compared systematically with evidence from each case (Eisenhardt, 1989). Some researchers argue for a deliberate process of joint data collection and analysis (e.g., Glaser and Strauss, 1967). We employed this joint process by frequently moving between the data and the emerging theory as we developed our model. The value-driver categories derived from our preliminary analysis of the initial data clearly influenced the design of the subsequent questionnaire that we used for further data collection.[9]

We used standard techniques for both the within-case and the cross-case analyses (Glaser and Strauss, 1967; Miles and Huberman, 1984; Eisenhardt, 1989; Yin, 1989). Within-case evidence was acquired by taking notes rather than by writing narratives. For this purpose, members of the research team answered the questions enumerated in the questionnaire, integrating facts from the various data sources mentioned above. As observed by Yin (1981: 60), "The final case studies resembled comprehensive examinations rather than term papers." Different members of the research team then analyzed these products sequentially and independently, and periodically discussed their observations in order to reach agreement about the findings. These analyses were the basis for verifying the business-model construct developed earlier, for generating initial hypotheses about the value-driver categories, and for gaining insight into what makes e-commerce firms tick.

The final model was shaped through intensive cross-case analysis. We first split the sample into two groups, with different researchers responsible for each set. Eisenhardt (1989) notes that this strategy of dividing the data by data source is valid for cross-case analysis. We then identified what we considered to be the predominant value drivers and compared these patterns across the sub-samples. In order to corroborate our findings, we tabulated the evidence underlying the value-driver constructs as suggested by Miles and Huberman (1984). The next section outlines the value driver model that emerged from this process.

The Value Driver Model

Figure 2.2 depicts our value driver model. As emphasized throughout the chapter, the term "value" refers to the total value created for all parties involved in the transactions that a business model enables. As stated earlier, this value can be measured as the sum of the values that can be appropriated by all participants in the business model across all transactions enabled by the business model. By considering a firm's business model as the unit of analysis, the value driver model facilitates an assessment of the value-creating potential of different e-commerce business models. Each of the four major value drivers that were identified in the analysis – efficiency, complementarities,

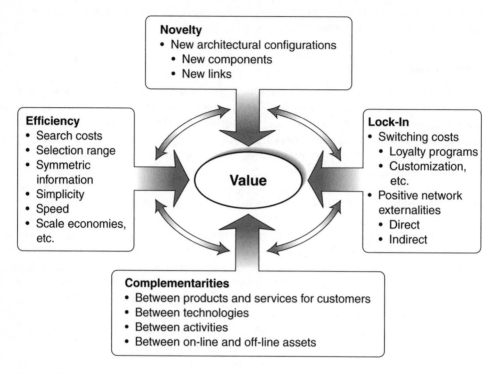

Figure 2.2   Value drivers of e-commerce business models

lock-in, and novelty – and the linkages among them, are discussed below. We suggest that the value-creating potential of any business model is enhanced by the extent to which these factors are present.

Efficiency

Efficiency refers to a particular transaction enabled by a business model. Transaction efficiency increases when the costs per transaction decrease, where "costs" are broadly defined, as elaborated in detail below. The greater the transaction efficiency gains that are enabled by a business model, the more valuable that business model will be. Efficiency enhancements relative to off-line business models (i.e., those of companies operating in traditional markets), and relative to other on-line business models (i.e., those of companies operating in virtual markets), can be realized in a number of ways. One is by reducing information asymmetries between buyers and sellers through the supply of more up-to-date and comprehensive information. Improved information can also reduce customers' search and bargaining costs, enable faster and more informed decision-making, provide for greater selection at lower costs by reducing distribution costs, streamline inventory management, simplify transactions and thus reduce the likelihood of mistakes, allow individual customers to benefit from scale economies through demand aggregation, and bulk purchasing, streamline the supply chain, and expedite transaction processing and order fulfillment, thereby benefiting both vendors and customers. Marketing and sales costs, transaction-processing costs, and communication costs can also all be reduced in an efficient business model.

Autobytel.com's business model is a good case in point. Potential auto buyers are supplied with detailed and comprehensive comparative shopping information on different models and the costs to dealers of these models. This information assists consumers in quickly making well-informed decisions. The buying process is also substantially simplified and accelerated, and bargaining costs are reduced. While vendors' margins on each sale might be lower, sales volumes increase at essentially no marginal costs.

Efficiency gains in highly networked industries are well documented in the management literature. A study of highly networked Japanese firms, for example, suggests that information flows and reduced asymmetries of information, among other factors, are important in reducing the potential transaction costs associated with specialized assets (Dyer, 1997). More generally, information technology is believed to lead to a reduction of the costs of coordinating and executing transactions (Evans and Wurster, 1999). These arguments can be related to the efficiency gains generated by e-commerce business models. They confirm that the appropriate level of analysis in studying value creation through e-commerce is the business model anchored in the transaction perspective.

Complementarities

Complementarities are present whenever having a bundle of goods together provides more value than the total value of having each of the goods separately. In the strategy literature, Brandenburger and Nalebuff (1996) have highlighted the importance of providing complementary outputs to customers.[10] They state that, "A player is your complementor if customers value your product more when they have the other player's product than when they have your product alone" (1996: 18).

e-commerce firms can leverage this potential for value creation by offering bundles of complementary products and services to their customers. These complementary goods may reflect vertical complementarities (e.g., after-sales service) or horizontal complementarities (e.g., one-stop shopping, and cameras and films) that are often provided by partner firms. They are often directly related to a core transaction enabled by the firm's business model. For example, E-bookers, a European on-line travel site, grants its customers access to weather information, currency exchange rate information, and appointments with immunization clinics. These services enhance the value of the core products (airline tickets and vacation packages) and make it convenient for users to book travel and vacations with E-bookers.

Similarly, off-line assets can complement on-line offerings. Customers who buy products over the Internet may value the possibility of getting after-sales service through bricks-and-mortar retail outlets, including the ability to return or exchange merchandise. This complementarity between on-line and off-line businesses is the essence of "click-and-mortar" business models, such as that of barnesandnoble.com. The business model used by barnesandnoble.com also creates value for its partners by cross-marketing their products in Barnes and Noble bookstores and offering on-line customers the opportunity to browse, order, and receive books in its bricks-and-mortar stores.

Customers may also benefit from a range of complementary goods that may not be directly related to the core transactions enabled by a business model. Consider, for example, the business model of Xoom.com, a company that facilitates community building among Internet users and exploits its customer base through a mix of e-commerce activities, such as auctions, sales, and direct marketing. Xoom.com attracts customers by offering an array of free Internet services, such as home page building and hosting, access to chat rooms and message boards, email, on-line greeting cards, downloadable software utilities, and clip art. These services are not directly related to the products Xoom.com sells or to the auctions they host. However, they fit well with the community aspect of Xoom's business model since they facilitate communication among members.

Business models may also create value by capitalizing on complementarities among activities (such as supply-chain integration), and complementarities among technologies (such as linking the imaging technology of one business-model participant with the Internet communication technology of another), thereby unleashing new value.

Efficiency gains made possible by information technology pave the way for the orchestration and profitable exploitation of complementarities. Weaving together transaction content delivered by distinct firms in a business model is economically compelling when transaction costs, and hence the threat of opportunism, are low. However, the reverse is also true: complementarities may lead to increased efficiency of a business model, at least from a customer's point of view. Customers may benefit from complementary products and services, for example, through reduced search costs (e.g., when purchasing a car with the help of Autobytel.com, one is automatically offered car insurance, a complementary product) and improved decision-making.

Lock-in

The value-creating potential of a business model also depends on the extent to which it is able to motivate customers to engage in repeat transactions. This characteristic can be described as the "stickiness" or "lock-in" property of a business model. It prevents migration to competitors and increases transaction volume through repeat transactions. Lock-in refers to the high switching costs faced by customers who consider using alternative business models.

There are several ways in which customer retention can be enabled by a business model. First, loyalty programs can be established that reward repeat customers with special bonuses (Varian, 1999). These programs are similar to airline frequent flyer reward programs. Second, firms can develop a dominant design proprietary standard (Teece, 1987) for business processes, products, and services (e.g., Amazon's patented shopping cart). Third, firms can establish trustful relationships with customers, for example, by offering them transaction safety and reliability guaranteed by independent and highly credible third parties. The business model of Consodata, a European direct mailing firm, demonstrates this ideal. Consodata promotes in-house systems to protect data from misuse, but, more importantly, also accommodates inspections by the French government agency CNIL (Commission Nationale Informatique et Libertés). To the extent that customers develop trust in an e-commerce company through such measures, they are more likely to remain loyal to the site rather than switch to a competitor.

Switching costs might include the costs of switching firms after an Internet user has customized products, services, or information to his or her needs. The companies that participate in the business model often use specific methods to personalize goods (products, information, and services), and thus increase switching costs. These methods might include the ability to set up personalized storefronts or conduct direct advertising, analyze submitted customer information, use cookies, analyze click streams, analyze past purchases, create a personalized interface, target emails, and target cross-selling on web pages. Furthermore, the creation of virtual communities bonds participants to a particular business model (Hagel and Armstrong, 1997). Such communities enable frequent interactions on a wide range of topics and thereby create loyalty and enhance transaction frequency.

Smith et al. (1999) contend that familiarity with the interface design of a web site represents customer learning and thus inhibits customers from switching to other sites. This argument gains strength when customization features such as "one-click ordering," a standard feature of many e-commerce sites, are available. Personalization can also be achieved with filtering tools that compare a customer's purchase patterns with those of like-minded customers and make recommendations based on inferred tastes. This mechanism exhibits the interesting property that the more the customer interacts with the system, the more accurate the matching results become. Customers thus have high incentives to use the system. This creates a positive feedback loop (Arthur, 1990). More important for our discussion of business models, however, is the idea that increasing returns (Arthur, 1996) and positive feedback may derive from network effects (Katz and Shapiro, 1985; Shapiro and Varian, 1999).

e-commerce business models connect various parties that participate in transactions and can thus be considered network generators. Networks may exhibit externalities in that the production or consumption activities of one party connected to the network have an effect on the production or utility functions of other participants in the network. This effect is not transmitted through the price mechanism. Network externalities are usually understood as positive consumption externalities in which "the utility that a user derives from consumption of the good increases with the number of other agents consuming the good" (Katz and Shapiro, 1985: 424). Henceforth, we will refer only to consumption externalities when discussing network externalities. In the context of a business model, network externalities are present when the value created for customers increases with the size of the customer base. Consider, for example, a community site such as FortuneCity, where a user benefits when there are more participants with whom she or he can interact in chat rooms, on bulletin boards, etc. After a new member has joined the community, it becomes even more attractive for other potential members to subscribe. The opposite is also true – if a site is unattractive and loses members, it becomes less attractive for existing subscribers, who may drop out. A dangerous downward spiral is set in motion, which, in the extreme case, can destroy the business.

There may also be *indirect* network externalities that arise when economic agents benefit from the existence of a positive feedback loop with another group of agents. Consider, for example, the business models implemented by on-line auction companies such as eBay or QXL. As mentioned earlier regarding eBay, a buyer on one of these auction sites has no immediate advantage from the presence of additional buyers. However, the presence of more buyers (a signal of current and future market liquidity) makes it more attractive for potential sellers to put their products up for sale at that particular site, thus enhancing the site's attractiveness to potential buyers. Both buyers and sellers thus benefit indirectly from increasing numbers of other buyers and sellers.

The indirect network effect, which Katz and Shapiro (1985) term the "hardware-software paradigm," can be attributed to the complementary nature of some of the major components of the network that constitutes a business model (Economides, 1996). In an auction business model, the complementary components of the network would be the buyers and sellers. Here, the total value created is a direct function of network size.

Although some business models (for example, those revolving around on-line communities and auctions) are more likely than others (for example, those focusing mainly on direct, on-line sales) to exhibit important network externalities, e-commerce business models can be designed to harness the power of this lock-in mechanism. Amazon.com, for example, has incorporated several community features into its business model (Kotha, 1998). Among other things, it has created a "community of interests" by allowing its customers to write book reviews. Even stronger are the network effects created by on-line vendors of video-game software, such as Cryo-Interactive or Gameplay.com, that provide a web location where customers can interact and play games (obtained from the web provider) with each other.

The efficiency and complementarities of value drivers can be helpful in fostering lock-in. A business model's efficiency features and complementary product and service offerings may serve to attract and retain customers and partners. The higher the relative benefits offered to existing and prospective participants, the higher their incentives to stick with or join the network established by the business model. The increasing return properties inherent to network effects then magnify the relative benefits offered, thus triggering positive feedback dynamics.

Conversely, when a business model creates lock-in, it can also have positive effects on its efficiency and on the degree to which it provides complementarities. For example, many auction sites enable buyers to rate sellers. This feature increases buyers' trust in the fairness of transactions and therefore fosters the stickiness of the respective business model. This feature also provides a strong incentive for repeat sellers to refrain from cheating, which clearly enhances transaction efficiency. Moreover, the promise of high-volume (repeat) business generated by a business model's strong potential for lock-in also constitutes an incentive for high-profile partners to become contributors of complementary products and services. There are thus important relationships between lock-in, efficiency, and complementarities. The potential value of an e-commerce business model depends to an important extent on the combined effects of all the value drivers.

Novelty

Schumpeter (1934) defined innovation as the introduction of new products or services, new methods of production, distribution, or marketing, or tapping new markets. None of these modes of innovation, however, captures the essence of the novelty introduced by the business models adopted by companies such as eBay, Priceline.com, and Autobytel.com. For example, eBay was the first to introduce customer-to-customer auctions in which even low-value items could be successfully traded between individual consumers. Priceline.com introduced reverse markets, whereby individual buyers indicate their purchase needs and reservation prices to sellers. Autobytel.com revolutionized the automobile-retailing process in the USA through linking potential buyers, auto dealers, finance companies, and insurance companies, thus enabling around-the-clock one-stop car shopping from home. These companies all introduced new ways of conducting and aligning transactions, thereby eliminating inefficiencies in the buying and selling processes. These cases indicate that the business model has become a locus of innovation. Innovative business models create value through addressing latent consumer needs (such as haggle-free car purchasing from the convenience of your home) and by creating new markets (e.g., auctions for low-ticket items).

The unique characteristics of virtual markets (i.e., the removal of geographical and physical constraints, possible reversal of information flows from customers to vendors, and other novel information bundling and channeling techniques) make the possibilities for business-model innovation appear almost endless. There are a vast number of business-model structures that can be constructed based on any given set of parties and transaction content. However, not every combination makes economic sense. Timmers (1998) claims that only 11 basic types of e-commerce business models can be observed, among them are the e-shop, e-auction, e-mall, virtual communities, and information brokerage.

e-commerce firms can uncover latent sources of value by identifying and incorporating valuable new complementary products and services into their business models in novel ways. One dimension of innovation in business models refers to the appropriate selection of participating parties. For example, firms can direct and intensify traffic to their web site by initiating affiliate programs with third parties, who are compensated for enabling the execution of transactions from their own web sites.

There can be substantial first-mover advantages for business-model innovators. Being first to market with a novel business model makes it faster and cheaper to create switching costs by capturing "mindshare," and by developing brand awareness and reputation. Business-model innovators can also gain by learning and accumulating proprietary knowledge, and by pre-empting scarce resources.

Novelty and lock-in, two of the four main value drivers in our model, are linked in two important ways. First, business-model innovators have an advantage in attracting and retaining customers, especially in conjunction with a strong brand. Second, being first to market is an essential prerequisite to being successful in markets characterized by increasing returns. First movers are in a good position to initiate the positive feedback dynamics that derive from network externalities, and to achieve a critical mass of suppliers and/or customers before others do. In "winner-takes-most" or "winner-takes-all" markets, it is paramount to enter a new market first.

Novelty is also linked with complementarities. The main innovation of some e-commerce business models refers to the complementary content of transactions. Cyberian Outpost, a US Internet-only computer retailer, lets customers select computer configurations along with accessories and peripheral solutions by giving them access to an up-to-date database containing over 170,000 products, including infor-

Table 2.1 Value drivers attributes of selected business models

	Efficiency	Complementarities	Lock-in	Novelty
Autobytel.com (ABT) (Automobile retailing) (US firms)	• Consumers benefit from informed decisions enabled by rich online content, valuation reports, photos of vehicles, and inspection reports for used vehicles • Dealers benefit from lower inventory costs due to automated online order taking, higher volume, lower selling costs, lower marketing, advertising, and personnel costs • Product research is faster than with off-line models	• Complementary services offered by business model participants (cars, insurance, financing) • Company combines the reach and richness of virtual markets with the bricks-and-mortar necessities (viewing, test drive, delivery, service) • Hence, ABT achieves important vertical and horizontal complementarities	• Repeat purchases supported by strong incentive schemes (reward points) • Affiliated dealers have high switching costs because of investments in the extranet connection and subscription contracts. • Products and services offered to end-users are personalized (click stream analysis, cookies, targeted emails, "Your Garage")	• Introduced reverse on-line markets to auto retailing • Compared with off-line competitors, the quality and depth of links between business-model members is novel • Company is recognized as a pioneer – continuously implementing tailored and innovative services (online vehicle auctions)
Cyberian Outpost (Ordering PCs software solution) (US firm)	• Customers can make informed decisions through use of extensive information • Online presence allows the company to offer a larger range of products than offline competitors (over 170,000 products) and powerful search capabilities • Warehouse, shipping, purchasing and order processing information are integrated in order to deliver "the next day"	• Online presence has no "shelf space" constraints therefore a wide range of complementary products is offered • Large number of participants and goods enable cross-selling • Vertical and horizontal complementarities are important for this business model (never achieved on such scale in bricks-and-mortar firms)	• Customers can customize products by comparing product features and choosing according to their preferences • Affiliate programs enable virtual store creation on individual affiliates' pages • Click Miles program is offered: for each purchase subscriber receives points	• Business model enables novel competencies division (Outpost focus on client acquisition, while suppliers on product innovation and competitive offerings) • Integration of information flows enables overnight and same day delivery • Outpost picks product returns at the client's house/office

| Ricardo.de (Auctions) (European firm) | • Transaction actors are either identified or reviewed, therefore clients can make informed decisions
• Information asymmetry reduced through photo and product descriptions
• Clients find online bidding easier than the off-line bidding | • Participants in business model offer many complementary products
• Company sometimes takes possession of items offered in auctions, thus provides complementary products itself
• Strong supply chain integration | • Offers loyalty program
• Partners promote transaction safety and reliability through goods insurance, password, and encryption technologies
• Participant lock-in is created through reputation, building upon transactions history, and participant rating system | • Online auction of low-cost goods
• New incentive for bidding has been introduced (i.e., entertainment)
• Continuous introduction of innovative solutions and offerings (expansion into B2B offerings, life auctions pioneering) |

mation on their functionality and compatibility. The database contains information on many complementary products from partner firms (computer hardware manufacturers, accessories producers, and software developers, to name a few). Each product is presented to interested buyers together with possible complementary solutions, including warranty options. Of course, the database also contains a wealth of information on substitute products. From the customer's perspective, however, information about any of these products is complementary because it enables them to make better choices. Cyberian Outpost's business model is thus a prime example of a novel business model that is based to a large extent on the logic of harnessing complementarities for consumers.

Finally, there is also an important relationship between novelty and efficiency. Certain efficiency features of a business model may be due to novel transaction content. For example, Artnet.com, a European company that has adopted a business model that enables on-line art auctions, reduces the asymmetry of information between buyers and sellers of art (traditionally a source of severe inefficiencies) through maintaining and expanding a database of transactions (including information on price) that is accessible to its clients. This information service, which allows participants in auctions to benchmark current transactions against historic art sales, is novel in the art auction business and increases transaction efficiency. Efficiency can also derive from novel business-model structures. That is, small reorganizations within existing business models may lead to considerable efficiency gains.

Table 2.1 illustrates, in summary form, the results of our in-depth, case-based analyses of the value drivers of the business models developed by six of the sample's firms. The table depicts the specific ways in which the value drivers are manifested in the business models of the three US based and three European firms that are displayed. These four value drivers emerged from multiple case analyses and are uniquely applicable to the examination of value creation through business models. While the traditional value chain, five-force industry analysis, and the RBV frameworks focus on the competitive advantage of firms (and hence on value creation for the firms' shareholders), the value drivers (depicted by Figure 2.1), on the other hand, focus on value creation by all participants in the business model. Put together, the four value drivers distinctively focus on the transaction enabled by the business model, and reflect the unique way in which the network of capabilities, which span firm and industry boundaries, has been configured to enable transactions. The novelty of the value driver model therefore lies in the linkage between the business-model construct and the configuration of the four drivers along with the interrelationships among them. The business model depicts the ways in which transactions are enabled by a network of firms, suppliers, complementors, and customers, while the value drivers capture the factors that enable value creation within the context of a business model.

Conclusion

In this chapter, we draw on a wide body of literature to link the unique characteristics of virtual markets with new approaches to value creation. The theoretical development leads to the introduction of the business-model construct as a unit of analysis that enables the examination of new ways in which value can be created. The business model, which refers to the content, structure, and governance of transactions, is applicable to both on-line and traditional, off-line firms. It derives much of its rationale from the possibilities for business-model innovation offered by the emergence of e-commerce. Armed with the business-model construct, we use a unique e-commerce data set we developed to conduct case analyses aimed at identifying common patterns of value creation in the process of enabling transactions. The analysis of the business models of the sample firms led to the development of the value driver model, which includes four factors that enhance the value creation potential of e-commerce business models: efficiency, complementarities, lock-in, and novelty.

This chapter is a first step in attempting to understand the strategic issues faced by e-commerce firms in the emerging context of the Internet. It raises a number of interesting and challenging paths for future research including such questions as: (1) What are appropriate strategies in a world where business-model innovation has become a dominant competitive force?; and (2) Are strategy tools that were formulated based on a competitive landscape inhabited by off-line firms still relevant in the new world of e-commerce? Our chapter suggests that a shift to business-model innovation may require a parallel shift in strategic thinking towards more dynamic, adaptive, and entrepreneurial strategies. The research also leads us to examine how business models emerge, and how they evolve. Although the possibility to deliberately design inter-firm networks and the importance of adapting business models are increasingly acknowledged in the strategy and entrepreneurship fields, we need more in the way of methodological approaches to the study of business-model dynamics and design.

Our chapter also offers important implications for practitioners of e-business. As managers consider whether to launch or invest in e-businesses, the business-model perspective and the related value driver framework offer a way to analyze the potential value. In analyzing the value-creation potential of current and future e-business opportunities, managers and entrepreneurs should consider the following questions:

- What is your firm's business model?
- Is this business model genuinely efficient (from the perspectives of the company, suppliers and customers)?
- Are complementarities with other related products and services exploited to add to the value of the business?
- Are opportunities exploited to create lock-in?
- Can novelty be used to challenge or transform the current business processes and offerings to gain advantage and create value?

This, of course, is an incomplete list of the questions that managers need to ask. The next step in analyzing a particular opportunity is to consider how this potential value can be appropriated through revenue models. If only little value is created, there may not be much to divide and appropriate. As more of the value in markets migrates to on-line firms, and as e-business moves from a relatively low-risk experiment to the core of major firms, this type of analysis will become increasingly central to business strategy. The ability to understand value creation in e-business is the first step to ensuring that e-business investments generate real value.

To summarize, in this chapter we have laid some of the foundations necessary for scholars and managers to analyze and design business models. The evolution from a focus on the firm to a focus on the business model, which spans firm and industry boundaries, is in its early stages and additional research to further develop the foundations of this perspective is called for. The rapid pace of technological developments and e-commerce growth gives rise to enormous opportunities for the creation of new wealth through the formation and growth of firms that deploy new business models. Research on business models should attempt to rise to the challenges that emerge from this new business landscape.

Appendix

US firms

Company	Core product business	Country	Foundation year	IPO date	No. of employees	Where traded
1-800-FLOWERS.COM	Flowers	USA	1992	08/03/99	2100	NASDAQ
Alloy Online	Portal	USA	1996	05/14/99	120	NASDAQ
Amazon.com	Books	USA	1994	05/15/97	7600	NASDAQ
Ask Jeeves	Search engine	USA	1996	07/01/99	416	NASDAQ
Autobytel.com	Automobiles	USA	1995	03/26/99	255	NASDAQ
Barnesandnoble.com	Books	USA	1997	05/25/99	1237	NASDAQ
Beyond.com	Computer accessories	USA	1994	06/17/98	389	NASDAQ
CareerBuilder	Job portal	USA	1995	05/12/99	179	NASDAQ
Careinsite	Healthcare portal	USA	1996	06/16/99	160	NASDAQ
CBSportsline	Sports content	USA	1994	11/13/97	453	NASDAQ
Cyberian Outpost	Hardware, software retailing	USA	1995	08/05/98	234	NASDAQ
E*TRADE	On-line brokerage	USA	1982	08/16/96	1735	NASDAQ
ebay	Auctions	USA	1995	09/24/98	138	NASDAQ
eToys	Toys	USA	1996	05/20/99	940	NASDAQ
Fashionmail.com	Clothing and accessories	USA	1994	05/21/99	43	NASDAQ
Fatbrain.com	Books and information	USA	1995	11/20/98	315	NASDAQ
Healtheon	Healthcare portal	USA	1995	02/11/99	1825	NASDAQ
Iturf	Community/retail for youth	USA	1995	04/09/99	153	NASDAQ
Log On America	ISP	USA	1992	04/22/99	13	NASDAQ
MapQuest.com	Mapping	USA	1996	05/04/99	335	NASDAQ
Medscape	Medical portal	USA	1996	09/28/99	298	NASDAQ
Musicmaker.com	Customized CDs	USA	1997	07/07/99	73	NASDAQ
N2H2	Internet filtering	USA	1995	07/30/99	179	NASDAQ
Net2Phone	Internet telephony	USA	1997	07/29/99	333	NASDAQ
NextCard	On-line credit	USA	1996	05/14/99	287	NASDAQ
Priceline.com	Reverse auction	USA	1997	03/30/99	373	NASDAQ

Company	Core product business	Country	Foundation year	IPO date	No. of employees	Where traded
Streamline.com	Delivery goods	USA	1993	06/18/99	350	NASDAQ
Talk City	Communities	USA	1996	07/20/99	197	NASDAQ
VerticalNet	Trade communities	USA	1995	02/11/99	669	NASDAQ
Xoom.com	Retail/auction/advertising	USA	1996	12/09/98	92	NASDAQ
EU firms						
AB Soft	Communications software	France	1987	12/03/97	69	Nouveau Marché
Amadeus	Airline tickets	Spain	1987	10/19/99	2,860	Madrid
Artnet.com	Art	Germany	1989	05/17/99	97	Neuer Markt
Beate Uhse	Erotic goods	Germany	1946	05/27/99	706	Frankfurt
Boursedirect	On-line brokerage	France	1996	11/10/99	22	Nouveau Marché
Buecher.de	Books	Germany	1996	07/05/99	45	Neuer Markt
Commtouch	Email	Israel	1991	07/13/99	214	NASDAQ NM
Consodata	Consumer data	France	1995	10/07/99	220	Nouveau Marché
Cryo-interactive	Computer games	France	1992	12/08/98	218	Nouveau Marché
e-bookers	Travel booking	UK	1999	11/11/99	160	NASDAQ NM/ Neuer Markt
Fortunecity	Community	Germany	1996	03/19/99	164	Neuer Markt
Freeserve	ISP	UK	1998	07/26/99	16	NASDAQ NM
Gameplay.com	Computer games	UK	1999	08/02/99	37	LSE
i:FAO	Travel booking	Germany	1977	03/01/99	112	Neuer Markt
Iceland Group	Grocery	UK	1970	10/16/84	11,895	LSE
ID Media	Community/software	Germany	1988	06/17/99	99	Neuer Marklt
Infonie/Infosources	ISP	France	1995	03/20/96	450	Nouveau Marché
Lernout & Hauspie	Speech-related software	Belgium	1987	06/23/97	2500	EASDAQ/ NASDAQ NM
QXL.com	Auctions	UK	1997	10/07/99	105	LSE/NASDAQ NM
Ricardo.de	Auctions	Germany	1998	07/21/99	73	Neuer Markt
Scoot.com	Directory services	UK	1993	03/10/97	1000	NASDAQ NM

Sportingbet	On-line betting	UK	1998	02/22/99	33	OFEX
Terra Networks	ISP	Spain	1998	10/29/99	928	Madrid/NASDAQ NM
The exchange	Financial services	UK	1991	08/06/99	235	LSE
Tiscali	ISP	Italy	1997	10/27/99	178	Nuovo Mercato
Topjobs.net	Job portal	UK	1996	04/28/99	64	NASDAQ NM
Town Pages	Directory services	UK	1995	05/05/99	270	AMEX
Vocaltec	Internet telephony	Israel	1994	02/07/96	343	NASDAQ

Acknowledgements

We thank Iwona Bancerek, Jon Donlevy, Dovev Lavie, and Alasdair Macauley for their research assistance. The authors are grateful to the Snider Entrepreneurship Research Center and to the Goergen Entrepreneurial programs at the Wharton School, to the Social Sciences and Humanities Research Council of Canada (Grant Number 412 98 0025), and to the 3iVenturelab, the R&D Department at INSEAD and eLab@INSEAD for generous financial support of this research. We also acknowledge the contributions of Jennifer Wohl, Janet Gannon, and the W. Maurice Young Entrepreneurship and Venture Capital Research Center at the University of British Columbia, with which both authors were previously affiliated. We received very useful feedback on an earlier version of this chapter from Howard Aldrich, Charles Baden-Fuller, Izak Benbasat, Max Boisot, Mason Carpenter, Yves Doz, Bo Erikson, Sumantra Goshal, Anita McGahan, Ian MacMillan, Paul Schoemaker, Craig Smith, Belen Villalonga, Bob de Wit, George Yip, and from participants at a faculty seminar at the Wharton School and at UBC.

Sections of this chapter originally appeared in R. Amit and C. Zott, "Value Creation in e-Business," *Strategic Management Journal*, 22 (6–7), 2001. © John Wiley & Sons Limited. Reproduced with permission.

Notes

1   Based on estimates made by the Center for Research in Electronic Commerce, University of Texas, Austin and Forrester Research.
2   Forrester Research.
3   Data available from Jupiter Communications.
4   The difficulty that some e-commerce firms experience in establishing a pan-European presence indicates that there still exist certain barriers, due, for example, to local languages and tastes, or to cross-border logistics. However, the importance of geographical boundaries still appears to be vastly reduced relative to the traditional "bricks-and-mortar" world.
5   Note that we are referring to the net effect of e-business on transaction costs here. Naturally, there may be increases in transaction costs (e.g., the costs of monitoring and enforcing transactions) due to the nature of virtual markets as well.
6   As of October 2000. Source: Nielsen/Netratings.
7   The decision to include US as well as European firms in our sample has several implications. e-commerce activity in Europe is dominated less by start-ups, as is the case in the US, and more by established companies (Morgan Stanley Dean Witter, 1999). For example, the UK's Freeserve is a spin-off of Dixons, a large "bricks-and-mortar" retailer, and Spain's Terra Networks is a spin-off of Telefónica, a large telecom firm. An affiliation (past or present) with established companies probably influences the particular business models of respective e-commerce firms. For example, some spin-offs may benefit from the alliance network of their parent companies, while others may suffer from imposed organizational constraints. However, a possible sample bias toward (mostly former) subsidiaries of established companies should not affect our ability to develop a general framework for evaluating the value creation potential of e-commerce firms. In fact, such a general framework should be independent of the mode of business creation.

8   We do not believe that our focus on "with-C" firms seriously affects the theory development. The business-model construct introduced in this chapter accommodates any type of transaction, and any type of participant in a transaction. In other words, it applies to "with-C" firms as well as to "B-to-B" firms and other types of firms. In addition, the value driver categories identified in the analysis apply to "B-to-B" models, albeit perhaps with different weights.

9   We started with an initial version of the questionnaire that reflected a working framework we had constructed early on to bring focus and clarity to the questions asked. This initial questionnaire had been pre-tested on several cases. Subsequently, we modified, added, and dropped questions about two months into the research project, and made similar revisions again about one month later. After every revision, all cases that had hitherto been examined were updated accordingly.

10   Complementarities can be defined with respect to outputs or inputs, that is, with respect to the determinants of a firm's profit function. A profit function that is well behaved (i.e., concave, continuous, and twice continuously differentiable) is complementary in its inputs if raising the level of one input variable increases the marginal return to the other input variable. This notion of complementarity goes back to Edgeworth. Milgrom and Roberts (1990, 1995) present a generalization of this idea that is relevant for the strategy field.

References

Amit, R. and Schoemaker, P. 1993: Strategic assets and organizational rent. *Strategic Management Journal*, 14, 33–46.

Anand, B. N. and Khanna, T. 2000: Do firms learn to create value? The case of alliances. *Strategic Management Journal*, 21, 295–315.

Arthur, W. B. 1990: Positive feedbacks in the economy. *Scientific American*, February, 80–85.

Arthur, W. B. 1996: Increasing returns and the new world of business. *Harvard Business Review*, 74, 100–9.

Balakrishnan, A., Kumara, S. R. T., and Sundaresan, S. 1999: Manufacturing in the digital age: Exploiting information technologies for product realization. *Information Systems Frontier*, 1, 25–50.

Barney, J. B. 1991: Firm resources and sustained competitive advantage. *Journal of Management*, 17, 99–120.

Barney J. B. 1997: *Gaining and Sustaining Competitive Advantage*. Reading, MA: Addison-Wesley.

Bartlett, C. A. and Ghoshal, S. 1989: *Managing Across Borders*. Boston, MA: Harvard Business School.

Baum, J. A. C., Calabrese, T., and Silverman, B. S. 2000: Don't go it alone: alliance network composition and startups' performance in Canadian biotechnology. *Strategic Management Journal*, 21, 267–94.

Bettis, R. A. 1998: Commentary on "redefining industry structure for the information age" by J. L. Sampler. *Strategic Management Journal*, 19, 357–61.

Blankenburg Holm, D., Eriksson, K., and Johanson, J. 1999: Creating value through mutual commitment to business network relationships. *Strategic Management Journal*, 20, 467–86.

Brandenburger, A. M. and Nalebuff, B. J. 1996: *Co-opetition*. New York: Doubleday.

Brandenburger, A. M. and Stuart, H. 1996: Value-based business strategy. *Journal of Economics and Management Strategy*, 5, 5–25.

Bresser, R. K. F., Heuskel, D., and Nixon R. D. 2000: The deconstruction of integrated value chains: practical and conceptual challenges. In R. K. F. Bresser, M. A. Hitt, R. D. Nixon and D. Heuskel (eds), *Winning Strategies in a Deconstructing World*. Chichester: Wiley and Sons, 1–21.

Burt, R. S. 1992: *Structural Holes: The Social Structure of Competition*. Cambridge, MA: Harvard University Press.

Center for Research in Electronic Commerce: www.forrester.com

Doz, Y. and Hamel, G. 1998: *Alliance Advantage*. Boston, MA: Harvard Business Press.

Dutta, S. and Segev, A. 1999: Business transformation on the Internet. *European Management Journal*, 17, 466-76.

Dyer, J. H. 1997: Effective interfirm collaboration: how firms minimize transaction costs and maximize transaction value. *Strategic Management Journal*, 18, 535–56.

Dyer, J. H. and Nobeoka, K. 2000: Creating and managing a high-performance knowledge-sharing network: the Toyota case. *Strategic Management Journal*, 21, 345–67.

Dyer, J. H. and Singh, H. 1998: The relational view: cooperative strategy and sources of interorganizational competitive advantage. *Academy of Management Review*, 23, 660–79.

Economides, N. 1996: The economics of networks. *International Journal of Industrial Organization*, 14 (October), 673–99.

Eisenhardt, K. M. 1989: Building theories from case study research. *Academy of Management Review*, 14, 532–50.

Evans, P. B. and Wurster, T. S. 1999: *Blown to Bits: How the New Economics of Information Transforms Strategy*. Boston, MA: Harvard Business School Press.

Galunic, C. and Eisenhardt, K. M. 2000: Architectural innovation and modular corporate forms. INSEAD Working Paper, January 2000, available at http://faculty.insead.fr/galunic/papers/rrcorpweb2.pdf.

Glaser, B. and Strauss, A. 1967: *The Discovery of Grounded Theory: Strategies of Qualitative Research*. London: Weidenfeld and Nicholson.

Green, H. 1999: Throw out your old business model. *Business Week*, 3621 (March 22), EB22–EB23.

Gulati, R. 1998: Alliances and networks. *Strategic Management Journal*, 19 (4), 293–317.

Gulati, R. 1999: Network location and learning: the influence of network resources and firm capabilities on alliance formation. *Strategic Management Journal*, 20, 397–420.

Gulati, R., Nohria, N., and Zaheer, A. 2000: Strategic networks. *Strategic Management Journal*, 21, 203–15.

Hagel, J. III and Armstrong, A. G. 1997: *Net Gain: Expanding Markets through Virtual Communities*. Boston, MA: Harvard Business School Press.

Hamel, G. 1999: Bringing silicon valley inside. *Harvard Business Review*, 77, 70–84.

Hitt, M., Harrison, J., Ireland, R. D., and Best, A. 1998: Attributes of successful and unsuccessful acquisitions of US firms. *British Journal of Management*, 9, 91–114.

Hitt, M. and Ireland, R. D. 2000: The intersection of entrepreneurship and strategic management research. In D. L. Sexton and H. Landstrom (eds), *The Blackwell Handbook of Entrepreneurship*. Oxford: Blackwell Publishers, 45–63.

Jupiter Communications: www.jupitercommunications.com

Katz, M. L and Shapiro, C. 1985: Network externalities, competition, and compatibility. *American Economic Review*, 75, 424-40.

Kotha, S. 1998: Competing on the Internet: how Amazon.com is rewriting the rules of competition. *Advances in Strategic Management*, 15, 239–65.

McGrath, R. and MacMillan, I. C. 2000: *The Entrepreneurial Mindset*. Boston, MA: Harvard Business School Press.

Miles, M., and Huberman, A. M. 1984: *Qualitative Data Analysis*. Beverly Hills, CA: Sage Publications.

Milgrom, P. and Roberts, J. 1990: The economics of modern manufacturing: technology, strategy, and organization. *American Economic Review*, 80, 511–28.

Milgrom, P. and Roberts, J. 1995: Complementarities and fit: strategy structure and organizational change in manufacturing. *Journal of Accounting and Economics*, 19, 179–208.

Morgan Stanley Dean Witter 1999: *The European Internet Report, Industry Report*. June.

Peteraf, M. A. 1993: "The cornerstones of competitive advantage: A resource-based view", *Strategic Management Journal*, 14, pp. 179–91.

Porter, M. 1985: *Competitive Advantage: Creating and Sustaining Superior Performance*. New York: Free Press.

Prahalad, C. K. and Ramaswamy, V. 2000: Co-opting customer competence. *Harvard Business Review*, 78, 79–87.

Rayport, J. F. and Sviokla, J. J. 1995: Exploiting the virtual value chain. *Harvard Business Review*, 73, 75–85.

Sampler, J. L. 1998: Redefining industry structure for the information age. *Strategic Management Journal*, 19, 343–55.

Schumpeter, J. A. 1934: *The Theory of Economic Development: An Inquiry into Profits, Capital, Credit, Interest, and the Business Cycle*. Cambridge, MA: Harvard University Press.

Shapiro, C. and Varian, H. R. 1999: *Information Rules: A Strategic Guide to the Network Economy*. Boston, MA: Harvard Business School Press.

Smith, M. D., Bailey, J., and Brynjolfsson, E. 1999: Understanding digital markets: review and assessment. In E. Brynjolfsson and B. Kahin (eds), *Understanding the Digital Economy*. Cambridge, MA: MIT Press.

Stabell, C. B. and Fjeldstad, O. D. 1998: Configuring value for competitive advantage: on chains, shops, and networks. *Strategic Management Journal*, 19, 413–37.

Teece, D. J. 1987: Profiting from technological innovations: implications for integration, collaboration, licensing, and public policy. In D. J. Teece (ed.), *The Competitive Challenge: Strategies for Industrial Innovation and Renewal*. Cambridge, MA: Ballinger Publishing Company, 185–219.

Timmers, P. 1998: Business models for electronic markets. *Electronic Markets*, 8, 3–8.

Varian, H. R. 1999: Market structure in the network age. Working Paper (August 1999), available at http://www.sims.berkeley.edu/~hal/Papers/doc/doc.html.

Venkatraman, N. and Henderson, J. C. 1998: Real strategies for virtual organizing. *Sloan Management Review*, 40 (Fall), 33–48.

von Hippel, E. 1986: Lead users: a source of novel product concepts. *Management Science*, 32, 791–805.

Wernerfelt, B. 1984: A resource-based view of the firm. *Strategic Management Journal*, 5, 171–80.

Williamson, O. E. 1975: *Markets and Hierarchies, Analysis and Antitrust Implications: A Study in the Economics of Internal Organization*. New York: Free Press.

Williamson, O. E. 1983: Organizational innovation: the transaction cost approach. In J. Ronen (ed.), *Entrepreneurship*. Lexington, MA: Lexington Books, 101–33.

Yin, R. 1981: The case study crisis: some answers. *Administrative Science Quarterly*, 26, 58–65.

Yin, R. 1989: *Case Study Research: Design and Methods*. Newbury Park, CA: Sage Publications.

CHAPTER THREE

An Intermediation-Based View of Entrepreneurship

Mike W. Peng and Heli Wang

Introduction

Entrepreneurial activities contribute toward significant productivity increase and economic growth in many economies. One of the most important roles that entrepreneurs play is intermediation. In the new information age with the rapidly changing global economy, at first glance it may seem that intermediation is being eliminated from many activities. For example, the development of Internet technology has been thought to be able to bring buyers and sellers together more efficiently, which may result in "disintermediation." However, we believe what has happened in the Internet age is not "disintermediation;" instead, it is "reintermediation" through a different set of channels enabled by new technology and discovered by new entrepreneurs. We further argue that, regardless of the technology level, intermediation activities have always represented the heart of entrepreneurship. Therefore, the aim of this chapter is to sketch the contours of an intermediation-based view of entrepreneurial activities through which entrepreneurs discover and exploit opportunities due to information asymmetries and market failures.

Although this perspective can be traced back to Schumpeter's (1934) classical insights which focused on entrepreneurs' role in "new combinations" and Kirzner's (1997) seminal work which equated entrepreneurship with "arbitration," it is very surprising that after decades of research, a more encompassing intermediation-based view of entrepreneurship has not emerged. This chapter begins to fill the gap by demonstrating how this new perspective which conceptualizes entrepreneurs as intermediaries is able to rigorously explain and predict (1) why entrepreneurs arise and exist at all; and (2) why some entrepreneurs outperform others, two of the key unanswered questions in entrepreneurship research (Amit et al., 1993; Bygrave and Hofer, 1991; Cooper, 1993).[1]

What Are Intermediaries?

Intermediaries perform an important function by linking individuals and organizations that otherwise would not have been connected (Cosimano, 1996; Rubinstein and Wolinsky, 1987; Winkler, 1989). Intermediaries are known to exist in sectors whereby information asymmetries between buyers and sellers of goods and services are strong and transaction costs are high, such as financial markets and international trade.

Borrowing and lending represent some of the most important functions of financial markets. For example, start-up firms often need to obtain financing from banks directly or from venture capital firms, and established public companies also seek financing from either banks or equity investors to finance new projects. In these markets, borrowers typically have better knowledge about the quality of their projects than do lenders. But due to potential moral hazard, borrowers cannot be expected to be entirely straightforward about the characteristics of their projects, since there are substantial rewards for exaggerating positive qualities. Specialized financial intermediaries emerge as a solution to this transaction cost problem, by signaling value to lender's markets as a function of the size of the stake that intermediaries take in borrowers (Allen and Santomero, 1997; Benston and Smith, 1976; Campbell and Kracaw, 1980). In addition, equity investors can rely on an intermediary's reputation or credit ratings to infer the true quality of the projects to be financed. For example, IPO firms which rely on investment banks or venture capitalists as intermediaries are often more successful in obtaining capital from equity markets than IPO firms which do not rely on these intermediaries. Thus, information asymmetries between borrower and lenders can be at least partially solved through intermediation. In a nutshell, "information asymmetries may be a primary reason that [financial] intermediaries exist" (Leland and Pyle, 1977: 383).

Similarly, information asymmetries are pervasive in international trade, which is characterized by the geographic and cultural separation between buyers and sellers (Peng, 1998). Given the uncertainties, international transaction costs, which are virtually by definition higher than domestic transaction costs, may deter a lot of exchanges from taking place. International trade intermediaries, such as export trading companies, thus serve as a bridge connecting domestic producers and foreign buyers (Peng and Ilinitch, 1998). Specifically, trade intermediaries can conduct market research for prospective exporters, negotiate the deal on their behalf, and help enforce the contract in order to minimize the information asymmetries between exporters and importers. While clearly under-studied, international trade intermediaries (e.g., the East India Company of Great Britain, the East Indies Company of the Netherlands, and Mitsui of Japan) played a significant role in the early development of the global economy, and, due to their inherent importance, have experienced a revival in recent international business practice and research (Peng et al., 2000; Peng and York, 2001; Perry, 1992).

In sum, it is widely acknowledged that intermediaries are especially likely to emerge in sectors whereby information asymmetries are considerable. Extending this logic, in the next section we suggest that many entrepreneur activities may be fruitfully conceptualized as intermediaries.

Entrepreneurial Activities and Intermediation

Markets are interlocking economic relationships among a diverse set of buyers and sellers of goods and services, coordinated by independent companies (and sometimes alliances). Entrepreneurs discover and exploit market opportunities (Spulber, 1998). In fact, the following analysis shows that many of these market-making entrepreneurial activities are exactly intermediation activities. While entrepreneurial activities can be found in almost all kinds of markets, here we illustrate four important markets: financial, labor, distribution, and technology.

As discussed earlier, the role played by intermediaries in *financial* markets is hardly disputed. They build market bridges by making unobservable aspects of the transaction more transparent (e.g., requiring and processing more information of borrowers for lenders), by signaling the soundness of the transaction (e.g., investing their own capital in start-ups), and by leveraging more observable aspects of the transaction (e.g., the reputation of financial intermediaries). For example, venture capitalists emerge to combat market failures in start-up financing by literally creating a new market (Amit et al., 1998; Bygrave and Timmons, 1992). Their growth in the 1990s underscores the importance of such a new market. In the United States, total venture capital investment rose from less than $5 billion in the early 1990s to $60 billion in 1999. The growth was particularly strong in the technology sector: approximately $84 billion of the $105 billion invested by venture capitalists in 2000 was sunk into Internet companies.[2] In recent decades, similar growth occurred in Europe (Bygrave and Timmons, 1992; Manigart, 1994).

However, intermediaries are not only active in financial markets. Traditional *labor* markets are similarly characterized by high search and negotiation costs between employers and laborers. Entrepreneurs such as Manpower discovered and exploited these market imperfections in traditional labor markets through the creation of a new labor market whose hallmark is temporary employment. Specifically, these entrepreneurs help both sides of the transaction save search and negotiation costs by serving as go-between agents for employers and employees. Otherwise, the search and negotiation costs between thousands of firms and millions of employees would have been prohibitive. In the late 1990s, Manpower annually provided training and employment to more than 2 million people, while General Motors, the largest "traditional" US employer, employed about 400,000 people. The fact that Manpower currently "employs" more people than General Motors indicates the importance of this new, temporary labor market carved out by entrepreneurs. According to one estimate (Matusik and Hill, 1998: 680), approximately 10 percent of the US workforce (over 12 million individuals) participated in this new labor market at the dawn of the twenty-first century.

Similarly, entrepreneurs in *distribution* industries bring buyers and sellers to one place by saving transaction costs for both sides. Consider, for example, Amazon.com, which carries 3 million titles of books and CDs (*Fortune*, 1999b). It buys from hundreds of publishers and sells to millions of buyers. Imagine in contrast the high costs of marketing and sales that would be incurred if publishers wanted to directly reach that many potential customers by themselves. Likewise, Amazon.com customers also gain tremendously in terms of reduced search costs, in the form of reduced (or eliminated) travel time to different bookstores as well as cheaper prices.

Finally, tremendous entrepreneurial activities in *technology* markets connect suppliers and end users in their own distinguished ways. Examples of these firms include software developers (e.g., Microsoft) and engineering firms (e.g., AMG), among others. The emergence of enterprise software firms serves as a case in point (*Fortune*, 1998). These firms (e.g., SAP, Oracle, PeopleSoft, and J. D. Edwards) use standard computer hardware and Windows-type applications from their suppliers, and then develop proprietary software to automate finance, manufacturing, and human resources for large corporations. Further, some enterprise software can electronically link companies to their customers, dealers, and suppliers. The new market they have created has been spectacular: from less than $1 billion sales in 1990, it grew to $23 billion in 1998, and is estimated to reach $84 billion by 2004 (*Fortune*, 1998).

Overall, many entrepreneurial activities in a variety of markets can be fruitfully conceptualized as intermediaries which are, in essence, *market makers* by connecting complicated sets of suppliers and customers. The presence of asymmetric information, thus high transaction costs, between pairs of transaction parties, such as lenders–borrowers, employers–employees, suppliers–buyers, and developers–end users, creates an opportunity for intermediation, which enables entrepreneurs who can save transaction costs for both sides to carve out new market niches.

Two Assumptions

Our arguments leading to an intermediation-based view of entrepreneurship hinge on two main assumptions. First, we assume a disequilibrium world in which entrepreneurial opportunities always exist (Shane and Venkataraman, 2000: 220–1). In an equilibrium, entrepreneurial opportunities either do not exist or are randomly distributed. Since the days of Joseph Schumpeter (1934), it is the dissatisfaction with the neoclassical equilibrium approach that has led to the development of entrepreneurship research (Kirzner, 1997). A second assumption is that there are persistent market failures due to information asymmetries, bounded rationality, and opportunism. Such market failures may result from transaction costs that are too prohibitive for transaction parties (Williamson, 1985). While markets do not always fail, transaction costs cannot be reduced to zero, thus always leaving room for further, innovative ways of transaction cost reduction, a role that entrepreneurs play.

These two assumptions enable us to provide insights in explaining and predicting (1) why entrepreneurs arise and exist at all; and (2) why some of them outperform others, which are two of the key building blocks for a theory of entrepreneurship (Amit et al., 1993: 815). Toward that end, the proposed new research agenda centers on an eclectic integration of two influential schools of thought, transaction cost and resource-based perspectives.

Why Do Entrepreneurs Exist? A Transaction Cost Perspective

Viewed from a transaction cost perspective, the fundamental role of entrepreneurs is to lower the transaction costs between two parties involved in a transaction. According to Williamson (1985), transaction costs can be divided into three key constituent components: the *ex ante* search costs and negotiation costs, and the *ex post* monitoring/enforcement costs. Sellers and buyers can trade directly (e.g., private firms go public directly without intermediaries; manufacturers export directly to overseas markets) or indirectly through intermediaries. Transaction cost theory posits that firms will attempt to minimize the combination of search, negotiation, and monitoring/enforcement costs when making governance choices. To succeed, entrepreneurs as intermediaries must lower the transaction costs relative to the other, direct trade mode; otherwise, there will be no rationale for their existence (Peng and Ilinitch, 1998; Peng and York, 2001).

Search costs are the *ex ante* costs to overcome information asymmetries. Buyers and sellers constantly search for the best deal to maximize the gains of trade. In a world of perfect information, entrepreneurial profits through intermediation are not likely to exist because nobody needs intermediaries to lower search costs. But such a condition is not likely to hold in the real world (Kirzner, 1997). As a result, entrepreneurs who can lower the search costs for buyers and sellers are likely to emerge. However, not all industry, sector, and geographic markets are characterized by the same degree of information asymmetry; some are more severe than others. The stronger the information asymmetries, the more likely the emergence of entrepreneurs to profit from intermediation or arbitrage activities. For example, complex industries, distant foreign markets, and chaotic economic transitions, all of which suffer from a high level of information asymmetries, may be a hotbed for entrepreneurs taking advantage of such asymmetries (Peng, 2001; Peng et al., 2000).

While search costs may be high for pairs of buyers and sellers under the condition of high information asymmetries, the same condition may also lead to high *negotiation* costs. In the extreme case, search costs may be too high for both parties to find each other, thus rendering any negotiation impossible. For buyers and sellers that do start to negotiate, they confront a high level of information asymmetries, because, *a priori*, both sides do not know the extent to which the other side is willing to compromise (Lewicki et al., 1994). Consider international trade negotiations, where both sides may speak different languages and have different negotiation norms and expectations. It is not surprising that intermediaries who can reduce the cultural distance between both sides by speaking multiple languages and understanding the needs of both sides can lower negotiation costs (Peng, 1998).

Supportive evidence comes from venture capital studies in the United States (Fiet, 1996), Canada (Amit et al., 1998), Western Europe (Manigart, 1994; Sapienza et al., 1996), and also transition economies such as Hungary (Karsai et al., 1997). Venture capitalists are disproportionately more prominent in industries where information asymmetries are high (e.g., biotechnology, software, and communications) than in "routine" industries (e.g., restaurants and retail outlets) (Amit et al., 1998). In contrast, in markets where information asymmetries are more manageable, search and negotiation costs for buyers and sellers may be more acceptable, thus reducing the demand for intermediaries. The recently emerged markets for on-line investing can serve as a case in point, whereby all sorts of high-quality data are available, most in real time, resulting in a movement which can be summarized as "Who needs a broker?".

In addition to minimizing both search and negotiation costs, buyers' and sellers' governance choice also needs to consider the *monitoring* and *enforcement* side of the cost equation. Once market research is finished, negotiations concluded, and contracts signed, the next thing that buyers and sellers are concerned with is the monitoring of contractual obligations and enforcing contractual performance, if necessary. Financial intermediaries, for example, specialize in delegated monitoring (Diamond, 1984). Rather than directly lending to companies, investors place their funds with financial intermediaries who then screen and lend to companies. There are mutual advantages for both investors and intermediaries. Investors can take advantage of intermediaries who are specialists in dealing with and monitoring certain kinds of start-ups in order to reduce information asymmetries between investors and companies. By monitoring many borrowers, intermediaries are able to reduce the costs of monitoring.

However, for the same reason information asymmetries between buyers and sellers may prevent some transactions from taking place, information asymmetries between either party (i.e., buyers or sellers) and entrepreneurs who stand in the middle as intermediaries may also lead to transaction hazards (Robbie et al., 1997). Specifically, intermediaries are agents for their clients on both sides (Gifford, 1997; Norton, 1995). These agents may have incentives to behave in ways not always in the best interest of their principals, such as monopolizing communication between buyers and sellers, not paying attention to their principals' needs, or simply failing to perform as promised. As a result, buyers and sellers employing entrepreneurs as their intermediaries need to compare the monitoring/enforcement costs of going through the intermediaries *vis-à-vis* the monitoring/enforcement costs of going direct to market (Peng and Ilinitch, 1998).

If these agency costs are deemed too high, buyers and/or sellers may (1) opt to integrate the intermediary function, i.e., going direct to market; (2) switch agents by using a new set of entrepreneurs as intermediaries; and/or (3) quit transacting at all. None of these options is attractive to entrepreneurs who want to preserve their intermediation profits. Therefore, entrepreneurs' chances of being selected and retained by their principals also depend on whether they can assure their clients that the potential agency costs will be less than the monitoring/enforcement costs these buyers or sellers would have incurred when engaging in direct trade. As a result, entrepreneurs have an incentive to minimize the information asymmetries between themselves and their principals in order to enhance entrepreneurs' chances of survival and success (Bowen and Jones, 1986).

As intermediaries, venture capitalists are found to employ a number of tactics to reduce information asymmetries between themselves and the start-ups in which they invest, such as formal business plan evaluation (MacMillan et al., 1985) and informal relationships with the venture team (Harrison et al., 1997). On the other hand, venture capitalists are also being monitored by their own investors in order to reduce their information asymmetries (Robbie et al., 1997). Specifically, venture capitalists have a marked preference for serial business founders, especially those with a good track record and/or previous deals with the same venture capitalists, because of reduced information asymmetries between the two sides.

Overall, entrepreneurs arise as intermediaries to take advantage of information asymmetries separating buyers and sellers. Specifically, they serve to lower search, negotiation, and monitoring/enforcement costs of the transaction process by linking buyers and sellers together. On the other hand, since transaction cost theory is often used to explain and predict the choice of organizational form, most existing work in this area takes the point of view of principals, examining their governance choices (e.g., export directly or via intermediaries). As a result, little is known about what determines the success or failure of entrepreneurs who stand in the middle of the process. In the next section, we employ a resource-based framework to approach the issue from the entrepreneurs' standpoint, investigating how some entrepreneurs outperform others.

How Do Entrepreneurs Perform? A Resource-Based Approach

Although transaction cost theory provides insights regarding why entrepreneurs as intermediaries exist, it assumes stronger bargaining power on the part of buyers and sellers as principals interested in structuring their governance choices, and implicitly treats intermediaries as passive agents waiting to be selected (or bypassed). This assumption, however, may not hold when we consider intermediaries as entrepreneurs. In contrast, entrepreneurs are likely to be aggressive, proactive, and interested in enhancing their own odds of being selected and successful by building up their competitive resources and capabilities (Barney, 1991; Teece et al., 1997). As a result, the resource-based view of the firm (Barney, 1991; Hitt et al., 1999) enables us to understand what leads to superior entrepreneurial performance. Simply put, the resource-based view argues that valuable, rare, and hard-to-imitate resources are sources of competitive advantage. Thus, entrepreneurs with these resources will be more likely to outperform their competitors. We will discuss these resources from the perspective of minimizing search, negotiation, and monitoring costs, and advance the proposition (see figure 3.1) that as long as entrepreneurs possess resources that will help buyers/sellers lower these three kinds of costs, their services will be sought, their survival viable, and their success likely (Peng and York, 2001).

First, in terms of search cost minimizing, entrepreneurs with unique and hard-to-imitate knowledge and expertise of the transaction process between existing and potential sets of buyers and sellers stand a better chance of being selected and successful (Grant, 1996). The best intermediaries are likely to have the best knowledge of the information asymmetries that make existing transactions inefficient and deter other transactions from taking place. Take the example of Amazon.com. It had to know what books would sell, and know how selling products via the Internet could result in lower costs. However, it is obvious that Amazon.com's knowledge of the book market was *not* unique. Barnes and Noble, for example, has been in the book business for 35 years. In 1998, Barnes and Noble sold $35 billion books with a 15 percent US market share, while Amazon.com sold $600 million with a 2 percent market share

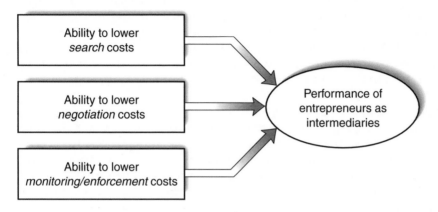

Figure 3.1   What determines the performance of entrepreneurs as intermediaries?
Source: Adapted from Peng and York (2001)

(*Fortune*, 1999c). Amazon.com's knowledge of how Internet would revolutionize the ways products are bought and sold was also not unique; consider Internet start-ups which ventured into other industries at about the same time, such as eBay and e.Schwab. However, the unique knowledge that Amazon.com did possess was that it was the first one to observe the information asymmetries separating two markets (books and Internet technology) and explored an innovative way to connect them. Amazon.com not only discovered that customers often have to search several traditional bookstores to get the books they want, but also leveraged such knowledge by building the world's largest book warehouses, which ironically are "brick-and-mortar," to fill on-line orders (Kotha and Dooley, 1999). Perhaps the ability to explore these opportunities, by itself, is not hard to imitate by competitors; however, the first mover advantage that Amazon obtained and the subsequent success due to path-dependent capabilities are not easily copied by other competitors.

Second, entrepreneurs who can most effectively lower negotiation costs of the transaction process for buyers and sellers will also perform better. Negotiation costs not only include the direct costs of personnel involved and the logistical and travel costs of conducting negotiations (which, for example, can be substantial in international trade), but also include the costs of potential hazard when dealing with unfamiliar negotiation norms (Lewicki et al., 1994). One important reason for negotiation breakdown is asymmetric information (Spulber, 1998: 147). For inexperienced buyers and sellers, their lack of knowledge in certain markets is often compounded by their lack of understanding of, and sensitivity to, the intricacies of industry- and/or culture-specific negotiation norms. Even when they try to handle the negotiations by themselves, they may find themselves parties to bad deals, i.e., "lemons" (Akerlof, 1970). As such, they may find negotiations with unfamiliar parties especially complex, frustrating, and troublesome.

In contrast, entrepreneurs with valuable and unique knowledge and expertise in negotiation can often lower negotiation costs to a level below their competitors. Such knowledge and expertise include their experience in negotiating such contracts and their ability to prevent and resolve misunderstanding due to language, cultural, and industry-norm gaps. And perhaps most importantly, the unique culture of the firm and the quality of teamwork are often the fundamental reason why some entrepreneurs excel at lowering negotiation costs. These resources and capabilities are rare and extremely difficult to imitate due to their causally ambiguous and socially complex nature.

Finally, entrepreneurs who can most effectively lower monitoring and enforcement costs by reducing information asymmetries between themselves and their principals will have better performance (Robbie et al., 1997). Entrepreneurs face a serious dilemma: on the one hand, their very existence depends on the information asymmetries between potential buyers and sellers; reducing such asymmetries is not only costly, but may also seriously undermine their business. Furthermore, a lot of entrepreneurial activities are not directly verifiable, even if entrepreneurs are willing to share such information. On the other hand, the new information asymmetries introduced in a principal–agent relationship between buyers/sellers and entrepreneurs may deter potential buyers and sellers from entering exchange relationships with entrepreneurs. The challenges for entrepreneurs, therefore, are (1) how to ensure that the monitoring/enforcement costs of using their services are lower than the monitoring/enforcement costs that buyers and sellers would have incurred should they trade directly (Fingleton, 1997); and (2) how to do so in a way better than their competitors (Peng and York, 2001).

A key strategy for entrepreneurs is to use observable actions, which "speak louder than words," to signal to principals that they are trustworthy (Harrison et al., 1997). In this sense, the best-performing entrepreneurs are likely to be those with the best signaling capability (Leland and Pyle, 1977; Spence, 1973). Two behavioral measures of signaling capability are highlighted here. First, a key behavioral measure is frequent, open, and timely communication in order to ensure goal congruence between entrepreneurs and their principals, as found in venture capitalist start-up relations (Cable and Shane, 1997; Gorman and Sahlman, 1989; Sapienza, 1992; Sapienza and Gupta, 1994; Sapienza and Korsgaard, 1996). Second, entrepreneurs can also leverage their reputation, which is often earned through years (and sometimes decades) of hard work, as a behavioral measure to signal their credibility as intermediaries to principals (Chemmanur and Fulghieri, 1994). This seems to be the case when established financial intermediaries entered electronic commerce with a strong existing reputation, such as e.Schwab (*Fortune*, 1999a).

However, not all entrepreneurs have the same signaling capability. In the case of venture capitalist firms, although a higher level of involvement with start-ups leads to better performance (Bruton et al., 1997; Fried et al., 1998; Lerner, 1995), some of them simply do not spend enough time with their principals (start-ups) (Gorman and Sahlman, 1989; MacMillan et al., 1989). Others simply do not have the reputation upon which they can leverage (Peng, 1998). Finally, many of them are unable to meet the stringent requirements imposed by their principals, such as taking title to the goods in export trade, due to a lack of resources (Peng and York, 2001). As a result, the ability to differentiate ways to signal to principals how monitoring/enforcement costs are reduced may differentiate the winning entrepreneurs from the losing ones.

Among the resources that enable an entrepreneurial firm to have lower monitoring costs than others, reputation and trust between an intermediary and its clients are probably the most important. Reputation cannot be built overnight. But once a positive reputation is built and widespread, it is very difficult for competitors to imitate at low cost. A trusting relationship built between intermediaries and its clients is also hard to be copied due to causal ambiguity and social complexity.

In sum, entrepreneurs with the unique capability to identify and explore intermediating opportunities, with a valuable organizational culture and team work environment, and a positive reputation and trusting relationship with clients will be more likely to excel in lowering search, negotiation, and monitoring/enforcement costs for the buyers and sellers they try to connect. Therefore, they will be more likely to be successful as intermediaries.

Conclusion

Why entrepreneurs arise and exist at all and why some of them outperform others have been two of the key unanswered questions in entrepreneurship research. In this chapter, we suggest that viewing entrepreneurs as intermediaries significantly helps answer these two questions. Currently, the field of entrepreneurship research lacks a conceptual framework that can be called its own. Following Bygrave and Hofer's (1991: 13) call "to develop models and theories built on solid foundations from the social sciences," we draw upon insights from transaction cost economics and resource-based view of the firm, two well-established theories which are often pitted against each other but are actually complementary (Peng et al., 2000), to enrich entrepreneurship research. The relationship between these two theories seems to be that "transaction cost economics informs the generic decision [of governance choices] . . . while competence [i.e., the resource-based view] brings in particulars" (Williamson, 1999: 1097). In this chapter, the transaction cost perspective answers the generic question of why entrepreneurs arise and exist, while the resource-based view provides the particulars on how some entrepreneurs outperform others. In other words, transaction cost reasoning seems to be "feeding into" the resource-based logic (ibid.: 1098), thus enabling us to address the essence of entrepreneurship.

For current and would-be entrepreneurs, our perspective suggests how entrepreneurs, and the buyers and sellers of their goods and services, may find competitive advantage in a world of heightened rivalry, lowered market barriers, and improved communications. Specifically, entrepreneurs are viewed as a bridge connecting their customers and their suppliers of capital, technology, services, and manufactured inputs. These market makers succeed by building the most effective market bridges, that is, by continuously developing innovative transactions linking different sets of buyers and sellers. To be successful, entrepreneurs must acquire, develop, and deploy resources which can lower their principals' search, negotiation, and monitoring/enforcement costs in the transaction process, thus benefiting their buyers and sellers.

While competition in many of the world's industries is changing, we believe that the essence of entrepreneurship, focusing on intermediation activities, remains the same. In this new "entrepreneurial millennium," it is useful to view entrepreneurs as intermediaries who connect buyers and sellers in innovative ways to enhance value added from exchange, and consider the best-performing entrepreneurs as the best market makers who create and win their markets. As academic entrepreneurs whose interests span several disciplines whereby linkages are characterized by information asymmetries, we have sought to act as intermediaries in this chapter by attempting to lower the barriers (or, if we may, "transaction costs") of interdisciplinary communication in order to maximize the gains from such scholarly exchanges. If as a consequence of this chapter more scholars and practitioners become interested in this entrepreneur-as-intermediary perspective, then the aims of our intermediation will have been well served.

Acknowledgements

This research was supported in part by the Center for International Business Education and Research, Center for Slavic and East European Studies, and Fisher College of Business Research Committee, The Ohio State University. An earlier version of this article was presented at the Strategic Management Society annual international conference in Vancouver, October 2000. We thank Jay Barney, Curt Haugtvedt, Roy Lewicki, Agnes Peng, Mike Wright, and Anne York for helpful discussion and comments, and the two editors for editorial guidance.

Notes

1   In this article, entrepreneurial activities are focused on the "creation of new organizations" (Shane and Venkataraman, 2000: 219). Although entrepreneurship can also occur within existing organizations, this type of entrepreneurship is not included in our analysis since our perspective may not always hold for existing organizations.
2   Source: National Venture Capital Association.

References

Akerlof, G. 1970: The market for lemons: quality uncertainty and the market mechanism. *Quarterly Journal of Economics*, 84, 488–500.
Allen, F. and Santomero, A. 1997: The theory of financial intermediation, *Journal of Banking and Finance* 21, 1461–85.
Amit, R., Brander J., and Zott, C. 1998: Why do venture capital firms exist? Theory and Canadian evidence. *Journal of Business Venturing*, 13, 441–66.
Amit, R., Glosten L., and Muller E. 1993: Challenges to theory development in entrepreneurship research. *Journal of Management Studies*, 30, 815–34.
Barney, J. 1991: Firm resources and sustained competitive advantage. *Journal of Management*, 17, 99–120.
Benston, G. J. and Smith, C. W. 1976: A transaction cost approach to the theory of financial intermediation. *Journal of Finance*, 31, 215–31.
Bowen, D. and Jones, G. 1986: Transaction cost analysis of service organization-customer exchange. *Academy of Management Review*, 11, 428–41.

Bruton, G., Fried, V., and Hisrich, R. 1997: Venture capitalists and CEO dismissal. *Entrepreneurship Theory and Practice*, 21 (3), 41–54.

Bygrave, W. and Hofer, C. 1991: Theorizing about entrepreneurship. *Entrepreneurship Theory and Practice*, 16 (2):13–22.

Bygrave, W. and Timmons, J. 1992: *Venture Capital at the Crossroads*. Boston, MA: Harvard Business School Press.

Cable, D. and Shane, S. 1997: A prisoner's dilemma approach to entrepreneur-venture capitalist relationships. *Academy of Management Review*, 22, 142–76.

Campbell, T. and Kracaw, W. 1980: Information production, marketing signaling, and the theory of financial intermediation. *Journal of Finance*, 35, 863–82.

Chemmanur, T. and Fulghieri, P. 1994: Investment bank reputation, information production, and financial intermediation. *Journal of Finance*, 49, 57–79.

Cooper, A. 1993: Challenges in predicting new firm performance. *Journal of Business Venturing*, 8, 241–53.

Cosimano, T. 1996: Intermediation. *Economica*, 63, 131–43.

Diamond, D. 1984: Financial intermediation and delegated monitoring. *Review of Economic Studies*, 51, 393–414.

Fiet, J. 1996: Fragmentation in the market for venture capital. *Entrepreneurship Theory and Practice*, 21 (2), 5–20.

Fingleton, J. 1997: Competition among middlemen when buyers and sellers can trade directly. *Journal of Industrial Economics*, 45, 405–27.

Fortune 1998: The E-ware war. December 7, 62–8.

Fortune 1999a: Internet defense strategy: cannibalize yourself. September 6, 121–34.

Fortune 1999b: Is there an Amazon.com for every industry? January 11, 159–60.

Fortune. 1999c: Title fight. June 21, 84–94.

Fried, V., Bruton G., and Hisrich, R. 1998: Strategy and the board of directors in venture capital-backed firms. *Journal of Business Venturing*, 13, 493–503.

Gifford, S. 1997: Limited attention and the role of the venture capitalist. *Journal of Business Venturing*, 12, 459–82.

Gorman, M. and Salhman, W. 1989: What do venture capitalists do? *Journal of Business Venturing*, 4, 231–48.

Grant, R. 1996: Toward a knowledge-based theory of the firm. *Strategic Management Journal*, 17 (winter), 109–21.

Harrison, R., Dibben, M., and Mason, C. 1997: The role of trust in the informal investors' investment decision. *Entrepreneurship Theory and Practice*, 21 (4), 63–81.

Hitt, M. A., Clifford, P. G, Nixon, R. D., and Coyne, K. P. (eds) 1999: *Dynamic Strategic Resources: Development, Diffusion, and Integration*. New York: Wiley.

Karsai, J., Wright, M., and Filatotchev, I. 1997: Venture capital in transition economies: the case of Hungary. *Entrepreneurship Theory and Practice*, 21 (4), 93–110.

Kirzner, I. M. 1997: Entrepreneurial discovery and the competitive market process: an Austrian approach. *Journal of Economic Literature*, 35, 60–85.

Kotha, S. and Dooley, E. 1999: Amazon.com. In M. A. Hitt, R. D. Ireland, and R. E. Hoskisson (eds), *Strategic Management*, C16–C31, Cincinnati: Southwestern.

Leland, H. and Pyle, D. 1977: Information asymmetries, financial structure, and financial intermediation. *Journal of Finance*, 32, 371–87.

Lerner, J. 1995: Venture capitalists and the oversight of private firms. *Journal of Finance*, 50, 301–18.

Lewicki, R., Litterer, J., Minton, J., and Saunders, D. 1994: *Negotiation*. 2nd edn. Chicago: Irwin.

MacMillan, I., Kulow, D., and Khoylian, R. 1989: Venture capitalists' involvement in their investments: extent and performance. *Journal of Business Venturing*, 4, 27–47.

MacMillan, I., Siegel, R., and Narasimha, P. N. S. 1985: Criteria used by venture capitalists to evaluate new venture proposals. *Journal of Business Venturing*, 1, 119–28.

Manigart, S. 1994: The founding rate of venture capital firms in three European countries (1970–90). *Journal of Business Venturing*, 9, 525–41.

Matusik, S. and Hill, C. 1998: The utilization of contingent work, knowledge creation, and competitive advantage. *Academy of Management Review*, 23, 680–97.

Norton, E. 1995: Venture capital as an alternative means to allocate capital: an agency theoretic view. *Entrepreneurship Theory and Practice*, 20 (2), 19–29.

Norton, E. and Tenenbaum, B. 1993: Specialization versus diversification as a venture capital investment strategy. *Journal of Business Venturing*, 8, 431–42.

Peng, M. W. 1998: *Behind the Success and Failure of U.S. Export Intermediaries*. New York: Quorum Books.

Peng, M. W. 2001: How entrepreneurs create wealth in transition economies. *Academy of Management Executive*, 15 (1), 95–108.

Peng, M. W., Hill, C., and Wang, D. 2000: Schumpeterian dynamics versus Williamsonian considerations: a test of export intermediary performance. *Journal of Management Studies*, 37 (2), 167–84.

Peng, M. W. and Ilinitch, A. Y. 1998: Export intermediary firms: a note on export development research. *Journal of International Business Studies*, 29 (3), 609–20.

Peng, M. W. and York, A. S. 2001: Behind intermediary performance in export trade: transactions, agents, and resources. *Journal of International Business Studies*, 32 (2), 327–46.

Perry, A. 1992: *The Evolution of U.S. International Trade Intermediaries*. New York: Quorum Books.

Robbie, K., Wright, M., and Chiplin B. 1997: The monitoring of venture capital firms. *Entrepreneurship Theory and Practice*, 21 (4), 9–28.

Rubinstein, A. and Wolinsky, A. 1987: Middlemen. *Quarterly Journal of Economics*, 102, 581–93.

Sapienza, H. 1992: When do venture capitalists add value? *Journal of Business Venturing*, 7, 9–27.

Sapienza, H. and Gupta, A. 1994: Impact of agency risks and task uncertainty on venture capitalist-CEO interaction. *Academy of Management Journal*, 37, 1618–32.

Sapienza, H. and Korsgaard, M. A. 1996: Procedural justice in entrepreneurs-investor relations. *Academy of Management Journal*, 39, 544–74.

Sapienza, H. Manigart, S., and Vermeir, W. 1996: Venture capitalist governance and value added in four countries. *Journal of Business Venturing*, 11, 439–69.

Schumpeter, J. 1934: *The Theory of Economic Development*. Cambridge, MA: Harvard University Press.

Shane, S. and Venkatraman, S. 2000: The promise of entrepreneurship as a field of research. *Academy of Management Review*, 25, 217–26.

Spence, A. M. 1973: *Market Signaling*. Cambridge MA: Harvard University Press.

Spulber, D. 1998: *The Market Makers*. New York: McGraw-Hill.

Teece, D. Pisano, G., and Shuen, A. 1997: Dynamic capabilities and strategic management. *Strategic Management Journal*, 18, 509–33.

Williamson, O. E. 1985: *The Economic Institutions of Capitalism*. Free Press: New York.

Williamson O. E. 1999: Strategy research: governance and competence perspectives. *Strategic Management Journal*, 20, 1087–108.

Winkler, G. M. 1989: Intermediation under trade restrictions. *Quarterly Journal of Economics*, 104, 299–324.

CHAPTER FOUR

How Real are Real Options? The Case of International Joint Ventures

Jeffrey Reuer

Introduction

Options theory has been employed for some time in many financial and economic applications (e.g., Brennan and Schwartz, 1985; Margrabe, 1978; McDonald and Siegel, 1986; Myers, 1977), yet during the last decade or so it has come of its own in the strategy literature. (e.g., Bowman and Hurry, 1993; Luehrman, 1998; McGrath, 1997, 1999; Sanchez, 1993). Whereas more familiar financial options provide investors with claims permitting the subsequent purchase or sale of a financial asset, real options instead relate to follow-on opportunities (i.e., to expand, switch inputs or outputs, stage investment, etc.) created by firms' strategic investments. By emphasizing the dynamic advantages stemming from such flexibility, rather than the static efficiencies described earlier by theories such as transaction cost economics, real options theory has also reoriented scholars' views on the merits of various strategic investments such as foreign direct investment (e.g., Kogut, 1983, 1985; Kogut and Chang, 1996; Kogut and Kulatilaka, 1994).

Specifically, the importation of options concepts, both in literal and metaphorical modes, has led to new insights and has presented new avenues for inquiry in the strategy and entrepreneurship fields. Novel aspects of real options treatments include suggestions that through discretionary investments managers can enhance value by embracing, rather than avoiding, uncertainties (e.g., Amram and Kulatilaka, 1999); that multinational networks are distinctive in enabling shifts in MNCs' value-chain activities across borders in response to changes in product, factor, and currency markets (e.g., Kogut, 1989); and that real options logic opens up a way for theory on entrepreneurship to overcome an antifailure bias (McGrath, 1999). By implementing a real options-based approach, entrepreneurs may be able to gain access to upside opportunities in the future while at the same time limiting downside risk in entrepreneurial activities such as investing in a new technology or exploring new markets (McGrath, 1997), but they also may face significant implementation hurdles.

Our particular interest centers on the question of how real options theory might further advance thinking on international joint ventures (IJVs). Kogut (1991) first extended real options theory to the domain of joint ventures. In essence, his theoretical argument was that by entering joint ventures, firms can limit their downside risk to the initial equity purchase and at the same time access the venture's upside potential. The actual upside is captured by the firm by buying out its partner if conditions prove favorable in the future. Thus, the growth option embedded in a joint venture is akin to a financial call option. Based on this reasoning, joint ventures can be helpful in entrepreneurial undertakings intended to test new products, technologies, or foreign markets as part of a sequential investment approach. While firms also use joint ventures to leverage existing assets, in the corporate entrepreneurship setting joint ventures can be useful in implementing more exploratory initiatives by taking on partners with different sets of resources.

Despite many advances in real options theory in recent years, a significant gap persists between theory and empiricism (e.g., Dixit and Pindyck, 1994). One significant challenge in studying real options further and attempting to push forward existing insights lies in specifying more clearly when particular options are present (Trigeorgis, 1997). As will be noted in an overview of the literature, empirical research has tended to examine firms' investment decisions as option purchase or exercise decisions under the assumption that a specific option is present for an investment. As Dixit and Pindyck (1994) emphasize, this approach has produced a significant body of *prima facie* evidence consistent with the theory. However, additional analysis is required to identify when firms actually purchase or exercise options as well as the benefits they truly derive from them. The alternative is to risk making overgeneralizations for a strategic investment or to miss relevant boundary conditions for the theory.

In response to these issues, I investigate the occurrence of explicit call option agreements in firms' international joint ventures (IJVs) and the factors influencing whether or not firms use such agreements. Understanding such micro-features of the design of IJVs is important for testing and advancing real options theory as it is applied to collaborative strategy for several reasons. For instance, as a practical matter, the *ex ante* negotiation of a call option mitigates *ex post* bargaining costs and the opportunities for the seller to hold up the buyer and capture the gains from sequential expansion. Contractual agreements that enable the buyer to expand its equity and control over the collaboration also can serve as valuable safeguards in joint ventures, particularly for minority investors lacking equity dominance up front. In a section below, I elaborate upon the reasons why the presence or absence of explicit options matters, and return to them in a section devoted to the development of research hypotheses.

The remainder of the chapter proceeds as follows: after a discussion of call options in joint ventures, an overview of recent real options research appears. This review highlights formal models of strategic investment under uncertainty, work on firm-level option strategies, and empirical studies of real options. A subsequent section develops hypotheses identifying contingencies shaping firms' use of call options in IJVs. The hypotheses suggest that such agreements can be useful to firms seeking to expand sequentially over time. I also develop the argument that firms will tend to use options as contractual safeguards when the right to shift the control structure of the venture is attractive. After a presentation of the research design, the empirical results follow. A concluding section discusses the implications of the study for future strategy and entrepreneurship research on real options.

Call Options in Joint Ventures

Why does the presence or absence of an explicit call option agreement in a JV matter? First, the gains the buyer potentially attains from acquiring equity in a JV *ex post* can be influenced by the *ex ante* specification of purchase terms. Consider, for example, a venture that experiences a positive change in demand for its product, and this leads one firm to seek to expand via acquisition of the partner's equity (Kogut, 1991). Under this scenario, the gains from expansion can be partially or fully appropriated by the selling party, who may also appreciate the business's enhanced value. Accordingly, option value at the formation stage depends upon the call holder's right to claim the upside, and this claim can be rendered uncertain if hold-up risks are present and the firm relies upon *ex post* re-negotiation of the venture arrangement. It is also plausible that firms benefit from the process of negotiating the option since executives in both parent firms think through and discuss details surrounding the future transition of the joint venture, thereby mitigating future misunderstandings and adjustment costs.

Second, the selling party may also obtain some level of protection from option agreements if its bargaining power erodes over time in the relationship (e.g., Ariño and de la Torre, 1998; Doz, 1996; Makhija and Ganesh, 1997). For instance, as a multinational firm accumulates knowledge from a local partner in an IJV, the uniqueness of the local partner's contribution may decline to a point that collaboration is no longer warranted from the multinational's perspective (Inkpen and Beamish, 1997). The option agreement can help the local seller by obtaining a price that was negotiated *ex ante* when its bargaining position was stronger.

Third, identifying the presence or absence of options to acquire equity in joint ventures is important from the standpoint of the researcher attempting to establish parent firms' intents for collaborative relationships. Although JVs lacking explicit option agreements can clearly have implied option value, viewing all JVs as call options presumes that all parent firms explicitly or implicitly enter into collaborations in order to limit risks with a view toward sequential expansion. However, the vast literature on joint venture formation motives suggests that firms enter into collaborative relationships for many different reasons (e.g., Contractor and Lorange, 1988; Doz and Hamel, 1998; Hennart and Reddy, 1997; Koza and Lewin, 1998), so the possibility of sequential expansion may be of secondary or negligible importance for one or both of the parent firms in a specific collaboration. By examining JVs with or without embedded call options, one can therefore partially address this heterogeneity in joint ventures.

Finally, the negotiation of call options in JVs can be viewed not only from a sequential expansion perspective, but also from a governance perspective. For instance, the right to acquire full ownership in the venture is tantamount to the right to convert a hybrid governance structure to an internal unit within the firm's hierarchy (e.g., Hennart, 1993; Williamson, 1991). Hence, options can have implications for partners' incentives and can provide safeguards for ventures, be they transitional by design or equilibrium arrangements. As a consequence, this contingent control property of real options in joint ventures can be particularly valuable for minority investors lacking the control provided by initial equity dominance. Thus, the governance properties of options potentially influence a parent firm's exposure to contractual hazards.

Research on Real Options

Building on options research in finance several decades ago, recent work has extended the tools and insights of options theory to a variety of firms' strategic investment decisions. Several recent books have provided extensive reviews as well as indications of the theory's potential reach. For instance, Dixit and Pindyck (1994) provide an overview of the mathematical foundations of option valuation and discuss applications such as sequential investment and capacity choice, among others. Trigeorgis (1997) reviews prior work on options to defer, stage investment, alter operating scale, abandon, switch, and grow. Amram and Kulatilaka (1999) indicate how the real options approach can be used to understand start-up valuation, investments in infrastructure, and competitor pre-emption.

Given the depth of the theory and its far-ranging possible applications, the literature review is not intended to be exhaustive. Rather, its objective is confined to providing a sketch of recent work conducted in the strategy, entrepreneurship, and international business areas to illustrate research approaches in these fields. Research in these areas using the real options lens tends to fall into three categories: (1) formal models of strategic investments; (2) conceptual treatments of firm-level option strategies; and (3) empirical research on real options.

Formal models of strategic investments

Following research in finance and economics, researchers have used formal models to examine the benefits and tradeoffs associated with investments in different strategic options. For instance, Kogut and Kulatilaka (1994) modeled the value of coordinating geographically dispersed subsidiaries subject to foreign exchange rate uncertainty. Multinationals obtaining the option to switch production across borders are in an advantageous position relative to domestic firms that have fewer degrees of freedom. Their model also explains hysteresis in firms' investment decisions and has implications for how multinationals evaluate performance and set transfer prices. Researchers in other disciplines have developed models that similarly demonstrate how operational flexibility contributes to value creation (e.g., Huchzermeier and Cohen, 1996; Mello et al., 1995). Related work has modeled the option to switch outputs or inputs to achieve product or process flexibility (e.g., Dixit and Pindyck, 1994; Trigeorgis, 1997).

In the IJV context more specifically, Chi and McGuire (1996) developed a stochastic model to assess how uncertainty about the market and uncertainty about the exchange partner elevate the value of a collaborative venture. Their model reveals that call, or growth, options fail to create value when the partners share the same *ex post* valuation of the IJV. *Ex ante* asymmetries in the partners' valuations of the option, potentially due to differential uncertainties about the venture's future or differential absorptive capacities, bring about a trade in option rights.

Firm-level option strategies

Set against these formal models are conceptual treatments of options that depict strategic decision-making at the firm level and tend to use options theory metaphorically. For instance, Bowman and Hurry (1993) discussed how real options reasoning can integrate diverse strategy concepts and organizational phenomena such as resource allocation, sense-making, organizational learning, and strategic positioning. Sanchez (1993) and Luehrman (1998) likewise discussed how strategy can be viewed as optimizing the firm's set of strategic options.

In the venture capital setting, Hurry et al. (1992) compared the venture capital industries in the USA and Japan and posited that Japanese venture capitalists tend to pursue an options strategy, whereas their US counterparts follow a more myopic, project-based approach. They portrayed an options strategy as a firm-level investment orientation that would be evidenced by a larger portfolio of ventures, smaller individual investments, and a higher percentage of loss-making ventures.

In the areas of technology strategy and entrepreneurship, McGrath (1997) offered a conceptual framework depicting the forces underlying the value of a technology option as well as the appropriate timing of its exercise. In a subsequent article, she detailed how real options theory might be used to design organizational processes and incentives in entrepreneurial initiatives in order to enhance gains while limiting downside risk (McGrath, 1999).

Empirical research on real options

Apart from formal models of strategic investments and these conceptual treatments of real options at the firm level, there is also a developing body of empirical work on real options that seeks to determine whether firms invest in accordance with real options predictions and whether they derive benefits from their investments that are consistent with real options theory. Thus, this research tends to ascribe options to certain investments and then seeks to garner support or disconfirming evidence for the theory based upon the consistency of firms' behavior or outcomes with the predictions of real options theory. Such work is exemplified by current empirical research on the multinational firm and joint ventures.

Real options theory suggests that firms with dispersed FDI benefit from the option to shift value-chain activities across country borders in response to changes in external conditions such as exchange rates, local demand, wage rates, and so forth (e.g., Kogut, 1983, 1985, 1989; Kogut and Kulatilaka, 1994). Empirical research has established that multinational corporations (MNCs) shift production and sourcing in response to exchange rate changes (Rangan, 1998), and that the breadth of the firm's subsidiary network relates positively to firm value (Allen and Pantzalis, 1996) as well as the market's response to earnings announcements (Tang and Tikoo, 1999). The "twin benefits" that multinational firms attain *vis-à-vis* their domestic counterparts – lower risk and higher returns – have likewise been attributed to the strategic options that multinationals possess (Kim et al., 1993). Related research shows that FDI decreases firms' economic exposures to foreign exchange rate movements (Miller and Reuer, 1998). Nevertheless, evidence that MNCs select lower financial leverage ratios (e.g., Lee and Kwok, 1988) and that systematic risk increases with the firm's degree of internationalization (Reeb et al., 1998) casts some doubt on the diversification benefits of international operation (e.g., Caves, 1996). Furthermore, recent evidence suggests that the dispersion of foreign direct investment across country borders has no bearing on various dimensions of firms' downside risk (Reuer and Leiblein, 2000).

A similar research approach has also been employed in empirical studies on joint ventures. As alluded to earlier, Kogut's (1991) investigation of JV termination revealed acquisition patterns consistent with call exercise behavior. Examining firms' initial collaborative investments as purchases of call options, Folta (1998) found that firms enter into equity collaborations with biotech firms rather than acquisitions when growth opportunities and technological uncertainties exist. However, in contrast to the predictions of real options theory, there is recent evidence that joint ventures increase, rather than decrease, firms' subsequent income stream risk and bankruptcy risk (Reuer and Leiblein, 2000).

In sum, while formal models indicate the value that is possible for firms to obtain from using a real options approach, conceptual treatments of options-based strategies have grappled with the application of insights from option theory to the strategy setting. The complexity associated with making this translation has typically meant that the tools of options theory have been imported in metaphorical, often loose, terms. In a similar fashion, existing empirical work has tended to proceed under the assumption that a specific option is present for a given strategic investment rather than attending to the basic questions of whether a firm actually has the right but not the obligation to take some follow-on action and whether the firm is truly in a position to limit its downside while simultaneously being able to claim upside opportunities. Thus, despite the *prima facie* evidence that exists in support of real options theory, empirical research is needed on these underlying contingencies and boundary conditions for various forms of options to add value in strategic and entrepreneurial initiatives.

Theory and Hypotheses

The introduction suggested that firms may employ call options in IJVs for at least two basic reasons. First, options in IJVs can facilitate sequential investment. They enable the call holder to place a limit *ex ante* on the price it pays for the venture *ex post*. By negotiating a call option, the ultimate buyer reduces hold-up problems that otherwise would allow the seller to appropriate the gains from expansion. The buying party can also reduce the *ex post* costs of the business's transition by achieving clarity on the hand-over process *ex ante*. Second, as tools affording contingent control, options can serve as safeguards in IJVs. This means that the firm holding the call option can shift the control structure of the venture to its advantage if the need arises.

In the hypotheses developed below, one or both of these forces may be at work in the firm's decision to use an option agreement in a given IJV. For some hypotheses, the two perspectives offer the same prediction. For instance, both the sequential expansion view and the governance view contend that option agreements are valuable for minority investors. For other determinants of firms' use of call options, the two views may give rise to alternative predictions, as is the case for the business relationship between the IJV and parent firm. We also consider the effects of the property rights regime and behavioral uncertainty on firms' use of real options in IJVs.

IJV ownership

Fundamental to the real options view is the notion that firms enter into IJVs to limit downside risk while at once securing access to upside opportunities by making a limited capital outlay and by subsequently monitoring market and other cues to determine if the IJV's value over time is such that expansion via the acquisition of additional equity is warranted. If, for example, a change in demand elevates the value of the IJV to a sufficiently high level, the firm can gain by acquiring equity; otherwise the option to expand is held open (Kogut, 1991). If V_c is the value the call holder places on the entire venture, α_{c0} is the call holder's initial equity, α_{ct} is the equity level the call holder has the right to attain (where $0 < \alpha_{c0} < 1$, $0 < \alpha_{ct} \leq 1$, and $\alpha_{c0} < \alpha_{ct}$), and P is the price at which the equity purchase occurs, then the firm will gain $(\alpha_{ct} - \alpha_{c0})V_c - P$ by expanding, and it will hold the option open if $(\alpha_{ct} - \alpha_{c0})V_c < P$.

It follows that firms will find call options more attractive for minority IJVs for several reasons. First, by taking a minority stake in the venture, the firm limits its initial sunk investment while obtaining access to future expansion opportunities. Second, during the option's holding period, the firm reduces its income stream risk in the IJV. Algebraically, the firm's expected profit each year is given by $\alpha_{c0}E(\pi_{IJV})$, where π_{IJV} is the IJV's profit, so the variance in the firm's profit is given by $\alpha^2_{c0}\sigma^2(\pi_{IJV})$, which declines in the firm's equity stake (i.e., where $\sigma^2(\pi_{IJV})$ is the variance in the IJV's profit). Third, the terminal value of the call option, $\max[(\alpha_{ct} - \alpha_{c0})V_c - P, 0]$, increases as the firm's initial equity stake decreases. Finally, the firm seeking the call option may bargain by making concessions in other areas, such as by providing greater residual claimancy to the partner (Chi and McGuire, 1996).

A governance perspective on call options also suggests that options will strengthen the position of minority investors having less control in IJVs. Transaction cost treatments of foreign direct investment have treated equity ownership as a summary indicator of the firm's control over foreign subsidiaries (e.g., Delios and Beamish, 1999; Gatignon and Anderson, 1988; Gomes-Casseres, 1989), but have not considered firms' abilities to obtain additional control through subsequent equity purchases. It is not uncommon for firms maintaining majority positions in IJVs to have a majority of seats on the venture's board and to exercise significant influence over the venture's day-to-day decisions and operations. In such circumstances, the right to acquire additional equity is less valuable given the control rights already provided by equity dominance. Conversely, firms lacking control in minority investments are more apt to find the contingent control property of call options attractive. In such IJVs, the firm without an option is exposed to contractual hazards since it lacks discretion over the IJV's operations and future direction. Hence, research on the coordination of MNCs' affiliates also suggests that call options are more attractive for minority IJVs and that greater equity *ex ante* will prove useful when the firm lacks the right to acquire more equity in the future.

Hypothesis 1:   The likelihood that the firm has an explicit option to acquire equity will be lower for noncore IJVs than for joint ventures operating in the firm's primary business.

Markete exploration and resource protection

The sequential investment and governance perspectives generate the same prediction relating IJV ownership to the utilization of options, yet they lead to alternative hypotheses when one considers the business relationship between the IJV and the parent firm. On the one hand, expanding sequentially will be valuable when the firm faces learning opportunities and uncertainties when investing outside of its core business. On the other hand, the control rights provided by call options are useful when the firm establishes a collaboration in its core business and thereby runs the risks of knowledge appropriation and building up a competitor.

Firms commonly invest in joint ventures outside of their core businesses (e.g., Stopford and Wells, 1972). Relative to organic growth and acquisitions, joint ventures are efficient mechanisms for exploring opportunities in new domains in order to gather new information and to establish a platform for future expansion (e.g., Kogut, 1991; Koza and Lewin, 1998). In noncore domains, the firm's knowledge base is comparatively weak and learning challenges are greater. Folta (1998) suggests, therefore, that investments outside of the firm's core business are subject to greater endogenous uncertainty, and equity investments are helpful until this uncertainty is resolved. The attractiveness of partnering and establishing growth options is enhanced since the firm can invest in multiple exploratory projects rather than committing funds to a single investment opportunity that requires greater resource commitment (e.g., Mody, 1993). The joint venture solution affords opportunities for gathering new information and re-evaluating the business's prospects, and it also allows the firm to switch at relatively low cost. The value the market attaches to diversifying joint ventures is broadly consistent with a learning, options perspective on collaborative strategy (Reuer and Koza, 2000).

Just as collaborators can use joint ventures to acquire competencies and information in new domains, parent firms will also tend to seek protection of their firm-specific advantages when partnering within their main line of business. It is in the parent firm's core business that its knowledge base tends to be stronger and, given the overall importance of this business, that risks such as negative IJV-parent firm spillovers, loss of key competencies, and building up a competitor are particularly great. Alliance studies have considered how competitors vie for each others' capabilities in alliances (e.g., Khanna et al., 1998), when firms need to act to prevent leaks of sensitive information (e.g., Hamel, 1991), and how firms might better protect themselves against knowledge misappropriation (e.g., Parkhe, 1993).

Options to acquire additional equity are one potential design alternative to deal with the risks of collaborating in the firm's core business. When firms are uncertain about their ability to alter their management of a venture, they can incur large costs and delays in attempting to renegotiate a change in the relationship. They can also risk losing nonrecoverable investments in the event of JV dissolution, which is likely in competitive relationships (Park and Russo, 1996). If a partner's actual behavior differs from the parent firm's initial expectations, due to opportunism or its lack of capabilities, the option holder can exert more control over the business. By providing the partner with a significant equity stake and negotiating an option to acquire equity, the firm can take steps to deter opportunistic behavior and safeguard resources if control changes are needed.

Given that the sequential investment and governance perspectives provide different explanations of firms' use of options in non-core versus core domains, respectively, we wish to test the following two competing hypotheses:

Hypothesis 2a: The likelihood that the firm has an option to acquire equity will be higher for noncore IJVs than for ventures operating in the firm's primary business.

Hypothesis 2b: The likelihood that the firm has an option to acquire equity will be lower for core IJVs than for ventures operating outside the firm's primary business.

Property rights

An external factor bearing on the contractual hazards faced by the firm and, therefore, the potential value of having an option to acquire equity and control, is the level of intellectual property protection in the host country. Although the institutional environment was taken as a given in early governance research, Williamson (1991) has provided a comparative statics framework to consider how differences in institutional environments affect firms' market entry strategies in different host countries. Prior research has given attention to how weakness in a host country's property rights regime reduces the firm's incentives to make investments involving technology- or marketing-based resources (Teece, 1986b), and more recent research has assessed how this dimension of the institutional environment encourages firms to increase its ownership position and hierarchical controls in alliances (e.g., Delios and Beamish, 1999; Oxley, 1999). When property rights are comparatively weak, the firm risks dissemination of knowledge or other resources to rivals and other local parties. Monitoring and enforcement costs in non-hierarchical governance modes are therefore significant, and firms using alliances to enter such markets turn to equity structures over non-equity arrangements in an effort to help align incentives as well as improve control and monitoring through shared board membership (Oxley, 1999).

Firms utilizing call options in IJVs are able to further increase their control over IJVs by acquiring equity. For instance, if knowledge begins to leak to a partner in a minority venture, the firm can alter the control structure of the venture (Chi and McGuire, 1996). When its resources are less easily protected due to the host country's property rights regime, the MNC is more likely to attach greater value to the option to acquire equity and control. This right also potentially reduces the incentives for misappropriation and thereby increases the firm's confidence that the partner will use the MNC's resources appropriately in agreed-upon domains.

Hypothesis 3:   The likelihood that the firm has an option to acquire equity will be greater for IJVs based in host countries with weaker property rights regimes.

Cultural distance

If call options in joint ventures facilitate sequential expansion and offer control rights that are valuable in light of risks of partner opportunism, such options to acquire equity will be attractive when the firm expands into culturally distant host countries. Research on the internationalization of firms, for example, suggests that the firm can use a joint venture as a stepping stone to acquire knowledge about local markets and reduce its initial liability of foreignness (e.g., Hymer, 1976; Johanson and Vahlne, 1977). As discussed earlier, the sequential expansion view suggests that firms can use options in IJVs to establish an investment platform, explore new domains in foreign markets, and embrace endogenous uncertainties.

A governance view of options similarly predicts that firms will implement options in culturally distant countries. Cultural differences have been theorized to contribute to internal uncertainties, inefficiencies in tailoring business practices abroad, and coordination costs (e.g., Gatignon and Anderson, 1988; Hennart and Reddy, 1997; Kogut and Singh, 1988) that decrease over time, which suggests that deferring the institution of control can enhance efficiency. Cultural differences are also thought to occasion perceptions of opportunism, which can undermine the collaboration and threaten firms' investments (e.g., Beamish and Banks, 1987; Parkhe, 1991). Options to shift the control structure of the joint venture may therefore reduce the firm's exposure to behavioral uncertainty.

Hypothesis 4:   The likelihood that the firm has an option to acquire equity will be greater for IJVs based in culturally distant host countries.

Methods

Sample

The base sample developed from the SDC database was comprised of all two-parent IJVs formed during the years 1995–7. For purposes of collecting data, at least one parent firm had to be a US firm, and this partner served as the sampled firm in the analyses. Ventures were considered international if they were based outside of the USA, which reflected the focus on the effects of the contracting environment on firms' decisions to negotiate option agreements. While full data were available on IJVs formed during this period, illustrative data are presented on the incidence of real options during the 1991–8 time period. As discussed below, to address the discrepancy between the number of IJVs with and without embedded real option agreements, the multivariate analyses focused on ventures in which the US party had a minority equity stake, and ventures were included with options that were formed during the extended 1991–8 time period. After accounting for missing data, the final sample for the multivariate analysis consisted of 121 IJVs, 8 percent of which had real options in place.

Model specification

The multivariate statistical model took the following basic form:

Call option = β_0 + $\beta_1$core IJV + $\beta_2$intellectual property protection +
$\beta_3$cultural distance + β_4IJV experience + $\beta_5$political turmoil risk +
$\beta_6$host market growth + ε_t.

As will be discussed in a subsequent section on the empirical data patterns, the incidence of call option agreements for US firms investing in IJVs abroad was low overall, particularly for ventures in which the US party held at least half of the equity. As one step toward redressing the imbalance between the number of IJVs with and without option agreements, the model was estimated for two-party IJVs in which the US firm holds a minority equity stake. The relationship between call options and equity ownership was then explored using a bivariate, non-parametric test for independence as well as a two-sample t-test.

While the goal was to develop a parsimonious model explaining when firms use option agreements, other controls were incorporated that may affect the sequential investment process and the value of having contingent ownership and control in the IJV. In particular, the models accounted for the firm's IJV experience, which may affect firms' behavioral uncertainties in IJVs as well as the sophistication of its collaborative strategy. Political risk was incorporated as a control since the MNC may seek to preserve the local party as a buffer rather than acquire ownership under conditions of political risk (Teece, 1986a). Finally, a control for the growth of the host market addressed the attractiveness of the host country and the corresponding bargaining power of local parties (e.g., Fagre and Wells, 1982; Gomes-Casseres, 1990).

Measures and data

Call option.   The dependent variable in equation (1) is a 0–1 variable indicating whether or not the US parent firm in the IJV held an explicit, contractually agreed-upon option to acquire equity in the venture. Equation (1) was estimated using logistic regression analysis to identify the conditions under which firms employ explicit options to acquire equity in IJVs (i.e., Call Option = 1). Data on IJVs obtained from the Securities Data Corporation (SDC) were used to determine if the US party held a call option in the IJV.

Explanatory variables.   The overlap between the domain of the venture and the parent firm was proxied based on the SIC of the IJV and the SIC of the parent firm's primary business. Core IJV equals one when the venture operates in the same four-digit industry as the parent firm's core business, and zero otherwise. Data on the SICs of the IJV and parent firm were obtained from the SDC database.

The measure for the protection of intellectual property in the host country was developed by Park and Ginarte (1997). Relative to other measures of the national appropriability regime (e.g., Rapp and Rozek, 1990), this measure offers the advantage of being broader in coverage. The index is available for 110 host countries. The Park and Ginarte (1997) index is constructed based on five elements of patent law: extent of coverage, membership in international agreements, provisions for loss of protection, enforcement mechanisms, and duration of protection. Each element is scored on a 0–1 scale, and the Intellectual Property Protection variable is a sum of the five values for the IJV's host country. Host country locations of IJV were provided by SDC.

Cultural distance was measured in two ways in common with prior analyses of MNCs (e.g., Barkema et al., 1996; Fladmoe-Lindquist and Jacque, 1995; Gatignon and Anderson, 1988). A weighted index was first constructed using Hofstede's (1980) scales for uncertainty avoidance, individuality, tolerance of power distance, and masculinity for the US and host countries:

$$\text{Cultural distance}_{US,k} = \frac{1}{4} \sum_{i=1} [(I_{iUS} - I_{ik})^2 / V_i],$$

where the left-hand side is the cultural distance between the USA and country k (i.e., the IJV's host country), I_{iUS} is the score for the United States on scale i, I_{ik} is the score of country k on scale i, and V_i is the sample variance of scale i (Kogut and Singh, 1988).

A second technique was used to examine the sensitivity of the results and examine specific host country groups. This categorical approach used binary variables to classify JVs into national culture clusters obtained from a meta-analysis of prior culture studies (Ronen and Shenkar, 1985). Due to the absence of IJVs in some of the culture clusters, the low incidence of real options overall, and the lack of variance in firms' option decisions within some clusters, two alternative model specifications were used. Focusing on IJVs in the culturally most similar countries for which model estimation is feasible, one model compares IJVs in Anglo (e.g., Australia, Canada, Ireland, New Zealand, South Africa, and the UK) and non-Anglo nations after controlling for other host country attributes such as host market growth and political risk. Similarly, focusing on IJVs in the culturally most distant clusters, a second model considers IJVs in the Far East (e.g., Hong Kong, Indonesia, Malaysia, Philippines, Singapore, South Vietnam, Taiwan, and Thailand) and Latin America (e.g., Argentina, Chile, Columbia, Mexico, Peru, and Venezuela), countries relative to those in other host countries that are culturally more similar to the USA Based on the predictions of Hypothesis 4, the parameter for Anglo should be negative, and the parameters for Far East and Latin America should be positive.

Control variables.   The firm's IJV experience was measured by counting the number of international joint ventures formed in the prior ten years. IJV experience was defined as the log of one plus the number of IJVs in which the firm had invested in the prior ten years in order to remedy significant positive skewness that was evident for the pre-transformed count measure. International joint venture formation data were obtained from searches using the SDC database.

Our control for political turmoil risk was obtained from 18–month forecasts from the Political Risk Service. Political turmoil risk forecasts are reported on a scale from "low" to "very high." Following Fladmoe-Lindquist and Jacque (1995), we converted these forecasts to numerical scores on a 1–4 scale. Data on political turmoil risk are compiled annually in the *Planning Review*. Finally, host market attractiveness was proxied as the host market's five-year growth rate in real GDP, expressed as a percentage. These data were also obtained from the Political Risk Service's tables published in *Planning Review*.

Results

Table 4.1 provides data on the incidence of real option agreements in IJVs over the years 1991–8. The data patterns indicate that the total number of IJVs formed by US firms peaked in 1995 after a steady increase from 1992, and 1998 saw the fewest number of IJVs being formed by US firms investing abroad during this time frame. The incidence of options is low overall at roughly 1 percent and is stable over the time interval under consideration.

Table 4.1   Incidence of call option agreements in IJVs over time[a]

Year	No. of IJVs with option clauses (%)	No. of IJVs without option clauses (%)	Totals
1991	11 (1.41)	770 (98.59)	781
1992	1 (0.28)	351 (99.72)	352
1993	3 (0.45)	668 (99.55)	671
1994	9 (0.91)	976 (99.09)	985
1995	9 (0.69)	1300 (99.31)	1309
1996	2 (0.37)	541 (99.63)	543
1997	4 (0.72)	555 (99.28)	559
1998	1 (0.50)	201 (99.50)	202
Totals	40 (0.74)	5362 (99.26)	5402

[a] All IJVs are equity joint ventures formed by at least one US parent firms and are based outside of the USA.
Source: SDC database

To examine the relationship between firms' equity ownership and their usage of options in IJVs (i.e., Hypothesis 1), table 4.2 presents relative frequencies of real options across the different ownership positions held by US parent firms in two-party IJVs formed in 1995–7. The distribution of IJVs across the four cells indicates that the presence of an option is negatively related to firms' equity ownership levels ($\chi^2 = 37.27$, $p < 0.001$). Consistent with expectations, the relationship between initial equity and the right to obtain ownership is substitutive in nature. For IJVs lacking an option agreement, the focal firm owns at least 50 percent of the equity in 89.69 percent of the cases, whereas firms with embedded options in their IJVs have minority stakes 70 percent of the time. The average equity position for firms with call options is

Table 4.2   Call option agreements in IJVs and equity ownership (1995–7)[a]

Number of Firms (%) (Row %) (Column %)	Equity stake < 50%	Equity stake ≥ 50%	Row total
Option to acquire ownership present	7 (0.38) (70.00) (3.59)	3 (0.16) (30.00) (0.18)	10 (0.55)
Option to acquire ownership absent	188 (10.26) (10.31) (96.41)	1635 (89.20) (89.69) (99.82)	1823 (99.45)
Column total	195 (10.64	1638 (89.36)	1833 (100.00)

[a] $\chi^2 = 37.27$ (p < 0.001). All IJVs involve two parent firms. Equity stake refers to the ownership position of the focal, US firm, and the option designation also refers to this firm's right to acquire equity.

50.2 percent, whereas the average equity position of firms without call options is 31.2 percent ($p < 0.01$).

Descriptive statistics and a correlation matrix appear in table 4.3. Seventy-five percent of the IJVs represented investments by parent firms outside of their core businesses. The sampled IJVs operated in 36 different industries at the two-digit SIC level and 25 different countries. Significant heterogeneity also was present in firms' IJV experience levels. For 32.2 percent of the parent firms, no IJV investments were made during the prior ten years, whereas roughly 5 percent of the firms formed more than 100 IJVs during this time frame. The median level of collaborative experience was five prior IJVs.

The bivariate results demonstrate that significant interdependencies exist among the explanatory variables. For instance, the host country's protection of intellectual property is weaker in host countries that are culturally distant from the USA, subject to political turmoil risk, and growing more rapidly (all $p < 0.001$). Such intercorrelation indicates the importance of using multivariate analysis to isolate the partial effects of the theoretical variables on the firm's decision to negotiate a call option agreement when investing in an IJV. However, it also suggests the possible existence of multicollinearity problems for model estimation. Accordingly, variance inflation factors (VIFs) were investigated, and the maximum VIF for all of the variables in the specifications employed was 3.51, which is well below the accepted cutoff value of ten for multiple regression models and therefore provides no indication of multicollinearity problems (Neteret al., 1985).

Table 4.4 provides estimates for the logistic regression analyses of firms' decisions on the negotiation of option agreements in IJVs. Model II is a specification using Kogut and Singh's (1988) index of cultural distance. Models III and IV rely on the categorical indicators from Ronen and Shenkar's (1985) culture clusters. To test

Table 4.3 Descriptive statistics and correlation matrix[a]

Variable	Mean	S.D.	(1)	(2)	(3)	(4)	(5)	(6)	(7)	(8)	(9)
1. Call Option	0.08	0.27	—								
2. Core IJV	0.25	0.43	0.18[b]	—							
3. Intellectual Property Protection	2.93	1.00	−0.21[c]	−0.06	—						
4. Cultural Distance	1.85	1.19	0.14	0.15[b]	−0.41[e]	—					
5. Anglo	0.14	0.35	−0.03	−0.12	0.10	−0.58[e]	—				
6. Far East	0.16	0.37	0.20[c]	−0.09	−0.23[c]	0.47[e]	−0.17[b]	—			
7. Latin America	0.11	0.31	0.19[c]	0.23[c]	−0.42[e]	0.51[e]	−0.14	−0.15	—		
8. IJV Experience	1.77	1.57	−0.08	−0.02	−0.06	−0.04	−0.22[c]	−0.10	0.07	—	
9. Political Turmoil Risk	1.52	0.74	0.15[b]	0.04	−0.52[e]	0.19[c]	−0.09	−0.06	0.26[d]	0.04	—
10. Host Market Growth	3.09	2.20	−0.04	0.10	−0.46[e]	0.57[e]	−0.25[d]	0.65[e]	0.21[c]	−0.03	−0.18[c]

[a] $N = 121$. All IJVs are two-party ventures in which the US firm holds a minority equity position. [b] $p < 0.10$, [c] $p < 0.05$, [d] $p < 0.01$, [e] $p < 0.001$.

Table 4.4   Estimates of logistic regression analyses[a]

Variable	Model I	Model II	Model III	Model IV
Intercept	4.44	6.36[b]	5.53	18.04*
	(3.15	(3.75)	(2.15)	(8.16)
Core IJV	1.86*	1.87*	1.82*	5.47*
	(0.82)	(0.90)	(0.83)	(2.64)
Intellectual Property	−1.65*	−2.07**	−1.73*	−4.56*
Protection	(0.64)	(0.78)	(0.68)	(1.93)
Cultural Distance	–	0.93*	–	–
		(0.47)		
Anglo	–	–	−0.93	–
			(1.35)	
Far East	–	–	–	9.70*
				(3.79)
Latin America	–	–	–	3.71[b]
				(2.26)
IJV Experience	−0.49	−0.58[b]	−0.52[b]	−0.56
	(0.31)	(0.33)	(0.31)	(0.51)
Political Turmoil Risk	−0.52	−1.39	−0.74	−3.36*
	(0.69)	(0.92)	(0.83)	(1.57)
Host Market Growth	−0.57[b]	−0.97**	−0.67[b]	−2.72*
	(0.30)	(0.36)	(0.34)	(1.11)
χ^2	15.37**	19.84**	15.90*	40.59***
Log Likelihood (β)	−26.82	−24.59	−26.56	−14.21
−2 [L(β₁) − L(β)]	–	4.46*	0.52	25.22***

[a] N = 121. All IJVs are two-party ventures in which the US firm holds a minority equity position.
[b] $p < 0.10$, * $p < 0.05$, ** $p < 0.01$, *** $p < 0.001$.

the impact of cultural distance on the firm's use of real option clauses, Model I serves as a baseline. Models I through IV are all significant ($p < 0.01$, $p < 0.01$, $p < 0.05$, and $p < 0.001$, respectively), and Models II and IV provide better fit than Model I ($p < 0.05$ and $p < 0.001$, respectively).

Hypotheses 2a and 2b offered alternative predictions regarding the investment contexts in which parent firms utilize option agreements. On the one hand, the benefits of learning and investing sequentially under uncertainty underscored by real options theory suggest that firms will employ call options when entering into non-core industries abroad (i.e., Hypothesis 2a), whereas the view that options provide safeguards in IJVs suggests that options will be valuable for ventures within the firm's core business where the risks of losing key advantages and creating competitors are greater (i.e., Hypothesis 2b). The positive effect of the Core IJV indicator across the four specifications (all $p < 0.05$) lends support for Hypothesis 2b. Furthermore, the point estimate of the odds ratio for this variable indicates that the odds of negotiating an explicit call option into core IJVs are 6.5 times greater than for IJVs operating outside the firm's primary business, holding constant the other covariates.

Hypothesis 3 posited that firms will tend to use option agreements in IJVs when the protection of intellectual property is weak in the host country. The Intellectual Property Protection variable is negative in all of the specifications ($p < 0.05$, $p < 0.01$, $p < 0.05$, and $p < 0.05$, respectively), supporting Hypothesis 3. This finding offers evidence that the presence of an option provides the firm with some level of control when investing in minority IJVs subject to significant behavioral uncertainty.

Finally, Hypothesis 4 suggested that firms will negotiate call options more frequently in culturally distant countries. Model II reveals that the likelihood that the firm will utilize an option agreement increases with cultural distance ($p < 0.05$). The parameter estimate for the Anglo variable in Model III takes on a negative sign as predicted, but it does not reach significance at the 0.10 level. Model IV provides more explanatory power than Model I, indicating that the Far East and Latin America indicators are jointly significant ($p < 0.001$). Firms are more likely to negotiate option clauses in Far East countries ($p < 0.05$) and Latin American ($p < 0.10$) nations than other host markets. Taken together, these findings provide support for the prediction that firms use option clauses in culturally distant investment contexts giving rise to behavioral uncertainty and learning challenges.

All of the controls are significant in one or more of the specifications. Firms inexperienced with IJVs appear to be more apt to use real option agreements ($p < 0.10$ in Models II and III). Model IV indicates that firms are less likely to use options in countries subject to political turmoil risk ($p < 0.05$), though the variable fails to reach significance in the other specifications. Finally, the four models suggest that firms are less apt to use call options in growing host markets ($p < 0.10$, $p < 0.01$, $p < 0.10$, and $p < 0.05$, respectively).

Discussion

The incidence of real options

The findings indicate that the percentage of IJVs with embedded call options is low, though one suspects that the absolute level reported in the SDC data may be biased downwards if firms are not revealing specific features of their IJVs due to confidentiality agreements. While this cautions against drawing conclusions on the overall incidence of real options in IJVs, other recent work on strategic alliances also documents that relatively few collaborations involve such options. For example, Ziedonis (1999) examined 669 licensing decisions during the years 1975 to 1992 involving the University of California. Sixteen percent of these decisions were preceded by an option to license. As the present analysis is limited to explicit call options in IJVs formed by US firms, extensions might investigate explicit or implicit options in different alliances.

Nevertheless, several substantive explanations may also account for firms' apparently low usage of explicit call options in IJVs. First, host country governments may restrict the equity foreign investors can acquire. Emerging countries have historically placed limits on outside ownership and the allocation of rights upon termination of the venture, yet such restrictions appear to be less and less common, with firms establishing wholly-owned subsidiaries in China and Western firms buying out their venture partners in countries in the former Soviet Union.

Second, the preponderance of joint venture investments takes place outside of the firm's primary business, and our findings show that firms tend to implement options when collaborating in their core business instead. This suggests that if the number of collaborations between competitors increases in some industries, there may also be an increase in the incidence of real options embedded in joint ventures in those industries.

Third, clearly firms enter into joint ventures for many different reasons (e.g., Contractor and Lorange, 1988; Doz and Hamel, 1998; Hennart and Reddy, 1997; Koza and Lewin, 1998), which suggests that sequential expansion may be of secondary or negligible importance for any given IJV. This observation and our findings caution against viewing all JV investments as call options, and it suggests that survey research able to categorize firms' strategic intents in IJVs may be able to identify ventures most likely to use, and benefit from, options.

Fourth, even if the normative facets of real options theory hold out opportunities for firms to create value and reduce risk through sequential investment, firms may lack either a willingness or ability to adopt call options in IJVs. A recent survey of senior finance officers provides some supportive evidence on this point. The study found that few firms had procedures in place to evaluate options, and respondents were concerned about reduced organizational commitment to projects with real options (Busby and Pitts, 1997). These findings suggest that there are research opportunities to study why firms might fail to negotiate options where the theory predicts they are valuable.

The determinants of real options

Perhaps more important than firms' low overall usage of options in IJVs is the finding that firms are selective in negotiating options in their cross-border collaborative agreements. In testing where firms use options, the analysis sought to examine situations in which options can facilitate sequential investment or provide valuable safeguards for firms' IJVs. In some cases, as in minority IJVs, these two explanations offer the same prediction regarding when firms will use options. For instance, by holding an option on a minority IJV, the firm can limit its initial investment, reduce its income stream risk prior to exercise of the option, and still secure a claim on venture's upside potential. Having the right to shift the ownership structure is also valuable for minority IJVs affording lower levels of control. Similarly, IJV investments in culturally distant countries were also more likely to be accompanied by option agreements. The use of IJVs with options in these circumstances can help firms establish platform investments under conditions of uncertainty. Implementing options in such IJVs can also reduce the firm's exposure to behavioral uncertainty. For instance, the right to defer the institution of organizational controls is valuable due to internal uncertainty and the initial inefficiencies of internalization.

However, the sequential investment and governance views of options can also sometimes generate alternative predictions on firms' use of options in IJVs. In support of the latter, firms tend to use options in core businesses rather than in non-core domains. In its core business, the firm is more concerned about misappropriation, the control of key resources, and behavioral uncertainty, whereas in non-core domains issues such as market uncertainty and learning opportunities come to the fore. Firms also seek the contingent control provided by options in minority IJVs when the property rights regime of the host country is comparatively weak. A novel aspect of the findings' implications, therefore, is that a call option also can be seen as a governance feature of IJVs. Together these results suggest that the presence or absence of options in IJVs may affect parent firms' exposure to contractual hazards.

The finding that firms tend to negotiate call options in core domains raises the question of what options might be present in non-core IJVs in which explicit calls are not embedded. Since firms will often enter into such ventures to experiment and subsequently exit at low cost, non-core alliances may often be options to exit or abandon rather than call options. Penrose's remarks on learning and investment reversals in non-core domains are fitting in this regard:

> Diversification of this kind leads firms into relatively unfamiliar areas of activity by definition. Some mistakes will be made and some expectations disappointed. The obvious way to rectify mistakes is to sell out . . . The existence of this kind of market has an important effect on the process of growth of firms: it both promotes and helps to eliminate "excessive" diversification. It facilitates the correction of "mistakes" and thereby reduces the risk of loss when a firm experiments with new lines of activity, thus encouraging such experimentation. (1995: 174–5; 179)

This observation and the findings reinforce the need for future research to identify when specific options are present in firms' strategic investments. It also underscores the more general notion that various options are available in joint ventures and other strategic investments for corporate entrepreneurship initiatives (Trigeorgis, 1997). The quote indicates that firms may obtain implicit inputs in some alliances, and it follows that more research attention needs to be paid to reversibility conditions in alliances. Data patterns on stock price reactions to IJV formation and termination announcements suggest that firms can use venture termination to sequentially adapt or gain more value from joint ventures that initially created value (Reuer, 2000). However, in contrast to evidence on divestitures of acquired units, firms face difficulties in using termination to correct prior IJV formation decisions that reduced firm value, perhaps because joint venture sales often involve bilateral negotiations with hold-up potential rather than the sale of assets in a more competitive market.

Conclusion

Although a number of research opportunities have already been mentioned in discussing the empirical findings, the present study's scope and limitations present a number of other avenues for additional research. First, I have focused on firms acquiring call options in IJVs, so future research could also examine why firms choose to sell calls *ex ante* rather than negotiate venture sales through *ex post* renegotiation. Such research might offer insights on the benefits and risks of collaboration for entrepreneurs, who may or may not wish to become the option held by their larger counterparts. Furthermore, since the focus of the current analysis of international alliances is on the multinational firm, future research might consider the negotiation of option agreements from the local party's perspective and the potential roles that smaller firms' value chain contributions and bargaining power play in the process. Because the multivariate analyses are limited to minority IJVs, additional comparisons could be made across the governance continuum in order to contrast the use of minority or majority joint ventures with embedded options versus acquisitions or wholly-owned greenfield expansions. Empirical implications could be derived from real options theory as well as transaction cost theory to make such comparisons in a large-scale statistical analyses.

Second, although the study is situated in the international context, many of the basic principles and predictions carry over to the domestic setting. Future studies that examine joint ventures in the domestic setting may be able to examine the buy and sell sides simultaneously and can also take up other sources of environmental uncertainty than those considered here by implementing proxies at the host country level. However, one would anticipate that many of the same concerns surrounding minority investments and the need to safeguard resources in the firm's core business will apply in the domestic context.

Third, firms may implement other contractual provisions for joint ventures termination such as shotgun agreements (Harrigan, 1985) or independent appraisals, so it would be valuable to investigate these and other contractual features of alliances empirically. Since the occurrence of explicit options and other contractual safeguards such as shotgun agreements appears to be rather low, insights might be gleaned through a clinical analysis of joint venture negotiations. Such field studies might also be able to characterize and study implicit options in joint ventures that are difficult to pin down in large-scale empirical studies. Further, since the present study focused on two-party joint ventures, extensions might consider the negotiation of options, shotgun agreements, and other contractual terms in more complex collaborations involving three or more parties. It is conceivable that the sequential expansion and safeguard properties of options will differ in importance in such collaborations.

Finally, as I have concentrated on firms' IJV investment decisions, or the issue of alliance design, future research might examine the implications of options for the management of IJVs and their future evolution. More generally, option theory can be pushed forward considerably from its current focus on the purchase and exercise of various options by specifying more precisely how firms can obtain the promise of reducing downside risk while simultaneously exploiting upside opportunities. In other words, greater consideration should be given to the strategic and organizational realities encountered when importing basic concepts from options theory in finance. Elsewhere, I have conjectured that a combination of attention to transaction design and execution as well as the development of appropriate firm-level systems and capabilities is needed (Reuer and Leiblein, 2001), yet clearly more research is warranted on the implementation of options-based approaches. The paradox, or challenge, is that entrepreneurial firms and others that likely stand to gain the most from implementing an options-based approach may often not be well positioned to do so. Research in directions such as these can advance real options theory as it is applied in the joint venture context and might also serve to work out its usefulness in other domains in the strategy and entrepreneurship fields.

Acknowledgements

In developing this chapter, I have benefited from comments and suggestions from Erin Anderson, Hubert Gatignon, Michael Leiblein, Subi Rangan, and the editors. Thanks also go to Dina Tirtey for assistance with the data collection. Research funding was provided by INSEAD's R&D Department.

References

Allen, L. and Pantzalis, C. 1996: Valuation of the operating flexibility of multinational corporations. *Journal of International Business Studies*, 27, 633–53.

Amram, M. and Kulatilaka, N. 1999: *Real Options: Managing Strategic Investment in an Uncertain World*. Boston, MA: Harvard Business School Press.

Ariño, A. and de la Torre, J. 1998: Learning from failure: towards an evolutionary model of collaborative ventures. *Organization Science*, 9, 306–25.

Barkema, H. G., Bell, J. H. J., and Pennings, J. M. 1996: Foreign entry, cultural barriers, and learning. *Strategic Management Journal*, 17, 151–66.

Beamish, P. W. and Banks, J. C. 1987: Equity joint ventures and the theory of the multinational enterprise. *Journal of International Business Studies*, 18: 1–16.

Bowman, E. H. and Hurry, D. 1993: Strategy through the options lens: an integrated view of resource investments and the incremental-choice process. *Academy of Management Review* 18, 760–82.

Brennan, M. and Schwartz, E. 1985: Evaluating natural resource investments. *Journal of Business*, 58: 135–57.

Busby, J. S. and Pitts, C. G. C. 1997: Real options in practice: an exploratory survey of how finance officers deal with flexibility in capital appraisal. *Management Accounting Research*, 8, 169–86.

Caves, R. E. 1996: *Multinational Enterprise and Economic Analysis*, 2nd edn. Boston, MA.: Cambridge University Press.

Chi, T. and McGuire D. J. 1996: Collaborative ventures and value of learning: integrating the transaction cost and strategic option perspectives on foreign market entry. *Journal of International Business Studies*, 27, 285–308.

Contractor, F. J. and Lorange, P. 1988: Why should firms cooperate? The strategy and economics basis for cooperative ventures. In F. J. Contractor and P. Lorange (eds). *Cooperative Strategies in International Business*. Lexington, MA: DC Heath, 3–30.

Delios, A.and Beamish, P. W. 1999: Ownership strategy of Japanese firms: transactional, institutional, and experience influences. *Strategic Management Journal*, 20, 915–33.

Dixit, A. K. and Pindyck, R. S. 1994: *Investment under Uncertainty*. Princeton, NJ: Princeton University Press.

Doz, Y. L. 1996: The evolution of cooperation in strategic alliances: initial conditions or learning processes? *Strategic Management Journal*, 17 (Summer Special Issue), 55–84.

Doz, Y. L. and Hamel, G. 1998: *Alliance Advantage: the Art of Creating Value through Partnering*. Boston, M.A: Harvard Business School Press.

Fagre, N. and Wells, L. T. 1982: Bargaining power of multinationals and host governments. *Journal of International Business Studies*, 11, 9–23.

Fladmoe-Lindquist, K. and Jacque, L. L. 1995: Control modes in international service operations: the propensity to franchise. *Management Science*, 41, 1238–49.

Folta, T. B. 1998: Governance and uncertainty: the tradeoff between administrative control and commitment. *Strategic Management Journal*, 19, 1007–28.

Gatignon, H. and Anderson, E. 1988: The multinational corporation's degree of control over foreign subsidiaries: an empirical test of a transaction cost explanation. *Journal of Law, Economics, and Organization*, 4, 305–36.

Gomes-Casseres, B. 1989: Ownership structures of foreign subsidiaries: theory and evidence. *Journal of Economic Behavior and Organization*, 11, 1–25.

Gomes-Casseres, B. 1990: Firm ownership preferences and host government restrictions: an integrated approach. *Journal of International Business Studies*, 21, 1–22.

Hamel, G. 1991: Competition for competence and interpartner learning within international strategic alliances. *Strategic Management Journal*, 12: 83–103.

Harrigan, K. R. 1985: *Strategies for Joint Ventures*. Lexington, MA: Lexington Books.

Hennart, J.-F. 1993: Explaining the swollen middle: why most transactions are a mix of "market" and "hierarchy." *Organization Science*, 4, 529–47.

Hennart, J.-F. and Reddy, S. 1997: The choice between mergers/acquisitions and joint ventures: the case of Japanese investors in the United States. *Strategic Management Journal*, 18, 1–12.

Hofstede, G. 1980: *Culture's Consequences: International Differences in Work-Related Values*. Beverly Hills, CA: Sage.

Huchzermeier, A. and Cohen, M. 1996: Valuing operational flexibility under exchange rate risk. *Operations Research*, 44, 100–13.

Hurry, D., Miller, A. T. and Bowman, E. H. 1992: Calls on high technology: Japanese exploration of venture capital investments in the United States. *Strategic Management Journal*, 13, 85–101.

Hymer, S. H. 1976: *The International Operations of National Firms: A Study of Direct Investment*. Cambridge, MA: MIT Press.

Inkpen, A. C. and Beamish, P. W. 1997: Knowledge, bargaining power, and the instability of international joint ventures. *Academy of Management Review*, 22, 177–202.

Johanson, J., and Vahlne, J. E. 1977: The internationalization process of a firm: a model of knowledge development and increasing foreign market commitments. *Journal of International Business Studies*, 9, 22–32.

Khanna, T., Gulati R., and Nohria, N. 1998: The dynamics of learning alliances: competition, cooperation, and relative scope. *Strategic Management Journal* 19, 193–210.

Kim, W. C., Hwang P., and Burgers W. P. 1993: Multinationals' diversification and the risk-return tradeoff. *Strategic Management Journal*, 14, 275–86.

Kogut, B. 1983: Foreign direct investment as a sequential process. In C. P. Kindleberger and D. B. Andretsch (eds),*The Multinational Corporation in the 1980s*. Boston, MA: MIT Press, 62–75.

Kogut, B. 1985: Designing global strategies: profiting from operational flexibility. *Sloan Management Review*, 27, 27–38.

Kogut, B. 1989: A note on global strategies. *Strategic Management Journal*, 10, 383–9.

Kogut, B. 1991: Joint ventures and the option to expand and acquire. *Management Science*, 37, 19–33.

Kogut, B. and Chang, S. J. 1996: Platform investments and volatile exchange rates: direct investment in the U.S. by Japanese electronic companies. *Review of Economics and Statistics*, 78, 221–31.

Kogut, B. and Kulatilaka, N. 1994: Operating flexibility, global manufacturing, and the option value of a multinational network. *Management Science*, 40, 123–39.

Kogut, B. and Singh, H. 1988: The effect of national culture on the choice of entry mode. *Journal of International Business Studies*, 19, 411–32.

Koza, M. and Lewin, A. 1998: The co-evolution of strategic alliances. *Organization Science*, 9, 255–64.

Lee, C. L. and Kwok, C. C. Y. 1988: Multinational corporations vs. domestic corporations: international environmental factors and determinants of capital structure. *Journal of International Business Studies*, 19, 195–217.

Luehrman, T. A. 1998: Strategy as a portfolio of real options. *Harvard Business Review*, 76, 89–99.

Makhija, M. V. and Ganesh, U. 1997: The relationship between control and partner learning in learning-related joint ventures. *Organization Science*, 8, 508–27.

Margrabe, W. 1978: The value of an option to exchange one asset for another. *Journal of Finance*, 33: 177–86.

McDonald, R. and Siegel, D. 1986: The value of waiting to invest. *Quarterly Journal of Economics*, 101, 707–27.

McGrath, R. G. 1997: A real options logic for initiating technology positioning investments. *Academy of Management Review*, 22, 974–96.

McGrath, R. G. 1999: Falling forward: real options reasoning and entrepreneurial failure. *Academy of Management Review*, 24, 13–30.

Mello, A., Parsons, J., and Triantis, A. 1995: An integrated model of multinational flexibility and financial hedging. *Journal of Industrial Economics*, 39, 27–51.

Miller, K. D. and Reuer J. J. 1998: Firm strategy and economic exposure to foreign exchange rate movements. *Journal of International Business Studies*, 29, 493–514.

Mody, A. 1993: Learning through alliances. *Journal of Economic Behavior and Organization*, 20, 151–70.

Myers, S. C. 1977: Determinants of corporate borrowing. *Journal of Financial Economics*, 5, 147–76.

Neter, J., Wasserman, W., and Kutner, M. H. 1985. *Applied Linear Statistical Models*, 2nd edn. Homewood, IL: Irwin.

Oxley, J. E. 1999: Institutional environment and the mechanisms of governance: the impact of intellectual property protection on the structure of inter-firm alliances. *Journal of Economic Behavior and Organization*, 38, 283–309.

Park, S.H. and Russo, M. V. 1996: When competition eclipses cooperation: an event history analysis of joint venture failure. *Management Science*, 42, 875–90.

Park, W. G. and Ginarte, J. C. 1997: Determinants of patent rights: a cross-national study. *Research Policy*, 26, 283–301.

Parkhe, A. 1991: Interfirm diversity, organizational learning, and longevity in global strategic alliances. *Journal of International Business Studies*, 22, 579–601.

Parkhe, A. 1993: Strategic alliance structuring: a game theoretic and transaction costs examination of interfirm cooperation. *Academy of Management Journal*, 36, 794–829.

Penrose, E. T. 1995: *The Theory of the Growth of the Firm*, 3rd edn. New York: John Wiley and Sons, Inc.

Rangan, S. 1998: Do multinationals operate flexibly? Theory and evidence. *Journal of International Business Studies*, 29, 217–37.

Rapp, R. and Rozek, R. 1990: Benefits and costs of intellectual property protection in developing countries. *Journal of World Trade*, 24, 75–102.

Reeb, D. M., Kwok C. C. Y., and Baek H. Y. 1998: Systematic risk of the multinational corporation. *Journal of International Business Studies*, 29, 263–79.

Reuer, J. J. 2000: Parent firm performance across international joint venture life-cycle stages. *Journal of International Business Studies*, 31, 1–20.

Reuer, J. J. and Koza, M. P. 2000: Asymmetric information and joint venture performance: theory and evidence for domestic and international joint ventures. *Strategic Management*

Journal, 21, 81–8.

Reuer, J. J. and Leiblein, M. J. 2000: Downside risk implications of multinationality and international joint ventures. *Academy of Management Journal*, 43, 203–14.

Reuer, J. J. and Leiblein, M. J. 2001: Real options: let the buyer beware. In J. Picksford (ed.), *Mastering Risk*. London: FT Prentice-Hall, 79–85.

Ronen, S. and Shenkar, O. 1985: Clustering countries on attitudinal dimensions: a review and synthesis. *Academy of Management Review*, 10, 435–54.

Sanchez, R. 1993: Strategic flexibility, firm organization, and managerial work in dynamic markets: a strategic-options perspective. In P. Shrivastava, A. Huff, and J. Dutton (eds). *Advances in Strategic Management*. Vol. 9: Greenwich, CT: JAI Press, 251–91.

Stopford, J. M. and Wells, L. T. 1972. *Managing the Multinational Enterprise*. New York: Basic Books.

Tang, C. Y. and Tikoo, S. 1999. Operational flexibility and market valuation of earnings. *Strategic Management Journal*. 20, 749–61.

Teece, D. J. 1986a: Transaction cost economics and the multinational enterprise: an assessment. *Journal of Economic Behavior and Organization*, 7, 21–45.

Teece, D. J. 1986b: Profiting from technological innovation: implications for integration, collaboration, licensing, and public policy. *Research Policy*, 15, 285–305.

Trigeorgis, L. 1997: *Real Options: Managerial Flexibility and Strategy in Resource Allocation*. Cambridge, MA: MIT Press.

Williamson, O. E. 1991: Comparative economic organization: the analysis of discrete structural alternatives. *Administrative Science Quarterly*, 36, 269–96.

Ziedonis, A. 1999: The influence of knowledge assets on the external technology licensing decision. Paper presented at the annual meeting of the Strategic Management Society in Berlin, Germany.

CHAPTER FIVE

More Good Things Are Not Necessarily Better: An Empirical Study of Strategic Alliances, Experience Effects, and New Product Development in High-Technology Start-ups

Frank T. Rothaermel and David L. Deeds

Introduction

The last twenty-five years of the twentieth century witnessed an explosion in entrepreneurial activity. New technologies such as personal computers, software, medical electronics, biotechnology, and the Internet led to the creation of entirely new industries. It has long been argued that the creation of new ventures and the emergence of new industries provide an opportunity for organizational forms to be both intentionally and unintentionally changed, and subsequently for new forms of organizations to be introduced (Hannan and Freeman, 1989). One of the variations in organization used extensively by these emerging new ventures is the strategic alliance (Hagedoorn, 1993).

Prior to the experimentation undertaken by these new ventures, the use of hybrid forms of organization was generally limited to non-critical projects with relatively low levels of complexity and uncertainty (Mowery, 1990). Projects that were critically important and had high levels of uncertainty and complexity were internalized due to a fear of opportunism on the part of the organization's partners (Williamson, 1985). However, due to necessity, most new technological ventures have relied heavily on strategic alliances to undertake highly complex, uncertain, and lengthy research and development projects. This is particularly true of the biotechnology industry, where alliances involving early stage research and development projects with non-profit organizations, other biotechnology firms, and large pharmaceutical companies are a way of life (Baum et al., 2000).

A primary determinant of enterprise success in emerging high-technology industries is the rate at which the firm develops new products (Stalk and Hout, 1990). The ability to rapidly develop new products and bring them to market is important because it allows new ventures to gain early cash flows, external visibility and legitimacy, and early market share, which increases their likelihood of survival (Stinchcombe, 1965; Schoonhoven et al., 1990). Moreover, the faster a firm develops new products and brings them to market, the more likely it is to capture first mover advantages including patent protection, market pre-emption, reputation effects, and experience curve effects (Lieberman and Montgomery, 1988). It is also a critical factor influencing a new venture's access to additional private investment capital and the public equity markets (DeCarolis and Deeds, 1999). In addition, the financial markets react favorably to strategic alliances, particularly when they are undertaken with renowned partners (Kelm et al., 1995; Stuart et al., 1999). All of this reinforces the fact that the rapid development of new products is critical for competitors in emerging or rapidly changing industries.

Prior research has demonstrated a positive relationship between the number of strategic alliances in which a firm is engaged and a firm's research productivity (Shan et al., 1994). It has also been shown that the relationship between strategic alliances and new product development is characterized by diminishing marginal returns, which eventually lead to negative marginal returns (Deeds and Hill, 1996). However, while the basic functional shape of the relationship has been demonstrated, we still lack a more detailed understanding of the relationship. What is the relationship between different types of alliances and their respective levels of diminishing marginal returns? In addition, we need a better understanding of how firm-specific factors influence the performance of individual firms with respect to alliance intensity.

The purpose of this study is to improve our understanding of the underlying nature of the connection between strategic alliances and new product development. Further, we shed some light on how a firm's experience affects its alliance management capability. Our study uses a database of 2,226 strategic alliances entered into by 325 new biotechnology firms (NBFs) fully dedicated to the development of human therapeutics and diagnostics between 1975 and 1997. We will begin by corroborating the earlier findings on our larger sample and then move on to examining the relative impact of different types of alliances on new product development. Finally, we will examine the impact of firm experience on the relationship between strategic alliances and new product development.

Hypotheses Development

It has been empirically shown that a positive relationship exists between a new entrant's total number of strategic alliances and its research productivity or its new product development, respectively (Shan, et al. 1994; DeCarolis and Deeds, 1999). It is important to point out that these prior studies have lumped all alliances into a single category. However, there are clearly different types of alliances that a firm can undertake.

Baum et al. (2000), for example, have pointed out that there are three primary types of alliances that a biotechnology firm can enter: (1) *vertical-upstream* alliances with universities, research institutions, government labs, hospitals and industry associations; (2) *horizontal* alliances with other biotechnology firms; and (3) *vertical-downstream* alliances with pharmaceutical and chemical firms.

Even though prior literature has proposed a positive relationship between alliance activity and research productivity or new product development, one must consider the fact that every firm faces limited managerial and financial resources. Eventually, the costs of simultaneously managing a large number of alliances will exceed the gains obtained by entering additional alliances. The relationship between the number of strategic alliances into which a firm enters and its new product development will eventually exhibit diminishing marginal returns and, past some point, possibly diminishing total returns, i.e., negative marginal returns for each additional cooperative arrangement (Deeds and Hill, 1996).

There are many reasons for this proposed relationship. For example, the more alliances a firm has formed, the higher the probability that management will be less effective in managing those alliances due to bounded rationality (Simon, 1960). In a similar fashion, an increasing number of alliances results in increasing managerial information-processing demands, which may contribute to an overall negative net effect at high levels of alliance intensity (Hitt et al., 1997). In addition, with an increasing number of alliances, an incumbent firm's transaction costs may rise up to, and possibly beyond, a point where the gains from additional alliances are outweighed by their costs, resulting in negative marginal returns for high levels of alliance intensity (Jones and Hill, 1988). A similar phenomenon has been proposed with respect to firm product diversification (Chandler, 1962). It has been shown that product and international diversification are positively related to firm performance at moderate levels, but exhibit a negative effect on firm performance at high levels (Hitt et al., 1994; Hitt et al., 1997).

We assume a similar curvilinear relationship with respect to a firm's alliances and its new product development. In particular, we propose that the relationship between the number of strategic alliances into which a firm enters and its new product development will exhibit diminishing marginal returns, and may even pass the point of diminishing total returns and thus eventually exhibit negative marginal returns for each additional cooperative arrangement (Deeds and Hill, 1996). This proposed relationship should also hold for each subcategory of alliances, i.e. vertical-upstream, horizontal, and vertical-downstream alliances.

Hypothesis 1:   The number of a new entrant's total strategic alliances is related to its new product development in a curvilinear (inverted-U shape) manner.

Hypotheses 1a–c: The respective number of a new entrant's vertical-upstream, horizontal, and vertical-downstream alliances is related to its new product development in a curvilinear manner.

In the biotechnology industry, the primary role of the new biotechnology firm is the commercialization of the basic science being developed in the laboratories of universities and other non-profit research institutions. A recent study found that over 85 percent of the patents cited in new biotechnology firms' patents were from non-profit institutions. In addition, this rate is significantly higher than that of large, diversified pharmaceutical companies (McMillan et al., 2000). The relationships between non-profits and biotechnology firms are clearly oriented towards the commercialization of the basic scientific knowledge created in the non-profit organization. In contrast, new entrants need to enter vertical-downstream alliances with incumbent pharmaceutical firms in order to commercialize the new technology. New entrants enter these alliances in order to gain access to capital, as well as the downstream value chain activities such as distribution, marketing, sales, and regulatory expertise. Thus, interfirm cooperation between biotechnology firms and pharmaceutical firms is motivated by the desire to exploit specialized complementary assets and is likely to occur in a later stage of the product development process (Rothaermel, 2001).

Uncertainty about the outcome of a cooperative arrangement should decrease as the focal point of interfirm cooperation moves downstream in the product development process. The reason for this is that lower levels of uncertainty, ambiguity, and complexity raise the odds of success for cooperative arrangements. The fundamental uncertainty of upstream alliances resides in the nature of the R&D process. In the biotechnology industry, vertical-upstream alliances can be viewed as *exploration alliances* (March, 1991). In contrast to downstream alliances where well developed assets, such as marketing assets, regulatory skills, or financial assets are being exchanged, upstream alliances require firms not only to combine pre-existing assets and capabilities, but also to co-develop new skills, capabilities, and knowledge that translate into tangible products. The co-development of new skills and capabilities requires the partners in an exploration alliance to get close enough to share tacit knowledge such as basic R&D (Lane and Lubatkin, 1998). This increases the potential for the expropriation of valuable information by partners, which in turn increases the monitoring requirements that the alliance places on the firm's managers. The underlying uncertainty and ambiguity surrounding upstream research collaborations also make it difficult to clearly define the scope of the project. Difficulty in limiting the scope of an alliance limits the number of alliances that a firm can effectively manage, because it increases the potential for conflicts between the alliances in the firm's portfolio and increases the difficulty of effectively monitoring a partner's performance. Under these circumstances, adding additional alliances creates ever-greater demands on the managerial capabilities of the firm.

Horizontal alliances are characterized by less uncertainty and may include exploration as well as *exploitation alliances*, while vertical-downstream alliances are characterized by the least uncertainty since they are generally exploitation alliances (March, 1991). Exploitation alliances focus on complementarities among the allied partners as they exchange explicit knowledge and well-defined assets (Teece, 1992). Generally, the NBFs provide access to commercializable new technology and the pharmaceutical firms provide regulatory capabilities, drug distribution, and financial assets (Arora and Gambardella, 1990). Downstream alliances are entered into to exploit the technology that the firm has developed internally or in conjunction with an upstream partner. More developed technologies bring lower levels of uncertainty and ambiguity to the alliance, making it easier to define the scope and boundaries of the alliance. This lowers the managerial challenge because the conflict between the scope and boundaries of the alliances in the firm's portfolio is much easier to manage. The scope of downstream alliances is generally defined around a particular product, class of molecules or specific indications, thereby limiting the uncertainty and ambiguity in the alliance. In addition, the lower level of uncertainty and ambiguity makes it easier to monitor partner performance and the decreased need for integration lowers the potential for expropriation. Prior research and theory development have emphasized that the managerial challenge posed by a strategic alliance depends in general upon the uncertainty, ambiguity, and complexity of the project (Gulati and Singh, 1998). Therefore, the combination of these forces should serve to lower the demands that downstream alliances place on the managerial capabilities of the firm, and allow the firm to efficiently manage a greater number of downstream alliances than upstream alliances. Hence, the overall frequency of alliance activity should increase as the focal point of interfirm cooperation moves downstream in the industry development process, i.e. from vertical-upstream alliances (highest level of uncertainty) to horizontal alliances (moderate level of uncertainty), and finally to vertical-downstream alliances (lowest level of uncertainty). Thus, we posit that the point of diminishing total returns (DTR) to alliance intensity will increase as we move downstream in the product development process. As such, vertical-upstream alliances will have the lowest point of DTR, followed by horizontal alliances, with vertical-downstream alliances having the highest point of DTR.

Hypothesis 2a: At the industry level, the alliance activity of new entrants increases as the focal point of interfirm cooperation moves downstream in the product development process.

Hypothesis 2b: At the firm level, the point of diminishing total returns varies according to the type of alliance, with vertical-upstream alliances reaching the point of diminishing total returns first, followed by horizontal alliances, and finally vertical-downstream alliances.

Prior literature has largely ignored the potential importance of firm-specific factors in explaining the relationship between alliance intensity and firm performance. We argue that firm experience is one firm-specific factor that influences a firm's capability to simultaneously manage multiple alliances. Ignorance of alliance management or lack of experience in managing collaborative endeavors has often been blamed as the main source of alliance problems and failures (Lei and Slocum, 1992). Previous experience has also been shown to lead to the emergence of a distinct form of collaborative know-how that allows the firm to achieve greater benefits from subsequent alliances (Simonin, 1999). This occurs because firms involved in the cross-boundary development of new technologies develop appropriate routines to manage the activity based on the accumulation of operating experience (Pisano, 1994). The development of the appropriate managerial routines from prior experience should increase the firm's capacity to manage alliances and improve the speed and accuracy of communication between the partners. Therefore, firms with more experience in managing strategic alliances should be able to simultaneously manage a larger number of alliances. Accordingly, the point of diminishing total returns to alliance intensity should be reached at a higher number of alliances for more experienced firms than for less experienced firms.

Hypothesis 3:   More experienced firms are able to manage a larger number of alliances than less experienced firms.

Research Setting and Design

Research setting

The research setting is the biotechnology industry. This term comprises the industrial sector composed of non-profit organizations conducting basic and applied research in biotechnology, such as universities and other research institutions, new biotechnology firms dedicated to commercializing the new technology, such as Amgen and Chiron, and traditional pharmaceutical companies such as Merck or Eli Lilly that participate in utilizing biotechnology for drug discovery and development. The "new" biotechnology (primarily recombinant DNA) allows the manipulation of the inner structure of microorganisms. In 1973, a research team led by Cohen and Boyer published their breakthrough study on recombinant DNA. This technique involves "cutting" DNA out of one cell (e.g., a human cell) and "pasting" it into a different host cell (e.g., *E-coli* bacterium). For example, if the DNA holds the genetic code for producing insulin, then the host cell will produce insulin external to the human body. In 1975, cell fusion techniques for producing highly purified proteins (monoclonal antibodies) were developed by Milstein and Köhler. Subsequently, research in biotechnology prospered, making it one of the stellar sciences in the late twentieth century.

Many new biotechnology firms emerged to commercialize this technological breakthrough. The year 1976 is often referred to as the start of commercialized biotechnology since the first NBF – Genentech – was founded by scientist Boyer and venture capitalist Swanson. The emergence of biotechnology can be interpreted as a process innovation that broke the barriers of entry into the pharmaceutical industry (Rothaermel, 2000). Between 1970 and 1997 alone, 1,049 companies entered the industry to commercialize biotechnology, the majority of them focusing on human pharmaceuticals. On average, 37 companies entered the industry per year in this time period, with 89 entries in 1992 alone. The new entrants represent a little more than 85 percent of all firms participating in the biotechnology industry (BioScan, 1997).

The commercialization of biotechnology is characterized by extensive cooperative arrangements (Burrill, 1999). Biotechnology is the industry with the highest absolute number of strategic alliances, and accounts for 20 percent of all strategic alliances (Hagedoorn, 1993). This figure represents more than double the rate of adoption of strategic alliances than can be found in the next most prolific industry, and is without precedent in business history (Harrigan, 1985). Thus, the biotechnology industry provides an ideal research setting to study interfirm cooperation and its impact on new product development.

Research design

Data and Sample. We identified all new biotechnology firms listed in the BioScan 1997 industry directory that were fully dedicated to human therapeutics and diagnostics, i.e., all firms that were engaged in developing *in vivo* therapeutics or diagnostics. This segment of the biotechnology industry comprises new biotechnology start-ups engaged in the R&D of drugs or diagnostics that are placed inside the human body (*in vivo*) as opposed to *in vitro* drugs or diagnostics that are used outside the human body. We chose to limit our sample to in vivo therapeutics and diagnostics since the firms engaged in this segment of biotechnology are exposed to extensive regulative requirements (FDA, etc.), which entails detailed reporting of products under development. Our sample includes 325 new biotechnology firms.

We then constructed a database of strategic alliances entered into by the new biotechnology firms in our sample with other participants in biotechnology over a time horizon of 25 years (BioScan, 1997). This database contains 2,226 strategic alliances. BioScan provides the most comprehensive publicly available directory covering the global biopharmaceutical industry. It has been used in a number of different studies (cf., Arora and Gambardella, 1990; Shan, et al., 1994; Deeds and Hill, 1996; Lane and Lubatkin, 1998; Rothaermel, 2001).

We focused exclusively on biotechnology-based drug discovery and product development alliances and did not consider marketing alliances, i.e., alliances where NBFs market the products of other NBFs. Biotechnology-based alliances lead to new product development, whereas pure marketing alliances are a consequence of product development. Considering marketing alliances by NBFs, which are the exception at this stage of industry development, would lead to a causal problem in the link between the start-up's alliance activity and its new product development. We did include, however, marketing alliances between NBFs and pharmaceutical companies, i.e., where a pharmaceutical company markets a product based on a technology developed by a biotechnology start-up. Thus, all 2,226 alliances are alliances in which some form of biotechnology-based drug discovery, R&D, and development is transferred between the alliance partners. The NBFs are either the receivers or transmitters of this new biotechnology.

Measures

Dependent variable.   One direct measure of how well a new biotechnology firm is performing is its *new product development.* This is the dependent variable of the firm-level analysis and has been used in a number of prior studies (Deeds and Hill, 1996; Rothaermel, 2001). We measured a new biotechnology firm's new product development by the number of its total products, which is the sum of products in development and products on the market.

Independent variables.   The *total number of alliances* is a count variable, and represents the strategic alliances a new biotechnology firm has entered into with other participants in biotechnology since the early 1970s and up to December 1997, which marks the publication date of the BioScan directory used for this study. We subsequently split the total number of alliances into three subcategories: vertical-upstream, horizontal, and vertical-downstream alliances. We proxied vertical-upstream alliances through alliances with non-profit organizations such as universities and other research institutions, horizontal alliances through alliances with other biotechnology firms, and vertical-downstream alliances through alliances with pharmaceutical firms (Baum, et al., 2000).

Control variables.   In order to control for age dependency, we calculated the average age in months of the strategic alliances and their subcategories. Older alliances are more likely to yield more innovative products than are younger alliances (Hannan and Freeman, 1989). We controlled for *equity alliances* (strong ties) versus *non-equity alliances* (weak ties) through the inclusion of the ratio of equity alliances over non-equity alliances. We further controlled for a new entrant's *firm size* by using the number of employees as a proxy (Shan, et al., 1994). In general, firm size is measured in revenues or market share, however, most NBFs do not have a positive revenue stream at this point. Thus, measuring firm size in terms of employees provides a reasonable alternative.

We controlled for the new entrant's *firm age*, assuming that older firms are likely to have more new product development than younger firms. We also used firm age as the basis for splitting the sample into three subsamples, i.e., oldest third, middle third, and youngest third, to test the experience-effect hypothesis (Hypothesis 3). We chose firm age to operationalize experience because a firm's experience in managing the different types of alliances should increase as its age increases. This should hold true since an older firm is able to establish routines and external reputation and thus is more likely to have overcome the liability of newness (Stinchcombe, 1965; Baum, et al., 2000).

We also controlled for potential *economies of scope* through the inclusion of a count variable representing the number of biotechnology subfields in which a new entrant firm participates (Shan, et al., 1994). We controlled for the ownership status of the firm (1 = *public* firm). We controlled for whether the firm was a subsidiary or independent (1 =*subsidiary*). Finally, we included the indicator variable *country* to distinguish between US-based biotechnology companies and non-US biotechnology companies (1 = *US firm*) in order to control for institutional differences (Hennart et al., 1999).

Model specification

Since the dependent variable (total products) is a count variable, OLS estimates of regression coefficients would have been asymptotically biased and inconsistent (Greene, 1997). Thus, the firm-level hypotheses were tested using a negative binomial regression model with a maximum likelihood estimation procedure. The negative binomial regression model was preferred over the Poisson model since equality of mean and variance is not given in the sample. The observed overdispersion in our data is characteristic of social science data (Kogut et al., 1992).

Results

The sample comprises 325 new biotechnology firms, which participated in 2,226 alliances in the biotechnology field. The 2,226 alliances split into 524 (23 percent) vertical-upstream alliances, 729 (33 percent) horizontal alliances, and 973 (44 percent)

Table 5.1 Descriptive statistics and correlation matrix

	Mean	Std. Dev.	1	2	3	4	5	6	7	8	9	10	11	12	13	14	15	16	17	18	19
1 New product development	6.34	4.97																			
2 Total SAs	6.81	6.82	0.63																		
3 Total (SAs)2	92.71	271.40	0.59	0.90																	
4 Vertical-upstream SAs	1.61	2.31	0.18	0.45	0.28																
5 Vertical-upstream (SAs)^2	7.93	22.38	0.12	0.40	0.25	0.90															
6 Horizontal SAs	2.24	3.44	0.58	0.84	0.84	0.17	0.14														
7 Horizontal (SAs)^2	16.83	77.91	0.53	0.73	0.89	0.11	0.06	0.88													
8 Vertical-downstream SAs	2.99	3.57	0.53	0.81	0.73	0.05	0.05	0.55	0.49												
9 Vertical-downstream (SAs)^2	21.68	71.69	0.45	0.71	0.76	0.04	0.04	0.49	0.50	0.86											
10 Age total SAs	35.75	23.20	0.04	0.09	0.09	0.10	0.08	0.02	0.02	0.09	0.09										
11 Age vertical-upstream SAs	21.93	28.12	0.15	0.32	0.21	0.50	0.28	0.17	0.11	0.12	0.07	0.39									
12 Age Horizontal SAs	25.11	26.72	0.09	0.23	0.16	0.10	0.08	0.22	0.08	0.17	0.16	0.50	0.22								
13 Age vertical-downstream SAs	29.21	28.63	0.19	0.18	0.14	-0.04	-0.03	0.11	0.08	0.25	0.15	0.60	0.10	0.25							
14 Equity vs. non-equity SAs	0.05	0.16	0.10	0.01	0.02	0.01	0.01	0.02	0.01	-0.01	0.01	-0.11	-0.03	-0.09	-0.08						
15 Firm size	161.17	573.19	0.55	0.62	0.73	0.08	0.04	0.75	0.86	0.43	0.38	0.03	0.07	0.06	0.08	0.02					
16 Firm age	9.61	4.62	0.32	0.30	0.29	-0.03	-0.04	0.28	0.24	0.33	0.28	0.32	0.13	0.22	0.37	-0.02	0.23				
17 Economies of scope	6.23	4.71	0.39	0.50	0.49	0.17	0.13	0.44	0.40	0.42	0.43	0.08	0.19	0.19	0.03	0.02	0.40	0.27			
18 Public	0.69	0.46	0.19	0.17	0.11	0.08	0.06	0.05	0.05	0.22	0.12	0.01	0.06	0.01	0.09	-0.01	0.09	0.17	0.06		
19 Subsidiary	0.08	0.27	≠0.04	0.01	0.03	-0.06	-0.04	0.04	0.04	0.01	0.01	0.18	0.03	0.12	0.13	-0.06	0.01	0.05	0.03	-0.18	
20 Country	0.78	0.42	0.07	0.11	0.09	0.07	0.05	0.07	0.06	0.10	0.06	-0.03	0.09	-0.01	0.01	0.04	0.06	0.01	0.04	0.11	-0.04

Correlations greater than or equal to 0.28 are significant ($p < 0.05$), N = 325.

Table 5.2   Regression results – full sample

	Model 1 NPD	Model 2 NPD	Model 3 NPD	Model 4 NPD	Model 5 NPD	Model 6 NPD
Constant	1.14922[d]	1.07284[d]	1.08742[d]	1.09923[d]	1.13521[d]	1.05476[d]
	(0.11468)	(0.11839)	(0.11631)	(0.11221)	(0.11464)	(0.11438)
Equity vs. non-equity SAs	0.42375[b]	0.39750[b]	0.40535[a]	0.36407[a]	0.44317[b]	0.36904[b]
	(0.2144)	(0.19852)	(0.21280)	(0.20511)	(0.20356)	(0.19657)
Firm size	0.00024[d]	0.00013[b]	0.00023[d]	0.00019[a]	0.00016[c]	0.00018[b]
	(0.00006)	(0.00006)	(0.00006)	(0.00010)	(0.00006)	(0.00010)
Firm age	0.02493[d]	0.01971[c]	0.02661[d]	0.01955[c]	0.01342[b]	0.01287[a]
	(0.00772)	(0.00764)	(0.00774)	(0.00759)	(0.00798)	(0.00783)
Economies of scope	0.02522[d]	0.01094	0.02302[c]	0.01822[c]	0.01809[b]	0.01313[b]
	(0.00776)	(0.00773)	(0.00774)	(0.00760)	(0.00803)	(0.00788)
Public	0.21397[c]	0.15777[b]	0.20709[c]	0.22952[c]	0.13617[a]	0.15074[b]
	(0.07788)	(0.07360)	(0.07719)	(0.07513)	(0.07623)	(0.07474)
Subsidiary	−0.05347	−0.03557	−0.02913	−0.03935	−0.09873	−0.04657
	(0.13217)	(0.12636)	(0.13150)	(0.12899)	(0.12808)	(0.12603)
Country	0.05082	0.00777	0.03382	0.04415	0.02891	0.01517
	(0.08278)	(0.07795)	(0.08249)	(0.07959)	(0.07963)	(0.07747)
Age total SAs		−0.00143				
		(0.00024)				
Age vertical-upstream SAs			−0.00058			−0.00172
			(0.00150)			(0.00146)
Age horizontal SAs				−0.00175		−0.00245[b]
				(0.00137)		(0.00140)
Age vertical-downstream SAs					0.00167[a]	0.00238[b]
					(0.00130)	(0.00129)
Total SAs		0.06073[d]				
		(0.00983)				
Toyal SAs²		−0.00081[d]				
		(0.00024)				
Vertical-upstream SAs			0.07113[b]			0.09525[c]
			(0.03922)			(0.03712)
Vertical-upstream SAs²			−0.00351			−0.00612[b]
			(0.00363)			(0.00341)
Horizontal SAs				0.10493[d]		0.07645[d]
				(0.02002)		(0.02095)
Horizontal SAs²				−0.00330[d]		−0.00299[c]
				(0.00137)		(0.00106)
Vertical-downstream SAs					0.07732[d]	0.05509[c]
					(0.01826)	(0.01907)
Vertical-downstream SAs2					−0.00183[c]	−0.00095
					(0.00078)	(0.00082)
Log likelihood ratio test	467.86[d]	510.56[d]	475.49[d]	494.76[d]	495.18[d]	519.79[d]
Improvement over base model		42.70[b]	7.63[b]	26.90[d]	27.32[d]	51.93[d]
N	325	325	325	325	325	325

[a] $p < 0.1$; [b] $p < 0.05$; [c] $p < 0.01$; [d] $p < 0.001$. Standard errors are reported in parentheses.

vertical-downstream alliances. The 325 firms split into 253 (78 percent) US-based firms and 72 (22 percent) foreign-based firms; 224 (69 percent) public firms and 101 (31 percent) private firms, and about 8 percent subsidiary firms. The average new biotechnology firm has entered into about 7 alliances, is about 9½ years old, and has 161 employees. A descriptive statistic of the variables as well as a correlation matrix can be found in table 5.1, while table 5.2 depicts the regression results for the full sample.

Model 1 depicts the base model including the control variables. Hypothesis 1 advances the notion that the relationship between the total number of a new entrant's strategic alliances and its new product development is curvilinear. Hypotheses 1a–c state that the relationships between a start-up's vertical-upstream, horizontal, and vertical-downstream alliances and its new product development are curvilinear. We find support for the hypotheses of diminishing marginal and subsequently diminishing total returns with respect to the new biotechnology firm's total number of alliances (Models 2 at $p < 0.001$), horizontal alliances (Model 4 at $p < 0.001$), and vertical-downstream alliances (Model 5 at $p < 0.01$). We fail to find support for a curvilinear relationship between vertical-upstream alliances and new product development (Hypothesis 1a) when analyzing vertical-upstream alliances in isolation (Model 3), even though the signs are in the expected direction and the linear term for vertical-upstream alliances is significant ($p < 0.05$). However, we find support for Hypothesis 1a at $p < 0.05$ in the full model (Model 6). In sum, we find support for Hypotheses 1 and 1a–c.

These results indicate that, given this sample and time period, there exists – on the average – a theoretically optimal number of alliances into which a new entrant firm should enter. To calculate the respective points of diminishing total returns (DTR), we took the partial derivatives with respect to the total number of strategic alliances (Model 2), vertical-upstream alliances (Model 3), horizontal alliances (Models 4), and vertical-downstream alliances (Model 5). The data suggest that new entrant firms reach their respective point of DTR somewhere around 10 vertical-upstream alliances, 16 horizontal alliances, 21 vertical-downstream alliances, and 37 total alliances. We would like to point out that these numbers are contingent upon the sample and time frame under investigation, thus, the result is more suggestive than prescriptive. The important message, however, is that at some point there are diminishing and subsequently negative returns to adding more alliances to an existing alliance portfolio.

Hypothesis 2a states that the alliance activity of new entrants at the industry level increases as the focal point of alliances moves downstream in the product development process, i.e., that the lowest number of alliances are expected to be vertical-upstream alliances, followed by horizontal alliances, while vertical-downstream alliances are the most prevalent. Overall, the new biotech firms entered into 2,226 alliances, which split into 524 vertical-upstream, 729 horizontal, and 973 vertical-downstream alliances. Applying a t-test, we find strong support for this hypothesis, as new entrants use vertical-downstream alliances at a significantly greater frequency than horizontal alliances ($p < 0.001$), and in turn, horizontal alliances at a significantly greater frequency than vertical-upstream alliances ($p < 0.01$).

Hypothesis 2b posits that the point of diminishing total returns for individual firms varies with the type of alliance partnership, with vertical-upstream alliances reaching the point of diminishing total returns first, followed by horizontal alliances, and finally

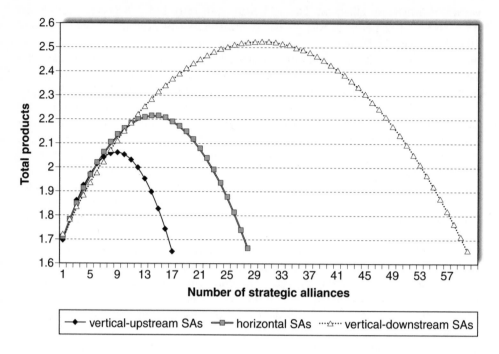

Figure 5.1   Alliance type, points of diminishing total returns, and new product development

vertical downstream alliances. Based on the calculations described above, we find that the point of DTR increases from about 10 vertical-upstream alliances to 16 horizontal alliances and finally to 21 vertical-downstream alliances. There is a substantial difference in the point of DTR for each of these types of alliances. In particular, there is a 60 percent increase in the number of alliances that a firm can manage when comparing vertical-upstream and horizontal alliances, and a 31.25 percent increase between horizontal and vertical-downstream alliances, as one moves down in the product development process. Overall, there is an approximately 110 percent increase in the number of alliances that can be managed when moving from vertical-upstream alliances to vertical-downstream alliances.

These findings provide some preliminary support for Hypothesis 2b. Additionally, we applied a Wald-type test to the full model (Model 6) to test whether the differences in the respective points of DTR are significant. We find that the point of DTR for vertical-downstream alliances is significantly larger than the point of DTR for horizontal alliances ($p < 0.001$) and that the point of DTR for horizontal alliances, in turn, is significantly larger than the point of DTR for vertical-upstream alliances ($p < 0.05$). Thus, we find support for Hypothesis 2b. Figure 5.1 depicts the relationship between the different types of alliances and their respective points of DTR for new product development based on the actual coefficients calculated in Model 6.

Hypothesis 3 posits that firm experience is positively related to a firm's capability to manage strategic alliances. To test this hypothesis, we split the sample into three

Table 5.3 Descriptive statistics for subsamples

Variable	Youngest third in age				Middle third in age				Oldest third in age			
	Mean	Std. dev.	Max.	Min.	Mean	Std. dev.	Max.	Min.	Mean	Std. dev.	Max.	Min.
New product development	4.77	3.16	17	1	6.28	4.37	25	1	8.00	6.34	29	1
Total alliances	4.84	3.39	22	1	6.84	5.26	24	1	8.76	9.69	58	1
Vertical-upstream alliances	1.50	2.23	11	0	1.99	2.82	14	0	1.35	1.72	8	0
Horizontal alliances	1.60	1.83	10	0	1.87	2.09	11	0	3.26	5.15	30	0
Vertical-downstream alliances	1.81	1.65	8	0	3.03	2.92	15	0	4.16	4.95	31	0
Age total alliances	26.26	14.61	89.5	2	38.78	25.40	159	6	42.30	25.00	174	3
Age vertical-upstream alliances	15.25	19.82	91	0	26.36	31.05	126	0	24.22	31.04	133	0
Age horizontal alliances	19.06	21.29	110	0	26.42	28.23	159	0	29.91	29.06	148	0
Age vertical-downstream alliances	17.68	15.16	63	0	29.45	20.67	102	0	40.60	39.45	258	0
Equity vs. non-equity alliances	0.05	0.16	1	0	0.05	0.18	1	0	0.04	0.13	1	0
Firm size	57.84	69.95	545	4	113.70	149.01	1300	3	312.91	965.06	7500	3
Firm age	4.87	1.32	7	1	9.15	1.10	11	7	14.84	3.30	27	11
Economies of scope	5.25	3.59	18	1	5.57	3.46	16	1	7.87	6.17	33	1
Public	0.56	0.50	1	0	0.74	0.44	1	0	0.77	0.42	1	0
Subsidiary	0.06	0.23	1	0	0.07	0.25	1	0	0.11	0.23	1	0
Country	0.72	0.45	1	0	0.84	0.37	1	0	0.78	0.42	1	0

Table 5.4   Regression results – subsamples

	Model 7 Old third age NPD	Model 8 Old third age NPD	Model 9 Mid third age NPD	Model 10 Mid third age NPD	Model 11 Young third age NPD	Model 12 Young third age NPD
Constant	1.17937[d] (0.31705)	1.41072[d] (0.28693)	0.761631 (0.54926)	0.44459 (0.55066)	1.07218[d] (0.26725)	0.81137[c] (0.27165)
Equity vs. non-equity SAs	1.16500[c] (0.39491)	0.96033[d] (0.30953)	0.13884 (0.35228)	0.15790 (0.33976)	−0.00153 (0.36225)	0.20282 (0.36251)
Firm size	0.00021[d] (0.00006)	0.00006 (0.00005)	0.00113[c] (0.00048)	0.00063[a] (0.00049)	0.00224[d] (0.00070)	0.00210[d] (0.00065)
Firm age	0.01639 (0.01679)	0.00562 (0.01506)	0.07138 (0.05791)	0.07709[a] (0.05618)	0.03334 (0.04359)	−0.01768 (0.04261)
Economies of scope	0.02612[c] (0.00976)	−0.00159 (0.00951)	0.03388[b] (0.01728)	0.02442[a] (1.44180)	0.01091 (0.01627)	−0.00551 (0.01597)
Public	0.26507[b] (0.13522)	0.17066 (0.11678)	0.09860 (0.15028)	0.09638 (0.14499)	0.10188 (0.12019)	0.03419 (0.11430)
Subsidiary	−0.17005 (0.18081)	−0.26800[a] (0.16259)	−0.52199[b] (0.29238)	−0.40389[a] (0.29961)	0.46801[b] (0.22953)	0.56823[c] (0.21348)
Country	0.07214 (0.13675)	−0.01785 (0.11822)	0.02877 (0.16585)	−0.00906 (0.16102)	0.04475 (0.12638)	0.02898 (0.11790)
Age total SAs		−0.00349[a] (0.00209)		0.00028 (0.00264)		0.00672[b] (0.00411)
Total SAs		0.06622[d] (0.01246)		0.07760[b] (0.03790)		0.11920[c] (0.04026)
Total SAs²		−0.00068[c] (0.00024)		−0.00212[a] (0.00168)		−0.00404[b] (0.00224)
Log likelihood ratio test	256.27[d]	286.37[d]	103.21[d]	112.50[d]	47.58[d]	63.75[d]
Improvement over base model		30.10[d]		9.29[b]		16.17[c]
N	108	108	108	108	109	109

[a] $p < 0.1$; [b] $p < 0.05$; [c] $p < 0.01$; [d] $p < 0.001$. Standard errors are reported in parentheses.

subsamples based on the age of the firm. The descriptive statistics presented in table 5.3 for each subsample support this assertion. The mean numbers of total, vertical-upstream, horizontal, and vertical-downstream alliances increase from the youngest to the middle-age subsample, and in turn, from the middle-age to the oldest subsample in all cases ($p < 0.1$ or smaller), except when comparing the number of vertical-upstream alliances between the middle-age and oldest subsample. In addition, the mean value of the dependent variable *new product development* increases significantly from the youngest to the middle-age subsample, and in turn, from the middle-age to the oldest subsample in all cases ($p < 0.05$ or smaller). Overall, the descriptive statistics indicate that our three subsamples are distinctly different on the variables of interest and support our choice of age as the basis for dividing the sample.

The results for the three subsamples are presented in table 5.4. On the average, firms in the oldest third subsample reach their point of DTR around 49 total alliances

(Model 8). Firms in the middle third subsample reach their point of DTR at around 18 total alliances (Model 10). Firms in the youngest third subsample reach their point of DTR at about 15 total alliances (Model 12). Applying a Wald-type test yields that firms in the oldest third subsample can manage more total alliances than the firms in the middle third and youngest third subsample ($p < 0.001$). Our results provide support for Hypothesis 3.

Conclusion

Taken as whole, the results of this analysis provide an interesting picture and three strong findings. The first finding supports and extends earlier work (Deeds and Hill, 1996). We find strong evidence of a curvilinear relationship between the number of strategic alliances in which a firm participates and its new product development. We extend prior research by demonstrating that this relationship holds at a finer level of analysis when alliances are split by type. This finding is important, because managers need to recognize that there are limits to the firm's ability to manage alliances. Past a certain point, one more vertical-upstream, horizontal or vertical-downstream alliance may not necessarily increase new product development as expected, but instead may actually decrease it. In addition to recognizing that there is an overall limit to the number of alliances a firm can effectively manage, it is important to note that different types of alliances pose more or fewer challenges to managers. Therefore, for different types of alliances, declining returns will set in at different levels of alliance intensity.

The second finding is that the type of the alliance also has an important impact on both the relationship to new product development and the number of alliances a firm can manage. Figure 5.1 indicates that the point of DTR increases when moving from vertical-upstream alliances to horizontal alliances and to vertical-downstream alliances. It further indicates that new product development is most frequent for vertical-downstream alliances, followed by horizontal alliances, and finally vertical-upstream alliances. We thus believe that the intensity of the managerial challenge posed by an alliance decreases as the focal point of the alliance progresses through the new product development process. Early stage alliances with high levels of uncertainty, ambiguity, and complexity appear to be much more demanding of the firm's managerial capabilities than later stage alliances. Therefore, managers need to recognize these differences and balance their portfolio of alliances accordingly.

The third finding is that there exists an experience curve in alliance management. More experienced firms can successfully manage a much larger number of alliances than less experienced firms. Experience effects in alliance management have been discussed in prior work, and our results provide some quantitative evidence in support of the concept. Future research should focus on other firm-specific factors that would explain interfirm differences with regard to their respective points of DTR. While we have focused on firm experience, other factors to be considered could be relative absorptive capacity (Lane and Lubatkin, 1998), operating routines (Stinchcombe, 1965), organizational structure and compensation systems (Henderson and Cockburn, 1994), early alliance networks (Baum, et al., 2000), and reputation of alliance partners (Stuart, et al., 1999).

While our results provide support for our hypotheses, we must also acknowledge that our focus on biotechnology raises questions about the generalizability of our study beyond this industry. Biotechnology has several unique characteristics, including a long product development and approval cycle, heavy reliance upon often arcane basic scientific research, and a very expensive product development process. In fact, biotechnology firms are facing extremely high levels of uncertainty, ambiguity, and complexity in the product development process. Despite these unique characteristics in our sample, we still believe that our results are generalizable beyond the biotechnology industry. Basic science appears to be playing a more significant role in the success and failure of individual firms (Dasgupta and David, 1994). This trend increases the levels of uncertainty, ambiguity, and complexity in many types of high-technology firms.

Another limitation of this study is that we were only able to study surviving alliances. In particular, given the higher degree of uncertainty involved in vertical-upstream alliances, one would expect them to exhibit a higher mortality rate relative to horizontal or vertical-downstream alliances. However, it is important to note that alliances in the biotechnology industry are characterized by longevity, since the product development process can take 15 years or more (Burrill, 1999). In addition, Shan et al. (1994) find that only 15 percent of the alliances entered since the early 1970s had expired by 1989. Another piece of evidence that only a small number of biotechnology alliances are terminated is provided by Green (1997), who reports that in 1996 only 21 alliances were terminated while 180 new alliances were formed. Given the low mortality rate of alliances in the biotechnology industry, we believe that our results are not materially influenced by a potential survivorship bias.

In the end our results provide a clear indication that both declining returns and experience curve effects apply to the problems of managing strategic alliances. In the future, both researchers and managers need to take these findings into account when considering strategic alliances. The entrepreneurs in biotechnology have provided important lessons that need to be understood by managers of both large and small firms. Strategic alliances are an important means of organizing work. They can clearly create value for the firms using them, but there are also substantial managerial costs that must be factored into the decision about when and what type of alliance to enter. It has long been known that entrepreneurial firms frequently "hit the wall" as they grow beyond the capabilities of the founding team and the simple organizational structure that they developed as early stage ventures. The consequences of "hitting the wall" are that projects and processes spiral out of control, productivity declines, and eventually, if the trend is not reversed, the new venture fails. The increased reliance upon strategic alliances as a means to access resources may decrease the cash needs of a new venture, but it clearly increases the demands on the managerial resources. Our results suggest that the requirement for better, more professional management may come earlier in new ventures that are relying heavily on alliances for resources, because the complexity of the managerial task in these firms is significantly greater. Entrepreneurs need to recognize that the demand for high-quality management skills and a well-developed organizational infrastructure are likely to come earlier and be more important to a firm balancing the tasks of complex R&D projects and numerous cross-boundary relationships. In fact, there are some indications that the benefits from alliance participation by new ventures has been mixed at best (Alvarez and Barney, 2000).

Our results also make it clear that entrepreneurs and mangers, particularly among high technology start-ups, must consider the impacts of a company's portfolio of alliances rather than looking at each alliance in isolation. Managers need to think about the impact of entering or exiting an alliance in the context of the firm's current portfolio of alliances. Will the additional alliance add value? Will it consume too much managerial time and energy? Is it an interesting enough opportunity that a firm should exit from one of its other alliances in order to properly pursue this one? These are the kinds of questions to which managers need answers and that the research on alliances should address. Researchers should build on the findings of this study and begin to examine other firm and alliance-level characteristics that impact the ability of the firm to achieve results using strategic alliances.

References

Alvarez S. A. and Barney J. B. 2000: *How Can Entrepreneurial Firms Really Benefit from Alliances with Large Firms?* Working paper. Fisher College of Business. The Ohio State University.

Arora, A. and Gambardella, A. 1990: Complementarity and external linkages: the strategies of the large firms in biotechnology. *Journal of Industrial Economics*, 4, 361–79.

Baum, J. A. C., Calabrese, T., and Silverman, B. S. 2000: Don't go it alone: alliance network composition and startups' performance in Canadian biotechnology. *Strategic Management Journal*, 21, 267–94.

BioScan The Worldwide Biotech Industry Reporting Service, 1997: December. Atlanta GA: American Health Consultants.

Burrill, G. S. 1999: *Biotech '99: Life Science into the Millennium*. San Francisco, CA: Burrill and Company.

Chandler, A. D. 1962: *Strategy and Structure: Chapters in the History of the American Industrial Enterprise*. Cambridge, MA: MIT Press.

Dasgupta, P. and David, P. A. 1994: Toward a new economics of science. *Research Policy*, 23, 487–521.

DeCarolis, D. M. and Deeds, D. L. 1999: The impact of stocks and flows of organizational knowledge on firm performance: an empirical investigation of the biotechnology industry. *Strategic Management Journal*, 20, 953–68.

Deeds. D. L. and Hill, C. W. L. 1996: Strategic alliances and the rate of new product development: an empirical study of entrepreneurial biotechnology firms. *Journal of Business Venturing*, 11, 41–55.

Green, D. 1997: Biotech partners: symbiosis puts down some roots. *Financial Times.* April 24.

Greene, W. H. 1997: *Econometric Analysis*. Upper Saddle River, NJ: Prentice-Hall.

Gulati, R. and Singh, H. 1998: The architecture of cooperation: managing coordination costs and appropriation concerns in strategic alliances. *Administrative Science Quarterly*, 43, 781–814.

Hagedoorn, J. 1993: Understanding the rationale of strategic technology partnering: interorganizational modes of cooperation and sectoral differences. *Strategic Management Journal*, 14, 371–85.

Hannan, M. T. and Freeman, J. 1989: *Organizational Ecology*. Cambridge, MA.: Harvard University Press.

Harrigan, K. R. 1985: *Strategies for Joint Ventures*. Lexington, MA: Lexington Books.

Henderson, R. M. and Cockburn, I. 1994: Measuring competence? Exploring firm effects in pharmaceutical research. *Strategic Management Journal*, 15, 63–84.

Hennart, J.-F., Roehl, T., and Zietlow, D. S. 1999: Trojan horse or workhorse? The evolution of U.S.-Japanese joint ventures in the United States. *Strategic Management Journal*, 20, 15–29.

Hitt, M. A., Hoskisson, R. E., and Ireland, R. D. 1994: A mid-range theory of the interactive effects of international and product diversification. *Journal of Management*, 20, 297–326.

Hitt, M. A., Hoskisson, R. E., and Kim, H. 1997: International diversification: effects on innovation and firm performance in product-diversified firms. *Academy of Management Journal*, 40, 767–98.

Jones, G. R. and Hill, C. W. L. 1988: Transaction cost analysis of strategy-structure choice. *Strategic Management Journal*, 9, 159–72.

Kelm, K. M., Narayanan, V. K., and Pinches, G. E. 1995: Shareholder value creation during R&D innovation and commercialization stages. *Academy of Management Journal*, 38: 770–86.

Kogut, B., Shan, W., and Walker, G. 1992: The make-or-cooperate decision in the context of an industry network. In N. Nohria and R. G. Eccles (eds), *Networks and Organizations: Structure, Form, and Action*. Boston, MA: Harvard University Press, 348–65.

Lane, P. J. and Lubatkin, M. 1998: Relative absorptive capacity and interorganizational learning. *Strategic Management Journal*, 19, 461–77.

Lei, D. and Slocum, J. W. 1992: Global strategy, competence-building and strategic alliances. *California Management Review*, 35, 81–97.

Lieberman, M. B. and Montgomery, D. B. 1988: First-mover advantages. *Strategic Management Journal*, 9: 41–58.

McMillan, G. S., Narin, F., and Deeds, D. L. 2000: An analysis of the critical role of public science in innovation: the case of biotechnology. *Research Policy*, 29: 1–8.

March, J. G. 1991: Exploration and exploitation in organizational learning. *Organization Science* 2: 71–87.

Mowery, D. C. 1990: The development of industrial research in U.S. manufacturing. *American Economic Review*, 80, 345–9.

Pisano, G. P. 1994: Knowledge, integration, and the locus of learning: an empirical analysis of process development. *Strategic Management Journal*, 15, 85–100.

Rothaermel, F. T. 2000: Technological discontinuities and the nature of competition. *Technology Analysis and Strategic Management*, 12: 149–60.

Rothaermel, F. T. 2001: Incumbent's advantage through exploiting complementary assets via interfirm cooperation. *Strategic Management Journal*, (22) (6–7), 687–99.

Schoonhoven, C. B., Eisenhardt, K. M., and Lyman, K. 1990: Speeding products to market: waiting time to first product introduction in new firms. *Administrative Science Quarterly*, 35, 177–207.

Shan, W., Walker, G., and Kogut, B. 1994: Interfirm cooperation and startup innovation in the biotechnology industry. *Strategic Management Journal*, 15, 387–94.

Simon, H. A. 1960: *The New Science of Management Decision*. New York: Harper and Row.

Simonin, B. L. 1999: Ambiguity and the process of knowledge transfer in strategic alliances. *Strategic Management Journal*, 20, 595–623.

Stalk, G. J. and Hout, T. M. 1990: Competing against time. *Research Technology Management*, 32, 19–24.

Stinchcombe, A. 1965: Social structure and organizations. In J. G. March (ed.), *Handbook of Organizations*. Chicago, IL: Rand McNally, 142–93.

Stuart, T. E, Hoang, H., and Hybels, R. C. 1999: Interorganizational endorsements and the performance of entrepreneurial ventures. *Administrative Science Quarterly*, 44, 315–49.

Teece, D. J. 1992: Competition, cooperation, and innovation: organizational arrangements for regimes of rapid technological progress. *Journal of Economic Behavior and Organization*, 18, 1–25.

Williamson, O. 1985: *The Economic Institutions of Capitalism*. New York: Free Press.

CHAPTER SIX

Knowledge Creation and Utilization: Promoting Dynamic Systems of Creative Routines

Ikujiro Nonaka and Patrick Reinmoeller

Introduction

Creative renewal in industries, organizations, and teams is the key to strategic thinking and acting in the entrepreneurial millennium. Routines of creative renewal are simple processes that create and exploit knowledge within large organizations. In these entrepreneurial times, when new ventures and start-ups threaten incumbents, knowledge management attempts to contribute to theory and practice of strategy. During the 1990s knowledge management focused on achieving operational excellence through explicit knowledge, closed systems for information processing and over looked the fact that knowledge resides in contexts.

The problems of creating and utilizing knowledge, however, are related to the degree of embeddedness (Granovetter, 1985). Explicit knowledge and best practices diffuse quickly (Boisot, 1997) and personal knowledge of employees can be rapidly lost, if it is not embedded in patterns of interaction (Teece, 2000). Recently researchers and practitioners have begun to emphasize dynamic relationships, interactions, and contexts (APQC, 2000). Information technology can assist knowledge management but organizations must develop dynamic business systems to create *and* utilize knowledge effectively *and* efficiently (Nonaka et al., 2001). Closed business systems aim at stabilizing organizational processes in order to develop routines apart from contexts, while dynamic business systems develop embedded routines to create and utilize knowledge for innovation, i.e. creative routines. Dynamic business systems are built from organically integrated structural and procedural components; they are open to continuously changing contexts. Creative routines for dealing with knowledge and using contexts emerge from the juxtaposition of structural and procedural technologies, and synchronic and diachronic processes.

This chapter develops the concept of creative routines and emphasizes dialogue and improvising. Creative routines make complex idiosyncratic relationships in dynamic business systems visible and trigger pragmatic action. Creative routines contribute to competitive advantage because they drive knowledge conversions on different levels, including the level of the so-called deep tacit knowledge that is authentic, hidden in contexts, distributed, and difficult to imitate.

First, creation and utilization processes in knowledge creation theory are briefly introduced. Then, the structural and procedural components of dynamic systems and the concept of creative routines are developed. We further distinguish three levels of creative routines and analyze the context-dependency of creative routines such as improvising and dialoguing. Three case studies of Seven-Eleven Japan, Toyota Motor Corporation, and Cisco Systems illustrate dynamic business systems and creative routines. The final section summarizes the concept of creative routines as pragmatic way to introduce entrepreneurial processes to organizations, to leverage deep tacit knowledge, and to harness the creative forces of dynamic contexts.

The SECI model: Knowledge Creation and Utilization

The set of standardized tools or best practices in knowledge management systems emphasizes the appropriating and sharing of existing knowledge; however, this is not enough to sustain competitive advantage through continuously innovating. Instead, dynamic systems are needed that support knowledge creation and utilization through reliable structures and processes (Amabile and Conti, 1999). There are two directions of developing dynamic systems for knowledge creation and utilization. First, information technology systems can be designed to trigger and invigorate action-reflection feedback (Nonaka et al., 1998). Second, models of dynamic business systems are developed to shape routines of interaction in shared contexts (Nonaka and Reinmoeller, 2000).

Operational structures and processes have to embed continuous creative destruction as creative routines. Routines preserve and refine organizational structures, but they can also be impediments to innovation and change (Nelson and Winter, 1982; Leonard-Barton, 1992). Therefore, creative routines and human intervention in contexts are necessary because they are the sticky media and modules of dynamic business systems to promote innovation through knowledge creation and utilization.

Organizations create and utilize knowledge through the interaction between explicit and tacit knowledge, the processes of knowledge conversion. There are four modes of knowledge conversion: socialization, externalization, combination, and internalization (SECI) (Nonaka, 1990; Nonaka and Takeuchi, 1995, see figure 6.1). Through these processes, tacit and explicit knowledge expand in terms of quality and quantity. Socialization and externalization are processes that emphasize the creation of knowledge. Combination and internalization focus on utilization of knowledge. Creation and utilization processes continuously unfold side by side (synchronic) and in sequence over time (diachronic); they are not limited to one organizational level.

Many organizations focus on utilization of knowledge through information technology, such as databases or enterprise systems, few emphasize the creation of tacit knowledge. Both approaches tend to become static, infused in isolated or automated

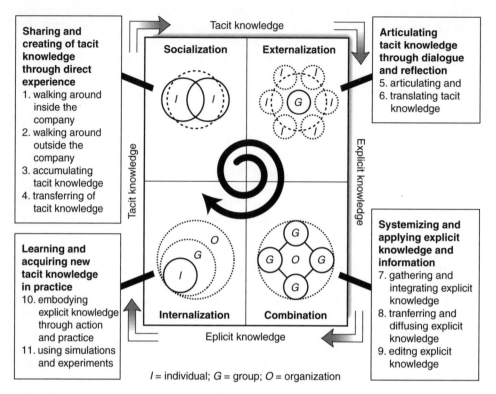

Figure 6.1   The SECI model of knowledge creation and utilization
Source: Nonaka and Takeuchi, 1995; Nonaka and Konno, 1999

processes. Dynamic systems establish a dynamic balance on the fine line between ex-ploration and exploitation (March, 1996). They develop creative routines to promote the spiral of the SECI processes, i.e., knowledge creation and utilization processes.

Knowledge is commonly utilized in everyday business routines. Routines are funda-mental to sustainable social life and organizational processes (Giddens, 1993; Nelson and Winter, 1982). Routines emphasize repetitive action, replication, rules, standardi-zation, and stability; they thus can become barriers to the exploration and creation of new knowledge. Changing such stabilizing routines is difficult, but it is even more difficult to develop routines of innovation and improvisation that continuously chal-lenge the ways things are done. Further, standardized routines are visible and can be quickly imitated; they therefore become diffused as best practices. Therefore, organi-zations need to develop creative routines for conversion of tacit knowledge, that is, to embed action patterns for innovation. Creative routines are dynamic action patterns promoting innovation by creating and utilizing authentic knowledge on a daily basis. Creative routines are simultaneously the media and the constituents of dynamic sys-tems for knowledge creation and utilization; they are continuously evolving technolo-gies, methods, and procedures for paying attention, sensing, and acting creatively when fluctuations occur.

Dynamic organizational systems are more than the aggregated creative routines of organizational members. Similar to particles in quantum theory, creative routines are both tacit patterns of creative action and explicit procedures of collective interaction. Dynamic systems promote such creative routines within a context of structures and processes to synchronically and diachronically create and utilize knowledge in everyday organizational practice.

Structural and Procedural Components for Dynamic Business Systems

Dynamic business systems provide shared contexts in motion (*ba* in Japanese) by integrating hard and soft components of dynamic business systems (Nonaka and Reinmoeller, 2000). Contexts encompass the resources provided by continuously changing conditions and circumstances of the before, later (diachronic context), and now (synchronic context). Contexts generate relationships or meanings, therefore knowledge is information in contexts. Actions and knowledge processes are juxtaposed in such contexts (Granovetter, 1985; Suchmann, 1987; Nonaka and Konno, 1998).

In the same way, the contextual interdependence of acoustics and visuals influences human perception of ensembles in the Japanese art of *kabuki*. *Kabuki* juxtaposes different resources including sound, rhythm, costume, movement, dance, text, and the spatial arrangement of stages during each performance. These resources are equally important components of the context, and as the performance proceeds they create a dynamic and meaningful context (Eisenstein, 1953; Ueno, 1999).

The ways actions and knowledge shape contexts are influenced by the use of time. Management practice and theory emphasize the importance of time to increase cost-efficiency (Stalk and Hout, 1990; Northey and Southway, 1994; Fine, 1998). Only recently has the potential in a variety of time concepts been discovered. The relevant time concepts include synchronicity (Jaworski, 1996), strategy under the condition of complexity (Brown and Eisenhardt, 1998; Eisenhardt and Brown, 1998), and time experience as an enabling context for knowledge processes (Reinmoeller, 1999).

Dynamic systems juxtapose structural and procedural components (figure 6.2). The resulting contexts are transient, unstable phenomena in time. They develop and evolve; thus they need to be seized at the right moment (timing). Dynamic systems promote such contexts on a constant basis and prepare creative routines. Artifacts (e.g., telephones, offices, interfaces), people (e.g., colleagues, competitors, personal networks), and contextual knowledge (information and shared experiences, ideas, ideals), or any interaction of these can elicit creative routines. Frequent face-to-face contact or virtual meetings on the Internet, as well as informal dialogues over lunch, at the copier, or in front of the water cooler, are creative routines that are embedded in integrated structural and procedural systems.

The structural perspective

The structural perspective allows us to analyze and increase the stability of business systems. It focuses on information technology (IT), such as enterprise systems or

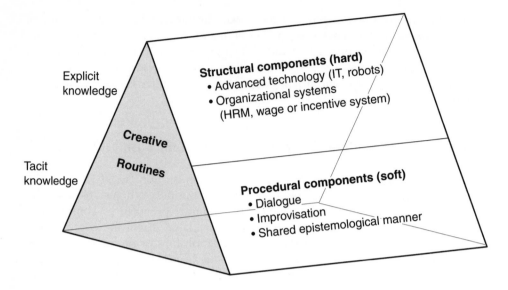

Figure 6.2   Creative routines and dynamic systems

organizational networks, and includes organizational systems. These systems are important in developing creative routines for knowledge utilization in everyday business. IT systems promote routines for systemizing and disseminating knowledge; organizational structure promotes routines for exercising and practicing new knowledge.

Information technology provides the structure in which explicit knowledge is created and exploited but it separates information from contexts. IT in knowledge management has three major advantages: efficiency, effectiveness, and velocity of appropriating, connecting, transmitting, utilization, access, and protection of knowledge (Choo, 1998; Churchill and Snowdon, 1998; Davenport and Pearlson, 1998; Davenport and Prusak, 1998; Ruggles, 1998; Earl, 1996; Turban et al., 1999).

There are, however, problems with this focus on IT tools in knowledge management that have been mentioned earlier. First, IT can support but not replace human creativity. Then, efficient IT is fast becoming standard practice and therefore less helpful in attaining competitive advantage (Davenport et al., 1998; Ishida, 1998; Schank, 1997). Finally, such tools to not take into account the contexts of knowledge and the embeddedness in social relationships (Clancey, 1997; Dyer and Singh, 1998). Recently, however, the increasing reach and richness of communication media and tools for visual real-time communication are addressing these problems.

The structural perspective includes specialized organizational systems. Knowledge is embedded in such organizational systems; they can be employed to effectively enhance learning and application. Human resource and career development programs are examples of systems promoting internalization of explicit knowledge. One important metaphor for organizational systems is the corporate university. Corporate universities are technology-enhanced learning environments in larger organizations. At Daimler-Chrysler, for instance, it combines the technological infrastructure of global computer networks for learning on-line, and the social architecture, including communities of practice and projects for virtual teams.

The procedural perspective

The procedural perspective represents the soft and transient side of dynamic systems, focusing on shared disciplines to sense and capture new meanings in changing contexts. Procedural systems integrate the capabilities, commitment, and discipline of people and contexts in motion through creative routines. Creative routines are dynamic action patterns; they emerge on the individual and the collective level. Creative routines including shared epistemological manner, dialogue, and improvisation help paying attention, sensing, and seizing opportunities. Thereby creative routines are essential to overcome impediments to knowledge processes such as lack of trust (Szulanski, 1996).

Deep dialogue is needed to promote externalization through sharing and articulating of tacit knowledge. Occasional contact with members of other departments, customers, or clients is not enough to share tacit knowledge. For deep dialogue, repeated face-to-face interaction is an effective way to capture the full range of physical senses and psycho-emotional reactions (e.g., joy, ease, or discomfort) and to transfer tacit knowledge synchronically and over a period of time (diachronically).

Improvising integrates individuals' mental models and skills through a dynamic process of co-creation. Individuals share mental models with others through joint acting and reflection, and by using creative language. The metaphor of improvising or jamming suggests the best of both worlds. Competition and playfulness, structure and openness, beginner's mind and professional experience, introspection and simultaneous extraversion increase the probabilities of serendipity and spontaneous emergence of meaning. Dynamic systems need to promote contexts that juxtapose multiple resources allowing individuals with complementary knowledge and capabilities to improvise. This chapter focuses on dialogue and improvising.

Shared epistemological manner is a set of processes based on the use of contexts in motion, the SECI spiral, and knowledge assets (Nonaka and Toyama, 1999). Leaders integrate these elements of knowledge creation to establish a company's "shared epistemological manner" so that effective and efficient knowledge creation becomes second nature in the organization. They increase the common base of contextual knowledge through shared vision and methods to pursue a common purpose.

Three Levels of Routines for Knowledge Conversion

Creative routines help to invent new ways of promoting knowledge processes including articulating knowledge by individuals or sharing knowledge in teams within or across organizational boundaries. Creative routines enable organizations to seize the opportunities for knowledge conversion that emerge with fluctuations.

For developing creative routines, three different levels of knowledge conversion processes need to be analyzed (figure 6.3). Knowledge conversions can involve, (1) only explicit knowledge; (2) tacit and explicit knowledge; and (3) only deep tacit knowledge. The three levels differ according to the intensity, depth of interaction, and

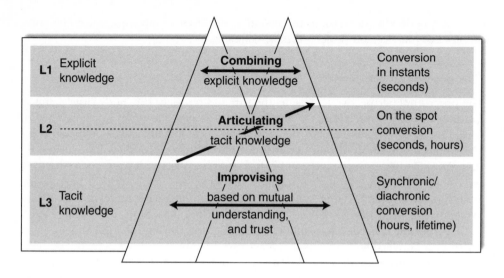

Figure 6.3   Three levels of creating and utilizing knowledge: duration of interaction between two parties
Source: Nonaka, et al., 1998; Nonaka and Reinmoeller, 2000

development of trust. Time is used as indicator of the potential for intensity, depth and trust on each level. Standard routines for connecting and learning help on the first level. Creative routines are needed to promote knowledge interactions on the second and third levels. Dynamic systems have to prepare and energize the creative routines on the three levels between two or more parties. The parties involved in the conversions can belong to internal departments or outside organizations; they can be individuals, groups, organizations, or wider networks.

Dynamic systems support these three levels in different ways. Each level comes with specific contexts and needs specific routines to maintain a dynamic balance between structural and procedural components. At level 1, explicit knowledge is gathered, combined, and utilized through communication media and standard routines. *Kaizen* models of incremental perfection (quality circles), apprenticeship, communities of practice (Brown and Duguid, 1991; Lave and Wenger, 1991; Senge, 1990; Wenger and Snyder, 2000), on-the-job training, and mentorship are well-known ways to structure skills and learning. They focus on learning by doing and/or guidance by experienced members. Such systems are important to convey and exercise specific practices to stabilize and refine routines. The time required to transmit explicit knowledge with information technology is increasingly reduced to real-time, that is, instants or points in time. Level 1 is the domain of current knowledge management. Digital technology and standard routines link explicit knowledge in real-time and provide instant access to large databases.

On this level three problems have to be solved. The first is a problem of technology. The transfer of explicit knowledge requires structural systems to make efficient transmission possible. Information technology and organizational systems can solve this problem effectively. Data mining or Intranets provide access or disseminate data inside organizations. Between organizations analogue and digital networks such as phone or Extranets and the Internet are used. The second problem is the problem of technology as commodity. Such technology and standard routines can be shared without context. These simple components can provide competitive advantage only for as long as the competitor needs to implement technology and best practices. The third problem is that of incentives. Organizational systems are the key to effective incentives. Within companies, the transfer of explicit knowledge needs to be systematically linked to compensation systems. Organizational members will share explicit knowledge when the incentive system and markets for knowledge provide compensation or rewards (Davenport and Prusak, 1998). The incentive systems are also important for external resources and absorption of best practices.

At level 2, the different parties help each other to articulate tacit knowledge. The second level of conversion from tacit to explicit knowledge requires intensive dialogue in shared contexts in motion (*ba*). The time that is required for such dialogue is a period of intensive and brief interaction. During this experience, the participants share tacit knowledge and partially understand each other's mental models. Mutual understanding and trust facilitate such synchronic articulation. If the time spent together is too short for sharing the same context, as for example through occasional chat on-line, the lack of intensity, depth, and trust is an impediment to mutual understanding or shared mental models. In knowledge management, some information technology, such as groupware, has become widely used on level 2. However, the dynamics of synchronous dialogue and improvisation in shared contexts have so far not been emulated by digital technology.

Two problems need to be solved on this second level. First, face-to-face interaction is important for dialogue. Face-to-face interaction delivers more than electronically mediated interaction because it includes contextual knowledge. However, long face-to-face time, for example, in more and longer meetings can be wasteful. Creative routines help to increase the effectiveness of face time. Second, for dialogue, creative routines that elicit the conversion of tacit into explicit knowledge are needed. However, people have to seize opportunities that emerge with fluctuations. People's skills determine the value of information technology in dynamic systems. Organizational systems such as human resource management, incentive systems, meeting schedules, operating procedures, patterns for problem solving, and dialogues are effective means of developing original and organization-specific creative routines.

Level 3 of knowledge creation and utilization is the most difficult but also the most important. Creative routines on this level are complex; they are idiosyncratic relationships embedded in dynamic systems. Such creative routines contribute to sustainable competitive advantage because tacit knowledge and processes are authentic, hidden in contexts, distributed, and therefore difficult to imitate. The essence of creative routines is to develop knowledge through the entrepreneurial process of continuous self-renewal. At level 3, both parties share their deep tacit knowledge and externalize it to promote innovation. The third level of conversion requires longer periods of time spent together. This includes longer diachronic experience for the sharing of rich tacit and contextual knowledge. Synchronic improvising in the course of a jam session is possible because trust and mutual understanding of deep tacit knowledge have been built through frequent and long experience over time (diachronic). On the third level, knowledge does not need to be articulated immediately; it can remain tacit. Deep tacit knowledge is created and utilized by improvising and bricolage, serendipity, crafting strategy, creative sparks, or jamming (Barrett, 1998; Crossan et al., 1996; Crossan, 1998; Leonard and Swap, 1999; Mintzberg, 1988; Mirvis, 1998). In the process of improvising, both parties interact by sensing and revealing deep tacit knowledge. In this sense, if mutual understanding and trust develop, knowledge is created on the spur of the moment and conceptual insight and practice are merged in action.

Creative Routines for Improvising

Creative routines for improvising include the use of symbolic language, distributed leadership, and cross-boundary teams. Such improvisation promotes sharing and articulation of new knowledge and connecting and learning of existing knowledge.

Symbolic language, including metaphors, analogy, and narratives, is based on common tacit knowledge. Symbols, images and narratives such as "war stories" of experiences at the "front line" convey insights and are intuitively understood (Shaw et al., 1998). 3M and Xerox have systemized creative routines for storytelling. At Xerox PARC, analogue storytelling is the basis for Eureka, a digital system that accumulates the personal success stories of copier repairmen.

Distributed leadership is necessary for the co-creation of prototypes in a group. Using experts with different complementary knowledge is important to broaden the scope of improvisation. When leadership is distributed simultaneously over place, time, and knowledge (expertise), creative routines help to integrate the different perspectives of people who share a common goal. Creative routines for distributed leadership allow flexible integration of individual knowledge, for instance, when people who promote knowledge creation and utilization become temporary leaders by volunteering tacit knowledge. Such leaders emerge from their peers by creating and utilizing knowledge in new ways. Creative routines foster the emergence of volunteers by facilitating improvisation in shared space and time.

Cross-functional teams link members with different expertise to support improvisation. A common base of tacit knowledge and a diversity of perspectives are important. Knowledge maps, knowledge yellow pages, or the design of offices with self-assigned seats facilitate the formation of cross-functional teams (Nonaka and Reinmoeller, 1999). Creative routines also provide cues that energize and sustain the dynamic balance between creation and utilization; teams often use milestones or deadlines. Cross-functional teams rely on a common perspective, specialized knowledge, and they improvise to realize the vision.

Creative Routines in Dynamic Business Systems: The Model

The model of creative routines and dynamic business systems is summarized in figure 6.4. The horizontal axis shows the external temporal context. It relates organizational activities in the value network to the diachronic development and the synchronic events of fluctuation or friction in everyday business. Headquarters govern these processes and these moments of occurrence. The vertical axis shows the three levels of knowledge creation and utilization. Level 1 is fundamental to dynamic systems and mainly built with tangible resources and structural components including information technology and organizational systems. Headquarters build this level and provide maintenance mainly to increase the efficiency of processes and create capabilities for real-time combination and sharing of knowledge.

On level 2, creative routines promote externalization and visualization. Creative routines are situated in shared contexts in motion (*ba*). Juxtaposed soft and hard systems support visualization, dialogue, and improvisation to articulate new ideas. Knowledge processes on level 3, including the internalization of skills and socialization with suppliers, colleagues, and customers in everyday business processes, take more time. Creative routines drive diachronic accumulation and continuous interaction that are the keys to anticipating and detecting fluctuation.

Creative routines enhance visualizing or articulating these fluctuations. Dynamic systems trigger creative routines of deep dialogue and improvisation to develop new hypotheses and to experiment. Means for visualization include images, metaphors, stories, visuals, and other techniques. Creative routines concentrate the distributed knowledge in the organization (people, perspectives) and energize processes of iterative testing and thinking (compassion, momentum) about new solutions to avoid fluctuations and improve business processes. Creative routines juxtapose testing and thinking, synchronic creation of new ideas, and diachronic utilization of expertise in shared changing contexts. They continuously generate the dynamic ensemble of new diachronic and synchronic patterns based on both procedural and structural systems. Creative routines, such as symbolic language, distributed leadership, and cross-functional teams are the keys to knowledge creation and utilization. Each case of a successful company is individually and authentically situated in specific contexts. However, creative routines that drive strategic creation and utilization of knowledge are common practice to leverage knowledge for innovation.

Case Studies: Adaptations of Dynamic Business Systems

The following cases, Seven-Eleven Japan, Toyota Motor Corporation, and Cisco Systems, show the different strategic adaptations of dynamic systems of creative routines in retail and manufacturing business. The three companies have built authentic dynamic business systems in which human intervention provides important contextual knowledge and new ideas. The case descriptions focus on how the organizations created and utilize knowledge through deep dialogue and improvisation; see figure 6.5 for a case study overview.

Seven-Eleven Japan

Ito-Yokado established Seven-Eleven Japan and opened the first Seven-Eleven stores in 1978. Since then Seven-Eleven Japan has become the most profitable

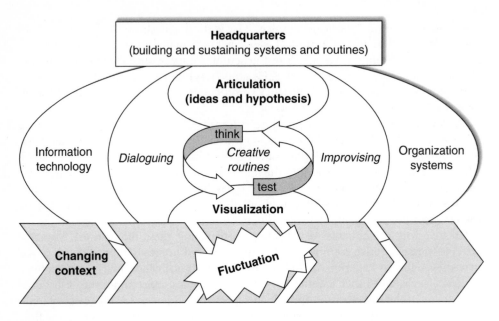

Figure 6.4   Dynamic systems and creative routines; using problems for knowledge conversion

retailer in Japan both in absolute and sales-profit ratio terms (Okamoto, 1998; Usui, 1998).

Each Seven-Eleven store of about 100 square meters sells some 2,800 items, of which about 70 percent change every year. To sustain this stream of innovations, Seven-Eleven makes extensive use of explicit knowledge such as manuals for store operation and employee training.

Recently Seven-Eleven has begun to implement an electronic commerce strategy that attempts to leverage the large retail network of 8,000 stores as a platform for cash and carry services of merchandise sold online.

Structural systems

Information technology.   Digital technology is an important part of Seven-Eleven's dynamic system (Mitsugi et al., 1998); it is used to eliminate mediocre products and to support innovation. The POS system (point of sale system) offers synchronic access to explicit knowledge from headquarters.

The POS system triggers the building and testing of hypotheses and to generate profitability listings. Constructing and verifying hypotheses are the key to Seven-Eleven's ability to innovate quickly. Each hypothesis is tested by actual orders and actual sales are again confirmed by POS data. Afterwards, successful hypotheses are collected and disseminated throughout the company.

The time needed to access databases and to combine knowledge is important on this

System components	Creative routines	Seven-Eleven Japan	Toyota Motor	Cisco Systems
Structural	Providing context	sevendream.com	Structure of Toyota Production Systems; vertical keiretsu	Internet, intranet; 24hrs virtual closure; network organization; Built-to-order
	Visualization	POS System; graphical user interfaces	ANDON system; Kaizen practice; poka-yoke	Internet, intranet, graphical user interface, browser
	Epistemological manners	"Adaptation to change", "adherence to fundamentals"	Persistent questioning, documenting	Exploiting change and generating customer value
	Articulation	Ordering by all employees; meetings, test luncheons	Workers/suppliers develop ideas in QC, assembly line	IT users (sales people) suggest improvements
	Dialoguing	Walking around employees, field counselors	Genbaism, QC circles;	Integration teams
Process	Improvising	Empirical intuitions on all hierarchical levels trigger change; realtime selection of products that do not sell	Trouble shooting at the place of work	Self-registered critical accounts

Figure 6.5   Case study overview: creative routines in business practice

level 1 of dynamic systems. Seven-Eleven analyzes new data on a daily basis and provides access in real-time. The new fifth-generation POS system includes satellite transmission from headquarters, data mining, and free access and queries from all stores.

Organizational systems

Seven-Eleven uses systematic training of store-owners and human resource development for employees to develop creative routines. The training of store-owners includes intensive periods of preparation and simulation for running a Seven-Eleven store.

Seven-Eleven emphasizes a mixed ordering-replenishing system that consists of automated processes with human intervention (Kunitomo, 1998, p. 243; Suzuki, 1998). The POS system is partly automated; it induces reflection upon simultaneous display of important data, visuals, and contextual information such as weather conditions. At headquarters, the sales data of all stores are analyzed on a daily basis. The POS system visualizes fluctuations and elicits new ideas from people at headquarters.

Human resource management at Seven-Eleven emphasizes OJT (on-the-job training) throughout the career path at Seven-Eleven. New employees start on the shop floor with their first learning experience, which is followed by assignments as store manager in one of the few directly managed stores, and later as field counselor. This variety of experiences is important for young entrants to internalize distributed knowledge in different contexts and to become familiar with different perspectives within the company. Managers who experience work in different positions become multiskilled; they internalize creative routines in different contexts. They are prepared to address fluctuations by utilizing past experiences and tacit knowledge to create new knowledge in the moments of crisis.

Procedural systems

Seven-Eleven's vision, "adapt to changes and pursue fundamentals," is linked to four guiding principles: freshness of goods; the best assortment of goods; cleanliness of stores, goods, and employee uniforms; and friendliness to customers. This vision provides criteria for all operational procedures and guidelines for store-owners, part-timers, and employees who are responsible for the customer interface (epistemological manner).

Dialogue and improvising.   Seven-Eleven has several systems for sharing the tacit knowledge of customers. Each shop floor is a place for face-to-face interaction between customers and employees. The shop-owners, field counselors, or walking-around employees are absorbing tacit knowledge by circulating inside and outside the company. Employees and owners on the front line continuously experience changes in customer mood and learn how to adapt to them. The changes in customer behavior are first spotted as fluctuations on the shop floor (synchronically) and later on a macro-level at headquarters (diachronically). Face-to-face interaction is important to improvise on these fluctuations on the spot (on the shop floor and at headquarters).

A system of meetings and other creative routines inspires thinking and testing. For example, knowledge of changes in customer needs is captured in the 8,000 stores of Seven-Eleven through short dialogues with customers (synchronic) and repetition of interaction over time (diachronic). Local employees share their knowledge with other employees and with operation field counselors (OFC). On level 2, creative routines of dialogue and improvisation are used to share and externalize images of experiences.

The OFCs visit stores frequently to consult the store-owners and engage in dialogue with customers and employees. The problems detected are augmented by the OFCs' knowledge (diachronic) and shared through OFC groupware and face-to-face dialogue (synchronic) at meetings in Tokyo. The OFCs collect problems and new ideas through dialogue with employees and observation. They concentrate distributed knowledge at the meetings in Tokyo (level 2).

All managers meet every Monday for the weekly face-to-face meeting (synchronic). President Suzuki expects the managers who are facing problems to leave the meeting to solve their problems immediately (improvising) and to return to the gathering and report on the strategies implemented, actions taken, and show early results. Thus,

President Suzuki triggers immediate action by synchronic face-to-face communication.

On the following day (Tuesday) all field counselors meet in Tokyo to attend a meeting; this synchronizes Seven-Eleven's market knowledge. During the meeting all field counselors listen to a speech by the energetic leader, Suzuki, who improvises on the company vision and current issues, including those discussed at the manager meeting. President Suzuki synchronizes Seven-Eleven's distributed expertise and prepares the integration of soft and hard technologies. He has generated creative routines to regularly create occasions for dialogue and improvisation.

Distributed leadership.   Seven-Eleven utilizes the distributed knowledge (expertise in local needs) of all employees and customers to improvise. Customer behavior and comments are observed and captured by employees on all hierarchical levels. Ordering responsibilities for product categories, for instance, are assigned to individual employees and jobbers who develop specific knowledge for hypothesis building.

Similarly, the testing of ideas through actual orders is done where new ideas are conceived. Thus, employees in each store are empowered to lead Seven-Eleven and introduce new ideas. Furthermore, employees are responsible for sales floor and service, store managers for the economic success of stores, OFC for regional performance, and people in headquarters for overall success; each addresses fluctuations at different levels of complexity.

Seven-Eleven utilizes distributed leadership in development teams that span the boundaries of organizations. Seven-Eleven systematically develops new products through strategic alliances with manufacturers that own complementary knowledge. This idea of creating and utilizing knowledge with (potentially competing) other organizations uses loosely coupled teams and face-to-face interactions.

The Seven-Eleven headquarters initiates the creative routine of team merchandising and forms a development team, together with experts from the manufacturers (supplier network). Finally, these new prototypes are evaluated at the officers' meeting at Seven-Eleven. If the approval of Seven-Eleven is gained, full support in terms of know-how and data is given to finalize the prototype and start production. Thus, the merchandising process at Seven-Eleven enables improvising within alliances through distributed leadership.

The team merchandising process is a creative routine that leverages the tacit knowledge of manufacturers with POS data and Seven-Eleven's dynamic system. However, the fast cycle of data analysis and replacement of poorly performing products creates continuously new products, but does not favor breakthrough innovations (Ogawa, 2000).

Toyota Motor Corporation

Toyota Motor Corporation, established in 1937, is the largest car manufacturer in Japan. The Toyota Production System is the prototype of "lean production." *Keiretsu* relationships with suppliers, and the design and development system have been critical for its success (Cusumano, 1985; Fujimoto, 1999; Sobek et al., 1999). During the economic crisis of the 1990s, Toyota emerged as the strongest independent Japanese carmaker and has been expanding its global reach by opening more factories abroad.

Structural systems

Information technology.   The so-called Toyota Production System includes just-in-time, automation, total quality control, and continuous improvement (*kaizen*), and other subsystems that are described in the literature (Fujimoto, 1999; Spear and Bowen 1999). These subsystems are based on the principles of reducing non-value-adding activities, reducing irregular pace of production and reducing workload. Digital information technology is gradually introduced to support the existing network relationships in the Toyota Production System.

Organizational systems

Organizational systems are very important for Toyota's dynamic system. This is illustrated by standard operating procedures, quality systems including quality circles, work teams or maintenance rules, and examples from human resource management.

Standard operating procedures for repetitive tasks explain specifics to the workers with visuals that are easy to understand. Such procedures are frequently revised to include successfully tested ideas that improve the overall result of the team, group, or assembly process. The visuals help all workers to quickly absorb the improvements made.

The system of quality circles is part of the organizational structure and culture. Standardized methods to increase the effectiveness of quality circles include the QC story (a standard sequence of analysis) and QC tools, a collection of visual material, all of which support workers in incremental innovation (Besser, 1996).

Total Productive Maintenance (TPM) and detailed rules regarding cleanliness, order, and discipline are disseminated throughout the organization. All workers, maintenance specialists, and engineers engage in preventive maintenance of the production equipment. Workers learn about the equipment they use by cleaning and checking the machines, occasionally performing minor repairs and tool changes. Such exercising and internalizing of knowledge about the equipment enables workers to develop creative routines in quickly assessing problems and finding solutions.

Skill accumulation is an important factor in Toyota's wage system. Toyota's human resource management fosters multi-skilled workers. Workers are paid by their ability to solve a variety of problems by creating and using knowledge. Leaders of small work teams, for instance, earn 5 percent more than team members because they have greater responsibility, coordination, and motivation tasks. This wage system is linked to job rotation and assignment of multiple tasks. Experience in different workplaces increases worker's knowledge and provides a wider set of creative routines.

The careers of shop floor supervisors are based on diachronic accumulation of knowledge during 10 to 15 years of experience at the assembly line (level 3). Shop floor supervisors are Toyota veterans with multiple experience of different jobs. These supervisors share and use creative routines in educational training or through troubleshooting at the production line.

Procedural systems

In January 1992 Shoichiro Toyoda announced the Toyota vision for the twenty-first century. The vision includes principles such as Toyota will develop individualism and team creativity within the organization and open buyer–supplier systems for mutually stimulating research and innovation. The new vision articulates Toyota's environmental responsibility and the need to emphasize creating and utilizing knowledge (epistemological manner).

Dialogue and improvising. Toyota's dynamic systems create contexts for creative routines. Visualization, distributed knowledge, leadership and cross-boundary teams trigger dialogue and improvising on the spot.

Toyota uses visualization to trigger and sustain improvisation. The automatic detection of defects makes problems evident by stopping the production line (*andon* system) and this is a strong signal of crisis. This is communicated visually together with detailed information to synchronize the worker's awareness of problems and to elicit a fast solution. Hypotheses are generated (externalization) and tested on the spot to overcome the fluctuations.

The standard operating procedures visualize actions that have proven to be superior in the past (diachronic). Displays, tables, and other visual cues communicate tasks, problems, and performance levels along the assembly line. Several systems such as the *kanban* system, vehicle specification sheets on each body, colored lines separating sections on the floor, and different colors to classify boxes make problems visible and create a shared knowledge base for all workers. The visual cues trigger actions such as ordering parts in the *kanban* system. The rules for cleanliness, order, and discipline create a homogeneous background of normality. This state of normality helps to detect problems visually because they are immediately visible as disorder.

Other visual cues are used to discourage and avoid action. The foolproof prevention of problems (*poka-yoke*) blocks the view on equipment parts that could cause false operation. Such fool-proofing focuses the context on important actions.

Distributed leadership. Toyota's detection of defects and shutdown of machines uses distributed knowledge in a systematic way. The *Andon* system interrupts the flow of production, if it detects a defect and creates a crisis for all workers on the line. It displays what kind of problem has occurred and where. This creates a crisis and concentrates attention on the actual spot and calls workers with relevant knowledge to join in improvising new solutions. This system visualizes problems and helps to integrate/synchronize the contextual knowledge distributed along the assembly line with the tacit knowledge of workers to improve overall performance. Furthermore, if a worker at the assembly line detects a problem, he can assume leadership by manually stopping the assembly line.

Problems can trigger improvisation in the supplier or sales network. In the supplier network, "face-to-face" competition (Ito, 1989) puts pressure on suppliers to cooperate and to innovate. The sales network of Toyota's dealers provides a continuous flow of customer knowledge that influences new product development.

Toyota emphasizes multiple skills and trains workers so that they have a variety of experiences and understand different perspectives. Shop floor supervisors are multi-skilled veterans. Some of them are work team leaders and others are group leaders responsible for several teams. Finding new solutions when problems occur requires a broad range of experience. This puts multi-skilled workers in charge of the improvisation process.

Distributed leadership is important for product development as well. The development of Prius, the first hybrid car worldwide (Iemura, 1999; Itazaki, 1999), goes back to different projects linked to Toyota's new vision of environmental responsibility. Development began in January 1996 with a new effort to build cross-functional teams and to use distributed expertise (Nonaka and Toyama, 1999). Each product development phase required knowledge different in scope and depth, and leaders changed accordingly. For the first time, Toyota installed a "team room" for the members of the cross-functional project team (levels 2 and 3), and used extensive computer networks to link team members, thereby facilitating communication and providing access to databases (level 1).

An important breakthrough was achieved by combining different areas of expertise. Unexpectedly, Vice President Wada forced the team members to abandon old mental models. This created a crisis and the need to improvise. The chief engineer and project team leader, Uchiyamada, managed to integrate the necessary technical and design knowledge inside and outside of the company boundaries by integrating different groups that were developing in parallel without knowing each other's intentions and mutual relevance (diachronic). The time pressure synchronized the groups' knowledge. Further, external expertise at Panasonic provided critical knowledge to develop the battery for Prius.

The Prius project was an important experience for Toyota. First, it triggered improvising with internally and externally distributed knowledge. Second, synchronizing different diachronic histories of professionals in cross-functional teams was very effective. Third, the project has generated new creative routines such as cross-boundary dialogue and improvisation; they are now used company-wide.

Cisco Systems

Cisco has become the worldwide leader in networking-related business on the Internet. Cisco sells Internet hardware and software to companies and exploits networks for its business processes. Before the end of the Internet boom, Cisco became briefly the most valuable company in the world on March 27, 2000. Cisco's networking solutions facilitate access or transfer of information. Routers and switches are Cisco's main business; it has 80 percent of global market share of Internet routers. The company has diversified into other networking hardware (Bunnell, 2000; Byrne, 1998; Greenfeld, 2000).

Cisco makes 84 percent of its sales over the web; more than 80 percent of its customer queries are answered on-line; technical support information is posted on the web, allowing customers to solve their problems by themselves (Chowdhury, 2000; Goldblatt, 1999; Pitta, 2000; N.N., 2000).

Structural systems

Information technology.   The Internet is the platform that links the organizational systems of Cisco's network. Cisco operates three firms directly; the remaining 35 manufacturing companies in the network are run independently by contractors. On-line connections pass incoming orders from Cisco's webpage directly to other companies in the network that produce according to the orders received (Hartmann and Sifonis, 2000).

Cisco's Intranet and Internet support organizational systems (Pottruck and Pearce, 2000). The most important constituents of IT-facilitated dialogue are Cisco Connection Online, Cisco Manufacturing Connection Online, Cisco Employee Connection Online and Client Fund Project.

Cisco Connection Online is the interface to customers. Some 150,000 active registered users use the Internet as a collaborative platform; they access this platform 1.5 million times each month. Cisco Connection Online is similar to a portal that offers access to Cisco's databases and 1.8 million webpages. The system has several components including a shopping center, technical support, and customer service. The integration of Cisco's Connection Online with its customers' database reduces cost by integrating the supply-chains and enables the partners to reduce order-processing time.

Cisco Manufacturing Connection Online (MCO) is an Extranet supply chain portal that leverages the Japanese just-in-time model exploiting the potential of the Internet. Since 1999 MCO has connected Cisco and contract manufacturers in a simple and secure integrated manufacturing environment. The MCO dynamically creates customized graphical interfaces drawing on several information systems and databases. Incoming orders are immediately visualized for Cisco's manufacturing partners and Cisco gains real-time access to supplier information. MCO increases efficiency of order processing and reduces cycle time; it is part of the strategy to create a virtual factory to create a manufacturing system for build-to-order for customers. Several concepts specify this strategy as, for example, extending the Cisco ERP (enterprise resource planning) to suppliers or implementing test cells for self-testing at the suppliers' site. Since 1997, suppliers have been shipping directly to customers. This reduces build-to-ship time to three days; this involves dynamic replenishment, orders go directly to manufacturers who check Cisco's inventory. MCO is a highly efficient platform for Cisco's cooperating network of companies. Currently 70 percent of Cisco's manufacturing is outsourced; outsourcing has enabled Cisco to quadruple output without building plants and to reduce time to market by one to three months.

Cisco Employee Connection (CEC) serves the needs of Cisco employees. This Intranet is used as a collaborative platform enabling employees to help themselves with information they need related to engineering, sales, marketing, training, financial, human resources, facilities, and procurement. Information provided includes everything from technical documentation to cafeteria menus.

Sales people receive daily updates about competitors' products, their prices and the discounts. This competitor information is easy to understand and relevant (displayed together with data on Cisco products). Sales people use the Intranet interactively; they fill in their sales estimates and new sales made to help manufacturing and planning (Dhaliwal, 2000).

The Client Fund Project (CFP) develops internal partnerships between the IT department and business units. It organizes the funding of information technology according to client–supplier relationships; it has helped to establish an enterprise-wide network foundation. The business units decide on the applications needed ("what") and the IT department on the technologies to make these available ("how"). The business units have to fund their own requests for information technology. The budget of the IT function remains large enough to support the normal growth of infrastructure.

Further, human resource management uses the Internet to streamline the hiring process. All job candidates apply on-line. The résumés of the candidates are distributed internally by email. This enables managers to check the files of each applicant and create rankings according to skills or experiences with prior employers more efficiently.

Finally, information technology is used to make business situations explicit. Visualization through the GUI browsers is an important trigger for sales people in the field checking newest updates for meetings with clients. The availability of information and high frequency of updates increase the speed of internal information flow. The emphasis on rapid visualization supports interpretation and activity by employees on different organizational levels. Visualization enables Larry Carter, Cisco's chief financial officer, to analyze the net revenue effect of each newly closed contract. His goal is the "virtual close," closing Cisco's accounts within a day, to get a real-time understanding of the financial situation.

Procedural systems

Since Chambers became CEO in 1995, he has changed the epistemological manner by emphasizing marketing and customer relationships over technology. Cisco articulates its epistemological manner through focus on customer value and fast exploitation of change (Chambers, 2000). Each of the 24,000 employees carries a plastic card listing Cisco's yearly top ten objectives. These objectives are the basis for evaluating business units and employees. Performance is measured in rates of customer satisfaction; this measure also influences the top executive's bonus.

Dialogue and improvising.   Cisco makes strategic acquisition decisions based on five elements: a company's vision; short-term performance; long-term strategy; cultural fit with Cisco; proximity. The preparation of acquisitions are periods of high speed, intensity, and ambiguity; routines for dialoguing, and improvising in face-to-face interaction help employees to adapt to the changing contexts.

The integration efforts after the acquisition aim to retain staff and facilitate assimilation of the new employees at Cisco. The integration process commences immediately after the contract is signed. The day the acquisition is announced, human resource teams and business development teams travel to the company employees in small groups. One-to-one dialogues shape employees' new roles at Cisco and convey that Cisco values their presence and commitment. Including the first orientation and training program for managers, the integration process takes 30 days.

Clients can self-register as critical accounts that require special attention. Cisco's

Intranet creates a ranking of critical accounts to help Cisco's top management increase customer satisfaction. This creative routine supports customers to make emergent dissatisfaction visible; thus it triggers the transcendence of inefficient routines.

Distributed Leadership.   Cisco has continued to enlarge its business through acquisition of companies and strategic alliances. Since 1993 Cisco has acquired 57 firms to become a full-service supplier of network solutions. Acquisitions provide fast access to talent, who are able to use and develop new technologies and markets.

Cisco has developed acquisition procedures to capture intellectual assets of individual companies efficiently and effectively and to utilize these assets creatively for the development of next-generation products. After Cisco bought Crescendo in 1993, the former CEO of Crescendo, Mario Mazzola still leads the business unit that includes his former company. Retention of employees of acquired companies is essential for superior performance because the companies acquired often compete in businesses that are new to Cisco. Entrusting these new businesses to experienced managers creates a distributed pattern of leadership by professionals.

Conclusion

The case studies show different dynamic business systems that are based on similar components. The examples of how integrating standard components such as POS systems, Just-in-time production or network technology create a complex system that is more than the sum of its parts. The design of each dynamic business system and its evolution through practice is the key to developing creative routines. The entrepreneurial usage of commodities and standards adapted to specific contexts enables the companies to develop unique patterns of knowledge creation and utilization. The creative routines at Seven-Eleven Japan, Toyota Motor Corporation and Cisco Systems were developed in the specific contexts of competition in the Japanese and US retail and manufacturing industries.

The differences between the individual systems co-exist with the family resemblance (Nonaka and Reinmoeller, 2000; figure 6.5). First, there is different emphasis on structural components. Cisco emphasizes network technology. Seven-Eleven uses information technology to combine explicit knowledge efficiently, but has only recently started to use the Internet for e-commerce. Toyota uses organizational systems as the main structural component and has linked the semi-automated systems with human intervention.

Second, the companies have developed different ways to visualize and articulate problems. Cisco uses Internet and Intranets in combination with the graphical user interfaces of browsers. Seven-Eleven Japan has integrated visualization devices in the 5th generation of its POS system. Toyota does not focus on visualization through information technology. It uses simple but effective foolproof devices or teams and group processes to link human intervention to the production flow so that deep tacit knowledge is captured when problems occur. All three companies have developed distinctive epistemological manners, visions, and rules for action.

Three, the way procedural components are used shows different ways to develop creative routines. Continuous dialogue and improvising help Seven-Eleven to share and capture hidden, tacit knowledge on a deeper level. Similarly at Toyota, the co-location at the place of work makes sharing of tacit knowledge an everyday experience. Cisco uses teams to foster dialogue on the occasion of acquisitions.

Hence, Cisco provides an example of a dynamic business system that is primarily based on Internet and networking technology. The example of Toyota shows that information technology is not necessary; organizational systems can develop creative routines when visualization and articulation are emphasized. Toyota has developed a system with creative routines to explore change and take advantage of problems that occur at the assembly line and in the vertical network structure (*keiretsu*). Seven-Eleven Japan points out that dynamic business systems are hybrids; they integrate structural and procedural components.

All knowledge is embedded in contexts. Human intervention is needed to create and visualize this knowledge. Dynamic business systems allow companies to share contexts in motion (*ba*) and to tap this source of knowledge by developing creative routines. When building such dynamic business systems it is important to leverage human intervention in automated processes to create and utilize knowledge when contexts change.

Creative routines are the key to develop dynamic capabilities (Teece et al., 1997; Eisenhardt and Martin, 2000). Static routines, such as imitation or assembly, are ineffective when contextual knowledge is involved. Organizations need creative routines to go beyond their present capabilities. Creative routines visualize problems and create, test, and develop new ideas by exploring the not-yet-known. Companies that develop dynamic business systems and creative routines continuously create and exploit knowledge. Future research needs to survey different types of dynamic business systems and to develop paths that help integrate such systems and build creative routines. These creative routines harness Schumpeter's gales of creative destruction (Schumpeter, 1951) on the organizational level by seizing opportunities to create and utilize knowledge.

Acknowledgements

The authors are greatly indebted to their anonymous reviewers.

References

Amabile, T. M. and Conti, R. 1999: Changes in the work environment for creativity during downsizing, *Academy of Management Journal*, 42, (6), December, 630–40.

APQC 2000: Showcasing successful knowledge management implementation, *Proceedings from APQCs 4th Knowledge Management Conference*, December, San Antonio, TX.

Barrett, F. J. 1998: Creativity and improvisation in jazz and organizations: implications for organizational learning," *Organization Science*, 9 (5), 605–22.

Besser, T. 1996: *Team Toyota: Transplanting the Toyota Culture to the Camry Plant in Kentucky*. Albany: State University of New York Press.

Boisot, M. 1997: *Knowledge Assets*, New York: Oxford University Press.

Brown, J. S. and Duguid, P. 1991: Organizational learning and communities of practice: towards a unified view of working, learning, and innovation. *Organization Science*, 2, 40–57.

Brown, S. L. and Eisenhardt, K. M. 1998: *Competing on the Edge: Strategy as Structured Chaos*. Boston: Harvard Business School Press.

Bunnell, D. 2000: *Making the Cisco Connection: The Story Behind the Real Internet Superpower*, New York: Wiley.

Byrne, J. A. 1998: The corporation of the future. Business Week, August 31, 1998, 56–8.

Chambers, J. 2000: *Foreword*. In A. Hartmann, and J. Sifonis (eds), *Net Ready: Strategies for Success in the E-conomy*, New York: McGraw-Hill.

Churchill, E. F. and Snowdon, D. 1998: Collaborative virtual environments: an introductory review of issues and systems. *Virtual Reality*, 3, (1), 3–15.

Choo, C. W. 1998: *The Knowing Organization*. New York: Oxford University Press.

Chowdhury, N. 2000: Cisco's Asian gambit. *Fortune*, January 10, 2000, 52–4.

Clancey, W. J. 1997: *Situated Cognition – On Human Knowledge and Computer Representations*. Cambridge: Cambridge University Press.

Crossan, M. M. 1998: Improvisation in action. *Organization Science*, 9 (5), 593–9.

Crossan, M. M., Lane, H. W., Klus, L., and White, R. E. 1996: The improvising organization: where planning meets opportunity. *Organizational Dynamics*, Spring, 24, (4), 20–35.

Cusumano, M. A. 1985: *The Japanese Automobile Industry : Technology and Management at Nissan and Toyota*. Boston: Harvard University Press.

Davenport, T. H., De Long, D. W., and Beers, M. C. 1998: Successful knowledge management projects. *Sloan Management Review*, Winter, 43–57.

Davenport, T. H. and Pearlson, K. 1998: Two cheers for the virtual office. *Sloan Management Review*, 39 (4), Summer. 51–65.

Davenport, T. H. and Prusak, L. 1998: *Working Knowledge*. Boston: Harvard University Press.

Dhaliwal, G. S., Senior Manager, Web Business, presentation at the 4th Knowledge Forum, University of California, Berkeley, September 27, 2000.

Dyer, J. H. and Singh, H. 1998: The relational view: cooperative strategy and sources of interorganizational competitive advantage. *Academy of Management Review*, 23 (4), 660–79.

Earl, M. J. 1996: *Information Management: The Organizational Dimension*. Oxford: Oxford University Press.

Eisenhardt, K. M. and Brown, S. L. 1998: Time pacing: competing in markets that won't stand still. *Harvard Business Review*, March–April, 59–69.

Eisenhardt, K.M. and Martin, J. 2000: Dynamic capabilities: What are they? *Strategic Management Journal*, 21 (10/11), 1105–21.

Eisenstein, S. M. 1953: *The Rhetorics of Movies*. Tokyo: Bunko.

Fine, H. 1998: *Clockspeed*. Boston: Harvard Business School Press.

Fujimoto, T. 1999: *The Evolution of a Manufacturing System at Toyota*. New York: Oxford University Press.

Giddens, A. 1993: *New Rules of Sociological Method*, Oxford: Polity Press

Goldblatt, H. 1999: Cisco's secrets, *Fortune*, November 8.

Granovetter, M. E. 1985: Economic action and social structure: the problem of embeddedness. *American Journal of Sociology*, 91, 481–510

Greenfeld, K. T. 2000: The network effect. *Time*, April 10, 47–8.

Hartmann, A. and Sifonis, J. 2000: *Net Ready: Strategies for Success in the E-conomy*, New York: McGraw-Hill.

Iemura, H. 1999: *Prius to iu yume – Toyota ga hiraketa 21 seiki no tobira* [*The Dream called Prius – Toyota Opened the Door Towards the Twenty-First century*]. Tokyo: Sanko Insatsu.

Ishida, T. (ed.) 1998: *Community Computing : Collaboration over Global Information Net-*

works. New York: John Wiley and Sons.

Itazaki, H. (1999): *Kakushin Toyota Jidosha – Sekai wo shinkan saseta Prius no shogeki* [Toyota Motor Innovation – The attack of the Prius that changed the world], Tokyo: Nikan Kogyo Shinbunsha.

Ito, M. (1989): Kigyo-kan kankei to keizoku-teki torihiki [Interorganizational relationships and continued exchange], K. Imai and R. Komiya (eds.) *Nihon no kigyo*, pp. 109–130, Tokyo: Tokyo University Press.

Jaworski, J. 1996: *Synchronicity: The Inner Path to Leadership.* San Francisco: Berrett-Koehler.

Kunitomo, R. 1998: *Seven-Eleven no Joho Shisutem [The Information System of Seven Eleven]*. Tokyo: Paru Shuppan.

Lave, J. and Wenger, E. 1991: *Situated Learning : Legitimate Peripheral Participation.* Cambridge: Cambridge University Press.

Leonard, D. and Swap, W. 1999: *When Sparks Fly: Igniting Creativity in Groups.* Boston: Harvard Business School Press.

Leonard-Barton, D. 1992: Core capabilities and core rigidities: a paradox in managing new product development. *Strategic Management Journal*, 13(5), 111–25.

March, J. G. 1996: Continuity and change in theories of organizational action. *Administrative Science Quarterly*, 41, 278–87.

Mintzberg, H. 1973: *The Nature of Managerial Work.* New York: Harper and Row

Mintzberg, H. 1988; Opening up the definitions of strategy. In H. Mintzberg, J. B. Quinn and R. M. James (eds), *The Strategy Process: Concepts, Contexts, and Cases.* Englewood Cliffs: Prentice-Hall, 13–20.

Mirvis, P. H. 1998: Practice Improvisation. *Organization Science*, 9 (5), 586–91.

Mitsugi, Y., Takimoto, T. and Yamazaki, M. 1998: Waga Kuni Kourigyo no Shinryutsu Senryaku to Johogijutsu" [New retail strategy and information technology in our country's retail business]. *Chiteki Shisan Sozo*, 6 (2), 18–29.

Nelson, R. and Winter, S. 1982: *An Evolutionary Theory of Economic Change.* Cambridge, MA: Harvard University Press.

Nonaka, I. 1990: *Chishiki Sozo Keiei: Nihon Kigyo no Epistemoroji"[Knowledge Creation Management: Epistemology in Japanese Companies].* Tokyo: Nihon Keizai Shinbunsha.

Nonaka, I. and Konno, N. 1998: The concept of "ba": building a foundation for knowledge creation. *California Management Review*, 40 (3), 40–54.

Nonaka, I. and Konno, N. 1999: *Chishiki Keiei no susume: Narejimanejimento to sono jidai [Recommending Knowledge Creation: The Age of Knowledge Management].* Tokyo: Chikuma Shinsho.

Nonaka, I. and Reinmoeller, P. 1999: "Knowledge creation architecture: constructing the places for knowledge assets and competitive advantage. *Internationales Management*, Wiesbaden: Gabler, pp. 22–46.

Nonaka, I. and Reinmoeller, P. 2000: Dynamic business system for knowledge creation and utilization. In C. Despres and D. Chauvel (eds), *Knowledge Horizons: The Present and the Promise of Knowledge Management.* Woburn, MA: Butterworth-Heinemann, 89–112.

Nonaka, I., Reinmoeller, P., and Senoo, D. 1998: The ART of knowledge. *European Management Journal*, 16 (6), 673–84.

Nonaka, I., Reinmoeller, P., and Toyama, R. 2001: Integrated IT systems for knowledge creation, In M. Dierkes, A. Berthoin Antal, J. Child and I. Nonaka (eds),*The Handbook of Organizational Learning and knowledge.* Oxford: Oxford University Press 827–48.

Nonaka, I. and Takeuchi, H. 1995: *The Knowledge Creating Company: How Japanese Companies Create the Dynamics of Innovation.* New York: Oxford University Press.

Nonaka, I. and Toyama, R. 1999: "Why do you create knowledge?: a shared epistemological manner of a firm. Paper presented at the Knowledge Forum 1999, Haas School of Business, University of California, Berkeley, CA.

Nonaka, I., Toyama, R., and Konno, N. 2000: SECI, ba, and leadership: a unifying model of dynamic knowledge creation. *Long Range Planning*, 33, 5–34.

Northey, P. and Southway, N. 1994: *Cycle Time Management*, New York: Productivity Press.

Ogawa, S. 2000: Nihon ni okeru ryuzukigyokiten no seihin kaihatsu [Product Development in the Japanese Retail Industry]. *Nihongata Marketing*, Tokyo: Chikura Shobo, 77–96.

Okamoto, H. 1998: *Yokado Group: Koshueki he no Shisutemu Kakushin [Yokado Group: The System Revolution towards High Profits*. Tokyo: Paru Shuppan.

Pitta, J. 2000: The Cisco kid, *Forbes*, January 10, 2000, 108–9.

Pottruck, D. S. and Pearce, T. 2000: *Clicks and Mortar*. San Francisco: Jossey Bass

Reinmoeller, P. 1999: Knowledge and time: a forgotten factor in knowledge management. Paper presented at European Group for Organization Studies Colloquium, July 4–6 1999, Warwick, Great Britain.

Ruggles, R. 1998: The state of the notion: knowledge management in practice. *California Management Review*. Special Issue. 40 (3), 80–9.

Schank, R. 1997: *Virtual Learning: A Revolutionary Approach to Building a Highly Skilled Workforce*. New York: McGraw-Hill.

Schumpeter, J. A. 1951: *The Theory of Economic Development*. Cambridge, MA: Harvard University Press.

Senge, P. 1990: *The Fifth Discipline: The Art and Practice of The Learning Organization*, New York: Doubleday.

Shaw, G., Brown, R., and Bromiley, P. 1998: Strategic stories: how 3M is rewriting business planning, *Harvard Business Review*, May–June, 41–50.

Sobek, D. K., Ward, A. C., and Liker, J. K. 1999: Toyota's principles of set-based concurrent engineering. *Sloan Management Review*, Winter, 67–83.

Spear, S. and Kent Bowen, H. 1999: Decoding the DNA of the Toyota Production system. *Harvard Business Review*, September–October, 96–106.

Stalk, T. M. and Hout, G. 1990: *Competing against Time: How Time-Based Competition is Reshaping Global Markets*. New York: Free Press.

Suchmann, L. 1987: *Plan and Situated Actions: The Problems of Human Machine Communication*. Cambridge: Cambridge University Press.

Suzuki, K. 1998: Tsuyoi "Ishi" to "Tetteiryoku" koso ga subete [Strong "intention" and "determination" are everything]. *2020AIM*, 156 (5), 40–5.

Szulanski, G. 1996: Exploring internal stickiness: impediments to the transfer of best practice within the firm. *Strategic Management Journal*, Winter, Special Issue, 17, 27–44.

Teece, D. 2000: Strategies for managing knowledge assets: the role of firm structure and industrial context. *Long Range Planning*, 33, 35–54.

Teece, D., Pisano, G., and Shuen, A. 1997: Dynamic capabilities and strategic management. *Strategic Management Journal*, 18 (7), 509–33.

The Economist. 2000: The dog food danger. April 8, 64–6.

Turban, E. McLean, E. and Wetherbe, J. (1999): *Information Technology for Management: Making Connections for Strategic Advantage*. New York: John Wiley and Sons.

Ueno, N. 1999: *Shigoto no naka de no gakushu: jokyoronteki apurochi* [Learning at Work: Situation Theoretical Approach]. Tokyo: Tokyo University Press.

Usui, M. 1998: Kigyo wo kaeru Web Kompyutingu – Henka Taiou to Atarashii Shisutemu Moderu [Web Computing changes the firm – adaptation to change and new system models]. *Seven-Eleven Japan, Information System Division* (presentation material).

Wenger, E. C. and Snyder, W. M. 2000: Communities of practice: the organizational frontier. *Harvard Business Review*, January–February, 139–45.

PART II

Exploiting Opportunities for Wealth Creation

An Optimal Stopping Model for the Exploration and Exploitation of a New Venture Opportunity

Young Rok Choi, Moren Lévesque, and Dean Shepherd

Introduction

Entrepreneurs discover new business opportunities. Discovering and exploring the potential of a new business opportunity, however, are not sufficient to obtain entrepreneurial rents; subsequent exploitation must be taken (Shane and Venkataraman, 2000). Successful entrepreneurs seem to shift from exploration (a focus on activities and/or investments to reduce technological and market uncertainties surrounding the potential opportunity) to exploitation (activities and/or investments committed to building efficient business operational systems to generate profits) at the most appropriate time.[1] For example, Boo.com, a UK-based on-line fashion retailer, incurred large losses from what appears to be a hasty decision to pursue full-scale operations. Value America, one of the pioneers of on-line retailing, also appears to have suffered problems associated with premature exploitation by beginning full-scale operations based on an incomplete business model.

Baumol (1993) suggests that the timing of a major innovative step involves a trade-off; by rushing a novel item to market an innovator can realize benefits earlier, but by delaying its introduction the innovator can benefit from further development and cost reductions in production. We argue that there exists a similar trade-off for an entrepreneur in deciding when to shift focus from exploring a new opportunity to its exploitation. Entrepreneurs can increase profit potential by exploiting the opportunity earlier and capitalizing on first mover advantages, but the entrepreneur can reduce the new venture's mortality risk by delaying exploitation, further exploring the opportunity, and thereby reducing its liabilities of newness (Stinchcombe, 1965).

Our research question is directed to this issue. When is the optimal time for an entrepreneur to shift focus from exploration to exploitation in order to maximize performance (i.e., optimize the trade-off between profit potential and mortality risk)? We construct an analytical optimization model to investigate this question, which is consistent with Baumol (1993), who argues for the appropriateness of an optimization technique to investigate the exploration–exploitation decision. That is, we propose an analytical model to better understand how entrepreneurs build a business entity so as to maximize performance (i.e., optimize profitability, mortality risk, and the cost of exploration). The model and its post-optimization analyses extend our understanding of the new venture creation process. For instance, built on Rumelt's (1987) assertion on the role of uncertainty in obtaining entrepreneurial rents, the optimality prescription further specifies how entrepreneurs choose the level of uncertainty at which they maximize overall performance. We also identify important properties of the entrepreneurial process (e.g., knowledge creation and imitation environments), which influence the timing decision. In our model, entrepreneurs of independent start-ups are in an exploration period and face two choices: continue with exploration or stop and begin exploitation. Our model applies to entrepreneurs who are strongly attached to their new opportunities, and therefore tend to avoid exit from the venturing process. Instead, they tend to modify an original idea – or move on to a new one – when that idea seems unviable (Bird, 1989). Consequently the time horizon ends when the entrepreneur begins exploitation.

This chapter proceeds as follows. We begin with an introduction to the entrepreneurship and strategic management literatures directed at the entrepreneurial process, profitability, and the mortality of new ventures. This review sets up our general model and characterizes an optimal decision rule. Next we translate the model's theoretical insights into propositions and offer explanations for each. We finally suggest implications from this framework for practitioners and scholars.

Theoretical Background, Model, and Optimal Strategy

Entrepreneurs begin their venturing process by exploring (experimenting on) a newly "theorized or believed" business opportunity in a highly uncertain environment. During exploration the entrepreneur attempts to reduce the uncertainty surrounding his/her new opportunity. Once entrepreneurs have accumulated sufficient information to assess the viability of the opportunity they need to shift focus from exploration to the exploitation of the opportunity. It is at this time of shifting focus that the entrepreneur must make major investments in building efficient production systems, training staff, and building relationships with customers. The decision to exploit an opportunity is an important one (Schoonhoven et al., 1990), since it seems to directly impact the overall performance of the new venture. We now describe each component of our model to optimize the time to shift focus from exploration to exploitation.

Uncertainty and knowledge creation

A primary uncertainty facing an entrepreneur is whether there will be sufficient demand for the new product/service (i.e., exogenous uncertainty) (Wernerfelt and Karnani, 1987). There is also supply side uncertainty (Wernerfelt and Karnani, 1987) – the entrepreneur must determine whether the new venture's products/services can be efficiently produced in a way that is sufficiently reliable and predictable (i.e., endogenous uncertainty). Let t represent time (i.e., the time since the entrepreneur began exploring the newly theorized opportunity) and U_t the entrepreneur's level of uncertainty (both endogenous and exogenous uncertainty) at t. The entrepreneur needs to reduce uncertainty to an acceptable level, one that provides the entrepreneur sufficient confidence to proceed with the substantial investments required to exploit an opportunity.

Exploration can reduce the uncertainty surrounding a new opportunity. Endogenous uncertainty can be reduced by learning through one's own exploration activities and exogenous uncertainty will likely decrease during the exploration period because, on average, such uncertainty decreases over time (e.g., customer preferences and technological trajectories are revealed) (Folta, 1998; McGrath, 1997).

Let X_t be the amount of knowledge *gained* by the entrepreneur as a result of exploration at t. Because of the unpredictable nature of market and technological uncertainties early in the entrepreneurial process, the magnitude of the gain in knowledge during each exploration period is likely to occur independently of that for previous periods. For example, while uncertainties in customer requirements may be resolved through trial and error (Robert and Meyer, 1991), the entrepreneur may not know *ex ante* how much knowledge can be gained in the next period of exploration (Lippman and Rumelt, 1982). Further, knowledge creation in a functional area at time t (e.g., technology development) will not necessarily be highly related to the knowledge creation in other functional areas (e.g., marketing fields) at time $t + 1$. Thus, we model X_ts as independent identically distributed random variables of non-negative mean μ_t.

Moreover, the X_ts decrease stochastically with exploration time, i.e., $P(X_t > K) \geq P(X_{t+1} > K)$ for all K and all t. Consequently, the expected (mean value) gain in knowledge will decrease over time (consistent with Ross [1983]). That is, as the marginal learning effect decreases over time along a typical learning curve, knowledge gain in each period of exploration will decrease over time. As a result, the total knowledge of the new venture will increase at a decreasing rate over time.

A gain in knowledge decreases the entrepreneur's level of uncertainty from one period to the next, which at t can be expressed by

$$U_t = U_{t-1} - \lambda X_t = U_0 - \lambda \sum_{n=1}^{t} X_n, \qquad (7.1)$$

where $\sum_{n=1}^{t} X_n$ indicates the entrepreneur's accumulated amount of knowledge at t. λ is the marginal decrease in uncertainty per unit of knowledge, and it takes on a positive value. U_0 is the initial level of the entrepreneur's uncertainty. When U_0 is large enough, uncertainty is kept non-negative.

Possible imitation by competitors

As discussed above, an entrepreneur learns about the viability of their new opportunity through exploration. Outsiders who can observe the entrepreneur's trials and outcomes also obtain this knowledge (Herriott et al., 1985; Mosakowski, 1997). "[C]ompetitors typically gain detailed knowledge about a firm's new products within one year of development, and much of the learning on production processes also gets diffused" (Ghemawat, 1986: 53). Therefore potential competitors can reduce their uncertainty in pursuing the same opportunity through observation alone (free riding on the entrepreneur's exploration activities), enabling them to proceed to exploitation with only a short exploration of their own. However, there are a number of obstacles limiting the ability of a competitor to learn from observation.[2] Nelson and Winter (1982) argue that the more the target knowledge involves idiosyncratic and "impacted" tacit knowledge, the more difficult and problematic imitation becomes. Therefore, the difficulty for competitors to imitate the entrepreneur likely varies from environment to environment and the entrepreneur may have some knowledge which is not imitable at all. This inimitable knowledge represents an irreducible gap in uncertainty between the entrepreneur and their (potential) competitors who do not conduct their own exploration of the opportunity.

We thus model uncertainty perceived by potential competitors, denoted by V_t, as a linear function of the entrepreneur's uncertainty where

$$V_t = \alpha_1 + \alpha_2 U_t. \tag{7.2}$$

α_1 (>0) represents an irreducible uncertainty for the competitor, and α_2 (>1) refers to the level of difficulty for a competitor to decrease reducible uncertainty. α_2 is greater than 1 because potential competitors usually perceive higher uncertainty with the entrepreneur's opportunity than does the entrepreneur. The gap in uncertainty between the entrepreneur and the potential competitor decreases over time: the entrepreneur's knowledge creation decreases over time, while the ability of the competitor to imitate through observational learning remains constant (from equation [7.2]).

Potential profitability, mortality risk, and exploration cost

We now describe the three elements of overall performance that entrepreneurs should optimize with their decision on when to shift focus from exploration to exploitation. First, we model *potential profitability* as a function of the new venture's lead-time over (potential) competitors. Second, *mortality risk* is introduced as a function of time and the uncertainty perceived by potential competitors. Finally, the *exploration cost* is presented as a function of time that increases at a constant rate.

Potential profitability.   The strategy literature suggests that a new venture should have a long *lead time* (the length of time the new venture's market offerings face no, or very limited, direct competition) to develop its first mover advantages and benefit from a sustainable increase in performance (Huff and Robinson, 1994). First mover advantages arise from several sources including technological leadership, learning curve effects, preemption of assets, buyer switching costs, and consumer preference formation (Carpenter and Nakamoto, 1989; Lieberman and Montgomery, 1988). In order to capitalize on these sources of a first mover advantage, the entrepreneur needs to focus on exploiting the opportunity through full-scale operations. For example, Lambkin (1988) showed that first movers must make a disproportionate level of investment in developing new markets.[3] Therefore, new ventures that are still

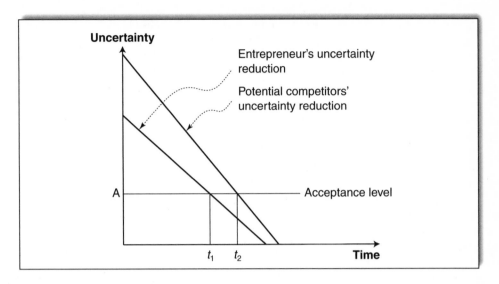

Figure 7.1   Difference in uncertainty and lead time between entrepreneur and potential competitors

exploring the opportunity are unable to capitalize on possible first mover advantages.

Since decision-makers perceive high risk in situations of uncertainty over future outcomes (Papageorgiou and Paskov, 1999), they should reach a particular level of certainty before making a decision. Thus we suggest that the length of lead time is determined by the size of the gap between the entrepreneurs' uncertainty over the new opportunity and that of their potential competitor's uncertainty. As shown in figure 7.1, given the condition that the entrepreneur and potential competitors require the same level of certainty, say A, before shifting their focus to exploitation, the entrepreneur will begin exploitation at t_1 and potential competitors will begin exploitation at t_2. The new venture's lead time will be $(t_2 - t_1)$, attributable to the size of the uncertainty gap.

From (7.2), the uncertainty gap at t is

$$V_t - U_t = \alpha_1 + (\alpha_2 - 1) U_t. \tag{7.3}$$

On one hand, there is a proportional relationship between the size of the uncertainty gap and the length of the lead time. On the other hand, profit is assumed linear in lead time. Therefore, profit potential at t is linear in uncertainty gap and expressed by, using (7.3):

$$P_t = \phi + \omega(V_t - U_t) = \phi + \omega\alpha_1 + \omega(\alpha_2 - 1) U_t, \tag{7.4}$$

where ϕ is the return associated with no lead time and ω is the marginal profit from an increase in the uncertainty gap.

Mortality risk.   Mortality risk refers to the probability that a firm will become insolvent and be unable to recover from that insolvency before being bankrupted and ceasing operations (Shepherd et al., 2000). Stinchcombe (1965) introduced the concept of the liability of newness to describe the high mortality risk facing new ventures. The sources of the liability of newness can be categorized as both internal and external to the firm. Internal sources of the liability of newness include the costs of learning new tasks, the strength of conflicts regarding new organizational roles, and the presence or absence of informal organizational structures (Singh et al., 1986; Stinchcombe, 1965). Choi and Shanley (2000) argue that these internal sources of the liability of newness can be reduced as exploration is extended. Therefore, we posit that the longer the exploration period, the lower the mortality risk at exploitation. We use an exponential functional form to mathematically express the decline over time in the mortality risk of a new venture at exploitation, which is consistent with learning curve studies (e.g., Yelle, 1979). Specifically, mortality risk is a probability and thus ranges from 1 to 0 (Levinthal, 1991; Singh et al., 1986).

An external source contributing to the liability of newness is the lack of stable links with key stakeholders (Singh et al., 1986) which new ventures have difficulty in establishing because of, in part, the high levels of uncertainty typically surrounding the venture. High levels of stakeholder uncertainty over the new venture have a negative effect on an entrepreneur's exploitation attempts, such as garnering additional financial resources and attracting key employees and customers. The level of uncertainty perceived by stakeholders is captured by a shifting up or down of the basic mortality risk curve. We use competitor uncertainty as a proxy for stakeholder uncertainty because potential competitors are generally the most interested in obtaining information about the entrepreneur's activities and hence build up knowledge about the new opportunity. This phenomenon can be mathematically represented by

$$M_t = V_t e^{-\beta t}, \qquad (7.5)$$

where β is the rate at which mortality risk declines over time.[4] When a stream of competitor uncertainty $\{V_m\}_{m=1,2,\,\ldots}$ lies beneath another stream $\{V_n\}_{n=1,2,\,\ldots}$, the mortality risk curve associated with the former stream lies below that for the latter stream.

Exploration cost.   Exploration cost, denoted by C_t, is an important factor in deciding whether or not the entrepreneur should continue exploration. If these costs are too high and its benefits from delaying exploitation (such as a decrease in mortality risk) are trivial, then the entrepreneur would be better off exploiting the opportunity. In a model of adaptive organizational search, Levinthal and March (1981) proposed that the search cost for innovation in each period depends on both a (changing) propensity to search and resources available for innovation. We assume that an entrepreneur's propensity to search is maintained and resources are available throughout the period of exploration. Thus, there is a constant exploration cost, c, per period where

$$C_t = ct. \qquad (7.6)$$

Entrepreneur's objective

Radner and Shepp's (1996) analytical model proposes that corporate strategy should aim at maximizing a *linear combination* of profit (the expected total dividends paid out during the life of the firm, discounted at some fixed rate) and bankruptcy (when the firm's cash reserve falls to zero and therefore ceases to operate). We follow the lead of Radner and Shepp (1996) and model the performance of new ventures as a linear combination of profit potential and mortality risk. In other words, the objective of a new venture is to maximize a linear combination of *profit potential* (the expected total return to investors during the life of the firm, discounted at some fixed rate), *mortality risk* (the probability that a firm will become insolvent and be unable to recover from that insolvency before being bankrupted and ceasing operations), and exploration costs. Schoemaker and Amit (1994) also indicate that firms' strategic actions constitute a trade-off between maximizing expected returns for stockholders and maximizing survival chances.

We draw on these previous studies and suggest that the entrepreneur's objective is to maximize performance, denoted by O_t, which is a linear combination of potential profit, mortality risk, and exploration cost, i.e., from (7.4), (7.5) and (7.6):

$$O_t = \{\phi + \omega(V_t - U_t)\} - \pi \, V_t e^{-\beta t} - ct, \tag{7.7}$$

where π is the entrepreneur's marginal reduction in performance from one more unit of mortality risk. Expected performances are next utilized to derive an optimal decision rule on when one should stop exploring and begin exploiting a new business opportunity.

Optimal exploration/exploitation strategy

By applying a classic optimal stopping approach to an entrepreneur's exploitation decision, we argue that if the performance from searching one more period is smaller than that from exploiting the new business opportunity now, the entrepreneur should exploit now. We demonstrate in the Appendix that this is equivalent to showing that there exists a stopping time N^* where

$$U_{t-1} \geq \frac{1}{\pi \, \alpha_2 e^{-\beta t}(e^\beta - 1)} \{c + \omega \lambda(\alpha_2 - 1)\mu_t - \pi\alpha_1 \, e^{-\beta t} (e^\beta - 1) - \pi \, \lambda\alpha_2\mu_t e^{-\beta t}\} \text{ when } t \leq N^* \tag{7.8}$$

$$\leq \frac{1}{\pi \, \alpha_2 e^{-\beta t}(e^\beta - 1)} \{c + \omega \lambda(\alpha_2 - 1)\mu_t - \pi\alpha_1 \, e^{-\beta t} (e^\beta - 1) - \pi \, \lambda\alpha_2\mu_t e^{-\beta t}\} \text{ when } t > N^*$$

The left-hand side of (7.8) is the entrepreneur's uncertainty level at $t - 1$, which is expected to decrease over time. The denominator of the right-hand side of (7.8) indicates the marginal performance from mortality risk reduction. The numerator of the right-hand side of (7.8) is a linear combination of (1) per period exploration cost; (2) lost profit from a decreased reducible uncertainty; (3) mortality risk reduction from decreased irreducible uncertainty (due to changes over time in the basic mortality risk function, $e^{-\beta t}$); and (4) mortality risk reduction from decreased reducible uncertainty (due to changes in knowledge creation). Put differently, the entrepreneur maximizes expected performance by delaying exploitation just as long as the expected gain in performance due to a reduction in mortality risk becomes less than or equal to the sum of the expected loss in performance from profitability and exploration cost. For later use, we denote the right-hand side of (7.8) by $L^{*}(t)$, and refer back to it as the *uncertainty threshold*.

> Hypothesis 1 (Optimal stopping rule): The optimal time to exploit a new opportunity occurs when the entrepreneur's uncertainty level reaches a specific threshold. This threshold (given by the right-hand side of (7.8)) corresponds to the net expected performance of additional exploration activity, which is weighted by the marginal performance of mortality risk reduction.

Post-Optimization Analysis

We next investigate the effects of the model parameters on the decision to shift focus from exploration to exploitation. To this end we observe the movement of the uncertainty threshold, $L^{*}(t)$, as a model parameter is increased. Figure 7.2 illustrates the uncertainty threshold as a function of time and demonstrates that, since the entrepreneur's realization of uncertainty at $\hat{t}$ is greater than the maximum threshold $(L^{*}(\hat{t}))$, it is not optimal to exploit the new opportunity during that period. [5]

At any given period t, movements of the threshold indicate an increase or decrease in the probability that an entrepreneur should exploit the opportunity earlier. The interval below the threshold – the acceptance interval in figure 7.2 – represents the acceptable entry decision space. As this interval increases, we argue that the probability an entrepreneur should exploit sooner rather than later increases, whereas this probability decreases when the interval decreases. The influence of increases in each key model parameter on the acceptance interval of exploitation is shown in the Appendix.

Parameters encouraging early exploitation

As the unit exploration cost increases, the entrepreneur will have a greater value in the right-hand side of (7.8), since exploration cost does not influence the relationship between profit potential and mortality risk. This higher cost to benefit ratio of further exploration should encourage earlier exploitation.

If the venture's lead time over its competitors has an increased marginal effect on profit potential, then the entrepreneur can afford to exploit earlier as it increases (on any given period) their profit potential without affecting either the risk of mortality or per period search cost. As the marginal effect of time on morality risk increases, mortality risk would decline at a faster rate and a decision maker's "acceptable" level of risk would thus be obtained earlier. In this situation, there are two alternatives that the entrepreneur can take. On the one hand, the decision-maker can choose earlier exploitation at the corresponding level of risk and benefit from higher profit potential. On the other hand, entrepreneurs can choose to exploit at the same time they would have

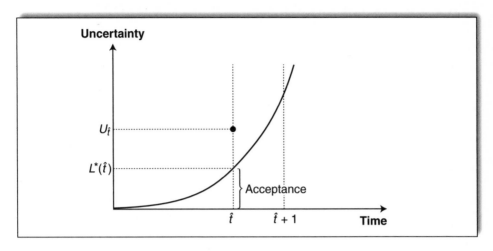

Figure 7.2   Uncertainty zone for exploitation entrance

had there not been an increase in the parameter, achieving the same profit potential but benefiting from a lower mortality risk. However, the model suggests the former. That is, the entrepreneur enters earlier because the benefit from lower mortality risk does not cover the loss from higher searching costs and lower profit potential.

> Hypothesis 2: The probability that the entrepreneur should exploit the new opportunity sooner increases when there is:

- an increase in the unit exploration cost (c);
- an increase in the marginal effect of uncertainty gap (and thus lead time) on profit potential (ω);
- an increase in the marginal effect of time on morality risk (β).

Parameters discouraging early exploitation

In the right-hand side of (7.8), an increase in the marginal effect of mortality risk on performance (π) has a negative impact on the entrepreneur's uncertainty threshold. As this marginal effect increases, we also observe that the entrepreneur should wait for an even lower mortality risk to overcome the greater loss in performance that each unit incurs. While this reduces profit potential, it is outweighed by the reduction in mortality risk. Therefore, the entrepreneur should delay exploitation.

Moreover, as the irreducible uncertainty gap (α_1) between the entrepreneur and his/her competitors increases, the entrepreneur should delay exploitation. The urgency to begin exploitation is significantly diminished, because the irreducible uncertainty is sustainable until the competitors begin their own exploration activities. This allows the entrepreneur time to further explore and further reduce mortality risk.

Hypothesis 3: The probability that the entrepreneur should exploit the new opportunity later increases when there is:

- an increase in the marginal effect of mortality risk on performance (π);
- an increase in the irreducible uncertainty (α_1).

Parameters having a dual impact on exploitation timing

We recall that potential profitability is decreased by a reduction in the uncertainty gap, which in turn is decreased by a reduction in the entrepreneur's uncertainty. This occurs because competitor uncertainty is a (linear) function of the entrepreneur's uncertainty. But it is plausible that imitators (competitors) learn at a faster rate than the new venture because second-hand learning of competitors is easier than the first-hand learning of entrepreneurs. Furthermore, recall that potential competitors' uncertainty is composed of reducible and irreducible uncertainties. The impact on the threshold line of a change in uncertainty reduction per unit of knowledge depends on whether the net change between marginal profit potential and marginal performance of mortality risk reduction – which is influenced by a change in reducible uncertainty – is positive or negative. Whenever this net marginal change is negative and the uncertainty reduction per unit of knowledge is increased, the entrepreneur should exploit sooner because delaying exploitation would lose more from reduced profit potential than gain from reduced mortality risk. However, when the net marginal change is positive, an increased uncertainty reduction per unit of knowledge results in the entrepreneur exploiting later.

Hypothesis 4: The probability that the entrepreneur should exploit the new opportunity sooner increases when the uncertainty reduction per unit of knowledge (λ) is:

- increased and the marginal reduction in profit potential from decreased reducible uncertainty $[\omega(\alpha_2 - 1)]$ is greater than the marginal gain in performance from decreased mortality risk arising from decreased reducible uncertainty $[\alpha_2 \pi e^{-\beta t}]$;
- decreased and $\omega(\alpha_2 - 1)$ is less than $\alpha_2 \pi e^{-\beta t}$.

Another dual impact on the decision of when to begin exploitation comes from the relationship between potential competitors' observational learning and an adjusted exploration cost. Because of time effect on mortality risk reduction, an entrepreneur can reduce mortality risk attributed to irreducible uncertainty by staying in exploration for an additional period. Therefore, the adjusted exploration cost indicates the net exploration cost left after accounting for the mortality reduction attributed to irreducible uncertainty. An unfavorable situation is where the loss in potential profit (recall that more uncertainty is associated with a longer lead time and therefore more potential profit) is greater than the adjusted exploration cost. In this unfavorable situation, if the competitors' ability to decrease reducible uncertainty through observation decreases (larger value for α_2), the loss in potential profit will further increase. Therefore the entrepreneur should exploit even sooner. On the other hand, if the loss in potential profit is below the adjusted exploration cost, entrepreneurs are in a favorable situation where they should delay exploitation and explore further.

Hypothesis 5: The probability that the entrepreneur should exploit the new opportunity sooner increases when the difficulty for a competitor to decrease reducible uncertainty (α_2) is:

- increased and profit potential reduction from the reducible uncertainty [$\omega\lambda\mu_r$] is greater than an adjusted exploration cost [$c - \pi\,\alpha_1 e^{-\beta t}(e^\beta - 1)$];
- decreased and [$\omega\lambda\mu_r$] is less than [$c - \pi\,\alpha_1 e^{-\beta t}(e^\beta - 1)$].

Discussion

We proposed an optimal stopping rule for an entrepreneur's decision on when to shift their focus from exploring an opportunity and begin its exploitation to maximize performance, i.e., optimize potential profitability, mortality risk, and exploration costs. The model characterizes the effects of various environmental/industrial factors (such as the length of a new venture's lead time and the nature of imitation) on the time to begin exploitation. The myopic but dynamic decision making rule drawn from the optimal stopping principle extends our understanding on a fundamental question in entrepreneurship: Rumelt (1987) asserts that entrepreneurial rent is the result of *ex ante* uncertainty. We believe that there has been insufficient attention in the field of entrepreneurship paid to the level of uncertainty entrepreneurs should face to maximize their performance. The dynamic decision rule presented in this chapter suggests that the entrepreneur, in deciding whether to continue exploration, should compare the marginal values of both benefit (mortality reduction) and costs (lost return in profitability and exploration cost) for each time period.

Scholars and practitioners involved in entrepreneurship have well recognized the phenomenon of high failure rates of new ventures. However, there is little scholarly attention paid to the role of mortality risk in the entrepreneur's decision process, which likely leads us to misleading implications. For instance, if mortality risk is removed from our framework (i.e., $\pi = 0$ in equation [7.7]), then the optimal decision for the entrepreneur to accrue maximum performance with the new opportunity will be to exploit it immediately after founding the new venture.[6] However, the optimal decision rule proposed in Hypothesis 1 suggests that such a strategy would be sub-optimal. This could provide insights in to the current failure of Boo.com and Value America who seemed to have too quickly shifted their focus to exploitation. Our model reflects the importance for entrepreneurs to consider both profitability and mortality risk in their decision of when to exploit an opportunity.

The overall nature of knowledge in the entrepreneurial process, which depends both on an entrepreneur's ability to make it idiosyncratic and the nature of the entrepreneurial process (influenced by industry and/or environmental factors), forms an irreducible uncertainty gap between entrepreneurs and potential competitors. The role of the irreducible uncertainty gap in the entrepreneurial process is worthy of attention. Our model prescribes that an entrepreneur should delay exploitation as the irreducible uncertainty gap increases (Hypothesis 3). This prescription challenges implications drawn from the current literature in strategic management and economics. Early entrants with a long lead time build strong first mover advantages (e.g., Carpenter and

Nakamoto, 1989; Huff and Robinson, 1994; Schmalensee, 1982), and hence obtain early cash inflows (Jovanovic and Lach, 1989). Furthermore, first mover advantages (including the lead time effect) are temporal (Lieberman and Montgomery, 1998) and barriers to imitation (i.e., uncertainty gap in this research's context) decay because of attritional effects of continued competitive action (Reed and DeFillippi, 1990). Taken together, these studies seem to imply that if entrepreneurs can obtain a long lead time, then they are more likely to exploit the opportunity early.

The above studies make a substantial contribution to the literature although they appear to ignore two important aspects of the entrepreneurial process. First, although the entrepreneur likely realizes earlier cash inflows through earlier exploitation, the level of uncertainty may hamper the entrepreneur from effectively and efficiently doing so, e.g., a higher mortality risk. Survivor biases exist in many first mover studies: "Forty-seven percent of market pioneers fail. In comparison, other researchers have found no pioneers that failed, or have not considered the survival problem to be serious" (Golder and Tellis, 1993: 169). Second, we argue that the literatures on strategic management and economics have not sufficiently specified those factors that provide a long lead time and whether they are reducible or not by a potential competitor's observation of an entrepreneur's exploration activities. Our framework explicitly models uncertainty and how it evolves over time and also depicts how a lead time is formed and influenced by potential competitors' actions.

Therefore, our model complements the current literature and provides new prescriptive insight into an entrepreneur's decision on when to begin the exploitation of an opportunity. With an increase in the irreducible uncertainty gap between entrepreneurs and their competitors, the urgency to begin exploitation is significantly diminished because the irreducible uncertainty is sustainable until the competitors begin their own exploration activities. The entrepreneur can thus delay exploitation and reduce mortality risk further.

Not only is the irreducible uncertainty gap important in understanding the decision of when to shift focus from exploration to exploitation, but the relative impact of the reducible uncertainty on changes in potential profitability and mortality risk also influence entrepreneurs' exploitation decision (Hypothesis 4). The greater the reduction in the reducible uncertainty, the greater the reduction entrepreneurs face in potential profitability, since the uncertainty gap (and thus lead time) reduces rapidly. This relationship is the same for mortality risk reduction.

Moreover, our model suggests that the profit potential reduction should be compared with the adjusted exploration cost (Hypothesis 5). That is, an entrepreneur should compare the advantage of being in exploration and reducing mortality risk (associated with irreducible uncertainty) with the disadvantage of potential profitability reduction (associated with reducible uncertainty) and exploration cost.

Conclusion

In this study we constructed an analytical model to explore the decision of when to shift focus from exploring the viability of a newly theorized opportunity to exploiting this opportunity. The model optimizes two main conflicting forces in the entrepreneurial process: begin exploitation earlier to increase profit potential or continue exploration to reduce mortality risk. Uncertainty embedded in the new business opportunity is the driving force of mortality risk as well as entrepreneurial rents. Mortality risk is an element that should be included in an entrepreneur's decision-making framework, particularly in the decision of when to begin exploitation. Future research is needed to empirically examine the propositions and analytically capture later stages of the entrepreneurial process.

Appendix

Proof of Hypothesis 1

Derman and Sack's (1960) theorem – Let $\{I_t, t = 1,2,...\}$ be a sequence of σ-fields of a sample Ω with I_t, $I_{t+1}, t = 1,2, ...$. Let $\{O_t\}$ be a sequence of random variables with O_t measurable with respect to I_t and such that EO_t exists and is finite for all t. Let Ψ be the class of all stopping rules such that $EN < \infty$. If there exists a stopping rule N^* with

  (i) $EN^* < \infty$
  (ii) $E[O_t | I_{t-1}] \geq O_{t-1}$ when $t \leq N^*(z)$
                    $\leq O_{t-1}$ when $t > N^*(z)$
for almost all $z \in \Omega$; and if there is some $\zeta < \infty$ such that
  (iii)   for all t, $E[|O_{t+1} - O_t| | I_t] \leq \zeta$,
   then $EO_{N^*} = \max_{N \in \Psi} EO_N$.

Applicability of the theorem – In the context of the present chapter, the σ-field I_t is generated by $(X_1, X_2, \ldots, X_t)$. The random variable O_t is the performance from exploiting the new business opportunity at period t with overall profit potential P_t, mortality risk M_t and exploration cost C_t, and it is expressed by

$$O_t = P_t - \pi M_t - C_t. \tag{A7.1}$$

Condition (i) is satisfied when the expected incremental benefit from delaying market entrance (due to a reduction in mortality risk) becomes eventually smaller than the expected incremental loss due to lost profit potential and additional exploration costs. The incremental benefit of delaying market entrance for exploitation (reduction in mortality risk) from one period to the next decreases as t increases, and ultimately approaches zero. The incremental loss in potential profit and exploration cost equals

$$(P_t - P_{t+1}) + (C_{t+1} - C_t) = \omega(\alpha_2 - 1)X_{t+1} + c, \tag{A7.2}$$

which is expected to decrease over time since the knowledge creation is expected to decrease over time, and ultimately approaches to c with a large t. Therefore, condition (i) holds and the optimal entrance delay is expected to be finite.
   Condition (ii) is equivalent to showing that, since U_t is a sufficient statistic for $\{X_1, X_2, \ldots, X_t\}$, there exists a stopping time N^* where

$$E[\phi + \omega(V_t - U_t) - \pi V_t e^{-\beta t} - ct \,|\, U_{t-1}]$$
$$\geq \phi + \omega(V_{t-1} - U_{t-1}) - \pi V_{t-1}e^{-\beta(t-1)} - c(t-1) \text{ when } t \leq N^* \tag{A7.3}$$
$$\leq \phi + \omega(V_{t-1} - U_{t-1}) - \pi V_{t-1}e^{-\beta(t-1)} - c(t-1) \text{ when } t > N^*$$

The expectation is taken on the random variables X_t from substituting U_t by $(U_{t-1} - \lambda X_t)$, as given by (7.1). Substituting the uncertainty gap using (7.3) and replacing $E[X_t]$ by μ_t offer an alternative form for (A7.3) where[7]

$$U_{t-1} \geq \frac{1}{\pi\,\alpha_2 e^{-\beta t}(e^\beta - 1)}\{c + \omega\,\lambda(\alpha_2 - 1)\mu_t - \pi\alpha_1\,e^{-\beta t}(e^\beta - 1) - \pi\,\lambda\alpha_2\mu_t e^{-\beta t}\} \text{ when } t \leq N^*$$

(A7.4)

$$\leq \frac{1}{\pi\,\alpha_2 e^{-\beta t}(e^\beta - 1)}\{c + \omega\,\lambda(\alpha_2 - 1)\mu_t - \pi\alpha_1\,e^{-\beta t}(e^\beta - 1) - \pi\,\lambda\alpha_2\mu_t e^{-\beta t}\} \text{ when } t > N^*$$

To ensure that (A 7.4) holds, we must verify that once the entrepreneur exploit the new opportunity (i.e., the threshold has been reached for the first time) the expected value of the uncertainty at any period following entry should not exceed the value of the threshold. It is sufficient to demonstrate that, for any t, $P(U_t > L^*(t + 1) \mid U_{t-1} < L^*(t)) = 0$. One has, since X_t is non-negative and $L^*(t)$ is increasing over time:

$$P(U_t > L^*(t + 1) \mid U_{t-1} < L^*(t)) = P(U_{t-1} - \lambda X_t > L^*(t + 1) \mid U_{t-1} < L^*(t))$$
$$= P(\lambda X_t < U_{t-1} - L^*(t + 1) \mid U_{t-1} < L^*(t)) \leq P(\lambda X_t < L^*(t) - L^*(t + 1) \mid U_{t-1} < L^*(t)) = 0.$$

Condition (iii) holds as long as the expected increment in performance from one period to the next is bounded. This condition is satisfied since P_t is bounded (and decreasing over time), $M_t \in [0,1]$ and c is finite.

Proof of Hypothesis 2

We are interested in the change on the acceptance interval from an increase in, respectively, the unit exploration cost, the marginal effect of uncertainty gap on profit potential and the marginal effect of time on mortality risk. We find, respectively:

$$\frac{\partial L^*(t)}{\partial c} = \frac{e^{\beta t}}{\pi\alpha_2\,(e^\beta - 1)} > 0, \quad \frac{\partial L^*(t)}{\partial\omega} = \frac{\lambda\mu_t(\alpha_2 - 1)e^{\beta t}}{\pi\alpha_2(e^\beta - 1)} > 0 \text{ and } \frac{\partial L^*(t)}{\partial\beta} > 0.$$

Proof of Hypothesis 3

We are interested in the change on the acceptance interval from an increase in, respectively, the irreducible uncertainty (α_1) and the marginal effect of mortality risk on performance (π). We find, respectively:

$$\frac{\partial L^*(t)}{\partial\alpha_1} = -\frac{1}{\alpha_2} < 0 \text{ and } \frac{\partial L^*(t)}{\partial\pi} = -\frac{(c + \omega\lambda\mu_t\alpha_2 - \omega\lambda\mu_t)e^{\beta t}}{\pi^2\alpha_2(e^\beta - 1)} < 0.$$

Proof of Hypothesis 4

We are interested in the change on the acceptance interval from an increase in the marginal effect of knowledge on uncertainty reduction (λ). We find:

$$\frac{\partial L^*(t)}{\partial\lambda} = \frac{\mu_t(\alpha_2\omega e^{\beta t} - \omega e^{\beta t} - \pi\alpha_2)}{\pi\alpha_2(e^\beta - 1)} > 0 \text{ if and only if } \omega(\alpha_2 - 1) > \alpha_2\pi e^{-\beta t}.$$

Proof of Hypothesis 5

We are interested in the change on the acceptance interval from an increase in the difficulty for a competitor to decrease reducible uncertainty (α_2). We find:

$$\frac{\partial L^*(t)}{\partial \alpha_2} = \frac{(-c + \omega\lambda\mu_t + \pi\alpha_1 e^{-\beta t + \beta} - \pi\alpha_1 e^{-\beta t}) e^{\beta t}}{\pi\alpha_2^2 (e^{\beta} - 1)} > 0 \text{ if and only if}$$

$$\omega\lambda\mu_t > c - \pi\alpha_1 e^{-\beta t}(e^{\beta} - 1).$$

Table 7.1 Summary of variables and parameters

	Symbol	Description
State variables	U_t	Entrepreneur's uncertainty level at t
	V_t	Potential competitors' (and stakeholders) uncertainty level at t
	O_t	New venture performance if he/she exploits the new opportunity at t
	P_t	Overall profit potential if he/she exploits the new opportunity at t
	C_t	Total exploration cost until t
	M_t	Mortality risk (i.e., the probability of failure) if the entrepreneur exploits the new opportunity at t
Random variable	X_t	Entrepreneur's knowledge creation through exploration activity at t
Parameters	λ	Marginal effect of unit knowledge on uncertainty reduction
	α_1	Irreducible uncertainty for a potential competitor's observational learning
	α_2	Difficulty for a competitor to decrease reducible uncertainty
	ϕ	Earning rate when there is no lead time
	ω	Marginal effect of uncertainty gap on profit potential
	c	Exploration cost per unit period
	β	Rate at which mortality risk decreases over time
	π	Marginal effect of mortality risk on an entrepreneur's performance
	μ_t	Expected knowledge creation at t

Notes

1 Our definitions of exploration and exploitation are based on March (1991).
2 For example, noise in the communication channels, inventors' and/or early adopters' un- willingness to dissipate information, and the knowledge being tacit in nature (Abrahamson and Rosenkopf, 1993).
3 There are, however, exceptions such as in the pharmaceutical industry where the mecha- nism for first mover advantage has little to do with scale since successful patenting will protect patent holders from imitation. But in most industries, there are multiple techno-

logical alternatives to circumvent the rights of patents (Afuah, 1999).

4   To insure that mortality risk (7.5) is a probability, the performance function in (7.7) will be scaled to take into consideration both the marginal effect of mortality risk on performance and the scaling of mortality risk between 0 and 1.

5   One can easily verify that the first and second order derivative of $L^*(t)$ with respect to t are positive. Although time is discrete in our model, we utilize a continuous representation of it in figure 7.2.

6   Technical details are available upon request from the first author.

7   $E[O_t \mid U_{t-1}] = \phi + \omega\alpha_1 + \omega(\alpha_2 - 1)U_{t-1} - \omega\lambda(\alpha_2 - 1)\mu_t - \pi\alpha_1 e^{-\beta t} - \pi\alpha_2 U_{t-1}e^{-\beta t} + \pi\alpha_2\lambda\mu_t e^{-\beta t} - ct.$

References

Abrahamson. E. and Rosenkopf, L. 1993: Institutional and competitive bandwagons: using mathematical modeling as a tool to explore innovation diffusion. *Academy of Management Review*, 18, 487–517.

Afuah, A. 1999: Strategies to turn adversity into profits. *Sloan Management Review*, 40, 99–109.

Baumol, W. J. 1993: *Entrepreneurship, Management, and the Structure of Payoffs*. Cambridge, MA: The MIT Press.

Bird, B. J. 1989: *Entrepreneurial Behavior*. Glenview, IL: Scott Foresman.

Carpenter, G. S. and Nakamoto, K. 1989: Consumer preference formation and pioneering advantage. *Journal of Marketing Research*, 26, 285–98.

Folta, T. B. 1998: Governance and uncertainty: the trade-off between administrative control and commitment. *Strategic Management Journal*, 19, 1007–28.

Ghemawat, P. 1986: Sustainable advantage. *Harvard Business Review*, (86) (5), 53–8.

Golder, P. and Tellis, G. 1993: Pioneering advantage: marketing logic or marketing legend. *Journal of Marketing Research*, 30 (May), 158–70.

Herriott, S. R, Levinthal, D. A., and March, J. G. 1985: Learning from experience in organizations. *American Economic Review*, 75, 298–302.

Huff, L. C. and Robinson, W. T. 1994: The impact of leadtime and years of copetitive rivalry on pioneer market share advantage. *Management Science*, 40, 1370–7.

Jovanovic, B. and Lach, S. 1989: Entry, exit and diffusion with learning by doing. *American Economic Review*, 79, 690–99.

Lambkin, M. 1988: Order of entry and performance in new markets. *Strategic Management Journal*, 9, 127–40.

Levinthal, D. A. 1991: Random walks and organizational mortality. *Administrative Science Quarterly*, 36: 397–420.

Levinthal, D. A. and March, J. G. 1981: A model of adaptive organizational search. *Journal of Economic Behavior and Organization*, 2, 307–33.

Lieberman, M. B. and Montgomery, D. B. 1988: First mover advantages. *Strategic Management Journal*, 9, 41–58.

Lieberman, M. B. and Montgomery, D. B. 1998: First mover (dis)advantages: retrospective and link with the resource-based view. *Strategic Management Journal*, 19, 1111–25.

Lippman, S. A. and Rumelt, R. P. 1982: Uncertain imitability: an analysis of interfirm differences in efficiency under competition. *Bell Journal of Economics*, 13, 418–38.

March, J. G. 1991: Exploration and exploitation in organizational learning. *Organization Science*, 2, 71–87.

McGrath, R. G. 1997: A real options logic for initiating technology positioning investments. *Academy of Management Review*, 22, 974–96.

Mosakowski, E. 1997: Strategy making under causal ambiguity: conceptual issues and empirical evidence. *Organization Science*, 8, 414–42.

Nelson, R. R. and Winter, S. E. 1982: *An Evolutionary Theory of Economic Change*. Cambridge, MA: Harvard University Press.

Radner, R. and Shepp, L. 1996: Risk vs. profit potential: a model for corporate strategy. *Journal of Economic Dynamics and Control*, 20, 1373–93.

Robert, E. and Meyer, M. 1991: New products and corporate strategy. *Engineering Management Review*, 19, 1, 4–18.

Ross, S. M. 1983: *Stochastic Processes*. Wiley: New York.

Rumelt, R. P. 1987: Theory, strategy, and entrepreneurship. In D. J. Teece (ed.), *The Competitive Challenge*. Cambridge, MA: Ballinger, 137–158.

Schmalensee, R. 1982: Product differentiation advantages of pioneering brands. *American Economic Review*, 72, 350–71.

Schoemaker, P. J. H. and Amit, R. 1994: Investment in strategic assets: industry and firm-level perspectives. *Advances in Strategic Management*, 10A, 3–33.

Schoonhoven, C. B., Eisenhardt, K. M., and Lyman, K. 1990: Speeding products to market: waiting time to first product introduction in new firms. *Administrative Science Quarterly*, 35, 177–207.

Shane, S. and Venkataraman, S. 2000: The promise of entrepreneurship as a field of research. *Academy of Management Review*, 25, 217–26.

Shepherd, D. A., Douglas, E. J., and Shanley, M. T. 2000: New venture survival: ignorance, external shocks and risk reduction strategies. *Journal of Business Venturing*, 15: 393–410.

Singh, J. V., Tucker, D. J., and House, R. J. 1986: Organizational legitimacy and the liability of newness. *Administrative Science Quarterly*, 31, 171–93.

Stinchcombe, A. L. 1965: Social structure and organizations. In J. G. March (ed.), *Handbook of Organizations*. Chicago: Rand McNally, 142–93.

Wernerfelt, B. and Karnani, A. 1987: Competitive strategy under uncertainty. *Strategic Management Journal*, 8, 187–94.

Yelle, L. 1979: The learning curve: Historical review and comprehensive survey. *Decision Sciences*, 10, 302–08.

CHAPTER EIGHT

Competition and the Electronic World: Does e-Commerce Require the Recognition of Channel as a Type of Diversification?

Esmeralda Garbi, Peggy Golden, and Brenda Richey

Introduction

Today, when attempting to apply core strategy concepts such as diversification to the creation of Internet-based companies or divisions, we are faced with a problem. The core competency for firms involved in electronic commerce is often the ability to share information, rather than a functional expertise such as manufacturing or new product technology. As a consequence, the ability to classify these businesses into different areas or industries, to define when more than one area is being reached, and to establish how they relate with each other becomes more difficult (Sampler, 1998). In this chapter, we examine the extent to which existing diversification concepts can adequately describe e-commerce and the world of the Internet, and argue that as a result of this new technology it may be necessary to reconsider diversification and include channel as a new type of diversification.

Here are some illustrations. Nordstrom is a full-service retailer that is geographically dispersed and sells a complex product line. Because of its historical growth, it developed its supply chain through conventional channels. Recently it has taken on a web-presence to reach customers (*Business Week*, 1999). Although its basic products and markets remain the same, the "click-and-mortar" presence offers a new distribution channel. It permits Nordstrom to choose whether it is more efficient to ship to a physical store or to bypass that point and ship directly from vendor to customer. Beyond just the distribution of goods, the electronic structure offers Nordstrom a new channel of communication with customers and suppliers as well as new means of acquiring vital market information.

Amazon.com is also a retailer that has increased its offerings. This company has never had a physical point of sale. Its products travel directly from the vendor to the customer. Amazon has expanded its offerings from books to music, toys, electronic equipment, and a variety of additional products. It has also added on functions of a marketplace, by bringing buyers and sellers together through its auction site, without participating in the actual exchange of goods or services (*Wall Street Journal,* 1999).

Using a broad definition of diversification as "reaching out into new areas, requiring the development of new competences or the augmentation of existing ones" (Rumelt, 1974: 10–11) we might surmise that both Nordstrom and Amazon had diversified. Using traditional categories of product or geographic market diversification, however, we could reach a different conclusion. Despite its extension into e-commerce, Nordstrom would not be considered to have diversified because its Internet operations do not include either a new set of products, or a real extension of geographic scope. Amazon, although arguably staying closer to its established skill-base in Internet retailing, might be considered to have diversified because its actions involve an extension of its product line. In this chapter, we ask whether these traditional diversification concepts are adequate to allow us to understand the unfolding world of e-commerce. At the core of this query lies a key issue: is it enough to define the business by the traditional notions of products and markets? Could we actually predict and/or explain outcomes in the e-commerce world based on our existing notions of product and market diversification? The examples described above, and many others like them, suggest that the answers to these questions are negative. For e-commerce, the most important challenge faced by managers expanding their range of activities seems not to be imposed by the products *per se*, or the new consumer markets, but by the extensions of the channels by which they reach customers and suppliers. In that case, the channel is the most defining component of these companies' operations.

The need for redefining strategy concepts has been stated by others in recent articles such as Bettis and Hitt (1995), Løwendahl and Revang (1998), and Sampler (1998). They provide a fertile background for this discussion, even though none of these works specifically addresses the challenges imposed on diversification theory by the advent of e-commerce. We propose that e-commerce, especially for traditional companies venturing into the electronic world, represents a different type of diversification, the logic of which is not based on products or markets but on the channel of communication and distribution.

We start by examining the new competitive endeavor that has been triggered and shaped by the increasing entry of electronic competitors in many industries, and the growing incursion of traditional companies into the electronic world. Next, we discuss the problem from the perspective of diversification theory. In particular, we review received theories of product and market diversification to attempt to explain the strategic moves recently observed in industries with extensive e-commerce competition. We next examine an alternative view of the problem from the perspective of strategic groups, seeing rivalry among traditional and new actors in e-commerce-intensive industries as competition within industries. Finally, we explore a third approach to the problem, proposing that e-commerce ventures imply a different type of diversification based on the channel of communication and distribution.

E-Commerce and the New Competitive Endeavor

Whether referred to as the information age, the "post-industrial society" (Bell, 1973), or the "third wave" (Toffler, 1981), the last quarter of the twentieth century will be remembered as the period in which information technologies reshaped all aspects of business operations. In fact, the shift in importance of information-intensive activities over manufacturing activities is one of the most important economic changes of recent years. For an excellent discussion on the economic transformations and challenges of the information age, see Sampler (1998). The most recent evidence of this transformation has been the striking proliferation of electronic companies and the effect they have had on their more traditional competitors. The surge of entrants, using electronic means to provide most or all of the value-added process, is forcing industry incumbents to modify their own structures, many of them responding by creating electronic counterparts or by modifying their traditional structures to operate electronically as well. For incumbents in many industries the process of incorporating e-commerce to respond to the threat of erosion of its customer base from a virtual or electronic company has become a top priority. Some companies are taking the path of extending their current operations to include an Internet side, while others are taking the more dramatic step of setting up new divisions or entirely new companies to compete in the online market place. For some, the changes are cosmetic, while others are changing their entire business system to incorporate the Internet at all stages of the value chain.

For firms that started life in the virtual world, we may also be seeing major shifts in strategy. Some have expanded beyond their roots to explore new products and markets. Amazon, for example, has entered both the international arena and substantially broadened the range of products handled. Others are migrating away from a totally virtual existence to add physical assets including storefront locations, such as E*Trade (*Business Week*, 2000).

As a result of these changes, we find a landscape shaped with different strategic configurations in the way firms use electronic commerce. A simplified breakdown of this landscape, necessary to provide a basis for further discussion, is shown in table 8.1. First, the e-company is the organization using the Internet and electronic communications technology to provide most or all of their value-added process including sourcing, operations, delivery, and all other elements of the value chain. Firms using e-commerce for auctions or direct sales, supply-chain management, and payments for products or services, such as Amazon.com, E*Trade, and eBay, are some of the most widely recognizable names to end-user consumers in this category. However, Charles Schwab, which started as a traditional broker and has now migrated to the e-world using the Internet and electronic channels for most of its commercial and business-to-business activities, is also an example of an e-company.

A second configuration of firms comprises the "click-and-mortars". These were "brick-and-mortars" that have now migrated some of their functions to the Internet, often in response to the moves of e-commerce competitors, while maintaining their traditional physical presence (Gulati and Garino, 2000). They might use the Internet to open a new business channel to complement existing channels, create a new company to duplicate their existing business in an electronic setting, or set up

Table 8.1   Organizational types observed in e-commerce

Type	Definition
e-company	Firm using electronic structures to provide most or all of the value-added process, including sourcing, operations, delivery, and all other elements of the value chain. Example: Amazon.com.
Click-and-mortar	Firm opening a new business channel to complement existing value-added channels, creating a new company to duplicate its existing business in an electronic setting or setting up a new division dedicated to electronic commerce. Example: Barnes & Noble.
Brick-and-mortar	Firm that maintains most of its activities outside the Internet, with the exception of the electronic data interchange required by suppliers or customers. Might be using electronic data interchange but as a limited extension of current operations. Example: Toys "Я" Us.

new divisions dedicated to e-commerce. An example of a click-and-mortar is Barnes and Noble, which is keeping its traditional presence and creating an electronic counterpart, barnesandnoble.com.

A third configuration is the traditional "brick-and-mortar", which maintains most or all of its functions outside the Internet (with the exception of the electronic data interchange required by suppliers or customers). These are firms using electronic data interchange as a limited extension of current operations, often to augment or replace existing communication or distribution links. The integration of electronic commerce with its traditional value chain is limited. An example of this configuration is Toys "Я" Us. Following its failed attempt to respond to heavy competition from eToys and others by entering into the on-line retailing in Christmas 1999, it has now partnered with Amazon for the on-line distribution of its products. All of Amazon's toy sales year-round will come from its Toys "Я" Us alliance, except for a few toys that Toys "Я" Us do not offer (*Wall Street Journal*, 2000). Amazon has insured its access to popular toys and Toys "Я" Us has established a web presence through this alliance, though it will basically operate as an outsourced distribution channel for them.

The question we now face is whether or not our extant theory and concepts will allow us to make sense of this new environment. In particular, we are interested in determining if we can use traditional diversification theory to survey and predict results.

A Traditional Diversification Approach to Understanding E-Commerce

In the context of e-commerce competition, the question of what constitutes related and unrelated diversification and what performance outcomes we can expect based on theories of related and unrelated diversification offers a challenge. Focusing on traditional definitions could impede our understanding. This section discusses e-commerce within the product-market diversification approach, addressing its limitations for a complete understanding of the e-commerce landscape.

Strategy researchers have widely studied corporate diversification (Grant et al., 1988; Palepu, 1985; Rumelt, 1974, 1982; Varadarajan and Ramanujam, 1987), mostly defining it as the increase in the range of products (entering new businesses across industries) or customer groups (entering new geographic regions, with new or traditional products) of a corporation (Dess et al., 1995; Ramanujam and Varadarajan, 1989). A key issue has been the understanding of the conditions allowing firms to create synergies that outweigh the costs associated with a more diverse organization (Hitt et al., 1997).

In product diversification, these synergies have been thought to occur when businesses are related (Bettis, 1981; Grant et al., 1988; Rumelt, 1974, 1982), allowing the company to share resources or leverage knowledge to the new activity. The concept of product-based relatedness has evolved from a focus on end products (usually defined by SIC codes), to shared competencies (resource-based analysis) and shared strategic orientation (dominant logic) (Chaterjee and Wernerfelt, 1991; Markides and Williamson, 1996; Robins and Wiersema, 1995). Studies of geographic diversification have focused on international expansions of firms and looked at relatedness as the distance between national cultures ('psychic' distance). Synergies occur when the savings from organizational integration exceed the costs associated with the needs of responding to local market differences or the costs of sales lost because of the failure to adapt to local market needs (Hitt et al., 1997).

In general, unrelated diversifications have been shown to be costly to the firm and have therefore impaired financial and market performance (Grant, 1988; Palich et al., 2000; Rumelt, 1974, 1982; Singh and Montgomery, 1987). Findings on the relationship between unrelated diversification and performance are mixed, however, particularly in regards to financial performance (Keats, 1990) and may reflect more complex interactions with firm strategy, structure and market conditions (Hoskisson and Hitt, 1990). The results and limitations of diversification studies have been widely discussed in the literature. For a review, see Hoskisson and Hitt (1990) and, recently, Palich et al., (2000).

All these studies have been driven by our ability as scholars to categorize the diversification behavior of the firm. Research has evolved from a product count based on SIC classifications to the entropy measures used more currently (Farjoun, 1998; Hoskisson et al., 1993; Qian, 1997). Diversification has been measured by deviations in assignment of two or four digit SIC codes, or by subjective inspection in relationship to the Department of Commerce categories (Robins and Wiersema, 1995). Implicit in much of these works is the concept of industry built around products. In the traditional literature, an industry is defined as a group of firms or business units producing close substitute products (Porter, 1980). For example, all firms supplying automobile door panels will be considered in the same industry whether the panels are made of plastic or metal, despite differences in plant facilities, raw material sourcing, materials handling, or manufacturing techniques.

We return to explore the questions we raised previously, using this traditional approach to diversification to look at the strategic moves undertaken recently by Amazon.com and Barnes and Noble. Using traditional diversification concepts, with a focus on product issues, we would identify Amazon's incursion into retail sectors as diverse as books, electronics, housewares, music, and toys as a form of diversification. It is at least arguable, however, that by doing so we would overemphasize the extent of the diversification undertaken by Amazon because of the wide range of product categories. If so, we would expect, based on our theories, Amazon.com to be outperformed by companies pursuing product-related diversification strategies.

Conversely, and possibly more importantly, using this same approach, the tendency would be to underemphasize the very real difficulties faced by "click-and-mortar" firms as they continue to sell their traditional product lines through alternative channels. When, for example, Barnes and Noble ventures into on-line sales, it is not diversifying its product portfolio. Should we expect, hence, that Barnes and Noble will be able to easily leverage synergies and knowledge from its traditional bookstore operations to barnesandnoble.com and outperform Amazon? Traditional product market diversification theory would suggest this is so. Companies such as Barnes and Noble and Nordstrom, which have gone on-line, may not consider these ventures diversification. Yet, in each case, the differences in resource needs such as knowledge, skills, physical assets, and of operational tasks and structures between the original business and the extensions may be tremendous. Therefore, we propose the following:

> Proposition 1: Diversification strategies in electronic commerce, and their degree of relatedness, cannot be captured by traditional product/market diversification constructs.

The inability of traditional product diversification theories to capture the level of diversification in e-commerce activity is aggravated by the use of SIC-based diversification measures to operationalize the constructs. Although not the only method, SIC codes are frequently used to develop measures for diversification and industry effect studies (McGahan and Porter, 1997; Powell, 1996; Rumelt, 1991; Wernerfelt and Montgomery, 1988). The inadequacy of SIC-based measures has been pointed out by others (Gassenheimer and Keep, 1998), so we will limit our discussion to aspects that present special issues for e-commerce firms.

Problems are twofold. First, because the code reflects a classification scheme developed to handle manufacturing firms, SIC-based measures are problematic in retail and service industries, where more diverse businesses tend to be lumped into a few categories. For instance, there is a lack of comparability in classification detail between manufacturing and retail categories (Gassenheimer and Keep, 1998). This suggests that, while traditional product diversification concepts would overestimate the level of Amazon.com's diversification, the operationalization of these concepts could lead to underestimation.

The second problem results from the self-reported nature of the information used to classify businesses activities. Two firms with similar activities may use different approaches in their SIC code reporting and so give rise to different determinations about diversification. Barnes and Noble reports its Internet operations under a different SIC code from its traditional bookstore operations. We might infer that their new activities represent a form of diversification if we only looked at the SIC code designations. On the other hand, Nordstrom's similar extension of traditional product lines into e-commerce channels would not be considered diversification because it has not reported them under separate SIC codes. These measurement issues only compound the theoretical issues that arise from the application of traditional product and market diversification theories to e-commerce.

An Alternative Approach to e-Commerce focusing on Strategic Groups

Another way to make sense of the e-commerce landscape is to analyze the problem from the perspective of intra-industry competition (with industry defined as a group of close competitors, not necessarily the same SIC category). A strategic group is a "group of firms in an industry following the same, or a similar strategy along the strategic dimensions" (Galbraith et al., 1994, quoting Porter, 1980). Research over the past twenty years has included discussions of whether strategic groups exist and are stable over time (Dranove et al., 1998), whether rivalry is greater within groups than across groups (Smith et al., 1997), and whether or not mobility barriers between strategic groups can be used to predict firm performance (Mehra, 1996; Wiggins and Ruefli, 1995). Though strategic groups are considered to be a theoretical construct, clusters of firms within industries using similar strategies or positioning themselves similarly along key strategic dimensions have been found empirically (Dranove et al., 1998; Nath and Gruca, 1997). An important consideration of strategic groups for describing competition is that, within industries, companies have closer competitors perceived to have higher potential for retaliation and imitation of a company's strategic moves. Managers will give more attention to those firms within their own strategic groups, because their strategies and resource positions are perceived as similar (Peteraf and Shanley, 1997). Firms within a group are seen as interdependent; their actions and results directly affecting other members in their group (Hatten and Hatten, 1987).

In this section, we use ideas generated by research in strategic groups to examine an alternative view of competition in the electronic world. The electronic commerce revolution seems to be having an effect on industry competition and the formation of strategic groups. In other industries, the diffusion of radically new technological changes also has had a significant impact on the configuration of strategic groups (Sabourin, 1999). That was the case of the steel industry where the emergence of flexible processes led to the formation of strategic groups in which medium-size manufacturers competed against large-scale traditional producers. From this perspective, strategic group formation and mobility barriers will have a role in determining differences in firm strategies and performance. The expected effect of strategic group membership on firm performance is based on theories of environmental adaptation as well as barriers to imitation. Because some strategic positions are going to be better "adapted" than other strategic positions to a particular industry environment, and because the effect of competitive forces differ across firms, it is assumed that firms in some groups have higher performance potential than firms in other groups (Hunt, 1972; Porter, 1979).

Once e-companies have entered an industry, they could be seen as representing a different strategic group from those companies using traditional channels. If incumbents in the traditional strategic group perceive the new entrants group as more attractive, they will attempt to migrate to it. But they may encounter mobility barriers, such as technological know how and customer knowledge, human resources, specialized programming, and organizational culture. This has been the case in other industries, such as banking, in which a technological change (i.e., ATMs) created a new market or industry "subfield" and represented new challenges for traditional competitors (Sinha and Noble; 1997).

We also expect to see mobility barriers acting to impede moves from the "virtual" to the "physical" channel strategy. New electronic entrants, such as E*Trade, are now trying to migrate away from a complete virtual existence and adding physical assets including storefront locations. E*Trade, Webvan.com, HomeGrocer.com, as well as several other e-companies are starting to behave more and more like their bricks-and-mortar counterparts. Webvan, for instance, needs warehouses, inventory flows, and delivery systems much like those of Publix or Vons Supermarkets. Acquiring and managing these real assets will present a challenge for these firms.

Mobility barriers need to be present for above normal returns to persist. Without mobility barriers firms will move to the higher performing group, eliminating performance differences in the long run. Therefore, the height of mobility barriers between groups is a key determinant of firm differential performance. We state the following proposition:

Proposition 2: Mobility barriers will develop between groups of firms using traditional channels and groups using electronic channels, and the height of these barriers may influence firm performance.

Furthermore, the height of mobility barriers appears to be asymmetric. The contrasting experiences of Toys "Я" Us and Charles Schwab reflect this issue. Toys "Я" Us experienced major difficulties in its attempt to sell on-line, while Charles Schwab appears to have successfully "moved" to the e-commerce group. The differing results may be attributed to differences in individual firm competencies, may be representative of differences between industries, or a combination of both. The nature of securities transactions, with infrequent physical transfer of the "product" (i.e., the securities) and its established automated processes, may have allowed Charles Schwab to avoid many of the delivery and information system problems that plagued Toys "Я" Us. Mobility barriers that prove to be immense in one industry may not be so in another. Therefore, we propose:

Proposition 3: In industries with electronic competition, there will be asymmetries in mobility barriers depending on the specific capabilities of firms and the nature of the industry.

The view of e-commerce endeavors as the switching of strategic groups might offer a new perspective to our understanding of the structural phenomenon associated with e-commerce. From this perspective, the question of synergies and relatedness between markets and businesses could be approached as a question of barriers to mobility among strategic groups. When an incumbent company expands its channels from traditional to electronic channels, it is not diversifying but entering a different strategic group. Issues would include the identification of mobility barriers and a determination of whether or not differences in performance reflect differences in the height of mobility barriers; i.e., higher barriers should result in greater profitability.

The strategic groups' perspective alone, however, is limited as a framework in understanding the competitive landscape of electronic commerce. A limitation of the framework is its focus on intra-industry competition, while one of the core issues in e-commerce is the inter-industry competition. E-companies have used "flanking maneuvers" to compete in traditional industries, overcoming pre-existing entry barriers such as brand name, economies of scale, and capital requirements. That was, for example, the approach of E*Trade, which entered the brokerage industry to compete with established firms such as Charles Schwab, Merrill Lynch, and the like. Other e-companies entry into the retail industry, such as eToys and Amazon, seem to reflect a similar situation: companies using technology to enter an established and mature industry and compete against firms with a greater physical base of assets and established relationships.

Another limitation of the strategic groups' perspective is the fact that some companies seem to be using mixed strategies (click-and-mortar), and even original e-companies seem to be moving to the mixed group, lessening the power of strategic group theory to explain differences in firm performance.

Channel as an Additional Type of Diversification

Using traditional diversification concepts and measures, a firm's excursion into on-line retailing of their traditional product line cannot be completely understood because traditional diversification types do not capture the very real challenges of the e-commerce extension. These challenges include dramatic changes in human resource management, technology base, skill development, and knowledge. These are the very types of changes that appear to have made some companies' venture into electronic commerce a failure. Conversely, a product/market diversification approach might also misread as diversification e-commerce companies' entries into diverse product/market lines that are actually not extending these firms' core capabilities and knowledge.

Similarly, observations using strategic groups theory would provide an incomplete analysis. Figure 8.1 highlights some of the issues presented by using this theory. In figure 8.1 we show a hypothetical competitive landscape with two industries and a variety of firms moving within and outside the industries. The movement of these firms is used to illustrate the discussion below. Using the concept of mobility barriers, we can develop insights into the constraints that slow the ability of bricks-and-mortar firms to compete with electronic competitors that have entered the industry (for example, the movement by firms C8a and C3a within Industry A). Mobility barriers may also explain the inability of some e-companies to move beyond the world of electronic commerce to compete on a broader base within their industry. It would not provide, however, a basis to explore the ability of electronic commerce to leap over the barriers to entering the industry initially (movement into Industry A by firm Cy), one of the most important issues in the electronic commerce landscape. Nor does strategic groups theory provide a basis for exploring issues across industry. As noted above, one of the more interesting questions may be that of whether or not the height of mobility

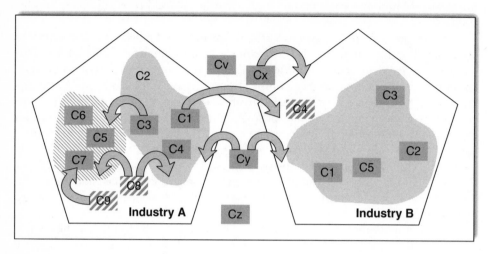

Figure 8.1   e-commerce competitive landscape

barriers varies across industry and under which circumstances do certain barriers become more important.

Earlier, we discussed traditional models that have allowed understanding of related and unrelated diversification in a manufacturing age. These arguments were made largely on the basis of market power theory and internal market efficiencies in manufacturing organizations (Grant, 1988). In the e-company and click-and-mortar firm, the efficiencies may not be related with synergies in manufacturing processes but with the use of information technology that creates organizational synergies in coordination, improving efficiency as well as customer responsiveness. St. John and Harrison (1999) allude to this argument in discussing a notion of manufacturing-based relatedness. We propose that traditional types of diversification do not address the inherent nature of electronic and click-and-mortar companies because their transformation processes are inherently information flows rather than assembly. For these reasons, we propose the notion of a channel diversification.

Proposition 4: Changes and extensions of the information and distribution channels represent important challenges to the dominant logic of a firm that can be viewed as a form of diversification.

Figure 8.2 highlights this idea. In figure 8.2, we attempt to show that the vertical and horizontal diversifications, as originally conceptualized, were based on the extent to which products were similar or on how they extended the involvement from the extraction of raw materials to the ultimate finished product. Traditionally, horizontal and vertical integrations dealt primarily with market power or with reduced transaction costs. In figure 8.2, we propose that the *de facto* vertical integration can occur much more easily in the e-commerce environment giving additional strength to the market arguments of Williamson (1975) and others.

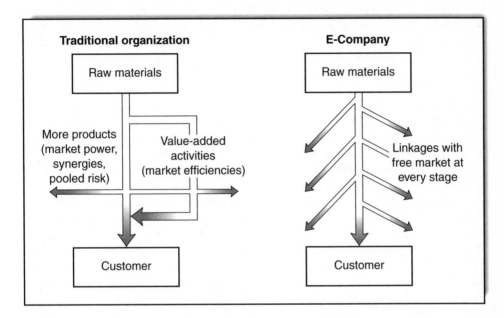

Figure 8.2   Vertical and horizontal diversification for traditional versus e-company

The e-commerce or click-and-mortar firm might be able to integrate forward and backward from the core competency without the burden of ownership and new learning involved in the stages of value-added and distribution. D'Aveni and Ravenscraft (1994) made similar arguments for the case of vertical integration. They proposed that vertically integrated firms over time could reduce both managerial and bureaucratic costs to improve financial performance. However, their results were mixed in supporting economies of scale and scope in vertically integrated firms. If the same study were done on an e-company, we would probably notice that the firm made no attempt to vertically integrate (under one CUSIP) through the value-added chain. The technological change that the e-company firm is based on permits an inherent hub from which it can source and supply without the burden of bureaucracy and ownership (Kaplan and Sawhney, 2000). A similar argument exists for horizontal diversifications: e-commerce and click-and-mortar firms might in some cases be able to add to their product portfolio without incurring the liability of newness in an industry. One of the challenges may be to identify the characteristics of the industries in which this is most likely to occur. In this respect, we post the following propositions:

Proposition 5: For channel-diversified firms, relatedness is based on information and distribution capabilities more than on product or market similarities.

Proposition 6: Channel diversified firms will be able to extend their product or market portfolios more easily than non-channel diversified firms in some industries.

Recognizing the information and distribution channels as a form of diversification allows us to examine and understand important differences that occur in the new competitive landscape. Frazier (1999) reviews the state of the distribution channel literature noting that, in spite of the wide range of understanding of distribution channels, there are still several missing pieces. These pertain to when the Internet should be used as a sales-distribution channel, and how coordination can be achieved. He notes increasing market fragmentation and reduced barriers to free and open competition. In order for a firm to maintain or develop asymmetries that lead to profitability in the quasi-vertical channel, one firm needs to take control of the channel. In the manufacturing era, this power was maintained by the member who had the most control over the distribution of resources. Viewing channel as a form of diversification may allow us to more easily explore these issues.

The approach to channels as a form of diversification will also allow us to apply some of the knowledge we have gained from traditional product and market diversification studies to this new landscape. For instance, traditional diversification studies have emphasized the importance not only of strategy (the decision to move into a new product line or market), but also of structure (the organizational form employed) in predicting the effect of diversification on firm performance. Once we have recognized channel as a form of diversification, we can begin developing the measures necessary to determine the relatedness of a firm's traditional channel (physical or virtual), its new channel, and the costs therein. We can then use diversification arguments to predict that in industries in which the shift to electronic commerce requires greater shifts in more areas of firm operations, it might be advantageous for the firm to house the new venture in a separate division or even a separate corporation. Our last propositions reflect issues suggested by both the product diversification literature and by the success and failure to date of various firms venturing into the world of electronic commerce.

Proposition 7: Firms that have acquired related channel experience will be more successful at diversifying into electronic channels than firms with less related experience.

Proposition 8: For firms that diversify into channels that are substantially unrelated to their existing ones, performance will be better if they do not attempt to integrate the new operations with existing operations or if they elect to outsource aspects of the new operations.

Conclusion

In this chapter we have argued that, in the context of technology change and the challenges imposed by e-commerce, core strategy terms need redefinition. For many firms there has been a shift from an emphasis on manufacturing and tangible assets to an emphasis on information and intangible resources. Although this shift is reflected in some of the conceptual work examining the firm, many strategy constructs still assume a manufacturing production model typical of the industrial age.

Traditional diversification types, in particular, seem insufficient to provide a full understanding of the electronic commerce landscape. By allowing for extensions in products and markets with only the limited acquisition of physical assets, electronic commerce simultaneously reduces the need of developing some new competencies for competing within these new products and markets, and increases the importance of developing competencies in other areas of the business. It is for this reason we suggest existing theory be supplemented by consideration of channel, interpreted broadly to encompass information flows, sourcing and distribution, as an additional type of diversification.

In many respects, what we propose is comparable to the process that accompanied the recognition of geographic market diversification. First, it was necessary to acknowledge that extending operations across national boundaries entailed substantial differences in multiple aspects of firm operations, and that these differences were not adequately captured by the existing studies of product diversification. Next, it was necessary to develop measures that would adequately capture both the level and the nature of these differences. Only then were we able to start exploring the effects of geographic market diversification on firm performance.

We anticipate a similar process in developing the concept of channel as a type of diversification. In this chapter, we have initiated the process. We argue for the acknowledgement that e-commerce requires differences in firm structures, operations and strategies that are not adequately captured by product diversification or strategic groups theory. As with market diversification, channel diversification should supplement, not supplant, traditional product diversification concepts. However, without this addition to existing theory we will have an incomplete picture of e-commerce and the competitive changes it has brought. The importance of developing concepts, constructs and measures to understand our new reality is paramount if, as a field, we want to be able to develop theories that explain and predict the outcomes of observed strategies.

Acknowledgements

This research project benefited from a FAU College of Business Dean's Summer Research Grant. We also would like to acknowledge the collaboration of John Leaptrott in the data collection, as well as comments by two anonymous reviewers and by attendees of the 2000 Strategic Management Society International Meeting in Vancouver, Canada.

References

Bell, D. 1973: *The Coming of the Post-industrial Society.* New York: Basic Books.
Bettis, R. A. 1981: Performance differences in related and unrelated diversified firms. *Strategic Management Journal*, 2, 379–93.
Bettis, R. A. and Hitt, M. A. 1995: The new competitive landscape. *Strategic Management Journal*, Summer Special Issue 16, 7–19.
Business Week. 1999: The big guys go online; and the likes of Nordstrom may make it tough for the e-tail veterans. September 6: 30.
Business Week 2000: Not just clicks anymore. August 28: 226–27.
Chaterjee, S. and Wernerfelt, B. 1991: The link between resources and type of diversification: theory and evidence. *Strategic Management Journal*, 12, 33–48.

D'Aveni, R.A. and Ravenscraft D. J. 1994: Economies of integration versus bureaucracy costs: does vertical integration improve performance? *Academy of Management Journal*, 37, 1167–206.

Dess, G. G., Gupta, A, Hennart, J. F., and Hill, C. W. L. 1995: Conducting and integrating strategy research at the international, corporate, and business levels: issues and directions. *Journal of Management*, 21, 357–93.

Dranove, D., Peteraf, M., and Shanley, M. 1998: Do strategic groups exist? An economic framework of analysis. *Strategic Management Journal*, 19, 1029–44.

Farjoun, M. 1998: The independent and joint effects of the skill and physical bases of relatedness in diversification. *Strategic Management Journal*, 19, 611–30.

Frazier, G. L. 1999: Organizing and managing channels of distribution. *Journal of the Academy of Marketing Science*, 27, 226-40.

Galbraith, C. S., Merrill, G. B., and Morgan, G.1994: Bilateral strategic groups: the market for nontactical navy information systems. *Strategic Management Journal*, 15, 613–26.

Gassenheimer, J. B. and Keep, W. W. 1998: Generalizing diversification theory across economic sectors: theoretical and empirical considerations. *Journal of Marketing Theory and Practice*, 6, 38–47.

Grant, R. 1988: On dominant logic, relatedness and the link between diversity and performance. *Strategic Management Journal*, 9, 639–42.

Grant, R. M., Jammine, A. P., and Thomas, H. 1988: Diversity, diversification, and profitability among British manufacturing companies. *Academy of Management Journal*, 31, 771–90.

Gulati, R. and Garino, A. P. 2000: Get the right mix of bricks and clicks. *Harvard Business Review*, 78, 107–15.

Hatten, K. J. and Hatten, A. P. 1987: Strategic groups, asymmetrical mobility barriers and contestability. *Strategic Management Journal*, 8, 329–42.

Hitt, M. A., Hoskisson, R. E., and Kim, A. P. 1997: International diversification: effects on innovation and firm performance in product-diversified firms. *Academy of Management Journal*, 40, 767–98.

Hoskisson, R. and Hitt, M. A. 1990: Antecedents and performance outcomes of diversification: a review and critique of theoretical perspectives. *Journal of Management*, 16, 461–509.

Hoskisson, R. E., Hitt, M. A., Johnson, R. A., and Moesel, D. D. 1993: Construct validity of an objective (entropy) categorical measure of diversification strategy. *Strategic Management Journal*, 14, 215–35.

Hunt, M. S. 1972: Competition in the major home appliance industry, *1960–1970*. Unpublished doctoral dissertation, Harvard University.

Kaplan, S. and Sawhney, M. 2000: E-hubs: the new B2B marketplaces. *Harvard Business Review*, 78, 97–104.

Keats, B. 1990: Diversification and business economic performance revisited: issues of measurement and causality. *Journal of Management*, 16, 61–72.

Lowendahl, B. and Revang, O. 1998: Challenges to existing strategy theory in a postindustrial society. *Strategic Management Journal*, 19, 755–73.

Markides, C. and Williamson, P. 1996: Corporate diversification and organizational structure: a resource-based view. *Academy of Management Journal*, 39, 340–67.

McGahan, A. M. and Porter, M. E. 1997: How much does industry matter, really? *Strategic Management Journal*, 18, Summer Special Issue, 15–30.

Mehra, A. 1996: Resource and market based determinants of performance in the U.S. banking industry. *Strategic Management Journal*, 16, 307–22.

Nath, D. and Gruca, T. S. 1997: Convergence across alternative methods for forming strategic groups. *Strategic Management Journal*, 18, 745–60.

Palepu, K. 1985: Diversification strategy, profit performance and the entropy measure. *Strategic*

Management Journal, 6, 239–55.

Palich, L. E., Cardinal, L. B., and Miller, C. C. 2000: Curvilinearity in the diversification-performance linkage: an examination of over three decades of research. *Strategic Management Journal*, 21, 155–74.

Peteraf, M. and Shanley, M. 1997: Getting to know you: a theory of strategic group identity. *Strategic Management Journal*, 18, Summer Special Issue, 165–86.

Porter, M. E. 1979: The structure within industries and companies performance. *The Review of Economics and Statistics*, 61, 214–44.

Porter, M. E. 1980: *Competitive Strategy: Techniques for Analyzing Industries and Competitors.* New York: Free Press.

Powell, T. 1996: How much does industry matter? an alternative empirical test. *Strategic Management Journal*, 17, 323–34.

Qian, G. 1997: Assessing product-market diversification of U.S. firms. *Management International Review*, 37, 127–49.

Ramanujam, V. and Varadarajan, P. 1989: Research on corporate diversification: a synthesis. *Strategic Management Journal*, 10, 523–51.

Robins, J. and Wiersema, M. 1995: A resource-based approach to the multibusiness firm. *Strategic Management Journal*, 16, 277–99.

Rumelt, R. P. 1974: *Strategy, Structure and Economic Performance.* Boston, MA: Harvard Business School Press.

Rumelt, R. P. 1982: Diversification strategy and profitability. *Strategic Management Journal*, 3, 359–69.

Rumelt, R. P. 1991: How much does industry matter? *Strategic Management Journal*, 12, 167–85.

Sabourin, V. 1999: Technological revolutions and the formation of strategic groups. *Journal of Engineering and Technology Management*, 16, 271–93.

Sampler, J. L. 1998: Redefining industry structure for the information age. *Strategic Management Journal*, 19, 343–55.

Singh, H. and Montgomery, C. A. 1987: Corporate acquisition strategies and economic performance. *Strategic Management Journal*, 8, 377–86.

Sinha, R. K. and Noble, C. H. 1997: The performance consequences of subfield entry. *Strategic Management Journal*, 18, 465–81.

Smith, K., Grimm, C., Wally, S., and Young, G. 1997: Strategic groups and rivalrous firm behavior: towards a reconciliation. *Strategic Management Journal*, 18, 149–57.

St. John, C. H. and Harrison, J. S. 1999: Manufacturing-based relatedness, synergy, and coordination. *Strategic Management Journal*, 20, 129–45.

Toffler, A. 1981: *The Third Wave.* New York: Bantam Books.

Varadarajan, P. and Ramanujam, V. 1987: Diversification and performance: a reexamination using a two-dimensional conceptualization of diversity in firms. *Academy of Management Journal*, 30, 385–97.

Wall Street Journal 1999: As eBay rivals emerge, some tips on bidding and selling on the Web. September 23, B1.

Wall Street Journal 2000: E-business: Toy wars II: Holiday cyber battle begins. September 25, B1.

Wernerfelt, B. and Montgomery, C. A. 1988: Tobin's q and the importance of focus in firm performance. *American Economic Review*, 78, 246-50.

Wiggins, R. R. and Ruefli, T. W. 1995: Necessary conditions for the predictive validity of strategic groups: analysis without reliance on clustering techniques. *Academy of Management Journal*, 38, 1635–62.

Williamson, O. E. 1975: *Markets and Hierarchies.* New York: Free Press.

CHAPTER NINE

Corporate Venture Capital and the Creation of US Public Companies: The Impact of Sources of Venture Capital on the Performance of Portfolio Companies

Markku Maula and Gordon Murray

Introduction

The role of large corporations as financiers of technology-based start-ups has increased dramatically during the last few years. Direct venture capital investments made by the subsidiaries and affiliates of industrial corporations have more than doubled during each of the last six consecutive years to a level of $18 billion in the year 2000 (see figure 9.1). In spite of this growth, and the many recent success stories on corporate venture capital appearing in the press, the true benefits and drawbacks for entrepreneurs in accepting strategic corporate investors as co-owners of their businesses are less clear. Although there has been a lot of discussion, there exists relatively little rigorous, empirical research on the influence of corporate investors on the performance of technology-based young companies.

Using a sample of 325 venture capital backed, information technology initial public offerings (IPOs) in 1998–99, we find that enterprises co-financed by multiple Global Fortune 500 information technology and communications corporations receive higher IPO valuations than comparable firms supported by venture capitalists alone. Similarly, this former group outperforms firms co-financed by venture capital and a single corporation. We explain the superior performance of co-financed ventures by complementary certification (increased legitimacy), the realization of operational synergies as well as better investment selection. The superior performance of enterprises with multiple corporate investors is posited as the result of incremental certification, validation

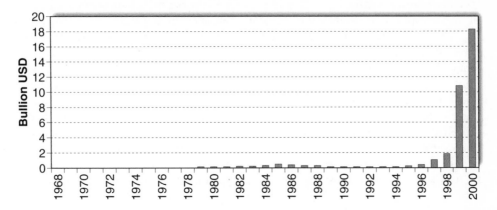

Figure 9.1   Annual corporate venture capital investments by subsidiaries and affiliates of nonfinancial corporations as reported in VentureXpert database in January 2001

of emerging dominant designs, and a reduced incidence of potential conflicts of interest between the investee firm and its investors.

These research results raise a number of profound implications for the three major constituencies, i.e. the corporate investor, the portfolio company, and the traditional venture capitalist investor. First, the figures clearly demonstrate that corporations can, and do, make extremely successful equity investments into new technology-based firms. Corporations are not "second-best" investors. Our results clearly show that the pejorative description of corporations as a source of "dumb money" has no contemporary basis in fact.

Second, the implications of the research for the portfolio company suggest that traditional venture capitalists and corporate venture capital (CVC) providers should not be seen as *alternative* sources of finance but more usefully as strongly *complementary* sources. The mix of resources provided by the traditional venture capitalists and the corporate partners to an investment syndication are qualitatively different and, when combined, enable the portfolio company to benefit directly from significant resource synergies. For example, the deep technological knowledge and foresight of a world-class technology company is unlikely to be available from all but a tiny minority of venture capital firms. Corporations also have hugely more international trading experience and operational capabilities to assist the rapid commercialization and sales roll-out of the portfolio firm's products and services. Conversely, experienced venture capitalists have a wealth of tacit experience in the "hands on" nurturing and development of the managerial capabilities of nascent, and often highly vulnerable, young firms. Venture capitalists can and frequently do build professional management teams from scratch. In this regard, corporate managers commonly have little pragmatic understanding of such early-stage entrepreneurial environments. Thus, they have frequently less relevant experience to offer directly in the earliest and most tentative stages of the formation of the venture. The key finding is that both of these skill sets are complementary and valuable to the portfolio firm.

Third, the research suggests that the number of corporations that the technology-based new firm can attract as investors has a direct impact on the subsequence success of the venture as perceived by the capital markets at the time of an initial public offering. The reasons for this performance effect are two-fold. First, the benefits offered by corporate investors, such as external certification, are usually cumulative to some extent and therefore the more investors, the higher the ensuing benefits to the portfolio firm. In addition, having more than a single corporate investor reduces the potential problems of conflict associated with the corporate investor becoming too dominant in the investor–investee relationship. The involvement of two or more corporate investors enables the creation of a more balanced, countervailing power structure between the portfolio company and its key investors. As such, the entrepreneurial team of the young start-up is likely to be able to enjoy more autonomy than might be conceded if the syndication included just one single, dominant investor. This more equitable distribution of interests in a multiple investor structure is also likely to be of advantage to the traditional venture capital partner.

Corporate Venture Capital

When we refer to the term "corporate venture capital", we mean that activity by which an established corporation sets up a new wholly-owned entity with the specific objective of investing its capital and other proprietary resources (i.e. technical and market knowledge) in a number of high potential young enterprises. The CVC acts in a similar fashion to a traditional, independent venture capital firm in that its management seeks to maximize the value of its investments. However, for the venture capital firm, value is exclusively measured by the net capital gain of its portfolio and the economic returns to its investors. For the CVC managers investing corporate funds, value is a more complex construct and includes economic gain in addition to more intangible strategic benefits to the parent corporation. Economic performance is a necessary but not sufficient objective for the CVC.

As noted, from the perspective of the corporate investor's interests, there are several potential advantages in creating a CVC activity. In addition to the opportunity for generating attractive financial returns, corporate venturing may provide the investors with several new strategic insights. Indeed, the "project hurdle rate" (defining *ex ante* an acceptable level of investment returns) may also primarily be used as a conditional means of identifying young companies with the best prospects rather than as the central economic rational (Hurry et al., 1992). Through CVCs' close association with new technology-based firms both as corporate investors and part owners, they can gain low risk "options to learn" about emerging business models in dynamic and immature markets and/or technologies. Thus, involvement in CVC, as a "commercial intelligence" mechanism, can be an important catalyst for the corporation's investment in new and strategically important industries. Such early-stage investments in young companies can also be employed to help pre-empt the actions of competitors by seeking first mover advantage in speculative but promising technologies. Similarly, some corporations also view CVC investments as an efficient way to search for and select future acquisition targets (McNally, 1997; Siegel et al., 1988; Sykes, 1990; Winters, 1988). Large technology-based corporations have long used acquisitions as an important mechanism to acquire new, or to enhance existing, competencies (Laamanen, 1997; Trautwein, 1989).

Corporate Venture Capital Fund – Parent Company Linkages and the Potential Threats for Portfolio Companies

In addition to the variance in their respective goals, there are two further differences between CVCs and independent venture capital firms. One difference is structural and the other is resource related. They each influence the nature of the inter-organizational relationships within the CVC–investee–VC "triad" and thus have important performance implications. First, the limited partner and the managing partner of the CVC fund are both from and part of the same corporation. This unity engenders a commonality of interests between the fund investor (parent corporation) and the CVC fund particularly when the CVC personnel are career managers from the same parent company. However, from the start-ups' perspective, this unity increases the potential for *moral hazard* problems. The portfolio companies bear a risk that their corporate investors might not strive to maximize the economic value of their portfolio firms. Indeed, if the corporate investor wishes to minimize the acquisition cost of the intellectual property created and owned by the investee, there are strong arguments for the corporate investor to seek to impede the growth in value of the portfolio firm. It is also possible that an emerging business area targeted by the portfolio company turns out to be too commercially important for the parent corporation to accept other than full control of the opportunity. Such circumstances can lead to a serious conflict of interests. Further, in a highly competitive environment where intellectual property is closely guarded, too close an association with one industry-leading corporation could prejudice the independence of the young enterprise. This, in turn, could limit other valuable, co-operation possibilities. This potentially value-compromising effect when a CVC is involved as a co-investor or syndicate partner is frequently cited by traditional venture capital firms. Too close an association or inter-dependency is deemed a particular concern if it adversely affects the exit opportunities and thus the value of the investee firm. Similarly, entrepreneurs worry about the threat of corporate investors covertly appropriating the firm's intellectual capital, a concern endemic to all alliance-type relationships involving the sharing of key competencies or intellectual property rights (Hamel, 1991). However, it is made more fraught when one partner is more established, many times larger and better financed than the other (Doz, 1988). Relative scale does not change the nature of the relationship but rather exacerbates its potential negative effects.

Parent Company Resources and Potential Benefits for a Portfolio Company

The second key difference from traditional venture capital firms resides in the ability of the CVC to provide direct operational assistance/support and high levels of industry-specific knowledge to the investee firm. The benefits that each party share from the complementarity of their unique and firm-specific resource endowments links this research directly to a growing interest in the "relational view" literature (Dyer and Singh, 1998). The dynamic association between the three heterogeneous parties to the investment can be usefully seen as an inter-firm network. This network facilitates the cooperative sharing of both tangible and tacit resources. Thus, being a participant in this network can reduce intra-firm constraints and increases the utility of each member of the network.

Corporate partners can provide technological support and some managerial expertise, as well as providing credibility and access to key distribution channels/markets. For example, many high-tech start-ups are increasingly either "born global" (i.e. selling to several countries as soon as they have a developed product) or internationalize at a very early age (Burgel and Murray, 1999; Oviatt and MacDougall, 1994). High knowledge intensity and rapid entry into foreign markets have each been shown to be associated with faster international growth (Autio et al., 2000). In addition to similarly confirming the growth benefits of internationalization to new high-tech small firms, Burgel et al. (2000) have also shown that the limited market credibility of young high tech firms can materially impede their ability to internationalize rapidly. Established firms are very wary of introducing the offerings of unknown young firms into their core technologies, products or processes. These authors term this sales constraint on young firms "the liability of alienness".

Logistics providers similarly see the distribution of the products of new technology-based firms as being frequently economically unattractive given that such commitments often require them to make a high investment in product knowledge for a very uncertain incremental revenue stream. Therefore, it can be hypothesized that global industry-leading companies can materially assist in the rapid internationalization of new technology-based firms by providing them with greater external credibility. In effect, the young firm's public association with highly established and respected larger companies is seen to reflect directly and positively on the reputation and potential of the young firm, i.e. a "halo effect". In addition to conferring an increased credibility on the young firm, CVCs may often provide several other forms of value-added. In a survey by McNally (1997), enhanced credibility in the market place was the most frequently mentioned major advantage of CVC over other sources of equity financing noted by investee firms. However, other more operational benefits from their relationships observed by McNally included: help with short-term problems, access to technical expertise, opportunities to establish further business relationships, and access to corporate management expertise. The successful CVC/investee relationship may include resource transfers across a wide spectrum of strategic and tactical demands.

Impact of Corporate Venture Capital on IPO Valuation

CVC provides an important means by which a young firm is able to access and share proprietary corporate resources of high strategic and operational value (for example, extensive R&D activity or market research knowledge) in addition to gaining core financing. Through an organizational relationship with CVC investors, the growth of a young company is no longer bound by its limited internal resources (Dyer and Singh,

1998; Eisenhardt and Schoonhoven, 1996; Hitt et al., 2000, Yli-Renko et al., 2001). Particularly in knowledge-based industries, which are characterized by high levels of uncertainty, intense competition and steep technology trajectories, such preferential access for small firms is likely to have a significant influence on the probability of economic success of the new enterprise (Stuart et al., 1999). The larger and more eminent the corporate partner, the greater the potential value of the shared resources to the recipient small firms (Stuart, 2000). Furthermore, earlier research by Gompers and Lerner (1998) demonstrated a higher likelihood of corporate venture capital-backed companies achieving an IPO than venture capital-backed companies. We would therefore expect to see that companies backed by industry leading corporations receive higher IPO valuations compared to the valuations of those ventures financed exclusively by independent venture capitalists.

Hypothesis 1: New technology-based firms co-financed by corporate venture capital organizations of industry-leading corporations receive higher IPO valuations than comparable firms financed exclusively by independent venture capital firms

There are three reasons why we surmise corporate venture capital backed companies should receive higher valuations from informed market makers at the IPO stage: (1) complementary certification; (2) the realization of operational synergies; and (3) advantageous selection, i.e. the better investment selection abilities of CVCs in identifying high potential young firms in related industries. These rationales are discussed below in more detail.

Complementary certification

We assume that corporate venture capital investors can, and do, provide their portfolio companies with increased certification benefits (Stuart et al., 1999). These benefits to the smaller companies are directly related to their public association with corporate investors enjoying international reputations. Whereas most new enterprises and traditional venture capital firms are familiar to only a very limited number of people, the majority of the portfolio companies' prospective customers and suppliers (including other suppliers of capital) are likely to recognize and accept the high credibility and status of Global Fortune 500 companies. The founder management of a new enterprise can leverage to their direct advantage the fact that an industry-leading corporation has chosen specifically to invest in their enterprise. That such a relationship has been offered by a corporation, through the agency of its CVC organization, is seen as being indicative of the investee firm's potential. This potential is a consequence of the young firm's technology/intellectual property rights rather than its production, sales, or marketing capabilities – each of which the corporate is likely to already command internally. The commercial advantages of this exploitation of the more powerful partner's status and social capital have been shown in several studies (Stuart et al., 1999; Stuart, 2000).

Realization of operational synergies

Building on the existing research literature on CVC, our understanding of the value-added provided by traditional venture capitalists (Sapienza, 1992), and the "relational view" extension of the resource-based theory of the firm (Dyer and Singh, 1998), we assume that industry-leading corporations are able to provide their portfolio companies with several kinds of complementary value-adding resources. Globally leading corporations normally have well developed and superior distribution channels. Preferential access to such channels is an asset of great value to a young and resource-constrained technology-based company. As already noted, the securing of appropriate channel access is particularly important at the early stages of a young firm's internationalization efforts (Burgel et al., 2000). Obtaining a presence in key overseas markets can be prohibitively expensive for a small, capital-rationed firm especially is there is a high level of client adaptation and support servicing required in the initial sales process. Thus, the association with a larger firm including preferential access to its established infrastructure and operating systems (e.g. sales support and distribution logistics) pushes the new incumbent rapidly along the experience curve while protecting it at least temporarily from the full forces of market competition.

It is also reasonable to assume that globally successful information and communications technology corporations have a comprehensive and deep technical expertise related to the specialist technical area of the young investee firm, if not to its specific technology application. Although it is often new entrants to an industry that engender radically novel ideas (Tushman and Anderson, 1986), industry leading companies in systemic business environments have a significant power to influence which new technologies are adopted by the sector. Technology-leading companies invariably create very detailed, strategic "road maps" as to how they see individual technologies and their market potential developing over time. This intelligence can be of major value to the young firm starting or expanding its sales activities. Thus, access to complementary, technological information from the corporation may generate major savings in cost and, critically, time. It may also represent a material reduction in both market and technology uncertainties, given the superior intelligence resources of the corporation.

Finally, given the strategic logic of the CVC to invest in related and contiguous technologies, it is likely that the portfolio of investee firms financed by the CVC each and collectively represents a deep resource of complementary technologies, processes, and market experiences. This *keiretsu* type network model presents advantages to both portfolio companies and to the CVC investor(s) alike. The cultivation of inter-firm synergies and linkages between their portfolio companies has not usually been a practice traditionally followed by professional venture capital firms. Indeed, the primary operational logic of venture capital firms may be to seek diversification benefits through investment in unrelated enterprises in order to manage diversifiable or unsystematic risk (Norton and Tenenbaum, 1993). The ability of CVCs to accommodate a relatively greater level of unsystematic risk – is a function of the strategic interests and greater industry knowledge of the parent and the relative small economic size of the CVC activity within the sum of the parent corporation's overall interests. This may result in the CVC having a greater ability to realize portfolio complementarities and synergies than is normally available to a traditional venture capital firm. For example, corporations could link new ventures to relevant but not publicly available technology expertise held by the corporation, and assist with building alliances around innovative ideas in order to support the rapid and pre-emptive establishment of new dominant designs (see McGrath et al., 1992 for earlier literature on factors influencing the emergence of new dominant designs).

Better investment selection

We assume that corporations will have certain advantages over independent venture capitalists in the execution of both market and technology-related due diligence as suggested by Gompers and Lerner (1998). Traditional venture capitalists are hugely constrained in the number of new investments they can investigate in detail given their scarce personnel resources (Zider, 1998). Gifford (1997) has shown that it is more rational for contemporary venture capitalists to optimize the value of their own scarce time across the totality of funds under their management rather than to optimize the value of single venture funds or their limited partners' investments. Having access to marketing and technology experts from the corporate parent's operating divisions or R&D laboratories removes major time and knowledge constraints which typically face traditional venture capitalists in their investment appraisals. The combining of the CVCs' and the venture capitalists' areas of specialist and particular knowledge could make the investment appraisal process both quicker and more effective in identifying high potential new businesses.

Differences between Single CVC and Multiple CVC-Backed Companies

We hypothesize that ventures with multiple industry leading corporate investors will receive higher IPO valuations when compared to ventures having only a single corporate investor.

> Hypothesis 2: New, technology-based firms receiving venture capital and co-financed by multiple corporate venture capital organizations receive higher IPO valuations than similar firms co-financed by a single, industry-leading corporate investor.

We believe that there are at least three reasons why ventures backed by multiple industry-leading corporations would receive higher valuations than comparable ventures backed by single corporate investor: (1) incremental certification; (2) enhanced opportunity to establish a new dominant design; and (3) lower incidence of CVC/investee agency conflict. These arguments are discussed below in more detail.

Incremental certification

We assume that certification by prominent partners is an incremental and cumulative function. This assumption is supported by Stuart et al. (1999). Thus, having two prominent partners is better than having only one. It is likely that the incremental beneficial effects will describe a curvilinear, inverted U-shaped function (Rothaermel and Deeds,

2001). Marginal endorsement benefits to the investee firm are likely to decrease rapidly after several industry-leading corporate investors have joined. However, the limited number and range of multiple CVCs in the sample did not allow us to test this relation. In our analysis we consider the difference between one and multiple corporate investors as an important factor because of the additional "counterbalancing effect" two or more industry-leading corporations may have compared to a syndication involving a single and potentially dominant corporation.

Enhanced opportunity to create a new dominant design

In high-tech industries, value is not only dependent of the technical superiority of a product or solution. Critically, the resultant value of a radically new innovative product or process also depends on its rapid and wide-scale adoption as the industry standard or dominant design. Analogous to Metcalfe's Law of network effects, the more universal the adoption of a new innovation, the greater its value to each of its users. Technology has long been known as a major influence on industry structure (Klein, 1977). The advent of a dominant design is likely to reduce the number of players in a particular product/technology space. As Suárez and Utterback (1995) show, new entrants that enter the industry *after* the development of a dominant design are less likely to survive than firms that co-existed before the advent of the new design. Most potentially disruptive new innovations will not become the dominant design but merely one of a number of alternative and subordinate solutions. The establishment of many industry-wide solutions has been as a result of a negotiated alliance between leading, and competing, corporations. Contemporary examples of this kind of alliances in wireless telecommunications include GSM, WAP, and Bluetooth. Critically, the advent of a dominant design also significantly reduces the uncertainty consequent on multiple technology choices for the purchasers or users of the technology and thereby increases their utility. The cooperative commitment of several CVCs to one portfolio company, and thus to a single technology solution, aligns closely the interests of the investors to that of the portfolio company and its technology. The more industry-leading companies that are committed to a common solution, the less likely the provision of serious support for alternative and competing technological offerings[1]. To deviate from the new technology orthodoxy is to risk failure as non-standard competencies quickly become irrelevant. Such concerted actions by powerful corporations, via their CVCs or through direct investment, materially improves the commercial opportunities for the new and innovating investee firm involved in developing the standard. In an efficient capital market, this advantage will be directly reflected in its enhanced market valuation.

Lower incidence of CVC/investee agency conflict

One of the important motives for corporations to engage in corporate venture capital is to learn from the start-ups they invest in. As investors, corporations gain access to the proprietary knowledge of their portfolio companies which may in some cases cause serious moral hazard problems such as misuse of intellectual property (Hellmann, 2000; Kann, 2000). Another objective commonly imposed on CVCs by their corporate parents is to find suitable, future acquisition candidates (McNally, 1997; Siegel et al., 1988; Sykes, 1990; Winters, 1988). Sykes noted that his CVC respondents made the observation that the owner-managers of entrepreneurial, portfolio companies were frequently antagonistic to the corporate investor using CVC investment activities as a low cost means of "buying an option" for future acquisition. More experienced entrepreneurs are likely to have a clearer view as to the potential value of their companies. They are also well aware that the ownership of a significant or controlling interest by one corporate investor may well pre-empt the opportunity for an attractive IPO. This is because the enterprise may subsequently be perceived by the market as *de facto* owned by its major investor. This will likely reduce the interest of other corporations that occupy a similar or related technology or market space in acquiring the firm. In most cases, experienced and well-informed entrepreneurs will not want to lose the option of taking their venture public at some future point. Even if the entrepreneur has purposely targeted a known trade buyer, the ability of the firm to elect to go to an IPO sets a constraint on the acquirer pricing too aggressively. Alternative exit options significantly increase the vendor's negotiating power in a competitive market for corporate control. The existence of two or more corporate investors attenuates this agency problem by reducing the perceived dominance of a single CVC over the future wealth-creating capability of the young investee firm. The behavior of any single investor has to be sanctioned by all other parties to the investment. Egregiously selfish actions in a relatively small and highly networked CVC/VC community are likely to be widely communicated and condemned. They risk the CVC subsequently being excluded from any future reciprocal deal flow. Aggressive private actions, which could create excessive agency costs, are likely to have to be moderated in the light of collectively imposed and accepted, investor responsibilities (Olson, 1968).

Empirical Setting

The empirical setting for this study is centered on technology-based young firms and Global Fortune 500 corporations operating in the information and communications industries. This focus was chosen because there is an incessant, strategic imperative for continued innovation in these dynamic, highly competitive and knowledge-based industries. Given these importunate demands on industry incumbents, it may be surmised that information and communications technology firms are likely to be heavily engaged in CVC-type activities for the multiple and inter-related reasons of innovation, IPR acquisition, competitive intelligence, and the encouragement/maintenance of a highly flexible and adaptive corporate culture. In this chapter, we include the companies from the following sector categories of the Global Fortune 500 list 1999 in our sample: computer services and software, computers, office equipment, electronics, electrical equipment, entertainment, publishing, printing, and telecommunications. These industries are a particularly attractive focus for a study of CVC because of their very high predisposition to engage in venturing activities over recent years. In our resultant list of 66 corporations from the Global Fortune 1999 list, 54 had CVC activities as reported in the Venture Economics database in January 2000.

Sample

The research sample consists of 325 venture capital-backed, information and communications technology companies that undertook a successful initial public offering (IPO) on NASDAQ between January 1998 and December 1999. The data was collected from the Venture Economics database. This commercial database contains information of over 118,000 private equity transactions from 1970 to the present time (Venture Economics, 1999). Venture Economics' data have been used in several academic studies on venture capital (e.g. Bygrave, 1988, 1989; Gompers, 1995). The information on IPOs was obtained from the New Issues database of Thomson Financial Securities Data. Merging the two databases yielded 405 venture capital-financed companies, of which 325 were information technology companies, according to the Venture Economics classification. Of the 325 companies identified, 60 (18 percent) had also received finance from a Global Fortune 500 information and communications technology corporation. Eighteen of these identified companies, i.e. approximately 1 in 20, had received finance from two or more corporate investors. Nearly half of all selected investments are related to Internet activities. The importance of this single category corroborates the intelligence and adaptation logic for CVCs given the potentially hugely disruptive effect of e-commerce on the core businesses of the parent corporations (Anderson and Tushman, 1990). This pattern closely reflects the trends in the traditional US venture capital industry. In 1999, \$31.8 billion was invested by venture capital firms in internet related companies. This figure, which was four times larger than the 1998 value, represented 66 percent of the total investments by US venture capitalists that year (National Venture Capital Association, 2000).

Measures

Dependent variables

Market value.   As the dependent variable measuring the IPO valuation, we measure the market value of the shares outstanding at the close of the offer. In contrast to Stuart et al. (1999), we use the market value at the close of the offer instead of a market value calculation based on the offer price. Using the market value at the close of the IPO is more consistent with earlier IPO studies assuming that the true value is the one determined by the public market at the first close of the offer. Also, the offer price is often purposefully under-priced to attract market interest (Loughran and Ritter, 1999; Rock, 1986).

The market value at the close of the IPO is calculated by multiplying the closing price of the first trading day and the number of shares outstanding after the IPO. We took the share price information from CRSP as the most reliable data set available. In cases where the values of CRSP and Thomson Financial Securities Data (TFSD) databases were different, we sought confirmative information from www.IPO.com and other sources. We found that both the New Issues database of TFSD and the CRSP data base contained erroneous entries for the number of shares outstanding after the IPO. Therefore, we collected manually prospectuses for the sample companies. We found prospectuses at www.sec.gov for 317 of 325 companies in the sample. For the eight missing companies, the correct number of shares outstanding was determined by combining several sources of information. The share price for the first trading day was obtained primarily from the CRSP data. However, to ensure accuracy, we compared the CRSP data with TFSD data and other sources in order to check for the existence of possible errors. CRSP data appeared accurate for the share prices. Having completed this somewhat laborious procedure, we are confident of the accuracy of our dependent variable.

In the regressions, we transform the market value using the natural logarithm in order to achieve a normal distribution. After transformation, the market value appeared to be normally distributed. Using logarithmic transformation also reduces the problem caused by heteroscedasticity in the regressions.

Independent variables

Existence of industry-leading corporate investors. We are trying to explain the impact of corporate venture capital investments on the IPO valuation. The existence of industry-leading corporate venture capital investors is measured using dummy variables. The first dummy variable indicates whether or not the venture is also backed by *one or more* Global Fortune 500 information and communications technology corporations in addition to venture capitalist(s). The second dummy variable accommodates the existence of *multiple* Global Fortune 500 investors. The combined use of these two binary, dummy variables allows a comparison of CVC/VC-backed companies with exclusively VC-backed companies. It also enables a comparison of multiple CVC-backed companies to single CVC-backed companies where all of the companies has also received VC finance. Purely for illustrative purposes, the final model contains dummies for single and multiple CVC-backed companies to illustrate the difference of these two categories compared to the reference category of exclusively independent venture capital backed companies. It is important to note that dummy variables were used rather than the number of CVC investors because of the very limited range of CVC investors. There are theoretical reasons to believe that there are rapidly diminishing returns for incremental numbers of CVC investors (Rothaermel and Deeds, 2001). However, in this study we are interested in the effect that the introduction of a corporate venture capital investor has on the investee firm's subsequent performance and whether or not multiple CVC investors have a further effect on performance.

Control variables

We include several control variables in the analyses to ensure that the outcomes we hypothesize are caused by corporate venture capital investments and not by other exogenous factors.

Revenues. In order to control for the differences in the firm size, we measure the revenues for the fiscal year before the IPO. The revenues are also transformed using the logarithmic transformation. Revenues are hypothesized to be positively related to the market value of the ventures.

Age.   In order to control the influence of age, we add the time from the date of founding to the date of IPO in the regressions.

Industry subsector.   In order to control for potential differences as a result of companies operating in different industries, we control for the impact of the five industry subsectors in the study by including four dummy variables. The subsectors in the study are: Communications, Computer Hardware, Computer Software and Services, Internet Specific, and Semiconductors/Other Elect. The 154 Internet-specific companies represent the majority of the sample of 325 companies and are used in the regressions as the "base case". Therefore, a dummy variable is assigned for each of the four other categories. The dummy variable is assigned "1" if the company belongs to the category and "0" otherwise.

Nasdaq index.   We control for the impact of stock market movements. During the two-year period, 1998–9, NASDAQ grew rapidly as a result of exceptionally bullish technology markets. The frequency of IPOs also increased towards the end of this period. In the regressions, we control for the impact of the bullish market conditions by including the NASDAQ share index at the time of the IPO in the regressions.

Proportion of outstanding shares offered at IPO.   We control the influence of the demand-supply balance at the time of the IPOs. If only a small proportion of the available shares are floated at the IPO, aggregate demand might easily exceed the supply, thereby leading to increasing prices. Controlling for the percentage of shares offered at the IPO (expressed as a percentage of the total post-IPO shares) addresses the demand-supply issue.

Number of venture capital investors.   We try to isolate the certification benefits provided by corporate venture capitalists by controlling for the certification influence of independent venture capitalists as syndicate partners. As argued by Barry et al. (1990) the presence of multiple venture capitalists indicates that the issuer has persuaded a larger number of sophisticated investors that the firm has favorable prospects and is willing to open itself up for scrutiny and guidance. Furthermore, the lead venture capitalist also has added incentives to monitor carefully because it has increased the risk to its reputation by soliciting the participation of other venture capitalists. Accordingly, Barry et al. (1990) suggest that higher number of venture capitalists should be associated with more intense monitoring, less uncertainty caused by bounded rationality or managerial slack, and therefore a better appreciation of the firm's prospects by the market. We control for this possible effect by including in the regression the number of venture capital investors at IPO as registered in the Venture Economics' database records.

Results

Table 9.1 presents the correlation matrix and descriptive statistics of the dependent, independent, and control variables used in testing the impact of CVC on the IPO

Table 9.1 Correlations, means, and standard deviations

Variable	1	2	3	4	5	6	7	8	9	10	11	12	13
1 Market cpaitalization at the close of IPO (log)	—												
2 Sales for the last 12 months (millions, log)	.03	—											
3 Age of the company at IPO	-.26[a]	.34[a]	—										
4 Company operates in communications sector	.19[a]	.17[a]	.08	—									
5 Company operates in computer hardware sector	-.11[b]	-.02	.08	-.08	—								
6 Company operates in computer software sector	-.22[a]	.10	.20[a]	-.29[a]	-.08	—							
7 Company operates in Internet specific sector	.10	-.32[a]	-.32[a]	-.49[a]	-.14[b]	-.54[b]	—						
8 Company operates in semiconductors sector	-.09	.23[a]	.14[b]	-.12[b]	-.03	-.13[b]	-.22[a]	—					
9 NASDAQ index at IPO	.25[a]	-.28[a]	-.09	.00	-.04	-.09	.14[b]	-.10	—				
10 Offer of total outstanding shares after IPO (%)	-.42[a]	-.08	-.03	-.05	.05	.03	.00	.00	.09	—			
11 Number of VC investors	.20[a]	-.28[a]	-.13[b]	.05	-.03	-.08	.08	-.10	.19[a]	.04	—		
12 Single GF500ICT investor (dummy)	.11[b]	-.04	-.06	-.06	.01	.06	.02	-.05	.00	-.07	.28[a]	—	
13 Multiple GF500ICT investors (dummy)	.16[a]	-.11[b]	-.07	.04	-.04	.05	-.04	-.06	.00	-.06	.15[a]	-.09	—
Mean	20.19	2.23	5.57	.21	.02	.25	.47	.05	2,608.49	29.32	6.31	.13	.06
Standard deviation	1.07	1.67	3.90	.41	.15	.43	.50	.22	488.09	17.36	4.10	.34	.00

[a] significant at the 0.01 level, [b] significant at the 0.05 level (2-tail).

Table 9.2   Comparative statistics by investor syndicate categories (medians)

	Medians		
	Pure VC	Single CVC	Multiple CVC
Sales, last 12 months before IPO, millions	$11.6	$10.2	$5.2
EBIT, last 12 months before IPO, millions	$−6.1	$−11.0	$−12.2
Net income last, 12 months before IPO, millions	$−7.0	$−12.2	$−13.7
Total assets, millions	$84.0	$85.0	$106.2
Years from the founding to IPO	4.5	4.2	3.5
Share of offering of the total outstanding shares	26.0%	22.3%	17.9%
Change in the management ownership	51.0%	48.6%	44.0%
Retained management ownership	−19.2%	−16.7%	−15.4%
Number of venture capital investors	5.0	8.0	9.0
Offer price	$14.0	$14.5	$16.5
Proceeds from the IPO, millions	$60.0	$60.0	$82.5
Market capitalization at the close of the IPO, millions	$467.7	$598.2	$1,047.6

Medians are reported separately for each group based on the number of Global Fortune 500 information and communications technology corporations.

valuation. As hypothesized, the existence of single and multiple CVCs is positively correlated with the market capitalization. All the control variables are also correlated with the market value in the direction hypothesized. The one exception is age, which is negatively correlated with market capitalization. This finding is consistent with the literature as age is known to be negatively correlated with the growth of small firms (Evans, 1987). It is future growth which the market is appraising and the bullish technology market during the sample period tended to indicate a preference for young as apposed to established enterprises. The correlations between the independent variables are relatively low, reducing possible problems with multicollinearity in the regressions.

Table 9.2 compares the median values of the dependent, independent, and control variables between the three groups categorized by investor syndicate. Looking at the medians of the variables of these groups lends support to the general hypothesis that ventures additionally financed by CVC corporations develop faster and are more highly valued than their counterparts. When compared to similar enterprises supported exclusively by traditional venture capital firms, those ventures financed by one or more CVC investors had:

- *lower* sales revenues in the 12 months before the IPO;
- *greater* losses in the 12 months before the IPO;
- *larger* total assets;
- floated at a *younger* age;
- *more* venture capital firms as investors;
- *smaller* IPOs in relation to the total outstanding shares;

Table 9.3 Impact of corporate venture capital on IPO valuation (logarithm of market capitalization at the close of the IPO)

Variables	Predicted sign	Model 1 (Base)	Model 2 (H1)	Model 3 (H2)	Model 4
Intercept		19.278[a]	19.221[a]	19.203[a]	19.202[a]
		(.317)	(.315)	(.315)	(.315)
Sales for the last 12 months before the IPO (millions, logarithm)	+	.141[a]	.141[a]	.146[a]	.146[a]
		(.034)	(.034)	(.034)	(.034)
Age of the company at IPO (logarithm)	+	−.074[a]	−.072[a]	−.072[a]	−.072[a]
		(.014)	(.014)	(.014)	(.014)
Company operates in a communications sector		.262[c]	.267[c]	.249[c]	.249[c]
		(.132)	(.131)	(.132)	(.132)
Company operates in a computer hardware sector		−.393	−.404	−.394	−.394
		(.340)	(.337)	(.337)	(.336)
Company operates in a computer software sector		−.293[c]	−.325[b]	−.333[b]	−.333[b]
		(.126)	(.126)	(.126)	(.126)
Company operates in a semiconductors sector		−.303	−.294	−.300	−.300
		(.241)	(.239)	(.239)	(.239)
NASDAQ index at IPO	+	.001[a]	.001[a]	.001[a]	.001[a]
		(.000)	(.000)	(.000)	(.000)
Percentage of shares offered of the total outstanding shares after IPO	−	−.026[a]	−.025[a]	−.025[a]	−.025[a]
		(.003)	(.003)	(.003)	(.003)
Number of independent venture capital investors	+	.045[a]	.035[b]	.035[b]	.035[b]
		(.012)	(.013)	(.013)	(.013)
Existence of GF500ICT investors (dummy)	+		.315	.205	
			(.133)	(.152)	
Single GF500ICT investor (dummy)	+				.206[d]
					(.152)
Multiple GF500ICT investors (dummy)	+			.366[d]	.571[b]
				(.244)	(.216)
Adjusted R^2		.394	.403	.406	.406
Number of observations		325	325	325	325

[a] significant at the 0.001 level, [b] significant at the 0.01 level, [c] significant at the 0.05 level, [d] significant at the 0.1 level. (1-tail). Unstandardized regression coefficients reported. Standard errors in parentheses.

- *lower* reductions, i.e. dilution, in management's' ownership post IPO;
- *lower* retained ownership by management post-IPO;
- *higher* offer prices;
- *higher* proceeds from the IPO;
- *higher* market capitalizations at the IPO.

Table 9.3 reports the results of the OLS regressions explaining the impact of CVC investors on IPO valuation. Model 1 presents the base model with only control variables included. As expected, sales were found to be significantly positively related to the market capitalization. In the regression, age at IPO was found to be negatively related to market value. Of the four dummy variables describing the industry subsectors, communications companies had a higher market capitalization when compared to Internet-specific companies. On the other hand, computer software companies had lower market capitalizations than Internet companies. For computer hardware and semiconductor companies, there were no statistically significant differences when compared to Internet-specific companies. Supporting our expectations regarding the impact of market conditions, the NASDAQ index was positively and highly significantly related to the market capitalization. Also in line with our expectations on the influence of the demand-supply balance at the time of the IPO, the percentage of total outstanding shares offered at the IPO was highly negatively related to the market capitalization. Finally, and again as expected, the number of venture capitalist investors at the IPO was highly positively related to the market capitalization at the close of the first trading day after the IPO.

In Model 2, the independent variable describing the existence of Global Fortune 500 investors is introduced. Supporting Hypothesis 1, the existence of Global Fortune 500 investors is positively related to the market capitalization ($p < 0.01$). Calculating from the regression coefficients, the involvement of corporations is associated with a 37 percent increase in market value (=exp[0.315]) when compared to purely independent venture capital-backed companies and controlling for the number of independent VC investors in the syndicate.

In Model 3, a dummy variable representing the existence of multiple Global Fortune 500 investors is included. This provides support for Hypothesis 2, as the valuation of IPOs with multiple CVC investors is higher ($p < 0.10$) than for IPOs with a single CVC investor. The implied increase in the market value from accepting the second CVC investor is 44 percent (=exp[0.366]).

Finally, Model 4 illustrates in a more intuitive format how the influence of multiple CVC investors is higher and more significant when compared to the effect of a single CVC investor. Calculating from the regression coefficients, controlling for other factors such as number of independent venture capitalists, inclusion of a single CVC investor increases the market value by 22 percent. (=exp[0.206]). On the other hand, inclusion of two or more corporate venture capital investors in the syndicate increases the market value by 77 percent (=exp[0.571]) compared to the situation with only independent venture capitalists.

Discussion

The most important result of this research is that it demonstrates that there are statistically robust differences in the IPO performance and valuation of venture capital-backed companies when compared with and without a Global Fortune 500 information and communications technology corporation as an additional investor. Furthermore, investee companies with multiple corporate investors were found to have superior performances when compared to companies with a single corporate investor. These latter companies were, in turn, also found have a superior performance to companies solely financed by traditional, independent venture capitalists. There appears to be a "pecking order" in IPO performance with those companies financed by multiple CVCs at the pinnacle.

We find the difference between single and multiple CVC-backed ventures worthy of further analysis. We assume that the greater certification provided by multiple CVC investors, endorsing both the value of the novel technology and the credibility of the investee firm developing the technology, might be an important explanation of the observed performance differences. Certification is in part a function of consensus. Generally, the larger the number of CVCs supporting a young, innovative firm, the better the firm's subsequent valuation. The same logic also applies for the number of traditional venture capital firms associated with an investment. The effect of multiple VC firms is shown to have a highly significant influence ($p < 0.01$) on the valuation at the IPO. These findings have important implications for new technology-based firms, corporate venture capitalists, and independent venture capital firms alike.

Our research results also can be interpreted as adding further empirical validity to the relational view extension of the resource-based view of the firm (Dyer and Singh 1998; Yli-Renko et al., 2001). In detailing the nature of these investment activities, we have *de facto* been describing the workings of specialist investment networks. Through the sharing of complementary resources, from such intangible assets as industry experience to the concrete assets of warehousing in the distribution channels, the CVC can add multiple sources of value to its investees' operational activities. Similarly, the traditional venture capital partners contribute other specific and not easily imitated skills including their considerable experience of the monitoring and governance of start-ups and young firms. Thus, the growth of a young company is no longer necessarily bound by its limited internal resources. Its participation in the investment syndicate increases its access to a wide array of multi-firm resources stemming from the network relationships.

Implications for new, technology-based firms

From the pragmatic perspective of the new technology-based firms, the study suggests that CVCs are attractive investment partners. Their value derives primarily from their strategic assets rather than the finance they also provide. Importantly, CVCs are attractive as a complement to, and not a substitute for, the skills of the traditional venture capital investors. However, the finding that multiple corporate investors are associated with more successful portfolio companies is open to several interpretations. It is possible that multiple investors resolve or ameliorate the negative (and value-destroying) effects of agency problems that can occur within a single investor/firm dyad. For an investment syndicate to survive, its members are obliged to act within a wider consensus that meets the minimum acceptable interests of all the inter-related parties including the investee firm. It is unlikely that the exercise of undue influence or control by a single CVC investor on behalf of its own private interests would be tolerated by its syndicate partners. All CVCs (and venture capital firms) have to be mindful of ensuring their continued access to the network and to the future deal flow of their investor partners.

However, the superior results for investee firms with multiple investors may just be a consequence of the fact that such firms represent a more attractive (i.e. potentially successful) cohort of portfolio companies. It may be that the greater number of investors does not add to the firm's success in any material way. Rather, the existence of several corporate investors signals to the market the existing attraction of the investment opportunity. Multiple industry-leading corporate investors, possibly given their superior sources of information and time to undertake evaluations, do not add value but merely recognize it in others. Essentially, they are just better at picking attractive firms. There may also be some economies of scale and scope in investee selection with multiple investors sharing knowledge in order to avoid adverse selection problems. These scale effects help them to identify and choose only the highest quality potential firms. However, recent research in venture capital syndication focusing specifically on selection versus value-added hypothesis has demonstrated that syndication is more about value-added through complementary assets than better selection (Brander et al., 1999). In syndication between independent and corporate venture capitalists, there is even more potential for value adding synergy benefits.

An additional but not necessarily conflicting explanation of our results is that the CVCs are not passive agents selecting attractive firms. Their very involvement alters the market's perception of the value of the firms in which they have invested. (A number of global Fortune 500 CVCs in discussions with the authors strongly argued the reality of this effect.) There is some evidence of a certification or signaling effect that works in the favor of the most attractive firms and their investors. In short, a potentially successful firm may signal the likelihood of its own success, thereby attracting more and better investors, and in consequence increasing the chances of its success. This latter, "self-fulfilling prophecy" explanation reverses the direction of causality of the agency argument. In this latter argument, the corporate investors do not actually make a tangible operational contribution to the subsequent success of the chosen firm. None the less, both arguments and their causalities could exist in tandem.

What is less in contention is that multiple and heterogeneous partners with a diversity of complementary and related assets, working in a reciprocal network in order to exploit multi-firm resources do contribute to the IPO performance of investee companies located within such structures. In short, from the viewpoint of the economic interests of the investee firm, a multiplicity and diversity of investors are clearly desirable.

Implications for industry-leading corporations

For industry-leading corporations, the present study suggests that syndication and co-operative strategies by CVCs can lead to superior results. In order to maximize relational benefits, the CVC should ensure a multiplicity of investors. These should include other CVCs and traditional venture capital firms, which control and are prepared to share unique and complementary resources including both tangible and intangible assets. CVCs are likely to be the main contributors of intellectual assets and operating experience. However, traditional venture capital firms can bring to the network/syndicate greater experience and competencies in, for example, deal structuring, contract negotiation, and other monitoring and governance issues associated with working with young and dynamic firms. It is perhaps the venture capitalist's clarity and singularity of purpose – i.e. the maximizing of net capital gain within a given time frame – that provide most value in a syndication of heterogeneous parties with invariably multiple and mixed interests.

As a form of diversification, syndication also has risk reduction advantages for the cooperating investors as the finite economic consequences of an adverse outcome, i.e. firm or investment failure, are shared among a greater number of principals. However, the syndicate also shares a greater array of assessment skills and therefore adverse selection should be a manageable problem. In the context of venture capital investment, the presence of CVCs also has additional, significant deal generation and information-sharing benefits (Bygrave, 1987, 1988). Thus, this study suggests a win-win strategy is possible. The investing corporations and the portfolio company each gain strategic and financial benefits from their association within the wider network. The participating venture capital companies also benefit from the involvement of additional venture capital firms and the CVC(s). The finding that the collective participation of several industry-leading corporations in a financing leads to superior results further suggests that co-investments by alliance partners might be an efficient way to shape industry development via the support of high potential companies. The powerful advantages of co-operative and synergistic actions between different investor types in order to rapidly establish an innovative firm and/or a new technological advance could be used as a vehicle for corporations seeking to influence the evolution of a technology. Such a strategic and pre-emptive role for CVC within the innovative process has not previously been noted in the literature.

Implications for independent venture capitalists

For independent venture capitalists, our study concludes that corporate investors are attractive syndication partners. In identifying, selecting, financing, and subsequently supporting start-ups and young firms until a successful market realization, no one type of equity provider has a monopoly on the diverse skill sets needed. Each party benefits from the involvement of the others. The existence of a pecking order of structures impacting on the investee firms' performance supports this assertion. Our findings suggest that corporate venture capitalists as network partners can bring a range of benefits including incremental certification and complementary value-added. The potential agency problem of conflicting interests in corporate venture capital investments may be attenuated by introducing more than one industry-leading corporation into the syndicate. Contrary to the belief of some venture capitalists, this study indicates that companies which also have corporate venture capitalists as investors are actually more successful in making initial public offerings when measured in market capitalization at IPO. However, venture capital firms may have to be mindful that CVC finance is a highly substitutable product for their own financial and related services. There is a possible danger that venture capital firms could get "crowded out" of attractive deals by their erstwhile corporate partners unless their own unique firm resources are emphasized. However, CVCs appear to have less interest and experience in a direct involvement in the governance of their portfolio firms than other types of investors. There may be an important and complementary "hands on" role for traditional equity providers as the primary managers of the syndicate/investee relationship.

Conclusion

Our study has several implications for future research. We indicate that the association of new enterprises with industry-leading corporations via the agency of corporate venture capitalists may lead to higher IPO valuations. We have also established the existence of a hierarchy or pecking order of performance with multiple CVC/VC investors being at the apex. However, the exact reasons why this advantageous ranking should occur are not fully resolved by our chapter although a number of further lines of analysis are suggested. Closer investigation of the exact nature of the value-added processes provided by both corporate and traditional venture capitalists is needed in order to better understand the multi-faceted relationships between investors and investees. This present study uses sector-specific data sets of IPO performance figures for Global Fortune 500 companies within the information and communications technology industries. In order to determine the full generalizability of our findings, additional research in, for example, the life-science sectors is an obvious empirical extension.

It might also be argued that there may be conditions where the technological competencies of large firms are not an advantage but act as a constraint on the success of the portfolio firms which they counsel. In highly volatile environments exhibiting disruptive and discontinuous change, the path dependent experience of presently dominant organizations may serve to imperil the future success of the innovative young firms with which they seek to ally. Our present findings are based exclusively on an analysis of secondary data over a relatively short time period. It may well add greater depth to our findings if we could also seek (subsequently testable) explanations for our results from the various players within the industry (i.e. the investee firms, venture capitalists and CVC personnel). The results of our quantitative analyses need to be viewed against practitioners' more qualitative and pragmatic understandings as to the role and importance of the various components of the value-added, relational process including network formation, alliance management, certification, and the benefits of sharing knowledge and other complementary resources. However, recent accounts by corporate venture capital practitioners appear to provide good support for our core argument of the complementary roles of corporate venture capital and venture capital investors (Christopher, 2000).

Acknowledgements

This chapter is based on a paper presented at the 20th Annual International Conference of Strategic Management Society in Vancouver 2000, which was awarded the McKinsey and Company/Strategic Management Society Best Conference Paper Honorable Mention. We thank the editors and anonymous reviewers for their helpful comments.

Note

1   It should perhaps be stressed that, in reality, major corporations will commonly back several new enterprises employing competing technologies in a dynamic and/or immature marketplace.

References

Anderson, P. and Tushman, M. L. 1990: Technological discontinuities and dominant designs – a cyclical model of technological-change. *Administrative Science Quarterly*, 35, 604–33.

Autio, E., Sapienza H., and Almeida, J. 2000: Effects of time to internationalization, knowledge intensity, and imitability on growth. *Academy of Management Journal*, 43, 909–24.

Barry, C. B., Muscarella, C. J., Peavy III, J. W., and Vetsuypens, M. R. 1990: The role of venture capital in the creation of public companies: evidence from the going public process. *Journal of Financial Economics*, 27, 447–71.

Brander, J., Amit, R., and Antweiler, W. 1999: Venture capital syndication: improved venture selection versus the value-added hypothesis. Forthcoming in *Journal of Economics and Management Strategy*.

Burgel, O., Fier, A., Licht, G., and Murray, G. C. 2000: *The Rapid Internationalisation of High Tech Young Firms in Germany and the United Kingdom*. London: London Business School and ZEW.

Burgel, O. and Murray, G. C. 1999: The internationalisation of start-up companies in high-technology sectors: differences between internationalisers and non-internationalisers. *Proceedings of the Frontiers in Entrepreneurship Research Conference*. Boston MA: Babson College.

Bygrave, W. D. 1987: Syndicated investments by venture capital firms: a Networking perspective. *Journal of Business Venturing*, 2, 139–54.

Bygrave, W. D. 1988: The structure of investment networks of venture capital firms. *Journal of Business Venturing*, 3: 137–58.

Bygrave, W. D. 1989: Early rates of return of 131 venture capital funds started 1978–1984. *Journal of Business Venturing*, 4, 93–105.

Christopher, A. 2000: Corporate venture capital: moving to the head of the class. *Venture Capital Journal*, November: 43–6.

Doz, Y. 1988: Technology partnerships between larger and smaller firms: some critical issues. In F. J. Contractor, and P. Lorange (eds), *Cooperative Strategies in International Business*. Lexington MA: Lexington.

Dyer, J. H. and Singh, H. 1998: The relational view: cooperative strategy and sources of interorganizational competitive advantage. *Academy of Management Review*, 23, 660–79.

Eisenhardt, K. M. and Schoonhoven, C. B. 1996: Resource-based view of strategic alliance formation: strategic and social effects in entrepreneurial firms. *Organization Science*, 7, 136–50.

Evans, D. S. 1987: Tests of alternative theories of firm growth. *Journal of Political Economy*, 95: 657–74.

Gifford, S. 1997: Limited attention and the role of venture capitalist. *Journal of Business Venturing*, 12, 459–82.

Gompers, P. A. 1995: Optimal investment, monitoring, and the staging of venture capital. *Journal of Finance*, 50, 1461–89.

Gompers, P. A. and Lerner, J. 1998: *The Determinants of Corporate Venture Capital Successes: Organizational Structure, Incentives, and Complementarities*. NBER Working Paper, No.

W6725. Cambridge, MA: National Bureau of Economic Research.

Hamel, G. 1991: Competition for competence and inter-partner learning within international strategic alliances. *Strategic Management Journal*, 12: 83–103.

Hellmann, T. 2000: *A Theory of Strategic Venture Investing*, Stanford University Working Paper, Stanford, CA: Stanford University Press.

Hitt. M. A., Dacin, T., Levitas, E., Arregle, J.-L., and Borza, A. 2000: Partner selection in emerging and developed market contexts: resource-based and organizational learning perspectives. *Academy of Management Journal*, 43, 449–67.

Hurry, D., Miller, A. T., and Bowman, E. H. 1992: Calls on high technology: Japanese exploration of venture capital investments in the United States. *Strategic Management Journal*, 13, 85–101.

Kann, A. 2000: Strategic venture capital investing by corporations: a framework for structuring and valuing corporate venture capital programs. Unpublished dissertation, Stanford University.

Klein, B. 1977: *Dynamic Economy*. Cambridge MA: Harvard University Press.

Laamanen, T. 1997: The acquisition of technological competencies through the acquisition of new, technology-based companies and through collaborative arrangements with new, technology-based companies. Unpublished dissertation, Helsinki University of Technology.

Loughran, T. and Ritter, J. R. 1999: Why don't issuers get upset about leaving money on the table in IPOS? *Review of Financial Studies*, Forthcoming.

McGrath, R. G. MacMillan, I. C., and Tushman, M. L. 1992: The role of executive team actions in shaping dominant designs: towards the strategic shaping of technological progress. *Strategic Management Journal*, 13, 137–61.

McNally, K. 1997: *Corporate Venture Capital: Bridging the Equity Gap in the Small Business Sector*. London: Routledge.

National Venture Capital Association 2000: *Yearbook 2000*. Arlington, VA: Thompson Financial Securities Data/Venture Economics Inc..

Norton, E. and Tenenbaum, B. H. 1993: Specialisation versus differentiation as a venture capital investment strategy. *Journal of Business Venturing*, 8, 431–42.

Olson, M. 1968: *The Logic of Collective Action: Public Goods and the Theory of Groups*. Schoken Books: New York.

Oviatt, B. M. and MacDougall, P. P. 1994: Toward a theory of international new ventures. *Journal of International Business Studies*, 25, 45–64.

Rock, K. 1986: Why new issues are underpriced. *Journal of Financial Economics*, 15, 187–212.

Rothaermel, F. T. and Deeds, D. L. 2001: More good things are not necessarily better: an empirical study of strategic alliances, experience effects, and new product development in high-technology start-ups. Chapter 6 in this volume.

Sapienza, H. J. 1992: When do venture capitalists add value? *Journal of Business Venturing*, 7, 9–27.

Siegel. R., Siegel, E., and MacMillan, I. C. 1988: Corporate venture capitalists: autonomy, obstacles, and performance. *Journal of Business Venturing*. 3, 233–48.

Stuart, T. E. 2000: Interorganizational alliances and the performance of firms: a study of growth and innovation rates in high-technology industries. *Strategic Management Journal*, 21, 791–811.

Stuart, T. E., Hoang, H., and Hybels, R. C. 1999: Interorganizational endorsements and the performance of entrepreneurial ventures. *Administrative Science Quarterly*, 44, 315–49.

Suárez, F. F. and Utterback, J. M. 1995: Dominant designs and the survival of firms. *Strategic Management Journal*, 16, 415–31.

Sykes, H. B. 1990: Corporate venture capital: strategies for success. *Journal of Business Venturing*, 5: 37–47.

Trautwein, F. R. 1989: Merger motives and merger prescriptions. *Strategic Management Journal*, 11, 283–95.

Tushman, M. L. and Anderson, P. 1986: Technological discontinuities and organizational environments. *Administrative Science Quarterly*, 31, 439–65.

Venture Economics. 1999:*Databases*. Online Document, URL: http://www.venture economics.com/databases.html. Accessed December 13, 1999.

Winters, T. E. 1988: Venture capital investing for corporate development objectives'. *Journal of Business Venturing*, 3, 207–23.

Yli-Renko, H., Autio, E., and Sapienza, H. J. 2001: Social capital, knowledge acquisition, and competitive advantage in technology-based young firms. Forthcoming in *Strategic Management Journal*. Special Issue on Entrepreneurial Strategies and Wealth Creation in the 21st Century, 587–613.

Zider, R. 1998: How venture capital works. *Harvard Business Review*, Nov./Dec. 131–9.

CHAPTER TEN

Strategic Decision-Making in the Entrepreneurial Millennium: Competition, Crisis and "Expert" Risk Assessment of Emerging Market Sovereigns

Gerry McNamara and Paul Vaaler

Introduction

This chapter examines strategic decision-making by expert organizations during periods of increased competitive and environmental turbulence. It is a rather low-risk prediction that an entrepreneurial millennium will see decisions affecting the very survival of organizations made less often in the cool, objective context that dominant market positioning and environmental placidness and predictability engender. Instead, decision-making in this emerging world assumes inherent instability, frequent change, and constant scanning for threats from rivals (D'Aveni, 1994). Reliance on stable industry structures and corporate competencies is problematic. Existing structures favoring incumbents in one period crumble in the next, leaving in the rubble confused incumbents prone to challenge from newcomers (Henderson, 1993). Internal corporate knowledge bases can be rendered obsolete or even misleading in this new environment (Argote, 1999). If there are persistently successful firms in this world, then they must be flexible enough to look within the firm for expertise on key decisions in one instance but then also look without to others linked by market and or network relationships (Gulati et al., 2000).

Of course, there are rich research streams in strategy and organizational theory ready for focus on decision-making in this emerging world. The upper echelons view (e.g., Hambrick and Mason, 1984; Wiersema and Bantel, 1992; Sambharya, 1996), for example, assesses decision-making tendencies based on the demographic background of top-managers within the firm. A decision-aids perspective (e.g., Schwenk, 1984; Lyles and Schwenk, 1992) investigates decision-making heuristics used by strategic actors and the consequent behavior to which they lead. Still another research stream from the dynamic capabilities viewpoint (e.g., Eisenhardt, 1989; Zaheer and Zaheer, 1997; Eisenhardt and Martin, 2000) examines the speed of internal decision-making processes linked to the inherent volatility of the business environment in which a firm operates.

Outside Experts, Decision-Making in Turbulence, and Bias

All three of these perspectives find increased relevance for researchers working in this emerging world. On the other hand, they also suffer from a common shortcoming which emerging trends in an entrepreneurial millennium highlight. These perspectives and others in the theoretical repertoire of strategy and related fields generally assume that the decision-making individuals and processes are *internal* to the firm. In increasing fact, many of the key decision-making individuals and decision-making processes may be externalized to others. Outside experts in law, accounting, finance, business, and various technical fields produce specialized information and services for firms seeking disinterested, objective advice as they mull over major decisions like mergers, acquisitions, new product and business expansions, and foreign ventures (Salacuse, 1994). Perhaps as importantly, particularly in cases where the firm faces great environmental uncertainty, these outside experts lend their reputations and provide legitimacy by "certifying" decision quality to firm stakeholders (James, 1992). For both sets of reasons, firms increasingly turn to such expert organizations for advice in connection with strategic decisions, especially as they face an increasingly diverse and volatile environment.

Strategy research in any era would benefit from deeper understanding of expert decision-making factors and processes, particularly during periods of heightened environmental uncertainty and turbulence for them and their clients. However, given trends associated with this entrepreneurial millennium, a deeper understanding of such expert decision-making individuals and contexts is crucial.

We address this by examining decision-making factors and processes familiar to one set of expert organizations important to the foreign investment decisions of firms and other organizations: international credit-rating agencies ("agencies"). Credit-rating agencies serve a critically important advisory role in the financial capital markets by providing objective assessments of the risk of various borrowers on a widely known multi-point (17 level) scale. Specifically, we examine agency risk assessments of emerging-market sovereign borrowers, and the occasionally turbulent environments in which they vie for sovereign risk-rating business. Previous empirical research almost universally modeled foreign investment risk-assessments based on objective evaluation of actual or perceived country factors, such as host-country macroeconomic, government policy, financial, legal and social conditions (e.g., Saini and Bates, 1984; Phillips-Patrick, 1989; Mahajan, 1990; Johnson et al., 1990; Ozler, 1991; Hashmi and Guvenli, 1992; Lee, 1993; Cosset and Suret, 1995, Cantor and Packer, 1996). The agencies themselves have taken positions consistent with this research approach, touting the comprehensiveness and objectivity of their risk-assessment of country factors (e.g., Standard and Poor's Ratings Services, 1997; Moody's Investors Service, 1999).

But unanticipated and prolonged crises in Asia in 1997 and in Europe and Latin America in 1998 sparked criticism from both scholars and practitioners that agency risk-ratings had become substantially skewed and reflected factors other than objective and comprehensive evaluation of the countries' macroeconomic, financial, legal, political, and social context (e.g., Radelet and Sachs, 1998; Karacadag and Samuels, 1999). One explanation for skewed assessments during the crisis highlights affective risk factors linked to agency surprise and over-reaction to revelations that certain emerging-market sovereigns were in more precarious economic and financial straits than previous research had indicated (e.g., Ferri et al., 1999). Another potential explanation relates to the growing competition among the agencies skewing their assessments in the run-up to the crisis years (McNamara and Vaaler, 2000).

Perhaps both explanations are important to understanding skewed risk assessment by these expert organizations. Research in strategy and organizational theory suggests that sudden, discontinuous changes in the firm's environment can induce greater uncertainty among top management (Tushman and Anderson, 1986), lead to higher perceived rates of change in market circumstances (Eisenhardt, 1989), and call into question the firm's standard operating procedures (Nelson and Winter, 1982) and behavioral assumptions (March and Olsen, 1976; Staw et al., 1981; Bourgeois, 1985). Risk-assessment under crisis conditions may lead firms to emphasize factors related to the background of individuals doing the assessment rather than to objective decision-making criteria about the creditworthiness of a particular foreign borrower (Kindleberger, 1978).

Strategy and organizational theory perspectives also link risk assessment by firms to their competitive context. Firm positioning as an incumbent or new entrant ("insurgent") in the industry (Lieberman and Montgomery, 1988; Mitchell, 1989, 1991) may shape perceptions of the risk associated with certain individuals and transactions. In an international context, firm risk assessment may also be shaped by geographic considerations such as the extent to which the firm operates on a regional or global scope (Doz and Prahalad, 1987) and depends on certain locales for business (Pfeffer and Salancik, 1978; Fiol and Lyles, 1985). Finally, firm risk assessment may be influenced by the level of rivalry the firm faces in a particular market context (Scherer, 1980).

We investigate the skewing effects of crisis and competition using agency risk-assessments of emerging-market[1] sovereign borrowers over the 1997–8 period. This empirical context provides clearly delineated markets, identification of rivals, competitive positioning as incumbent or insurgent, and extent of geographic specialty in business. The time period studied is also opportune: 1987–96 saw substantial growth both in emerging-market investment and in the number of agencies assessing attendant risks. This growth in risk-rating markets and rivals came to an abrupt halt with the onset of financial crisis in Thailand in mid-1997 and its spread to other emerging-market countries later in 1997 and 1998. The confluence of emerging-market growth, industry entry and rivalry, and then crisis gives us an ideal opportunity to examine whether and how expert risk assessments may be biased at the very moment when, arguably, their assessments command most attention from stakeholders.

Summary of Findings

We develop and test six hypotheses. Our results indicate first that crisis conditions are linked to negative deviations from objective risk assessment models used by the agencies. Specifically, we find that ratings during the 1997–8 crisis period are, on average, nearly two rating notches lower than an objective risk assessment warranted during the crisis. Because, ratings are highly correlated with the cost and availability of credit, these agency miscues probably exacerbated the impact of the crises on local firms and governments and conveyed inaccurate information to foreign investors.

Second, the results suggest that the extent of such negative deviations relate to competitive factors among the agencies themselves. We find significant links between an agency's deviation from objective risk assessment in crisis and industry positioning as an incumbent versus insurgent agency, and as an agency with global coverage versus regional specialization and dependency. Specifically, we find that insurgent agencies are less negatively biased than incumbents. Insurgency status is associated with one rating notch closer to objective risk assessments during the 1997–8 crisis period. Agencies with business focused substantially in one region of the world, however, exhibit more negative bias during the crisis period – almost two rating notches lower than objectively warranted if 40 percent of an agency's business derives from sovereigns in one particular geographic region.

We conclude that close examination of these trends in the data help explain rating miscues by the agencies in emerging-market countries during the 1997–8 crisis period. The examination also provides us with research insights and managerial prescriptions for other expert organizations making risk-assessments in other contexts where the twin stresses of crisis and competition – strategy hallmarks of an entrepreneurial millennium – are likely to interact.

The Research Setting

What sovereign risk ratings are

Sovereign risk-ratings, also known simply as "sovereigns," assess the relative likelihood that a state borrower will default on its obligations. Governments generally seek credit ratings to ease their access to international capital markets, as well as to ease the access of individual business firms and organizations domiciled within their borders. Many interested investors, particularly US-based investors, prefer rated securities to unrated securities of similar risk profiles. Institutional US investors in sovereign securities generally require ratings by one or two agencies designated as Nationally Recognized Statistical Rating Organizations ("NRSROs") by the US Securities and Exchange Commission (SEC, 1994).[2] The requirement of NRSRO status constrains entry into the sovereign credit risk market. It effectively limits the number of rivals and potential entrants able to rate offerings targeted to US institutional investors.

Typically, sovereign risk ratings are expressed in ordinal letter-rankings. The ordinal scale is most often given on a 16-level basis starting with "AAA" (16) and descending through "AA+" (15), "AA"(14), "AA-" (13), and so forth to "B-" (1). The scale may

Table 10.1   Agency letter ratings, grades, numerical equivalents, and interpretations

Moody's	S&P and the other three NRSROs	Grade	Numerical equivalent on 17-level (0–16) scale	Interpretation
Aaa	AAA	Investment	16	Extremely strong capacity to meet its financial commitments.
Aa1	AA+	Investment	15	Very strong capacity to meet its
Aa2	AA		14	financial commitments.
Aa3	AA–		13	
A1	A+	Investment	12	Adequate capacity to meet its financial
A2	A		11	commitments.
A3	A–		10	
Baa1	BBB+	Investment	9	Less vulnerable than lower rated
Baa2	BBB		8	obligors but facing adverse conditions
Baa3	BBB–		7	which could lead to obligor's inadequate capacity to meet its financial commitments.
Ba1	BB+	Speculative	6	More vulnerable than the obligors rated
Ba2	BB	(Junk)	5	above. Obligor currently has the
Ba3	BB–		4	capacity to meet its financial commitments but adverse conditions will likely impair this capacity.
B1	B+	Speculative	3	Currently vulnerable and dependent on
B2	B	(Junk)	2	favorable conditions to meet its
B3	B–		1	financial commitments.
C	C		0	

also expand to 17 levels with the inclusion of a "C" (0) rating. Table 10.1 lists the most commonly used proxy for sovereign risk-rating from each of the five agencies we studied along with their 17-level ordinal rankings for long-term foreign-currency-denominated sovereign debt securities.

Sovereigns generally invite an agency to give a rating. Once the invitation is accepted, the rating process can last several weeks or even months. A team of from three to seven analysts typically begins by reviewing a broad range of data on the sovereign and its country both from the agency's home office and in the field. Team members frequently interview government officials, business executives, and other individuals for an overview of risk factors. A preliminary report on the sovereign along with a prospective risk rating from the team is forwarded to the agency's rating committee back in the home office. There, the committee evaluates findings of the preliminary report and makes recommendations on the final rating. At this stage in the process, agencies characteristically invite the sovereign's participation including presentations to the committee and related agency personnel. Once a prospective final rating has been agreed to in committee but before its publication, agencies may allow sovereigns to "appeal" their decision and provide additional information and or analyses. When finally published, the rating is subject to ordinary review on a regular annual or semi-annual basis. It may also come up for extraordinary review should, for example, the rated sovereign request it or if the agency decides that key circumstances related to the sovereign have changed markedly (Linden, 1997).

The final rating issued by the agency is extremely important. The sovereign's risk rating is strongly associated with its cost of borrowing in international capital markets. Indeed, sovereign ratings are highly correlated with interest rate spreads on sovereign debt issued over the same period (Cantor and Packer, 1996). Additionally, the availability of credit is also commonly related to a sovereign's credit rating since many creditors limit the amount of lending they will make to borrowers at lower rating levels to limit their risk exposure with some lenders refusing to participate at all in sub-investment grade bond offerings. Ratings influence the cost and availability of credit for more than just governments and their agencies as borrowers in international capital markets. The sovereign risk rating also acts as a credit "ceiling" for other sub-sovereign governments, firms, and other locally domiciled individuals (Moody's Investors Service, 1999). Piercing the sovereign ceiling is still rare and costly (Torres and Zeiter, 1998; Zissu and Stone, 2001). Thus, nationality is crucial to determining whether and at what price credit may flow to sub-sovereign firms and other individuals, indirectly having a substantial impact on the economic well-being of a nation.

Agencies only started charging fees to individuals seeking ratings in the 1960s. Often, the rating is completed in connection with the issuance of securities. Accordingly, the agencies often compensate themselves for providing this initial rating with a fee based on a percentage of the face amount of the securities issued. The fees paid by sovereign issuers can range as high as 2 percent of the face amount. Agencies may also seek fees for subsequent issuances and for periodic reviews of the sovereign rating between issuances. Sovereign credit ratings may also be a source of related fees from issuing firms and other organizations domiciled within the sovereign's borders. Agencies may, therefore, seek sovereign risk-rating business as an entrée into rating prospective sub-sovereign governmental, corporate and other issuers more accurately and efficiently (Sinclair, 1995).

How emerging-market sovereign risk-rating business expanded: 1987–96

In 1987, only 30 sovereigns were rated by two NRSRO agencies: US-based Moody's Investor Service ("Moody's"); and Standard and Poor's Ratings Services ("S&P"). Of the 30 sovereigns rated by the end of 1987, 18 were from developed countries while only 12 were from emerging-market countries. By the end of 1996, things had changed dramatically: 74 sovereigns had obtained ratings from one of five US NRSRO agencies, which now included incumbents, Moody's and S&P, and insurgent agencies, US-based Duff and Phelps Credit Rating Company ("Duff"); Canada and US-based Thomson Bank Watch ("Thomson"); and UK-based International Bank Credit Analysis ("IBCA" or "Fitch IBCA").[3] Over this period, growth in emerging markets was explosive. The number of rated emerging-market sovereigns more than quadrupled to 51. By 1997, annual financing (loans, bonds and equity issued) by emerging-market sovereign governments and firms domiciled within their borders totaled nearly

Table 10.2   Rated emerging market sovereigns by geographic region, 1987–98

Africa/Middle East	Asia	Central/Eastern Europe	Latin America	Western Europe/ North America
Bahrain	China	Croatia	Argentina	Cyprus
Egypt	Hong Kong	Czech Republic	Brazil	Greece[a]
Israel	India	Hungary	Chile	Malta
Jordan	Indonesia	Lithuania	Colombia	Portugal[a]
Kuwait	Kazakstan	Poland	Costa Rica	
Mauritius	Korea	Romania	El Salvador	
Oman	Malaysia	Russia	Mexico	
Qatar	Pakistan	Slovakia	Paraguay	
Saudi Arabia	Philippines	Slovenia	Peru	
South Africa	Singapore		Uruguay	
Tunisia	Taiwan		Venezuela	
Turkey	Thailand			
United Arab Emirates	Vietnam			

[a] Greece and Portugal were classified as emerging-market countries through 1989.

$200 billion, up from less than $60 billion only five years earlier (OECD, 1998). Dramatic increases in sovereigns rated and the amounts borrowed on such ratings indicate the importance of emerging markets for these NRSRO agencies. The 51 emerging-market sovereigns rated by the end of 1996 are arranged by geographic region in table 10.2.

The crisis period: 1997–8

A series of emerging-market country financial crises began in mid-1997 in South-east Asia and then spread to several other Eastern European and Latin American countries. International monetary authorities described this shock as "foreseeable" several months in advance and "unprecedented" in terms of the financial, economic and even political dislocations it caused (IMF, 1998). Sovereign risk-rating changes during the 1997–8 period reflected the surprise of the agencies. For example, Moody's sovereign risk rating for Thailand was as an "A2" at the beginning of 1997 but had sunk to a grade of "Ba1" at the close of 1998. The surprise is conveyed not only in the sheer drop in rating notches (5) but also that the rating was changed by Moody's four times in a period of eight months after having remained at the same level for over seven years. On a practical level, this drop moved Thailand's sovereign debt from "investment grade" (> BBB) to "non-investment grade" or "junk" status (< BBB). The cost of credit for sovereigns crossing the "junk" line increases dramatically. In Thailand's case, companies borrowing at spreads of 250 basis points (2.5 percent interest rate points) above the London Interbank Overnight Rate, a commonly used gauge for the base cost of credit globally, saw spreads triple or quadruple, if credit was available at all after

Table 10.3   Summary of hypotheses for empirical study

Hypothesis number	Hypothesis description	Research basis	Skewing effects
H1	Industry-wide shock	Threat rigidity and uncertainty avoidance	All agencies (−)
H2a	Entry order	First-mover advantage	Insurgent agencies (−)
H2b	Entry order	Institutional and behavioral theories	Insurgent agencies (+)
H3a	Regional specialization	Learning and resource dependency	Regional focus (+)
H3b	Regional specialization	Threat rigidity	Regional focus (−)
H4	Market structure	IO economics and competitive dynamics	Greater rivalry (+)

downgrade to BB. Academic circles and the popular press reacted to the agencies' downgrades with accusations of irrationality and over-reaction (Radelet and Sachs, 1998; Karacadag and Samuels, 1999). By the end of 1998, even the agencies suggested revisiting certain emerging-market sovereign ratings after their hasty downgrade when the crisis began (FitchIBCA, 1998).

Theory and Hypotheses

In this context of market growth, increasing competition and crisis, we proposed that there might be less reliance on standard objective approaches to sovereign risk assessment. Instead, the vagaries of risk assessment during crisis require closer examination of the agencies and biases they may have linked to their position within the broader sovereign risk-rating industry as well as to their position within specific sovereign markets. Drawing on theoretical perspectives from strategy and organizational theory, we develop six hypotheses related to this general research proposition. Two hypotheses (H1 and H4) predict specific directions in agency bias once crisis unfolds. But the other four hypotheses (H2a, H2b, H3a and H3b) we evaluate suggest alternative directions in agency bias based on competing theoretical views in strategy and organization theory relevant to crisis decision-making. Each of these specific and alternative hypotheses are summarized in table 10.3 and described in detail below.

Crisis decision-making and deviation from objective assessment

Both anecdotal evidence we noted and established organizational theory suggest that crisis may prompt agencies to deviate substantially from standard decision-making models, resulting in skewed assessments of emerging-market sovereign risk. This reaction is consistent with organizational literature on response of firms generally to sudden changes in the surrounding environment. Tushman and Anderson (1986), for example, conclude that "punctuated" change in an organization's environment increases perceived uncertainty, triggers deviations from existing decision routines, and increases search and scanning efforts by the organization (Cyert and March, 1963; Greve and Taylor, 2000). Dramatic, unforeseen swings in the perceived creditworthiness of sovereign borrowers are likely to increase uncertainty among the agencies and less reliance on the risk-rating models and procedures they normally use.

The likely outcome for agencies is greater pessimism in risk-ratings than objective review would warrant. Previous research on foreign market entry suggests that uncertainty associated with market conditions dissimilar to those in which the firm is already positioned increases risk-aversion (Davidson, 1980). Additionally, decision-makers typically respond negatively to increasing ambiguity in decision targets, especially in situations where the decision-maker believes that others will scrutinize their decisions *ex post* (Ellsberg, 1961; Curley et al., 1986). Agencies used to the increasing creditworthiness of emerging-market sovereigns over the late 1980s and early 1990s may be less confident, and possibly less competent, in assessing the downward trajectories associated with crisis in these same countries. Ambiguity in the environment can also breed a threat-rigidity response from decision-makers (Staw et al., 1981; Bourgeois, 1985). This response may come in the form of greater oversight and control over the decision-maker's operations (Keats and Hitt, 1988). Or where such oversight and control mechanisms are not available, it may arise in the form of discount on the value of such operations. In the case of agencies rating sovereigns over this crisis period, control over the actions of seemingly errant sovereigns is minimal, thus the threat-rigidity response comes in the form of greater "discounting" (decrease) in the sovereign risk rating they assign. Along with agency risk aversion and uncertainty avoidance, threat rigidity response is also likely to result in sovereign risk-ratings that deviate negatively from objective assessment models and procedures.

Hypothesis 1: Agency sovereign risk-ratings will exhibit negative deviation from objective assessments during a crisis period.

Crisis decision-making and industry positioning

Aside from an industry-wide downward deviation in risk assessment in times of crisis, individual agencies may exhibit deviations from objective risk assessment linked to their particular intra-industry positioning. Strategy perspectives emphasize the importance of hard-to-replicate positioning within an industry (Rumelt, 1987). Among agencies competing for business in emerging-markets, a key resource or positioning factor relates to entry order. Incumbency may confer several "first-mover" advantages (Lieberman and Montgomery, 1988), including those related to reputation, learning and pre-emption of ratings business with preferred sovereigns. Given their established reputations, history, and experience in previous international credit cycles, incumbent agencies may have a more modest reaction to exogenous shocks. In contrast, prior management research suggests that building legitimacy in the eyes of key stakeholders is a central mission for new entrants to an industry (Deephouse, 1996). Newly designated NRSRO agencies may perceive greater oversight from regulators such as the US Securities and Exchange Commission, and other industry stakeholders. Consequently, they may be driven by institutional pressure to "buy" legitimacy with regulators through more swift and dramatic negative responses to shocks.

Consistent with this reasoning, Meyer (1982) concluded, in his study of hospitals' responses to an environmental shock, that firms with stable market positions, diversified market portfolios, and large slack resource bases were less responsive to environmental shocks. Mitchell's (1989, 1991) research on entry-order in emerging medical equipment industry sub-fields suggests that industry incumbents (but not recent industry entrants) enjoyed greater latitude to determine when, if at all, to react to market shocks caused by new product introductions. Recent theorizing by McEvily et al. (2000) argues that an industry incumbent's advantage derives largely from the network of informational resources it can draw on to mitigate some or all of the heightened uncertainty crisis conditions engender. Such empirical and theoretical work suggests that incumbent agencies, with established network, reputation and financial resource positions, would exhibit less pronounced negative responses to a crisis than insurgent agencies without all of these advantages.

> Hypothesis 2a: Insurgent agency sovereign risk-ratings will exhibit greater negative deviation from objective assessments than incumbent agency sovereign risk-ratings during a crisis period.

An alternative hypothesis linking negative deviation from objective risk assessments to industry incumbency predicts a negative relationship between the two in times of crisis. Recent work by McNamara and Vaaler (2000) found that in the period leading up to the 1997–8 crisis period, insurgent agencies actually published *lower* sovereign risk-ratings than incumbents after controlling for other relevant factors. In essence, the insurgent agencies appeared to be tougher on sovereigns than the incumbent firms, perhaps to "buy" legitimacy with regulators and other important industry stakeholders. Incumbent agencies, on the other hand, might have had fewer incentives to build legitimacy within a sovereign risk-rating business they had largely created prior to the promulgation of formal regulations on industry entry and behavior. This privileged position may have rendered the agencies less observant when warning signs of crisis cropped up in the mid-1990s. The crisis period, during which the ratings provided by all agencies faced increased scrutiny, may have been especially threatening to incumbent firms. To protect their legitimacy in the market, they may, therefore, have perceived the need to take more substantial action in response to the crisis in order to regain perceived control of the situation (Staw et al, 1981). Similarly, consistent with behavioral models of decision assessment (March and Olsen, 1976), unwarranted optimism among the incumbent agencies prior to the crisis could then necessitate a more pronounced negative response than their conservative insurgent rivals during the crisis.

> Hypothesis 2b: Incumbent agency sovereign risk-ratings will exhibit greater negative deviation from objective assessments than insurgent agency sovereign risk-ratings during a crisis period.

Crisis decision-making and regional specialization

Temporal positioning within the industry is not the only competitive factor that may affect agency response to crisis. Negative deviation from objective risk assessment may also be affected by an agency's positioning defined in geographic terms. The degree to which an agency specializes in rating sovereigns from a given geographic region may mute its crisis response. Consider the theoretical basis for this proposition from two perspectives familiar to organization theory. First, from a learning perspective (Fiol and Lyles, 1985; Lyles, 1995), agencies are likely to have deeper and broader informational resources on which to base a sovereign risk rating in regions in which they specialize. As Oxelheim and Wihlborg (1997) note, many risk elements related to one country have spillover effects on neighboring states. Agencies specializing in specific geographic regions have more opportunity to leverage these informational synergies. Consequently, these specialized agencies are likely to perceive warning signs earlier and will perceive less uncertainty once the turbulence becomes more evident. The additional information they have and lower level of perceived uncertainty may mute negative deviations during crisis within their geographic region of specialization.

Second, agencies that rely on rating sovereigns from a particular geographic region may perceive pressure to remain optimistic about the risk of sovereigns within that region due to resource dependency pressures (Pfeffer and Salancik, 1978). Agencies typically rely on sovereigns to request ratings and derive income from sovereigns when they are one of the raters of record for a financing transaction. Given the nature of close social ties that often exist within geographic regions, agencies are likely to perceive pressure to rank sovereigns favorably in order to gain the rating business on a particular issuance, and build market share and fee income in the broader market. Together, resource dependency and learning perspectives indicate that any negative deviation from objective sovereign risk assessment during a crisis period will be less pronounced as the agency's core business becomes more focused regionally.

Hypothesis 3a: The more an agency's business is focused on a given geographic region, the less pronounced will be the agency's negative deviation in sovereign risk-ratings from objective assessments for sovereigns from that region during a crisis period.

Again, there is an alternative hypothesis to consider in connection with regional specialization and deviation from objective assessment during crises. Negative deviations may be more pronounced for sovereigns from regions in which they specialize due to overly optimistic ratings they previously provided to sovereigns from that region. McNamara and Vaaler (2000), for example, found that agencies favored sovereigns in regions in which they specialized during a period of relative environmental tranquility, 1987–96. Consequently, the agencies may have perceived greater pressure to respond dramatically in the regions in which they specialize in order to maintain their perceived legitimacy as an expert in this region as well as to re-establish their self-perceived level of control in this critical geographic area (Staw et al, 1981; Keats and Hitt, 1988).

Hypothesis 3b: The more an agency's business is focused on a given geographic region, the more pronounced will be the agency's negative deviation in sovereign risk-ratings from objective assessments for sovereigns from that region during a crisis period.

Crisis decision-making and market structure

In addition to temporal and geographic dimensions, industry positioning may be assessed in terms of behavior within specific supplier market segments. In this case, supplier markets are defined nationally by the sovereign and related sub-sovereign borrowers needing the rating to access US institutions for capital. Agencies face varying degrees of rivalry in particular national markets. The number of firms operating in a given national market segment is a fundamental structural characteristic influencing the bargaining power of firms (Porter, 1980) as well as the ability of firms to collude (Fershtman and Muller, 1986). This, in turn, influences the strategic conduct and performance of individual firms in the industry (Scherer, 1980). As the industry moves from a simple monopoly to oligopolistic structures, the ability of incumbent firms to affect the competitive intents and actual behaviors of other market participants decreases (Chen, 1996). In our context, a lone agency operating as a monopolist may be able to interpret information about the sovereign and sub-sovereigns in a national market more deliberately and perhaps, less favorably, with little fear of losing business to others. As additional agencies enter, however, downward ratings pressure prompted by crisis is more likely to be constrained lest borrowers take their business elsewhere. Such change in national market structure will, therefore, result in less pronounced downward deviation from objective assessments for sovereign risk-ratings during crisis periods.

Hypothesis 4: The greater the number of rival agencies publishing a rating for a given sovereign, the less pronounced will be an agency's negative deviation in sovereign risk-ratings from objective assessments for that sovereign during a crisis period.

Methodology

Data collection and sampling

To test these six hypotheses, we collected data on sovereign credit risk-ratings made by NRSRO agencies as of December 31 in each year of the 1987–98 period. Our total sample includes 1,599 sovereign risk-ratings for 71 countries. Within this sample, 741 of the ratings were for emerging-market countries. For each of these countries, we collected information on the risk-ratings they received measured on a 17-point (0–16) scale. We also collected information on the agencies that rated these sovereigns, including sovereign characteristics normally used by the agencies to make their assessments.

Objective risk-rating model estimation

As a first step in our examination of the agencies' response to economic and financial crises, we developed a model to reflect the underlying objective risk-ratings of sovereigns over the 1987–98 period. Recent empirical studies using single-year cross-sectional data (Cantor and Packer, 1996) and multiple-year panel-data (McNamara and Vaaler, 2000) indicated that a parsimonious regression model utilizing only seven or eight sovereign factors could explain substantial variation in sovereign risk-ratings. Our objective model of sovereign risk-ratings utilizes eight sovereign factors identified in this prior research. Unless otherwise noted, measures for these factors over the 1987–98 period were taken from the World Development Indicators (World Bank, 1999). They included:

- *Per capita income.* Variable measuring per capita GNP in thousands of constant US dollars.
- *GDP growth.* Variable measuring average annual real GDP growth rate over the previous three years.
- *Inflation.* Variable measuring average annual consumer price inflation over the previous three years.
- *Fiscal balance.* Variable measuring average annual overall budget balance relative to GDP for the previous three years.
- *External balance.* Variable measuring average current accounts balance relative to GDP for the previous three years.
- *External debt.* Variable measuring the present value of debt relative to exports of goods and services for the current year.
- *Default history.* 0–1 indicator variable indicating if the sovereign has defaulted on foreign currency debt in the last 25 years (1 if default; 0 if no default). This variable was taken from Standard and Poor's Ratings Services' sovereign credit default report (Standard and Poor's Ratings Services, 1999).
- *Stage of economic development.* 0–1 indicator variable indicating if the country was identified as non-industrialized according to the International Monetary Fund (1 if non-industrialized; 0 if industrialized).

We use ordinal logistic regression to estimate objective sovereign risk-ratings since the ratings reflect a 17–level ordinal scale (Zavoina and McElvey, 1975; Maddala, 1983; Ederington, 1985). Results from the estimation of sovereign risk-ratings using 17-level ordered logistic regression are given in table 10.4. For our 17-level ordered logistic model estimation, we randomly selected 19 observations (the total number of ratings for a "B" (2) risk rating) from each of the 17 risk-rating levels, for a total of 323 observations. We used an equal number of observations in the model estimation to ensure that the model was not biased toward predicting the most common risk-rating levels (McNamara and Bromiley, 1997). The model provides a good overall fit ($\chi^2 = 436.79$, $p < .01$), with six of the eight coefficients exhibiting the expected sign and significance.[4]

Table 10.4   Objective model results: relationship between foreign currency sovereign risk-ratings and fundamental sovereign risk factors, 1987–98

Dependent variable: foreign currency sovereign risk-rating	Ordered logistic regression results	
Independent variables	*Parameter estimate*	*Standard error*
GNP per capita	2.13[a]	0.24
GDP growth rate	0.31[c]	0.17
Inflation rate	0.10	0.10
Fiscal balance	0.25[b]	0.12
External balance	−0.06	0.16
External debt	0.63[a]	0.18
Default history	0.89[a]	0.12
Stage of economic development	1.01[a]	0.22
χ^2	436.79[a]	

$N = 323$, [a] $p < .01$, [b] $p < .05$, [c] $p < .10$

Risk-rating deviation model estimation

To test our hypotheses concerning the crisis response of the agencies, we then constructed a deviation measure using the objective risk-rating model results reported above. We defined our central dependent variable, the agency's deviation from objective risk assessment, as the overall change in risk assessment compared to the objective risk-rating model's assessment over the crisis period (1997–8). Using the objective risk-rating model, we first estimated each agency's sovereign risk-ratings for emerging-market sovereigns it rated on December 31, 1996 and December 31, 1998. This period begins just before the initial outbreak of crisis in South-east Asia in mid-1997 and subsequent spread to other Asian, European and Latin American countries during the rest of 1997 and 1998. We then compared these estimated risk ratings to the actual risk ratings published by the agencies during the same period. The difference between actual and estimated risk ratings represented the extent of deviation exhibited by an agency at the beginning and end of this crisis period. We then calculated the change in deviation over this period by calculating the difference between the beginning-period and ending-period deviation measures. For example, the objective risk-rating model assesses Moody's sovereign risk rating for Malaysia at the close of both 1996 and 1998 as an "A" (11). Yet, the actual Moody's risk rating for Malaysia at the close of 1996 was an "A+" (12). At the close of 1998 it was a "BBB-" (7). Accordingly, we would measure Moody's deviation in response to crisis for Malaysia as a −5, that is, the difference between 12–11 = +1 in 1996 and 7–11 = −4 in 1998. It appears that Moody's had a rather substantial crisis response for Malaysia, becoming much more pessimistic about its credit worthiness relative to an objective evaluation of the risk of this particular sovereign.

We used this deviation measure to test all six hypotheses. We used a t-test for

Hypothesis 1, testing whether agency risk-rating deviations from objective risk assessment at the end of the period (December 31, 1998) were significantly negative compared to just prior to the crisis period (December 31, 1996). Hypotheses 2 through 4 were tested using the 17-level ordered logistic regression model. The dependent variable for this model was the deviation measure. The following terms related to the agencies and to the geographic regions of their work over the crisis period served as the independent variables.[5]

- *Agency insurgency.* 0–1 indicator variable indicating if the agency is a new entrant to the industry (1 if insurgents Duff, Thomson or Fitch IBCA; 0 if incumbent Moody's or S&P).
- *Agency regional specialization.* Variable ranging from 0 and 1. It measures the proportion of all sovereign risk ratings by an agency in a particular year coming from one of five geographic regions: Western Europe/North America, Latin America, Central/Eastern Europe, Africa/Middle East, and Asia.
- *Sovereign market structure.* Variable ranging from 1 to 5. It measures the total number of agencies publishing risk-ratings for the sovereign in a given year, and provides a *prima facie* indication of structural factors shaping market conduct and performance (Viscusi et al., 1995; McNamara and Vaaler, 2000).

We also created indicator variables for each of the five geographic regions which contained emerging markets, and include four of them in the analysis to control for regional specific factors that may have influenced the agencies' response to the crisis (Oxelheim and Wihlborg, 1987; Ferri et al., 1999). We exclude the indicator variable for the Latin American region from the analysis to avoid perfect collinearity.

Results

Results from our tests of the six hypotheses are summarized in table 10.5 and then described in greater detail below. To test Hypothesis 1, we asked whether the risk-ratings for all emerging-market sovereigns more negatively deviated from objective risk assessments at the end of the period (December 31, 1998) compared to deviations from objective risk assessments made just prior to the onset of crisis (December 31, 1996). Comparison of these measures indicated support for Hypothesis 1. We found that there was a significantly greater negative deviation from objective risk assessments of emerging-market sovereigns at the end of the crisis period compared to the beginning of it ($t = 3.54$, $p < .01$). On average, emerging-market sovereign risk-ratings in 1998 were nearly two (1.95) levels lower than the objective risk assessment model indicated.

Hypotheses 2 through 4 were tested with the ordered logistic regression model described immediately above. Statistical results are presented in table 10.6. Overall, the model provided significant explanatory value ($\chi^2 = 50.60$, $p < 01$). Not surprisingly, we found the agencies' overall greater negative deviation from objective risk assessments varied across different geographic regions, with the most substantial regional effect in Asia where the crisis began. Location in Asia or Central/Eastern Europe

Table 10.5 Summary table of results

Hypothesis number	Hypothesis description	Research basis	Skewing effects	Results from test
H1	industry-wide shock	threat rigidity and uncertainty avoidance	all agencies	support ($p < .01$)
H2a	entry order	first-mover advantage	insurgent agencies (−)	no support
H2b	entry order	institutional and behavioral theories	insurgent agencies (+)	support ($p < .05$)
H3a	regional specialization	learning and resource dependency	regional focus (+)	no support
H3b	regional specialization	threat rigidity	regional focus (−)	support ($p < .05$)
H4	market strcture	IO economics and competitive dynamics	greater rivalry (+)	no support

is associated with more significant negative deviation than in Latin America, the omitted region (parameter estimate = −2.49 for Asia and −1.44 for Central/Eastern Europe, $p < 01$).

Hypotheses 2a and 2b predicted a statistical link between industry positioning as an incumbent or insurgent agency and the negative deviation from objective risk assessments exhibited by an agency. Hypothesis 2a argued that resource and institutional problems afflicting insurgent agencies would compel them to react more excessively and negatively than incumbent agencies during the crisis. Hypothesis 2b countered

Table 10.6 Risk-rating bias model results: relationship between deviation from objective risk assessment and positioning factors among agencies

Dependent variable: deviation in sovereign risk-ratings from objective risk assessment, 12/96–12/98	Ordered logistic regression results	
Independent variables	*Parameter estimate*	*Standard error*
Insurgent agency indicator	0.83[b]	0.34
Regional specialization	−0.96[b]	0.47
Market structure	−0.23	0.17
Asian sovereign indicator	−2.49[a]	0.49
Central/Eastern European sovereign indicator	−1.44[a]	0.47
Africa/Middle Eastern sovereign indicator	0.32	0.53
Western Europe/North American sovereign indicator	0.43	1.17
χ^2	50.60[a]	

N = 130, [a] $p < .01$, [b] $p < .05$, [c] $p < .10$

that previous over-optimism by incumbent agencies would prompt them to be more excessive and negative in their response than insurgents. Consistent with Hypothesis 2b, we found evidence that insurgency was associated with the probability of less negative deviation from objective risk assessments compared to incumbent agencies, even after controlling for other sovereign conditions. The indicator for agency insurgents was positive (0.83) and significant ($p < .05$). In practical terms, this result implies that incumbent agency risk-ratings exhibited negative deviations from objective models that on average, were nearly one rating level greater (.95) than negative deviations exhibited by similarly situated insurgent agencies. For example, take Moody's and Thompson's ratings for Thailand. Moody's, an incumbent agency, provided a A2 (A) rating that was one level higher than an insurgent firm, Thompson, (A−) at the end of 1996. In response to the crisis, Moody's dropped their rating five notches to Ba1 (BB+) while Thompson dropped their rating only three notches, down to BBB−.

Hypotheses 3a and 3b linked deviation from objectivity in risk assessment to the degree an agency specialized in sovereigns from a given geographic region during the same period. Hypothesis 3a predicted that regional specialization would be linked to less substantial deviation from objective risk assessments during the crisis period; Hypothesis 3b made the opposite prediction. We found that regional specialization was associated with the probability of greater negative deviation from objective risk assessments during the crisis period (-0.96, $p < .05$). In practical terms, an agency with, say, 40 percent of its ratings from one geographic region would have deviated more negatively from objective risk assessments by approximately 1.6 rating notches for sovereigns from that region compared to an agency with only 10 percent of its ratings from that same region. For example, IBCA specialized in European sovereigns, providing 26 percent of their ratings to the Eastern European market. In contrast, Moody's did not focus on the Eastern European market, which accounted for only 13 percent of their ratings. During the crisis, IBCA dropped their rating six notches from BB+ to C while Moody's lowered their rating four notches, from Ba2 (BB) to B3 (B−). Consequently, Moody's had a lower rating at the beginning of the crisis but a higher rating at the end of the crisis than the more regionally-focused IBCA.

Finally, Hypothesis 4 predicted that the degree of rivalry in a market would be associated with a more muted response (change in bias) in the risk-ratings for that sovereign during the crisis period. The sign on this coefficient estimate is negative (-0.23), contrary to Hypothesis 4, but is not statistically significant. This result indicates that rivalry among the agencies in any one particular sovereign market has no statistically significant impact on deviations from objective risk assessment.

Conclusion

Central findings of the study

The questions we addressed in this study were whether and how competition and crisis relate to expert organization risk assessment. Our main responses are that crises appear to engender an over-reaction on the part of the experts, and that certain competitive factors appear to have a significant and substantial impact on these agency over-reactions. Overall, the emerging-market risk ratings published during the crisis period appeared to deviate negatively and, it appears, unwarrantedly from an objective assessment approach. These findings are consistent with Hypothesis 1, which predicted that organizations would excessively respond during a crisis period due to ambiguity/uncertainty avoidance and threat rigidity pressures. The results also support the view that the positioning as an industry incumbent or insurgent is important as is the geographic focus of an expert's business when and where crises strike. This reaction to the crisis may have been a consequence of prior complacency or over-optimism in the risk assessments of incumbent and geographically focused agencies. Individual national market structure and rivalry, however, had no statistically significant impact on the risk assessments made by agencies during crisis periods. If positioning is largely shaped by "time" (incumbency versus insurgency), "place" (regional specialization versus global scope) and "manner" (monopoly versus competitive market structure) of an expert organization, then our study indicates that time and place but not manner matter for understanding deviations from objective decision-making.

Our results do not negate the importance of understanding intrinsic, objective characteristics associated with a strategic decision. In our empirical context, this implies that a thorough understanding of the countries and individual borrowers involved in a credit transaction is still central to any agency assessment. Recall the significance of terms in our objective risk-rating model, which served as the basis for measuring deviations and assessing their determinants. Certainly economic, financial and political factors commonly analyzed in the foreign investment risk literature remain important. But our results suggest that accounting for these sovereign characteristics alone may ignore important additional information about the nature of risk assessment by expert organizations, particularly in crisis circumstances such as during the two-year period we examined. Agencies rendering risk assessments for emerging-market investment are not merely detached experts providing objective analyses. Their opinions may also be the result of competitive positioning within the industry as well as the chance result of assessing sovereigns within certain regions. Researchers will, therefore, benefit from accounting for these strategic factors in foreign investment risk assessment both during and between crisis periods.

The results from this study also do not limit discussion of positioning to agencies alone. Recall that we found insurgency, on its own, to be associated with less dramatic response during the crisis period. Newcomers to the sovereigns industry seemed to be less vulnerable to excessive swings in their risk ratings over the crisis period. One explanation for this followed from an institutional theory perspective on positioning. As they expand from their regional bases and learn more about the sovereign industry generally, insurgent agencies may try to compensate for competitive disadvantages against incumbents by building up legitimacy with other salient stakeholders such as regulators, investment banks, and other players in the industry. In this case, the drive to build legitimacy becomes associated with less volatility in risk ratings during crisis compared to incumbents. This invites further investigations into institutional switching costs (Klemperer, 1987) associated with downgrading more radically, or other institutional anchoring effects (Tversky and Kahneman, 1974) that may slow a sovereign's risk-rating descent. In any case, the nature of positioning within this industry requires a broader view of strategic players. Research in foreign-investment risk assessment will benefit from assessment of not only sovereign and agency characteristics as analyzed in this study, but from assessment of other industry stakeholders and the coercive pressures they may be able to bring to bear. As we said at the outset of this chapter, strategy in an entrepreneurial millennium will almost surely require greater inter-organizational cooperation and networking. Such industry stakeholders may therefore also demand a say in the way experts approach the risk assessment process and render advice in strategic decision-making contexts.

We think it interesting that certain agencies that firms might associate with more sober risk assessment and greater legitimacy during crisis actually exhibit greater over-reaction during crisis. Both incumbent agencies and those agencies specializing in sovereigns from certain geographic regions displayed the most substantial negative response during the crisis period. This suggests that expert organizations to which top managers would more likely turn during periods of crisis may, in fact, be *less* capable of displaying the dispassionate, objective perspectives that the top managers value most and vitally need. Again, this result informs our original view of strategic decision-making in an entrepreneurial millennium. In this world, incumbency does not necessarily provide an advantage to agencies when crisis unfolds and stakeholders affected by it look to the agencies of objective advice. By contrast, insurgent agencies less wed to past rating approaches (and the inertia it may generate) exhibit closer adherence to objective models of assessment during crisis times. Perhaps there is a similar liability associated with incumbency in other industries experiencing dramatic growth and change, competitive entry, and environmental turbulence (e.g., Henderson, 1993).

Implications for strategy research and practice

The value in expanding exploration of expert reactions to environmental crises and competitive positioning is a central research implication we draw from this study. Our findings provide a strong indication that researchers in strategy and organizational theory can and should play a more prominent role in investigating expert organization risk assessment factors and processes, which until recently have been examined almost exclusively by financial economists and public policy researchers. We have, perhaps, underplayed or ignored the competitive aspects of firms also providing quasi-governmental services. True, agencies play a key role in the broader public regulation of global capital markets. In this study, we note that they act as quasi-public regulators limiting access to US institutional investors. More recently, the same agencies have been accorded status to investigate and assess for international regulatory purposes, the adequacy of commercial bank capital in most countries (Crouhy et al., 2001). Yet, these are *private* firms in competition with each other for fees, market share and, ultimately, profits for their owners. It is crucial, therefore, that we bring research and practice from strategy and related fields to understand this increasingly important set of players crossing private and public sectors in global finance and business.

Within the industry setting studied, perhaps the main accomplishment of this study is to demonstrate the research benefits of revising issues about foreign investment risk-assessment into issues about foreign investment risk assessors and their environment. We uncover preliminary evidence that agencies stake out different positions regarding the riskiness of emerging-market countries and their sovereigns during periods of crisis. Those distinctive positions follow not only from honest differences in interpreting information about sovereign characteristics, but also from competitive positions as industry incumbent or insurgent, and as a regional specialist or global player within the industry. Perhaps such geographic positioning and related bias are an inevitable part of doing business as an agency. If so, then studies like ours lay bare the direction and extent of such bias and thereby warn consuming firms, investors, and others interested in the prudent use of experts for emerging-market investment decisions.

Similar results may follow when researchers examine risk assessments in other contexts where the decision-makers involved are less effusive than our expert agencies regarding the comprehensiveness and objectivity of their advice. Consider, for example, the pronounced negative reaction of many investment advisers to turbulence in high technology, Internet-related industries during the year 2000. Their arguably overly-reactive response to announcements of several business failures and lower growth prospects for many other businesses in 2000 may have followed from earlier over-confidence, portfolio over-commitment, and complacency about the investment fundamentals of high-technology, Internet-related firms. Our study suggests how and why experts might be prone to excessive positive and negative swings with industries undergoing sudden growth and change.

We think our study has important prescriptive implications for managers active in emerging-market countries. For managers involved in foreign investment risk-assessment, the study counsels caution about the extent to which they may rely on any one risk-assessment by expert organizations. The agencies are assessing the sovereign, competing with each other for business, and perhaps, "retaliating" against individual sovereign borrowers or whole regions for having recently undermined their credibility with industry stakeholders through the unexpected revelation of financial weakness and instability. In this context of multiple agendas, it behooves managers to refrain from excessive reliance on any single agency assessment and poll several on sovereign risks, particular during crisis. Indeed, agency risk ratings may be *least* reliable during crises; so, where time and resources permit, managers would also be advised to do their own risk assessments for comparison with "expert" agencies. In an emerging period of new business opportunities and challenges, firms should not delegate mindlessly to one expert or many, key investment and lending decisions.

Additionally, the results suggest that the ability of countries and corporate borrowers to gain access to plentiful and affordable financing needed to exploit the opportunities available in this entrepreneurial millennium may be subject to unwarranted volatility. The inability of these expert organizations to effectively respond to heightened volatility may cause increasing problems as the flow of financing to nascent economies may be significantly affected by vacillating – some might think even manic – optimism and pessimism from the rating agencies. Such vacillation may provide a significant advantage for large multinationals based in developed economies versus smaller firms based in emerging economies, especially during periods of economic turbulence. The large multinationals may have preferential access to financing since they are potentially able to receive higher credit ratings than firms based in emerging market countries. The sovereign credit ceilings under which both compete are likely to be higher and more stable for emerged versus emerging-market countries. Appreciating this difference may also provide a secondary advantage to large multinationals if they "keep a level head" during periods of crisis. Indeed, the reward may be opportunities to acquire cash-starved businesses with good "fundamentals" except for their unfortunate location in an emerging market country. In an entrepreneurial millenium, bias in decision-making by agencies means that a firm's national sovereignty may shape the firm's competitive destiny, particularly in turbulent times.

Acknowledgements

We thank Phil Bromiley, Frank Linden, Carnes Lord, Joel Trachtman and Phil Uhlmann for research assistance and/or helpful comments on earlier drafts of this chapter.

Notes

1 The definition of an "emerging-market" country varies across commentators. Most definitions (e.g., IFC 1999) refer to industrializing countries with high rates of economic growth, per-capita incomes and domestic stock-market capitalization. Following previous research on risk-rating determinants for emerging-market countries (McNamara and Vaaler, 2000; Trevino and Thomas, 2000), we define the term broadly to include any country *not* classified by the IMF as industrialized. A list of the countries included in our study is provided in Table 10.2.
2 Twelve current US federal regulations promulgated between 1931 and 1994 require credit ratings by NRSROs. They are listed in Cantor and Packer (1994: 6) and Sinclair (1995: 126–8).
3 Moody's and S&P were given NRSRO designation in 1975. Duff received NRSROs. status in 1982. IBCA obtained NRSRO status in 1990 and Thomson followed in 1991. Thomson began publishing sovereign ratings for emerging-market countries in 1991. Duff and IBCA began in 1993. Another NRSRO agency, Fitch Investor Services ("Fitch") was given NRSRO status in 1975 and began publishing sovereign risk-ratings in 1994. Fitch was merged into IBCA in December 1997 leaving only five NRSROs in operation at the end of the period we studied. More recently, Fitch IBCA announced a merger with Duff in March 2000. For more on the history of credit agency NRSRO designation, see Cantor and Packer (1994), Sinclair (1995: 101–6) and Linden (1997).
4 As an additional check on the precision of this objective model, we compared the model's risk assessment with the actual risk assessment provided by the agencies for all observations not used in the estimation of the objective model. Of the 1,276 observations used in this test, the model predicted the same risk-rating for 322 observations (25 percent) The model assessed the sovereign risk within one rating level of the agency's actual rating for more than 55 percent of the observations (709 observations). These results compare extremely well to random risk-rating rating assignment, which would match the rating agencies' assessment exactly less than 6 percent of time and would be within one risk level less than 17 percent of the time. We also tested the objective model's ability to identify bias in agency risk assessments. To do this test, we examined instances of disagreement between objective and actual risk-ratings, and then saw how these disagreements resolved themselves over time. In instances of such disagreement, we re-examined the ratings two years later to see whether the actual risk-rating had moved toward or away from the objective model's prediction. In 232 instances of such disagreement, actual risk ratings two years

later moved toward the objective model's prediction 154 times (66 percent) while the risk ratings moved away from the model's prediction only 78 times (34 percent). A binomial test of the likelihood that this movement toward the objective model was a random occurrence could be rejected at the 1 percent level ($p < .01$). These analyses suggest that we identified a precise and parsimonious objective model of sovereign risk assessment that also facilitates the identification of bias by the agencies.

5   We also examined Hypotheses 2 through 4 using ordinary least squares regression and found the results consistent with those from the 17-level ordered logistic regression analysis reported in this chapter. Results from this additional analysis are available from the authors upon request.

References

Argote, L. 1999: *Organizational Learning*. Boston: Kluwer Academic Publishers.

Bourgeois, L. 1985: Strategic goals, perceived uncertainty, and economic performance in volatile environments. *Academy of Management Journal*, 28, 548–73.

Cantor, R. and Packer, F. 1994: Sovereign credit ratings. *Federal Reserve Bank of New York Quarterly Review*, Summer–Fall Volume, 1–26.

Cantor, R. and Packer, F. 1996: Determinants and impacts of sovereign credit ratings. *Federal Reserve Bank of New York Economic Policy Review*. October, 37–53.

Chen, M. 1996: Competitor analysis and interfirm rivalry: toward a theoretical integration. *Academy of Management Review*, 21, 100–34.

Cosset, J. and Suret, J. 1995: Political risk and the benefits of international portfolio diversification. *Journal of International Business*, 26, 301–18.

Crouhy, M., Galai, D., and Mark, R. 2001: The new capital adequacy framework and the need for consistent risk measures for financial institutions. In L. Jacque, and P. Vaaler (eds), *Financial Innovations and the Welfare of Nations*. Norwell, MA: Kluwer Academic Publishers, 61–86.

Curley, S., Yates, J., and Abrams, R., 1986: Psychological sources of ambiguity avoidance. *Organizational Behavior and Human Decision Processes*, 38: 230–56.

Cyert, R. and March, J. 1963: *A Behavioral Theory of the Firm*. Englewood Cliffs, NJ: Prentice-Hall.

D'Aveni, R. 1994: *Hypercompetition*. New York: The Free Press.

Davidson, W. 1980: The location of foreign direct investment activity: country characteristics and experience effects, *Journal of International Business Studies*, 11, Fall, 9–22.

Deephouse, D. 1996: Does isomorphism legitimate? *Academy of Management Journal*, 39. 1024–39.

Ederington, L. 1985: Why split ratings occur. *Financial Management*, 15, 37–47.

Eisenhardt, K. 1989: Making fast strategic decisions in high velocity environments. *Academy of Management Journal*, 31, 543–76.

Eisenhardt, K. and Martin, J. 2000: Dynamic capabilities: what are they? *Strategic Management Journal*, 21, 1105–21.

Ellsberg, D. 1961: Risk, ambiguity and the savage axioms. *Quarterly Journal of Economics*, 75, 643–69.

Ferri, G., Liu, L., and Stiglitz, J. 1999: The procyclical role of rating agencies: evidence from the East Asian Crisis. *Economic Notes*, 28, 335–55.

Fershtman, C. and Muller, E. 1986: Capital investments and price agreements in semi-collusive markets. *Rand Journal of Economics*, 17, 214–26.

Fiol, M. and Lyles, M. 1985: Organizational learning. *Academy of Management Review*, 10, 803–13.

FitchIBCA. 1998: After Asia: some lessons of the crisis. *FitchIBCA Sovereign Comment,* January, 1–20.

Greve, H. and Taylor, A. 2000: Innovations as catalysts for organizational change: shifts in organizational cognition and search. *Administrative Science Quarterly,* 45, 54–83.

Gulati, R., Nohria, N., and Zaheer, A. 2000: Strategic networks. *Strategic Management Journal,* 21, 203–15.

Hambrick, D. and Mason, P. 1984: Upper echelons: The organization as a reflection of its top managers. *Academy of Management Review,* 9, 193–206.

Hashmi, M. and Guvenli, T. 1992: Importance of political risk-assessment function in US multinational corporations. *Global Finance Journal,* 3, 137–44.

Henderson, R. 1993: Underinvestment and incompetence as response to radical innovation: evidence from the photolithographic alignment equipment industry. *Rand Journal of Economics,* 24, 248–70.

IFC. 1999: *Emerging Stock Markets Factbook 1999.* Washington, DC: International Finance Corporation (World Bank).

IMF 1998: *World Economic Outlook,* May.

James, C. 1992: Relationship-specific assets and the pricing of underwriter services. *Journal of Finance,* 48, 1865–85.

Johnson, R., Srinivasan, V., and Bolster, P. 1990: Sovereign debt ratings: a judgmental model based on the analytic hierarchy process. *Journal of International Business Studies,* 21, 95–117.

Karacadag, C. and Samuels, B. 1999: In search of the market failure in the asian crisis. *The Fletcher Forum of World Affairs,* 23, 131–44.

Keats, B. and Hitt, M. 1988: A causal model of linkages among environmental dimensions. *Academy of Management Journal,* 31, 570–608.

Kindleberger, C. 1978: *Manias, Panics and Crashes,* New York: Basic Books.

Klemperer, P. 1987: The competitiveness of markets with switching costs. *Rand Journal of Economics,* 18, 138–50.

Lee, S. 1993: Relative importance of political instability and economic variables on perceived country creditworthiness. *Journal of International Business Studies,* 24, 801–12.

Lieberman, M. and Montgomery, D. 1988: First mover advantages. *Strategic Management Journal,* 9, 41–58.

Linden, F. 1997: The rater matters: understanding the determinants of sovereign risk-ratings and the idiosyncrasies of sovereign risk-rating agencies. Unpublished masters thesis. Medford, MA: Fletcher School of Law and Diplomacy, Tufts University.

Lyles, M. 1995: The impact of organizational learning on joint venture formations. *International Business Review,* 3, 459–67.

Lyles, M. and Schwenk, C. 1992: Top management, strategy and organizational knowledge structures. *Journal of Management Studies,* 29, 155–74.

Maddala, G. 1983: *Limited Dependent Variables and Qualitative Variables in Econometrics.* Cambridge: Cambridge University Press.

Mahajan, A. 1990: Pricing expropriation risk. *Financial Management,* 19, 77–86.

March, J. and Olsen, J. 1976: *Ambiguity and choice in organizations.* Bergen: Universitetesforlaget.

McEvily, S., Das, S., and McCabe, K. 2000: Avoiding competence substitution through knowledge sharing. *Academy of Management Review,* 25, 294–311.

McNamara, G. and Bromiley, P. 1997: Decision making in an organizational setting: cognitive and organizational influences on risk assessment in commercial lending. *Academy of Management Journal,* 40, 1063–88.

McNamara, G. and Vaaler, P. 2000: Competitive positioning and rivalry in emerging market risk assessment. *Journal of International Business Studies,* 31, 337–47.

Meyer, A. 1982: Adapting to environmental jolts. *Administrative Science Quarterly*, 27, 515–38.

Mitchell, W. 1989: Whether and when: probability and timing of incumbents' entry into emerging industrial subfields. *Administrative Science Quarterly*, 34, 208–30.

Mitchell, W. 1991: Dual clocks: entry order influences on incumbent and newcomer market share and survival when specialized assets retain their value. *Strategic Management Journal*, 12, 85–100.

Moody's Investors Service 1999: Moody's Sovereign Ratings: A Ratings Guide. *Global Credit Research (Special Comment)*, March, New York.

Nelson, R. and Winter, S. 1982: *An Evolutionary Theory of Economic Change*. New York: Belknap Press.

OECD 1998: Emerging markets. *Financial Market Trends*, 69, 53–8. Paris: Organization for Economic Cooperation and Development.

Oxelheim, L. and Wihlborg, C. 1987: *Macroeconomic Uncertainty: International Risks and Opportunities for the Corporation*, New York: John Wiley and Sons.

Ozler, S. 1991: Evolution of credit terms: an empirical examination of commercial bank lending to developing countries. *Journal of Development Economics*, 38, 79–87.

Pfeffer, J. and Salancik, G. 1978: *The External Control of Organizations*, New York: Harper and Row.

Phillips-Patrick, F. 1989: The effect of asset ownership structure on political risk: evidence from Mitterand's election in France. *Journal of Banking and Finance*, 13, 651–71.

Porter, M. 1980: *Competitive Strategy*. New York: Free Press.

Radelet, S. and Sachs, J. 1998: The East Asian financial crisis: diagnosis, remedies and prospects. *Brookings Papers on Economic Activitiy*, 1, 1–74.

Rumelt, R. 1987: Theory, strategy and entrepreneurship. In D. Teece (ed.), *Strategy and Organization for Industrial Innovation and Renewal*. Cambridge, MA: Ballinger, 137–58.

Sambharya, R. 1996: Foreign experience of top management teams and international diversification strategies of US multinational corporations. *Strategic Management Journal*, 17, 739–46.

Saini, K. and Bates, P. 1984: Statistical Techniques for Determining Debt-Servicing Capacity for Developing Countries: Analytical Review of the Literature and Further Empirical Results. Research Paper No. 7818. New York: Federal Reserve Bank of New York.

Salacuse, J. 1994: *The Art of Advice: How to Give it and How to Take it*. New York: Times Books.

Scherer, F. 1980: *Industrial Market Structure and Economic Performance* (2nd edn). Chicago: Rand McNally.

Schwenk, C. 1984: Cognitive simplification processes in strategic decision making. *Strategic Management Journal*, 5, 111–28.

SEC. 1994: Nationally Recognized Statistical Rating Organizations. US Securities and Exchange Commission Release No. 33–7085, August 31, Washington, DC: US Securities and Exchange Commission.

Sinclair, T. 1995: Guarding the gates of capital: credit rating processes and the global political economy. Unpublished doctoral thesis. North York, Ontario, Canada: York University.

Standard and Poor's Ratings Services. 1997: Sovereign credit ratings: a primer. *Credit Week*, April 16.

Standard and Poor's Ratings Services. 1999: Sovereign defaults: hiatus in 2000? *Credit Week*, December 22.

Staw, B., Sandelands, L., and Dutton, J. 1981: Threat-rigidity effects in organizational behavior: A multilevel analysis. *Administrative Science Quarterly*. 26, 501–24.

Torres, G. and Zeiter, J. 1998: Rating securitizations above the sovereign ceiling. *FitchIBCA*, December 29.

Trevino, L. and Thomas, S. 2000: Systemic Differences in the Determinants of Foreign Currency Sovereign Ratings by Rating Agency. Discussion Papers in Accounting and Management Science, No. 00–153, University of Southampton.

Tushman, M. and Anderson, P. 1986: Technological discontinuities and organizational environments. *Administrative Science Quarterly*, 31, 439–65.

Tversky, A. and Kahneman, D. 1974: The framing of decisions and the psychology of choice. *Science*, 185, 1124–31.

Viscusi, W., Vernon, J., and Harrington, J. 1995: *Economics of Regulation and Antitrust*. Cambridge, MA: MIT Press.

Wiersema, M. and Bantel, K. 1992: Top management team demography and corporate strategic change. *Academy of Management Journal*, 35, 91–121.

World Bank. 1999: *World Development Indicators, 1997*. Washington, DC: World Bank.

Zaheer, A. and Zaheer, S. 1997: Catching the wave: alertness, responsiveness and market influence in global electronic networks, *Management Science*, 43, 1493–509.

Zavoina, R. and McElvey, W. 1975: A statistical model for the analysis of ordinal level dependent variables. *Journal of Mathematical Sociology*. Summer, 103–20.

Zissu, A. and Stone, C. 2001: Engineering a way around the sovereign ceiling: securities backed by future export receivables. In L. Jacque, and P. Vaaler, (eds), *Financial Innovations and the Welfare of Nations*. Norwell, MA: Kluwer Academic Publishers, 267–82.

CHAPTER ELEVEN

Strategic Decision-Making in High Velocity Environments: A Theory Revisited and a Test

Kevin Clark and Chris Collins

Introduction

A decade ago, Eisenhardt (1989) proposed a model of strategic decision-making speed for firms facing high-velocity environments. This theory, while important at the time, has become even more relevant to the strategy-making bodies of firms in the entrepreneurial millennium. The model differed in important ways from much of the existing literature on decision-making speed (Frederickson and Mitchell, 1984; Janis, 1982; Mintzberg, et al., 1976; Nutt, 1976). Eisenhardt's ideas were based on a series of inductive case studies of eight firms competing in the fast-paced micro-chip industry. As such, it was an important theory-building effort in a central area of strategy process, strategic decision-making. To date, however, there have been no attempts to comprehensively test the model with a larger sample of firms.

The changes the economy is experiencing in this new millennium are astounding. In short, the hyper-competitive forces faced a decade ago by micro-chip makers have become pervasive throughout many of our top industries (D'Aveni, 1994; Grimm and Smith, 1997). Thus, the prescriptions of Eisenhardt's model would appear to be critical for today's firms as they seek entrepreneurial approaches to gaining competitive advantage. Top management teams (TMTs) capable of making rapid decisions can enable their firms to be the entrepreneurial first movers in their respective segments. To our knowledge, however, there has been only one attempt to replicate Eisenhardt's preliminary findings. Judge and Miller (1991) tested a portion of the model on a small sample (n = 32) of firms in three industries. The research tested two of the five "tactics" mentioned by Eisenhardt, did not incorporate the intervening processes, and produced mixed results. Thus, there have been no successful attempts to test the entire model on a large cross-section of firms. This is due in part to the difficulty researchers face in gaining access to a large sample of top executives, especially those facing fast-paced environments. This research tests Eisenhardt's model on a sample of 66 high technology firms competing in the IT, telecommunications, and engineering services industries.

Research on Strategic Decision-Making

Interest in top management teams has developed out of a belief on the part of researchers that the composition and functioning of this "dominant coalition" do a better job of describing organizational outcomes than does the study of the CEO alone (Cyert and March, 1963; Mintzberg, 1973; Kotter, 1982). Much of this literature has focused attention on the role the TMT plays in formulating organizational strategy through the decision process (Child, 1972). The strategic decisions top executives make have important impacts on organizational outcomes such as financial returns, sales growth, and survival (Finkelstein and Hambrick, 1996).

Much of the early work on TMT strategic decision-making focused on the ability of the group to reach agreement on important issues (e.g., consensus), and the level of comprehensiveness demonstrated in their decision process (Bourgeois, 1980, 1985; Fredrickson and Mitchell, 1984; Fredrickson and Iaquinto, 1989). A summary of this literature is found in Appendix A. The general results of these streams of literature were that consensus speeds issue resolution, but perhaps at a cost to quality (e.g., comprehensiveness), and that comprehensiveness is not feasible in all environments. These results were generally in line with the long-standing debate in the decision-making literature concerning the rationality of decision processes. Beginning with March and Simon (1958), decision theorists began to realize that actual decision processes deviated considerably from the rational ideal. Decision-makers were seen as cognitively limited, having conflicting goals, and proceeding through the decision process in a much less orderly fashion than rational models would suggest. As a result of "bounded rationality" and time and resource pressures, decision-makers often settled or "satisficed' on the first solution that addressed the problem rather than continuing to search for the optimal solution. Adding to the messiness of real decision processes was the acknowledgment that multiple and conflicting goals (and sometimes no goals at all) motivated decision-makers. Thus, three major schools of thought on decision-making emerged: (1) the rational school; (2) the incremental or boundedly rational school; and (3) the political school. Table 11.1 summarizes the major differences of these three schools of decision theory.

Eisenhardt (1989) found that actual decision processes in high technology TMTs facing turbulent environments deviated from the rational ideal, but not to the extent incrementalists would suggest. In addition, Eisenhardt and Bourgeois (1988) found that political processes were present in these TMTs, particularly in the slow TMTs. This was because fast TMTs realized the inefficiency of politics and employed tactics to minimize the use of politics in their teams. Further, she found that certain TMTs were able to inject a considerable level of rationality into their decision processes with no penalty in decision speed. Thus, Eisenhardt observed actual decision processes in TMTs of high technology organizations to be a combination of the three theoretical perspectives on decision-making. Rather than a purely incremental approach, as empirical

Table 11.1   Three schools of decision theory

Characteristic	Rational	Incremental	Political
Search process	Maximizing	Limited	Haphazard
Selection of solution	Maximizing	Satisficing	Based on Power and Influence
Managers are:	Efficient processors	Cognitively limited	Non-rational, self-interested
Decision process unfolds:	Sequentially	Sequentially	Randomly, iteratively
Information is:	Available	Costly	Controlled by the powerful
Decision pace is:	Slow	Fast	Varies, but typically slow
Process suitable for:	Stable environment	Turbulent environment	Ambiguous environment

research would suggest, fast TMTs incorporated aspects of rationality into their process while attempting to minimize the propensity for political behavior at these levels of the organization. Finally, based on a small sample of inductive case studies, she developed a model of fast decision-making consisting of five decision "tactics" and three mediating processes that fast TMTs used to increase both the comprehensiveness and the pace of their strategic decision process.

Three studies have built on Eisenhardt's ideas during the ten years since the model was introduced. Judge and Miller (1991) confirmed a portion of the model and demonstrated a link between fast strategic decision-making and firm performance in turbulent industries. Wally and Baum (1994) developed a model of decision pace based loosely on the ideas of Eisenhardt and tested on a sample of 151 firms in various industries. Finally, Hambrick et al. (1996) developed and tested a model of competitive speed (e.g., speed of implementation of firm actions and responses) based in part on demographic proxies for TMT decision process. In general, these models provide a fair level of support for the Eisenhardt model for firms facing turbulent environments. The contributions and contextual insights of these studies are mentioned below as they relate to the components of the Eisenhardt model.

Decision-making tactics

Eisenhardt (1989) found that fast TMTs used five "tactics" to speed up the decision-making process. Moreover, the slower TMTs either failed to use these, or differed substantially in the implementation of the tactics. Importantly, some of these tactics are not only associated with increases in the speed with which strategic decisions are made, but also impact the level of rationality of the process.

Real-time information use.   Fast TMTs made extensive use of scanning and reporting to continuously update their understanding of the position of the company, its competitors, and environment. Eisenhardt hypothesized that this activity allowed the members of the group to be on the same page, and to minimize the time needed to gear up for important decision issues facing the firm. Thus, the use of real-time information tactics by the TMT increased the pace of cognitive processing in the teams and led to smooth group process (e.g., consensus and conflict resolution) since all team members had access to similar information. Interestingly, in addition to increasing the pace of decision-making, the use of this tactic resulted in a more rational decision process.

Multiple simultaneous alternatives.   Eisenhardt also found that fast TMTs tended to look at multiple alternatives side-by-side, rather than in a serial fashion. Typically, this process was proceeded by a brainstorming session where TMT members attempted to generate a comprehensive list of possible courses of action. The use of simultaneous comparison aided the teams in their ability to discern subtle differences between alternatives and to quickly discard those that were inferior. This led to a speedy identification of a small number of worthy courses of action from which to choose. Thus, the side-by-side decision tactic allowed the TMT to accelerate its processing of the important issues. Further, Eisenhardt proposed that the process of generating a large number of alternatives and narrowing them down using a clear method increased the confidence of the TMT to act on the decision. As Eisenhardt notes, the use of multiple simultaneous alternatives resulted in a more comprehensive or exhaustive development of alternatives, and thus incorporated elements of the rational ideal.

Wally and Baum (1994) proposed that increases in the cognitive ability of TMT members would enable them to assess multiple alternatives simultaneously. Using a cognitive test and a education-level proxy, they determined that cognitive complexity of TMT members was positively related to decision pace. Though cognitive ability could reasonably affect decision process in multiple ways, this result lends some insight into the Eisenhardt model.

Decision integration.   Eisenhardt found that fast TMTs attempted to integrate decisions to fit into an overall pattern or plan. Again, the "fit" requirement served as an additional decision rule with which the TMT could differentiate between seemingly sound alternative courses of action. Thus, TMTs that integrated decisions with past decisions were able to quickly resolve ambiguities of choice and felt confident that the current decision matched previous efforts. Thus these TMTs experienced accelerated cognitive processing and an increased decision efficacy.

Two-tier advice process.   Eisenhardt also found that fast TMTs used two practices in order to break deadlock within the team. One such practice was the use by the CEO of an experienced "counselor" that resulted in a two-tier advice process. The "counselor," as described by Eisenhardt, was an experienced executive who had reached a career plateau, and thus could be trusted to give sound advice based on extensive experience. Wally and Baum (1994) found that experienced executives sometimes used heuristics to speed the decision-making process. The use by the CEO of an experienced counselor may also be relying to some extent on the unmeasured use of heuristics as well. Furthermore, Wally and Baum (1994) found that centralization was related to decision pace. This is because centralized decision processes use less consultation and decision-makers in a centralized structure may have greater feelings of control and thus be more confident to act. In the context of the TMT, the reliance by the CEO on a trusted advisor is a form of centralization.

Eisenhardt did not differentiate insider vs. outsider status, but clearly either situation could fit the counselor profile. The counselor aided the decision process by providing the CEO with a sounding board on tough issues that the TMT was having difficulty in resolving. The existence of a counselor benefited the decision process by breaking the deadlock (e.g., thus accelerating the decision process); increasing smooth group process by virtue of resolving the conflict, and in providing additional confidence on the part of the CEO to act on the decision.

Consensus with qualification.   Fast TMTs were also using a tie-breaker rule termed "consensus with qualification." Under this tactic, TMTs specified a set amount of time to attempt to reach consensus on strategy, after which the CEO was authorized by the group to make the call. Because the group pre-authorized the use of fiat by the CEO after having an opportunity to be heard, such TMTs experienced smooth group process. Obviously, the stalemate breaker tactic increased the decision speed of teams facing such a crisis. Consensus with qualification is an explicit compromise between the rationality of extensive attempts to reach consensus, and the very real need highlighted in incrementalism to cut the debate at some point. Hambrick et al. (1996) postulated that diverse TMTs would be able to conceive of and launch new actions rapidly because of expansive repertoires for action. At the same time, they acknowledged the large body of research that demonstrates the association between diversity and dissensus. Thus, Hambrick et al. proposed and found that TMT heterogeneity increased the propensity for action but at a cost to speed. Eisenhardt's model suggests the consensus with qualification tactic as a method with which to avoid the penalty of diversity to decision speed.

Intervening processes

Although Eisenhardt did not measure process, she did explain the linkages between decision "tactics' and decision speed as working through process. These linkages have been described above, however, the link between process and decision speed requires further discussion.

Accelerated cognitive processing.   Accelerated cognitive processing refers to the ability of the TMT to rapidly consider larger amounts of, often ambiguous, information. TMTs that have greater cognitive capacity of this sort are better equipped to resolve decision issues quickly, especially those being made under conditions of uncertainty and time pressure. Thus accelerated cognitive processing was proposed to be a primary factor in decision speed.

Smooth group process.   In addition to the ability to deal with large amounts of information, Eisenhardt proposed that TMTs experiencing smooth group process would make quicker decisions. Although the conceptualization of what exactly constitutes "smooth process" is not clear from the Eisenhardt piece, in a general sense she is referring to the ability of the TMT to resolve conflict and reach agreement on difficult decision issues.

Confidence to act.   Finally, Eisenhardt developed the argument that an important element of decision speed would be the confidence of the TMT to act on their decisions.

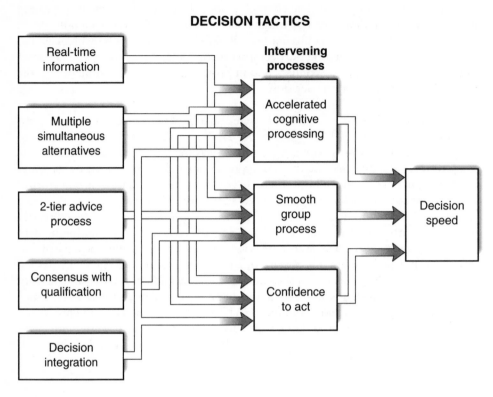

DECISION TACTICS

Figure 11.1   Eisenhardt's model of fast decision-making

In the case studies, she found that slower groups often vacillated back and forth in their quest to be absolutely certain, the result being a very drawn-out decision process. By contrast, fast TMTs developed the necessary confidence to make the decision once the solution became clear. Such efficacious decision processes dramatically improved the pace of decision-making in these teams. Wally and Baum (1994) also found that the confidence to act was a determinant of decision speed. In their study, confidence to act was viewed as stemming from personality characteristics of the TMT members. For example, TMT members with an internal locus of control and those with a high tolerance for risk were found to be more confident. Thus, in addition to decision tactics employed by TMT members, individual attributes may play a significant role in decision process. Figure 11.1 shows the model of fast strategic decision-making as proposed by Eisenhardt.

Method

The target population for the study was high-technology public and private organizations located in the mid-Atlantic region of the USA. Within each company, data was collected from multiple respondents: (1) detailed questionnaires were completed by members of the top management team; and (2) a structured interview was conducted with the CEO of each firm.

Sample and research procedures

Companies were selected for participation based on three key conditions. First, to ensure that the firms in the sample were similar across a number of basic characteristics, the companies had to conform to the definition of high-technology firms. This research was focused on high technology firms because many of these firms face "high-velocity" environments, which require constant change and innovation (Eisenhardt, 1989). Milkovich (1987: 80) defined the relevant features of high-technology industries as "firms that emphasize invention and innovation in their business strategy, deploy a significant percentage of their financial resources to R and D, employ a relatively high percentage of scientists and engineers in their workforce, and compete in worldwide, short-life-cycle product markets." Second, because of the time commitments involved in conducting the interviews for the study, organizations needed to be located within a three-hour driving distance from the research location. Third, the sample was restricted to firms meeting a size threshold of 50 or more employees (most were much larger, see below). This eliminated the inclusion of high technology startup firms that face constraints on decision-making stemming from venture-capital involvement.[1]

A list of high technology companies meeting these criteria was developed by using two sources. Initially, firms were identified through the 1998 *Mid-AtlanTech Almanac*. This almanac, published by TechCapital (a regional high-tech publication) contains company profiles, including information about the core business of the firm, contact addresses and phone numbers, number of employees, and names of top managers. Additional organizations were identified through a regional high-technology council. Following these procedures we identified 110 public and 40 high technology firms that were actively operating in the region.

To gain access to organizations, the research team followed a three-step protocol. First, the research team sent a package of four letters to the CEO/President outlining and endorsing the study. The first letter was from the research team introducing the project and outlining the goals of the research. Support letters from the Dean of the Business School, the University's Center for Entrepreneurship, and TechCapital were used to lend credibility and legitimacy to the research project and reinforce the importance of the study. In the second step, the research team called each CEO to schedule interviews (after allowing for sufficient time for the letters to be received and read).

In the final step, each CEO or President was interviewed for approximately one hour. There were three main purposes for the site visit with the CEO. First, the interview was a way to gain the support and endorsement of the CEO (including the signed letter of support and internal contact person). Second, the interview was used to collect information on the competitive environment (turbulence, munificence, complexity, etc.) of the firm. Finally, the CEO was asked to identify the members of their top management team. As part of this interview, each CEO was asked to sign a letter encouraging identified executives to complete questionnaires, and to identify an internal contact who could help the research team distribute and collect surveys. This step was necessary to obtain a full set of responses from employees inside each organization.

Of the 110 public firms contacted, we obtained full responses from 48 for a participation rate of 44 percent. Of the 40 private firms contacted, we obtained full responses from 18 for a participation rate of 46 percent. The average number of top managers that responded per firm was 3.24. The companies agreeing to participate were not significantly different from those not participating in terms of reported sales (t_{110} = 1.364, p > .05), or number of employees (t_{110} = 1.695 , p > .05). There was a large variance in the size of firms in the sample, both in terms of number of employees (45 to 16,668) and in revenue ($1.2 million to $4 billion). The average size of organizations in the study was 1,742 full-time employees, with a standard deviation of 3,391 employees.

Variable definition and measurement

All of the items used in this research were five-point Likert type scales. Each variable consists of between two and four items. For each variable, items and scale reliabilities are contained in Appendix B.

Real-time information.   Eisenhardt suggests that fast decision-making groups are often more comprehensive in their search than their slower counterparts. However, fast decision-making groups only use real-time information about competitors or their environment. We measured TMT use of real-time information with items such as: every member of the TMT knows where our organization is in its progress toward our goals; and, This TMT continuously monitors how our organization is performing.

Multiple simultaneous alternatives.   Though the literature suggests that the consideration of many alternatives (comprehensiveness) can slow the decision-making process, Eisenhardt proposed that the number of alternatives considered was not important, rather, it was the manner in which they were considered. Fast TMTs were able to simultaneously consider many possible courses of action. We measured the comprehensiveness of the TMTs search with items like: Our TMT develops an exhaustive set of alternatives before making important management decisions; and, Our TMT seeks advice from all the firm's functional areas when making important strategic decisions.

Two-tier advice process.   Eisenhardt proposed that fast TMT decisions often occurred when the CEO used a two-tiered process. First, the CEO would consult the entire TMT, and then would rely on a smaller subset, perhaps an individual counselor, to make the final decision. We measured the tendency of the CEO to rely on a small group of "counselors" with the following items: When the group cannot reach consensus easily, the CEO will often consult a senior member of the TMT to reach a decision; and, the CEO often makes decisions with the aid of one or two members of the TMT.

Consensus with qualification.   A particularly effective strategy for reaching quick decisions was termed "consensus with qualification". Fast TMTs operated under the rule that if consensus was not forthcoming, the CEO would make the decision. We measured the use of such strategies with items like: When members of the TMT disagree on an important decision, the CEO often has to step in to make the final decision; and, when TMT members disagree on an important decision, the CEO ends up listening to different viewpoints but making up his/her own mind.

Decision integration. Fast TMTs were those that evaluated each decision in the context of prior decisions. TMTs that were better able to integrate their decision-making, were also able to make decisions in a shorter amount of time. We measured the degree to which TMTs integrated their decisions into an overall framework with items such as: We consider the impact of one strategic decision on the other strategic decisions we have made; and, we try to place strategic decisions into an overall pattern or plan.

Accelerated cognitive processing. To the extent that TMTs use strategies (e.g., consensus with qualification, decision integration), rely on experienced members, and keep up to date (e.g., real-time information) they are better able to quickly process the information with which they are faced. We measure this ability in TMTs with the following items: When the need arises to make key decisions, the members of this TMT are already "on the same page," and, when making strategic decisions, we often have to re-familiarize ourselves with the key issues involved (reversed).

Smooth group process. Eisenhardt observed that fast TMTs often had developed smooth group processes. TMT members were familiar with one another, and avoided unnecessary conflict. We measured the "smoothness" of TMT process with items like: Members of the TMT get along with each other well.

Confidence to act. Fast TMTs were confident of their ability to make the right decisions. This confidence was based in part on the strategies they used (multiple simultaneous alternatives, decision integration), and on their up-to date knowledge of the current situation (real-time information). We measured the confidence of TMTs to act with the following items: The quality of this TMT's decisions gives me the confidence to act, and I feel this TMT can solve any problem we encounter; and I have confidence in the TMT's ability to make sound decisions.

Decision speed. Decision speed has been linked to performance, particularly for firms facing turbulent environments. We measured the decision speed of TMTs with the following items: This TMT moves quickly to make key strategic decisions; It takes this TMT too long to make important decisions (reversed); and, this TMT routinely makes important decisions in under one month. This approach differs slightly from that used by Eisenhardt. First, Eisenhardt assessed quick decisions as those made in under four months, and measured the length of the decision process as a continuous variable. Secondly, we incorporate a relative measure of decision speed to complement the absolute measure used in previous studies. We believe this approach better captures the meaning of "fast" decisions in the even more turbulent environment now faced by firms.

Results

The results of the study provide moderate support for the Eisenhardt model. As can be seen in table 11.2, the correlations amongst many of the key variables of Eisenhardt's model are very strong. High levels of multi-collinearity between independent variables can result in unstable betas, though this does not affect the overall R-squared for the model (Pedhazur, 1982). Green (1978: 227–8) suggests three strategies for dealing with high levels of intercorrelation in predictor measures: (1) ignore it; (2) delete one or more of the correlated variables; or (3) transform the predictors into a new set of mutually uncorrelated variables by use of a data reduction algorithm like factor analysis. Option 1 seems cavalier, however, Green suggests that under certain circumstances this may be the best course of action. First, when standard errors are high, multicollinearity is likely to be a problem. Second, regressions may be re-run after randomly dropping some observations (Green suggests 20 percent). If the results of the reduced sample are similar to the original results, then multicollinearity is not likely to be a problem. In the present analysis, the standard errors were not large. Furthermore, they remained stable when the sample was randomly reduced. The mediated regression was re-run after randomly dropping 10 observations (approximately 20 percent). The results were virtually identical to the full-sample regressions. Thus, it appears that the moderate levels of intercorrelation in the independent variables do not cause problems of interpretation of the results. A factor analysis was also performed and the results are reported later.

Mediated regression analysis was utilized to better understand the relationships amongst the independent variables, the intervening processes, and decision speed. Table 11.3 shows the results of the direct and mediated regression on decision speed. Tables 11.4, 11.5, and 11.6 show the regressions of the independent variables on the mediating processes. Figure 11.2 shows the direct relationships between decision "tactics" and decision speed.

The results of our analysis show strong support for three of Eisenhardt's five propositions with respect to the link between decision tactics and decision speed. Indeed, the model explained 76.9 percent of the variance in decision speed for this sample of firms. In support of Eisenhardt's first proposition, real-time information use was found to affect decision speed ($\beta = .417$, $p < .001$) through its impact on the TMT's accelerated cognitive processing ($\beta = .390$, $p < .001$) and through their confidence to act ($\beta = .392$, $p < .001$). In support of proposition two, the consideration of multiple simultaneous alternatives by the TMT affected decision speed ($\beta = .324$, $p < .001$) through its impact on the TMT's accelerated cognitive processing ($\beta = .367$, $p < .001$) and through their confidence to act ($\beta = .363$, $p < .001$) (P2). Contrary to Eisenhardt's model, the use of real-time information was not found to be linked to smooth group process, however, it was linked to TMT confidence ($\beta = .392$, $p < .001$, not predicted by Eisenhardt). Smooth group process was not found to be linked to decision speed. No other independent variables were found to be related to either accelerated cognitive processing or TMT confidence to act. Finally, some support for proposition five was demonstrated as decision integration was found to affect decision speed ($\beta = .251$, $p < .05$), not through the mediating processes as proposed, but directly (P5).

Table 11.2 Correlation table

	RT	SA	2-tier	CQ	DI	AP	SP	CA	DS
Real-time information	1.000								
Simultaneous alternatives	.747[a]	1.000							
Two-tier advice	−.419	−.542[a]	1.000						
Consensus w/qualification	−.189	−.415[a]	.708[a]	1.000					
Decision integration	.581[a]	.639[a]	−.483[a]	−.228	1.000				
Accelerated processing	.715[a]	.762[a]	−.470[a]	−.360[a]	.572[a]	1.000			
Smooth process	.628[a]	.703[a]	−.612[a]	−.423[a]	.566[a]	.815[a]	1.000		
Confidence to act	.734[a]	.784[a]	−.558[a]	−.345[a]	.580[a]	.879[a]	.829[a]	1.000	
Decision speed	.753[a]	.730[a]	−.354[a]	−.145	.667[a]	.816[a]	.727[a]	.804[a]	1.000

N = 66. [a] significant at $p < .01$ level (2-tailed)

Table 11.3 Predicting decision speed

Step	Variable	β	t
1	Real-time information	.417[c]	3.908
	Simultaneous alternatives	.324[c]	2.680
	2-tier advice	.048	.401
	Consensus with qualification	.081	.745
	Decision integration	.251[a]	2.516
2	Real-time information	.158	1.714
	Simultaneous alternatives	.095	.882
	2-tier advice	.089	.859
	Consensus with qualification	.147	1.598
	Decision integration	.196[a]	2.359
	Smooth group process	.105	.920
	Confidence to act	.225[a]	2.245
	Accelerated cognitive processes	.322[a]	2.687

Dependent variable = Decision speed, step 1 R^2 = .658; step 2 R^2 = .769
N = 66
[a] $p < .05$, [b] $p < .01$, [c] $p < .001$

Table 11.4 Predicting smooth group process

Variable	β	t
Real time	.238[a]	1.475
Simultaneous alternatives	.282[a]	2.006
2-tier advice	−.204	−1.168
Consensus with qualification	−.079	−.626
Decision integration	.139	1.197

Dependent variable = Decision speed, R^2 = .530
N = 66, [a] $p < .05$, [b] $p < .01$, [c] $p < .001$

Table 11.5 Predicting confidence to act

Variable	β	t
Real time	.392[c]	3.719
Simultaneous alternatives	.363[c]	3.034
2-tier advice	−.167	−1.426
Consensus with qualification	−.014	−.134
Decision integration	.038	.387

Dependent variable = Decision speed, R^2 = .660
N = 66, [a] $p < .05$, [b] $p < .01$, [c] $p < .001$

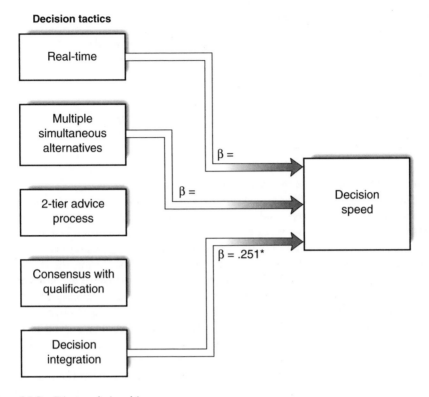

Figure 11.2   Direct relationships

Table 11.6   Accelerated cognitive processing

Variable	β	t
Real time information	.390[c]	3.487
Simultaneous alternatives	.367[b]	2.895
2-tier advice process	.055	−.438
Consensus with qualification	−.169	−1.482
Decision integration	.098	.937

Dependent variable = Decision speed, R^2 = .618
N = 66, [a] $p < .05$, [b] $p < .01$, [c] $p < .001$

Figures 11.2 and 11.3 show the direct and mediated models. Note that the direct links to decision speed for both real-time processing and multiple simultaneous alternatives drop when the mediating processes are introduced to the model. Only decision integration links directly to decision speed rather than through mediating processes as Eisenhardt proposed. In conclusion, the results of our analysis provide moderate

Table 11.7 Factor analysis of decision tactics

	Parallelism	Tie-Breaker
Decision integration	.819	−.185
Real-time information use	.896	−.009
Multiple simultaneous alternatives	.839	−.345
Consensus w/qualification	−.008	.950
Two-tier advice system	−.386	.834

support for the propositions of Eisenhardt's inductive case studies.

A principal components factor analysis with varimax rotation was also performed to further validate the results reported above. This data reduction strategy transforms the correlated predictors into uncorrelated factors. Factor scores can then be entered in to the regression model in the place of intercorrelated predictor measures. The downside of this method is that some level of richness and detail is lost during the transformation. The factor analysis (table 11.7) extracted factors: the first factor was comprised of the real-time use of information, consideration of multiple simultaneous alternatives, and decision integration tactics. This factor was labeled "parallelism" since each of the components refers to a tactic that involves analysis in parallel. The second factor was comprised of the consensus with qualification and two-tier advice system tactics. The second factor was labeled "tie-breaker" since both components are tactics used to resolve dissensus. The results of the regression of decision speed on the two decision tactics factors was consistent with the results reported above. The parallelism factor was related to decision speed ($\beta = .823$, $p < .001$), while the tie-breaker factor was not ($\beta = -.069$, $p = .345$.

Discussion

In general, the results of this research support Eisenhardt's central, if unstated, claim that fast TMTs are able to simultaneously inject a measure of rationality into their decision process without an adverse impact on decision speed. Certainly, we found that fast TMTs did this through the use of such tactics as the use of real-time information, side-by-side consideration of alternatives, and by integrating current decision issues with existing plans. The story is much more complex, however, and a closer examination of the results yields insights into the true functioning of fast TMTs. Figure 11.3 (below) contains the revised model of fast strategic decision-making.

Real-time information use.   As Eisenhardt proposed, the use of real-time information increased strategic decision-making indirectly through decision process. As predicted, real-time information use accelerated cognitive processing in the TMT leading to increased decision speed. Eisenhardt hypothesized that accelerated cognitive processing in such teams would be the result of the development of real-time information tactics of intuition. An alternative explanation is that TMTs whose members keep current are

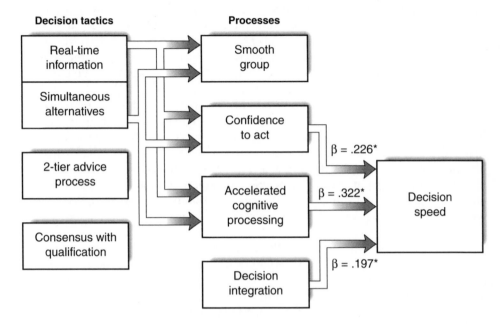

Figure 11.3   Revised model of fast strategic decision-making

able to begin processing *earlier* than those TMTs whose members have to spend time gearing up for decisions.

This research found that the use of real-time information gave the TMT increased confidence to act ultimately increasing decision speed. It is interesting that Eisenhardt did not propose the linkage between real-time information and confidence to act, which would appear to be fairly straightforward. Simply put, TMTs that continually update their knowledge bases concerning the state of the firm, the activities of rivals, and changes in the competitive environment are likely to perceive that they have a good grasp of the current situation. Such teams are likely to feel that they have left no stone unturned. The perception in the team that they have prepared themselves and have been comprehensive (e.g., up-to-date) in their search will directly bolster their confidence to act on such information. Such teams may experience what Hambrick and colleagues (1996) termed a higher propensity to act. This explanation is supported by evidence provided by Eisenhardt concerning the inability of certain TMTs to make decisions. She describes one team that continually sought more and more information, due to a fear that they were overlooking some key factor.

Finally, while real-time information use was associated, as Eisenhardt predicted, with smooth group process, this linkage did not impact decision speed in this sample.

Consideration of multiple simultaneous alternatives.   Again, the predictions of the Eisenhardt model are strongly supported. TMTs that were able to simultaneously assess several alternatives experienced increased confidence to act and accelerated cognitive processing. As Eisenhardt explained, the practice of comparing alternatives side-by-side helps TMTs to readily discern and evaluate slight differences and ambiguities. These differences may be very difficult for TMT members to recall and evaluate given a serial decision process. Indeed, TMTs may have to revisit earlier alternatives to resolve ambiguities adding time to the decision process. The insights garnered from a simultaneous comparison process helps solidify the preferences of TMT members resulting in increased conviction in the solution that is chosen.

Although such groups experienced smoother group process, this was not related to decision speed. Even though not directly relevant to this study, smooth group process has been associated in the literature with various desirable outcomes. The argument is that the use of a side-by-side comparison process drastically reduces the chance for divergent perceptions of the "facts" by forcing TMT members to evaluate alternatives simultaneously. Serial, particularly if temporally dispersed, modes of evaluation contain much greater opportunity for such misunderstandings to occur and to fester, ultimately leading to decreased functionality of group process.

Decision integration.   Eisenhardt (1989) proposed that the attempt to match current decisions with an existing overall pattern of strategy would speed the decision process by accelerating the cognitive processing of the team, and by increasing their confidence to act. While this research found that decision integration is related to decision speed, the link is direct, rather than through mediating processes.

There are several clues as to why the form of the relationship identified in this research deviates from the model as originally proposed. From Eisenhardt (1989), "[TMTs] maintained mental maps of how decisions fit together" and "[they] simultaneously kept in mind multiple decisions" (ibid.: 567) and "such integration may limit discontinuities between decisions" (ibid.: 566). These statements suggest that decision integration is an on-going process that transforms "batch" to "process" decision-making. Because fast TMTs view decisions as a continual integrated procession, they do not have to gear up for new issues – they remain in a state of heightened readiness. Importantly, this concept is distinct from Eisenhardt's "accelerated processing" in that it is really continual rather than speedy processing. Perhaps an apt analogy is that of the tortoise (continual processing) vs. the hare (accelerated processing). Of course, the most speedy decisions will be made by a tortoise with a kick. Additional support for this explanation can be found in Eisenhardt's observation that slow TMTs often shifted from stalemated inactivity to making "snap" decisions. In summary, decision integration is likely a standalone process, rather than an antecedent to accelerated cognitive processing.

Intervening processes.   Two of the three intervening processes, confidence to act and accelerated cognitive processing, were found to be strong predictors of decision speed. These findings lend good support for the Eisenhardt model and are generally consistent with the results reported by Wally and Baum (1994).[2] The present research cannot assess whether the confidence certain TMTs felt to act was based predominantly on the decision tactics employed by the team (e.g., use of real-time information and the simultaneous evaluation of alternatives), on certain personality factors as Wally and Baum propose, or on other factors such as past performance.

Accelerated cognitive processing was also found to be a strong predictor of decision speed. Although Eisenhardt describes accelerated cognitive processing as emanating from "deep personal knowledge of the enterprise that allows (TMTs) to access and interpret information rapidly when major decisions arise" (1989: 570), it may be that the use of real-time information simply allows these teams to begin the processing component of decision-making earlier than other teams. Regardless of the actual mechanism, TMTs that experience accelerated cognitive processing do make quicker decision.

Finally, the non-finding for the proposed linkage between TMT smooth process and decision speed is worthy of some discussion. Smooth process has been the topic of substantial research on TMT decision-making (Hickson et al., 1986; Mintzberg, 1973). Implicit in many of these studies is the idea that smooth process, particularly consensus, will lead to faster decision-making. It is, therefore, intriguing that this relationship was not detected in this study. There are two plausible explanations for this: (1) differences in the operationalization of the smooth process construct; and (2) smooth process may work through another construct.

In this study, smooth group process was operationalized as a linear combination of the standardized team scores for cohesion, consensus, and conflict. In Eisenhardt's study group process was referred to as the ability of the TMT to deal constructively with conflict and thus move the group to a decision. Though our definition of smooth process does not, on the surface, appear to deviate mu0ch from what Eisenhardt intended, the research findings regarding the effects of cohesion and conflict have been varied. For example, as Amason (1996) details, the upper echelons stream has consistently proposed that conflict is dysfunctional for decision-making groups, while others have indicated that certain types of conflict may actually help the decision process (Murray, 1989; Amason, 1996; Amason and Sapienza, 1997). Similarly, the impact of cohesion on group outcomes has been varied (Janis, 1972; Bourgeois, 1980, 1985). Therefore, a more careful operationalization of the construct may sort out the linkage between smooth process and decision speed.

An alternative explanation may be that smooth group process works through increased confidence to act. The logic for this specification of the model comes from the "groupthink" literature (Janis, 1972). In essence, groups that experience extremely smooth process may develop interaction norms such that the ideas of team members quickly converge, with little or no dissent. What may occur in such teams is a self-reinforcing escalation of confidence. Team members may develop hubris with respect to the group decision based in part on the lack of disconfirming voices. While this scenario is clearly dysfunctional from the perspective of decision quality, it may help explain the strong linkage detected in this research between decision efficacy and decision speed.

Conclusion

In a nutshell, Eisenhardt was on to something. Firms facing turbulent environments can take greater control over their decision-making processes by instituting certain tactics and by developing certain processes. Further, these TMTs can actually increase the speed with which they make decisions while simultaneously improving decision rationality. While the essence of Eisenhardt's arguments is correct, the findings of this research highlight the critical role theory testing plays in conjunction with inductive theory development research. Ultimately, it is the interplay of these two approaches to research over multiple iterations that leads the field to new insights and greater understanding. Just as inductive research seeks to clarify the questions that should be studied, and proposes potential linkages to be tested, so too deductive research should propose new directions for further study. It is to this task that we now turn.

Figure 11.2 contains a modified model of fast decision-making based on the results of this cross-sectional study. The model is not complete, however, since there are many factors that could reasonably be expected to impact decision speed, but which were omitted from the model as originally proposed by Eisenhardt. Many of these factors have been alluded to in the preceding discussion, however, it is important to reiterate them here for ease of reference.

Controls.   There are several compositional factors that might reasonably be expected to impact TMT decision speed. Chief among these is the cognitive capacity of the individual executives that comprise the TMT. Wally and Baum (1994) found that TMTs whose members had greater cognitive complexity were able to make quicker decisions. A second factor that may affect the speed of decision-making in the TMT is the propensity of executives to take risks. To the extent that TMT members are willing to "roll the dice' the decision process should progress more rapidly. Such teams are less likely to experience the "analysis paralysis" described by Eisenhardt. Wally and Baum (1994) also suggest the use of a team size control. This is consistent with earlier research that demonstrates the process difficulties of larger teams. A final control that should be included in subsequent studies of decision pace is the rate of change found in the firm's primary industry (note: Eisenhardt controls for this by virtue of conducting a single industry study, while Judge and Miller (1991) determined that this was an important contextual variable for strategic decision-making).

Leader behavior.   Eisenhardt focuses considerable attention on the behaviors the CEO exhibits during times of stalemate (e.g., seeking counsel, instituting tie-breaker rules), but she does not incorporate the variety of other CEO behaviors that could reasonably be expected to impact the pace at which decisions occur in the TMT. For example, a transactional leader may develop in their TMT a very different process than an autocrat – one that most certainly would impact decision speed. The approaches detailed by Eisenhardt appear to be hybrids that incorporate some aspects of decentralization (some form of consultation with other members of the TMT), while still retaining a semblance of autocracy (ultimately, the CEO calls the shot). Neither of these tactics was found to be associated with increased decision speed. In the interest of informing future research efforts, possible explanations for these non-findings are offered below.

Two-tier advice process.   The counselor tactic suggested by Eisenhardt was not something that the fast TMTs in our sample incorporated into their decision process. Indeed, in addition to failing to achieve statistical significance in the regression, the sign was reversed. There are two very plausible explanations of this non-finding: the first deals with way in which the "counselor" was conceptualized; and the second deals with the "tie-breaker" flavor of two-tier advice tactics.

Eisenhardt explains the "counselor" process she observed in the fast TMTs as the use by the CEO of an experienced member of the top management team who acted as a knowledgeable and unbiased sounding board. In their 1991 study, Judge and Miller conceived of the "counselor" as an external member of the board of directors. This highlights a fundamental flaw in the model proposed by Eisenhardt, and in the way we operationalized the counselor construct. A critical distinction future researchers should make in the conceptualization of the counselor centers on who that person is, more particularly, whether the counselor is internal to the TMT or an outsider. The reasoning for this is that other members of the top management team may react to the existence of a counselor very differently depending on the status of the advisor – internal vs external. The use by the CEO of an internal counselor is likely to be visible to other members of the team. Depending on the composition of the team, the individual motivations of team members, and a host of other factors, team members may react unfavorably to the increased influence the counselor appears to have with the CEO. There is some evidence for this scenario from Eisenhardt and Bourgeois' paper on politics and decision-making in TMTs. "(our meetings are) open and forthright" . . ."It's very open . . . we talk as a group, not committees" (1988: 752). One instance related in the paper described several team members voicing their displeasure at the coalition of three members (including the CEO) who tended to have off-line, but visible, conversations that were perceived to result in the decision being made. Certainly the reliance of the CEO on an internal counselor could be viewed by other TMT members in a similar light. The likely response to such a situation is bi-modal: (1) TMT members may decide they do not matter and thus decrease participation in decision-making; or (2) TMT members may deal with the influence of the counselor by forming a counter-coalition and employing various political tactics.

In contrast to the potential for dysfunctional behavior associated with internal counselors, the use of an external counselor may better aid the decision process. First, the jealousy and feelings of devalue risked in the first scenario are unlikely when an outsider is used. The outsider is much less likely to be known, or visible to the TMT, thus the CEO can portray counselor-aided decisions as their own, and use other tactics (e.g., consensus with qualification) to mitigate the process loss that typically accompanies autocratic decision-making. Second, an external counselor is even more likely to be unbiased than the plateaued executive Eisenhardt describes in her study. As compared to the plateaued executive, the outsider really has very little at stake – they do not work for the firm, they may have little to no equity holdings in the firm, and are likely providing the advice for no other reason than friendship with the CEO. The implication of this goes beyond the reliability of the advice the CEO is likely to receive. The real impact on decision speed comes in the increased efficacy the CEO will feel when making decisions based on the advice of a person with no stake in the organization, or agenda to pursue.

Thus, in order to determine whether the counselor tactic is associated with more rapid strategic decision-making, it is necessary to separate internal from external advice systems. At a minimum, researchers should ascertain what the specific impact of the use of a counselor has on group process, politics, and CEO decision efficacy.

Consensus with qualification.   In order to avoid prolonged dissensus, Eisenhardt found that fast TMTs specified that efforts to reach consensus would persist for a pre-ordained amount of time, after which the CEO would make the call. Again, our research findings did not support the role of this tactic in speeding decisions. There are two plausible explanations for this non-finding: (1) tie-breakers may homogenize decision duration, rather than minimize it; and (2) fast TMTs may rarely experience prolonged dissensus.

There is a fair amount of support for the idea that TMTs may routinize their decision processes over time. That is, decision-making techniques, if successful, may become a relatively permanent part of a team's repertoire of behavior. Indeed, Eisenhardt (1989) and others (Wally and Baum, 1994) argue that the development of experience-based intuition, and routines for decision-making may speed the process in some teams. The corollary to this argument is that routines may continue to be followed even in circumstances where they are dysfunctional. Habits may be formed based on early evidence of usefulness, but may persist in the absence of continued functionality.

In the present case, TMTs may have developed tie-breaker rules such as "consensus with qualification" and experience these to be effective ways of dealing with stalemate. One example of such a rule might be that the team agrees to discuss the various viewpoints surrounding an important decision issue for one month, after which they will spend an additional week to attempt to reach consensus on the proper course of action. If consensus is not forthcoming, the CEO will make the decision. Such a rule would certainly constrain the duration of major decisions to five weeks and most TMTs would consider this a fairly speedy process. The unintended consequence of such a rule, were it to become routinized, is the propensity of the TMT to take five weeks to make decisions even when the issues may be much more easily and quickly resolved. The structure introduced by the tie-breaker tactic could, therefore, actually lengthen the duration of decision-making in some instances, the end result being the homogenization rather than maximization of decision pace.

A second possibility exists that might also explain the non-finding for the "consensus with qualification" tactic. It is quite feasible that fast TMTs simply do not experience prolonged stalemates, and thus are not in a position to need or develop such tie-breakers. The results of our analysis lend some support for this view. Fast TMTs were very likely to depend heavily on real-time information, to use side-by-side comparison of alternatives, and to integrate current decisions into a coherent pattern of strategy. The use of these three "tactics" forces teams to deal in real time with all of the issues involved in making the decision. There are no time gaps or discontinuities which may lead to differential understanding of the issues. The process that emerges through the use of these three tactics may be much more objective, thus facilitating the rapid resolution of factual and perceptual differences amongst team members. Simply stated, fast decision-making teams may rarely get to point where they have occasion to utilize tie-breakers.

Finally, Eisenhardt specifies only two ways in which the CEO can actively deal with dissensus, however, there are many other means of conflict resolution that are not included in the model. An important way to distinguish between alternative conflict management styles may be the degree of passivity. Active management of conflict by the TMT should result in rapid decision-making.

Smooth process.   Smooth process, as has been discussed above, is a fuzzy label that could encompass multiple constructs. In addition to cohesion, conflict, and consensus, smooth process might reasonably be interpreted to mean a lack of political behaviors within the TMT. A full model of decision speed would necessarily incorporate various political behaviors, discriminate between cognitive and affective conflict in the TMT, and measure cohesion and consensus separately. In this way, the field can determine with much improved precision exactly which sorts of processes are driving decision speed. The non-finding for smooth process reported here highlights this need.

Decision speed.   The pace of decision-making is a multifaceted construct. One common conceptualization of decision speed is in terms of the absolute amount of time that passes between issue identification and the choosing of a course of action. Another way to think of pace is in terms of the *relative* speed with which a TMT makes decisions. Further, there are at least two ways to conceptualize relative speed: (1) are we quicker than our rivals?; and (2) are we quick enough to meet or exceed the rate of change in our environment? Future research should explore these variations on the theme of decision speed to determine which types of speed are most important to competitive advantage.

Managerial implications

The results of this study hold important implications for management practice. In providing further empirical support for Eisenhardt's decision-making model, we can reiterate with additional confidence and increased precision the behaviors and strategies that managers can employ to make rapid decisions.

First, managers can be confident that quick decisions do not have to be low quality decisions. While this research does not directly measure decision quality, a more comprehensive decision process should reasonably lead to better decision outcomes (Wally and Baum, 1994). Top management teams that made very quick decisions were also able to consider multiple alternatives. Moreover, use of restricted search by some teams did not help to speed the team's decision. The key factor was the manner in which the TMTs went about comparing the alternative courses of action. Fast TMTs were able to look at several options concurrently, to quickly determine which options were of highest quality, and then to focus on just these few. In contrast, TMTs that looked at alternatives in a serial fashion were very slow to come to a decision.

Second, managers who are "up on things" are in a much superior position to make quick decisions. Eisenhardt suggests that there may be various ways TMTs can ensure that they are up to speed when the decision is at hand. The critical factor is for the managers in the top management team to have real-time access to key information about the state of the firm, what competitors are doing, and any important changes in the external environment. We propose that the utilization of nested information systems, and Internet notification services (e.g., automated daily searches based on key words) can help managers have the information they need at all times.

Third, managers need to attempt to make decisions in the context of previous actions. The ability to integrate current decisions with the overall decision history of the organization actually increases the speed with which executives make decisions. This is in addition to the obvious advantages an overarching integrated plan can provide a firm.

Finally, while our results did not support the role of smooth group process in facilitating decisions, it did not preclude the possibility that certain types of cooperative behaviors of TMTs might be functional. More study is needed to determine whether smooth process is a good thing for decision-making bodies, and if so in what ways.

In conclusion, it appears that the top management teams of firms will continue to face increasing levels of uncertainty and competitive pressure. TMTs that are able to quickly assess the competitive landscape and make good quality decisions in a timely fashion will provide their organizations with the best chance to succeed in the entrepreneurial millennium.

Appendix A

Selected studies of concepts related to TMT decision-making

Year	Study	Demographic concept	Associated decision concept
1975	Taylor	Age	Slow decision-making and increased information seeking during decision-making
1984	Dollinger	Education	Tolerance for ambiguity
	Wagner, Pfeffer, and O'Reilly	Job tenure heterogeneity	Turnover, conflict
1988	Goodstein and O'Reilly	Past joint work experience	Trust and cohesion
	Goodstein and O'Reilly	Tenure	Trust and cohesion
1989	Zenger and Lawrence	Past joint work experience	Communication frequency
		TMT size	Lower communication frequency
1990	MacCrimmon and Wehrung	TMT age	Risk aversion
1995	Bantel and Finkelstein	TMT size	Lower cohesion
1991	Haleblian and Finkelstein	TMT size	Lower cohesion, less communication, higher creativity, higher organizational performance
1991	Hitt and Tyler	TMT age	Risk aversion
1991	Jackson et al.	Heterogeneity	Decreased social integration
1991	Miller	Tenure	Restricted information gathering
1991	Smith	Education	Increased competitive response
1991	Smith, Grimm, Gannon, and Chen	Industry experience	Increased competitive response
1992	Jackson	Heterogeneity	Dissensus

1992	Wiersema and Bantel	TMT size	Lower cohesion, lower communication frequency
	Wiersema and Bantel	Heterogeneity	Use of more sources of information, more creative, decreased social integration
1993	Bantel	Education	Increased demand for detailed information
1993	Hambrick, Geletkanycz, and Fredrickson	Age	Solidification of executives mental models
1994	Smith et al.	TMT size	Communication formality
	Smith et al.	Experience heterogeneity	Formality of communication
1994	Wally and Baum	Education	Cognitive complexity
1995	Jackson, May, and Whitney	Heterogeneity	Increased variance in decision-making alternatives
1996	Hambrick, Cho, and Chen	Education heterogeneity	Increased actions, decreased action speed
	Hambrick, Cho, and Chen	Heterogeneity in organizational tenure	Increased actions
	Hambrick, Cho, and Chen	Functional heterogeneity	Decreased action speed
	Hambrick, Cho, and Chen	Education	Increased actions
	Hambrick, Cho, and Chen	Tenure in organization	Lower propensity to act
1997	Amason and Sapienza	TMT size	Increased cognitive and affective conflict
1998	Miller, Burke, and Glick	Cognitive diversity	Decision-making comprehensiveness long-range planning
1998	Papadakis, Lioukas and Chambers	CEO organizational tenure	Decentralization of decision-making
1999	Knight et al.	Heterogeneity	Decreased strategic consensus

Appendix B

Items and reliabilities

Variable	Items (five-point Likert-type)	α
Real-time information	Every member of the TMT knows where our organization is in its progress toward our goals. This TMT continuosly monitors how our orgnization is peforming. Members of this TMT track our progress over time concerning our ideas and new developments.	.80

Year	Study	Demographic concept	Associated decision concept
	Multiple simultaneous alternatives	Our TMT develops an exhaustive set of alternatives before making important management decisions. Our TMT seeks advice from all the firm's functional areas when making important strategic decisions. Our TMT is extremely thorough in its evaluation of strategic alternatives.	.77
	Two-tier advice process	When the group cannot reach consensus easily, the CEO will often consult a senior member of the TMT to reach a decision. The CEO often makes decisions with the aid of one or two members of the TMT. All members of the TMT are actively involved in making important strategic decisions. (reversed)	.75
	Consensus with qualification	When members of the TMT disagree on an important decision, the CEO often has to step in to make the final decision. When TMT members disagree on an important decision, the CEO ends up listening to different viewpoints but making up his/her own mind.	.68
	Decision integration	We consider the impact of one strategic decision on the other strategic decisions we have made. We try to place strategic decisions into an overall pattern or plan. We make strategic decisions independent of our day-to-day operations. We consider each strategic decision in its own unique context. (reversed)	.76
	Accelerated cognitive processing	When the need arises to make key decision, the members of this TMT are already "on the same page." This TMT doesn't need to spend much time "gearing up" when a key decision issue is at hand. When making strategic decisions, we often have to re-familiarize ourselves with the key issues involved. (reversed) We are always ready to make key decisions when they need to be made.	.69
	Smooth group process	Members of the TMT get along with each other well. Members of the TMT really stick together. Members of this TMT are ready to defend each other from criticism by outsiders.	.81
	Confidence to act	The quality of this TMT's decisions gives me the confidence to act. I feel this TMT can solve any problem we encounter. I have confidence in the TMT's ability to make sound decisions. I believe this TMT's decision-making capabilities can lead this firm to achieve high performance.	.89
	Decision speed	This TMT moves quickly to make key strategic decisions. It takes this TMT too long to make important decisions. (reversed) This TMT routinely makes important decisions in under one month.	.71

Notes

1   One organization included in the sample had only 45 employees. Because this organization was not a start-up and met all other requirements of the research, it was deemed acceptable for inclusion in the study.
2   Although Hambrick and colleagues (1996) reported no significant correlation between action propensity and action speed, the constructs and measures used in their study differed substantially from our conceptualization of decision speed and confidence to act.

References

Amason, A. 1996: Distinguishing the effects of functional and dysfunctional conflict on strategic decision-making: resolving a paradox for top management teams. *Academy of Management Journal,* 39 (1), 123–49.

Amason, A. C. and Sapienza, H. J. 1997: The effects of top management team size and interaction norms on cognitive and affective conflict. *Journal of Management,* 23: 495–516.

Bantel, K. A. 1993: Top team, environment, and performance effects on strategic planning formality. *Team and Organization Management,* 18: 436–58.

Bantel, K. A. and Finkelstein, S. 1995: The determinants of top management teams. In B. Markovsky, K. Heimer, and J. O'Brien (eds) *Advances in Group Processes,* 12: 139–65. Greenwich, CT: JAI Press.

Bourgeois, L. J., III. 1980: Performance and consensus. *Strategic Management Journal,* 1 (2), 227–48.

Bourgeois, L. J. III. 1985: Strategic goals, perceived uncertainty, and economic performance in volatile environments. *Academy of Management Journal,* 28 (3), 548–73.

Child, J. 1972: Organizational structure, environments, and performance: the role of strategic choice. *American Sociological Review,* 6, 1–22.

Cyert, R. M. and March, J. G. 1963: *A Behavioral Theory of the Firm.* Englewood Cliffs, NJ: Prentice-Hall.

D'Aveni, R. A. 1994: *Hyper Competition: Managing the Dynamics of Strategic Maneuvering.* New York: Free Press.

Dollinger, I. 1984: Environmental boundary spanning and information processing effects on organizational performance. *Academy of Management Journal,* 27: 351–68.

Eisenhardt. K. 1989: Making fast strategic decisions in high velocity environments. *Academy of Management Journal,* 32 (3), 543–76.

Eisenhardt, K. and Bourgeois, L. J. III. 1988: Politics of strategic decision making in high velocity environments: Toward a midrange theory. *Academy of Management Journal,* 31, 737–70.

Finkelstein, S. and Hambrick, D. A. 1996: *Strategic Leadership: Top Executives and Their Effects on Organizations.* St. Paul, MN: West Publishing.

Fredrickson, J. and Iaquinto, A. 1989: Inertia and creeping rationality in strategic decision processes. *Academy of Management Journal,* 32: 516–42.

Frederickson, J. and Mitchell, T. 1984: Strategic decision processes: comprehensiveness and performance in an industry with an unstable environment. *Academy of Management Journal,* 27, 399–423.

Goodstein, J. and O'Reilly, C. 1988: *It's what's up top that counts: The role of executive team demography and team dynamics in determining firm success or failure.* Working paper. Berkley: School of Business Administration, University of California.

Green, P. E. 1978: *Analyzing Multivariate Data*. Dinsdale, IL: Dryden Press.

Grimm, C. and Smith, K. G. 1997: *Strategy As Action*. Ohio: South Western College Publishing.

Haleblian, J. and Finkelstein, S. 1991: Top management team size, CEO dominance, and firm performance: The moderating roles of environmental turbulence and discretion. *Academy of Management Journal*, 36: 844–63.

Hambrick, D. C., Cho, T. S., and Chen, M. 1996: The influence of top management team heterogeneity on firms' competitive moves. *Administrative Science Quarterly*, 41: 659–84.

Hambrick, D. C., Geletkanycz, M. A., and Fredrickson, J. W. 1993: Top executive commitment to the status quo: Some tests of its determinants. *Strategic Management Journal*, 14: 401–18.

Hickson, D., Butler, R., Cray, D., Mallory, G., and Wilson, D. 1986: *Top Decisions: Strategic Decision Making in Organizations*. San Francisco: Jossey-Bass.

Hitt, M. A. and Tyler, B. B. 1991: Strategic decision models: Integrating different perspectives. *Strategic Management Journal*, 12: 327–51.

Jackson, S. E. 1992: Consequences of group composition for the interpersonal dynamics of strategic issue processing. *Advances in Strategic Management*, 8: 345–82.

Jackson, S. E., Brett, J. F., Sessa, V. I., Cooper, D. M., Julin, J. A., and Peyronnin, K. 1991: Some differences make a difference: Individual dissimilarity and group heterogeneity as correlates of recruitment, promotions, and turnover. *Journal of Applied Psychology*, 76: 675–89.

Jackson, S. E., May, K. E., and Whitney, K. 1995: Understanding the dynamics of diversity in decision-making teams. In R. A. Guzzo and E. Salas (eds) *Team Effectiveness and Decision-making in Organizations*. 204–61. San Francisco: Jossey-Bass.

Janis, I. 1982: *Victims of Groupthink*. rev. edn. Boston: Houghton-Mifflin.

Judge, W. O. and Miller, A. 1991: Antecedents and outcomes of decision speed in different environmental contexts. *Academy of Management Journal*, 34, 449–63.

Knight, D., Pearce, C. L., Smith, K. G., Olian, J. D., Sims, H. P., Jr., Smith, K. A., and Flood, P. 1999: Top management team diversity, team process, and strategic consensus. *Strategic Management Journal*, 20: 445–65.

Kotter, J. 1982: *The General Managers*. New York: Free Press.

MacCrimmon, J., and Wehrung, R. G. 1990: Characteristics of risk-taking executives. *Management Science*, 36: 422–35.

March, J. G. and Simon, H. A. 1958: *Organizations*. New York: Wiley.

Milkovich, G. T. 1987: Compensation systems in high tech companies. In C. S. Anderson, and A. Kleingartner (eds), *Human Resource Management in High Technology Firms*. Lexington, MA: Lexington Books.

Miller, C. C., Burke, L. M., and Glick, W. H. 1998: Cognitive diversity among upper echelon executives: Implications for strategic decision processes. *Strategic Management Journal*, 19: 39–58.

Miller, D. 1991: Stale in the saddle: CEO tenure and the match between organization and environment. *Management Science*, 37: 34–52.

Mintzberg, H. 1973: *The Nature of Managerial Work*. New York: Harper and Row.

Mintzberg, H., Raisinghani, D., and Theoret, A. 1976: The structure of "unstructured" decision processes. *Administrative Science Quarterly*, 21, 246-75.

Murray, A. I. 1989: Top management group heterogeneity and firm performance. *Strategic Management Journal*, Special Issue, 10, 125–41.

Nutt, P. 1976: Strategic decision processes. *Academy of Management Journal*, 17, 234–52.

Papadakis, V. M., Lioukas, S., and Chambers, D. 1998: Strategic decision-making processes: The role of management and context. *Strategic Management Journal*, 19: 115–47.

Pedhazur, E. J. 1982: *Multiple Regression in Behavioral Research*, 2nd Edition. Ft Worth, TX: Harcourt Brace.

Smith, K. A. 1991: The link between top management team dynamics and strategy and performance. Unpublished Doctoral Dissertation. University of Maryland.

Smith, K. G., Grimm, C. M., Gannon, M. J., and Chen, M. 1991: Organizational information processing and competitive responses. *Academy of Management Journal*, 34: 60–86.

Smith, K. G., Smith, K. A., Olian, J. D., Sims, H. P., Jr., O'Bannon, D. P., and Scully, J. A. 1994: Top management team demography and process: The role of social integration and communication. *Administrative Science Quarterly*, 39 (4): 412–38

Taylor, R. 1975: Age and experience as determinants of managerial information processing and decision making performance. *Academy of Management Journal*, 18: 74–81.

Wagner, W. G., Pfeffer, J., and O'Reilly, C. A. 1984: Organizational demography and turnover in top management groups. *Administrative Science Quarterly*, 29: 74–92.

Wally, S. and Baum, R. 1994: Personal and structural determinants of the pace of strategic decision-making. *Academy of Management Journal*, 37: 932–56.

Wiersema, M. F. and Bantel, K. A. 1992: Top management team demography and corporate change. *Academy of Management Journal*, 35: 91–121.

Zenger, T. R. and Lawrence, B. S. 1989: Organizational demography: The differential effects of age and tenure distributions on technical communication. *Academy of Management Journal*, 32: 353–76.

CHAPTER TWELVE

The Ties That Bind: Managing Supplier Relationships in the High-Growth Firm

Amy Beekman and Richard Robinson

Introduction

Rapid globalization of markets and technology characterized the final years of the twentieth century. The impact not only changed the way companies compete, it has contributed to a new business millennium that is as dramatic in its sudden altering of the nature of global business as when Hans Solo's *Millennium Falcon* spaceship suddenly warped into light speed to flee pursuing storm troopers in the first edition of Star Wars. John Naisbett (1994) predicted it in his excellent book, *Global Paradox* when he said:

> The bigger the world economy, the more powerful its smaller players . . . The study of the smallest economic player, the entrepreneur, will merge with the study of how the big bang global economy works . . . As the world integrates economically, the component parts are becoming more numerous and smaller and more important. At once, the global economy is growing while the size of the parts are shrinking . . . The bigger and more open the world economy becomes, the more small and middle-sized companies will dominate . . . and strategic alliances between larger suppliers and smaller, market focused firms allow partners to gain added muscle and speed in responding to customers creating competitive advantage without getting bigger. (1994: 12, 13, 16, 17, 19)

The paradox he saw is the new, entrepreneurial millennium we have so quickly time-warped into. And one of the key areas that strategies are being restructured and re-thought in this entrepreneurial millennium is in the area of managing supplier relationships in the high-growth, entrepreneurial firm.

Firms in this new millennium are under increased pressure to quickly and accurately identify opportunities to sustain success. Just as importantly as identifying opportunities, however, companies must be poised to take advantage of opportunities as well as manage the growth that results from the successful pursuit of those opportunities. Although the issue of how to manage growth is important to all firms, the issue is particularly important in entrepreneurial ventures. For many entrepreneurial firms, growth is the essence of the firm (Carland et al., 1988). Further, entrepreneurial ventures are critical to the economic fabric of American business and have significant job creation capacity (Kirchhoff and Phillips, 1987). Consequently, examining the growth process in new ventures is crucial.

While sales growth is an important company goal, rapid sales growth can present a host of problems as well. For example, in a study of 30 companies, Hambrick and Crozier (1985) focus on critical issues for rapidly growing firms. The authors cite four key problems: (1) instant size, which creates problems of inadequate employee skills and organizational systems; (2) a sense of infallibility because of past success; (3) an increasing level of internal turmoil and frenzy that arises from the hectic pace that accompanies growth; and (4) extraordinary financial resource needs to fund growth. A company's inability to effectively deal with these issues does not bode well for the firm's continuing success. Other research also highlighting high-growth firms has addressed the relationship between growth and the strategy making process (cf. Shuman, et al., 1985; Shuman and Seegar, 1986), strategy content (cf. Dsouza, 1990; Cooper et al., 1986) or the link between environmental variables and strategy process and/or content in high-growth firms (cf. Bourgeois and Eisenhardt, 1988; Dsouza, 1990).

Although research has focused on the internal problems created by a firm's growth, the impact of growth on relationships external to the firm has not been as well investigated. For example, clearly relationships with key suppliers are critical to the organization's ability to meet demand, but how should these supplier relationships be managed? Should the organization that has undergone a period of rapid growth institute relationships with new suppliers and buyers to take advantage of opportunities that growth can create, or does the firm retain established relationships with which they are familiar to facilitate the growth process?

Evidence suggests that firms are increasingly engaging in long-term collaborative strategies with suppliers as well as other firms to improve their competitive position (Harrigan, 1988). Nielsen (1988) defines cooperative strategies as voluntary or contractual relationships where mutual collaboration results in risks or gains. While these strategies can range from value-chain partnerships with suppliers and buyers to equity joint ventures, the use of collaboration in general is viewed as a continuing trend (Smith et al., 1994).

Hudson and McArthur (1994) suggest that both entrepreneurial firms and established firms seek to establish collaborative strategies but that entrepreneurial firms have different reasons for pursuing these strategies. For example, new ventures typically do not have established ties or a track record of success. The absence of stable relationships as well as sufficient resources creates a liability of newness or a liability of smallness that contributes to a high failure rate (Baum et al., 2000). Consequently, establishing partnerships or other forms of collaboration offers many benefits. Young firms can facilitate and enhance learning from their partners (Hamel, 1991; Grant and Baden-Fuller, 1995). Alliances provide access to resources (Dyer and Singh, 1998; Gulati, 1998). Alliances also signal to future potential partners social status, reliability or reputation (Stuart, 2000).

According to Aldrich and Auster (1986), the use of long-term contracts with other organizations increases the chances of small firm survival. Larson (1988) suggests that entrepreneurs who establish relationships with key suppliers and buyers realize a competitive advantage that facilitates the ability of a small firm to compete with a larger firm. Jarillo (1989) and Stevenson and Jarillo (1990) argue that the use of external resources, acquired through long-term relationships, can generate growth and pursue opportunities. In a recent study, Baum et al. (2000) found that firms that established alliances at founding (particularly vertical alliances) performed better than firms that decided to go it alone.

Most of this research implies that the successful partnerships are those that are long-term in nature. This further suggests that firms maintain these relationships even during periods of high growth. Research on high-growth entrepreneurial firms by Beekman and Robinson (1999) found that high-growth firms tend to retain and in fact expand these long-term relationships with key suppliers in periods of growth.

The obvious question suggested by these findings, and the focus of this proposed chapter, is why high-growth firms stay with suppliers. Is it just the familiarity of the supplier or is it the effectiveness of the relationship that is positively related to percentage purchased? Is a strong working relationship with a key supplier the reason why the relationships survive periods of growth or can this be explained by looking exclusively at strategic factors like price, quality and availability?

In order to successfully seize opportunities, firms must understand the basis to establish and evaluate relationships with key suppliers. To that end, this chapter will present two contrasting theoretical perspectives, an economic exchange perspective and a social exchange theoretical framework, to propose and test hypotheses. The results of the tests will then be presented and discussed. The chapter will conclude with the implications of the research and directions for future research.

Conceptual Perspectives and Hypotheses

In evaluating why high-growth firms expand relationships with key suppliers in periods of growth, two contrasting theoretical perspectives suggest radically different rationalizations for this behavior. From an economic exchange perspective, the decision to stay with an established supplier is based on rational factors like performance. From a social exchange perspective, however, this behavior is rooted in the strength of the relationship. Each perspective will be considered separately.

The economic model of exchange

The economic model of exchange posits that the decision to engage in continuing exchange is based primarily on the effectiveness of the supplier relationship. Thus, performance factors like reducing costs, improving product quality, and increasing efficiency are critical as is the extent to which the relationship allows the focal firm to concentrate more on its core business. Supplier relationships that help firms improve their performance can be characterized as effective and are likely to be expanded as the firm grows. This model can be derived from multiple theoretical perspectives. This chapter will focus on two: the transaction cost economics perspective and the resource-based view.

From a transaction cost economics view (TCE), firms seek alliances in response to market failures (Williamson, 1985). Although TCE recognizes that partnerships can create joint value, TCE focuses on the dependence that alliances create and emphasizes the increased transaction costs associated with partnerships such as governance mechanisms to guard against opportunism, investment in specific assets and administrative governance burdens (Williamson, 1975, 1985). As these transaction costs must be factored into the alliance formation decision, firms will only engage in relationships where the expected benefits exceed the anticipated costs of the relationship.

According to Chiles and McMakin (1996), two perspectives have merged on how to assess costs: a long-term perspective where objective transaction costs drive decision-making and a shorter-term perspective where subjective cost estimates are based on evaluations of risk. Regardless of the perspective, supplier relationships that lower transaction costs and create value will be perceived as effective. Following this reasoning, these effective relationships are likely to be valued relationships that a company will want to preserve and even expand as sales grow.

Similarly, a resource-based view is based on economic analysis. According to this view, firms look for partners that have the resources they lack (Nohria and Garcia-Pont, 1991). These partnerships help firms achieve a sustained competitive advantage (Dyer and Singh, 1998). The resources can be resources they can leverage or capabilities they can learn which will improve their current competencies. (Hitt et al., 2000). Research on the selection of appropriate alliance partners is still evolving. Chung et al. (2000), for example, found that resource complementarity and status similarity are positively related to the formation of alliances. Lane and Lubatkin (1998) found that firms tend to learn the most from firms with similar basic knowledge but different specialized knowledge. Thus, partnerships with critical suppliers provide both access to resources and the opportunity for learning.

Another factor in the resource-based view that plays a role in selecting and maintaining relationships is cost. The resource-based view maintains that firms who possess rare, valuable, nonsubstitutable, and difficult to imitate resources will develop competitive advantage that leads to sustained above-normal profits (Barney, 1991, 1995). This suggests that firms will partner only to the extent that the relationship provides access to resources at a cost that will help the firm realize profits downstream and lead to a competitive advantage (Ahuja, 2000). Combining these criteria suggests that supplier relationships that both provide access to resources and help a firm reduce costs in an effort to achieve sustained superior financial performance can be characterized as effective. Although the resource-based view does not specifically address the impact of this, it can be inferred that effective relationships are likely to be expanded in periods of high growth.

Consequently, based on the two perspectives in the economic model of exchange, TCE and the resource-based view, effective supplier relationships are those that help reduce costs and improve operating efficiency. Effective relationships not only provide access to resources but they also create value. Because of these reasons, we expect effective relationships to be expanded in periods of high growth.

Hypothesis 1: In high-growth firms, the change in the percentage purchased from that critical supplier is positively related to the perceived effectiveness of the supplier relationship.

Supplier relationships as a social exchange

A social exchange model of supplier relationships offers a contrast to the economic model of exchange. The social exchange model suggests that factors other than price and delivery terms contribute to the "closeness" or the strength of the partnership. The motivations for entering alliances and subsequent behavior regarding partnerships include a broader consideration of the social and political context of relationships in addition to economic factors (Gulati, 1995; Dacin et al., 1999). To a large extent, both the TCE perspective and the resource-based view negate the role of a behavioral component in the management of supplier relationships. Williamson states that calculated self-interest is central to TCE and denies the development of trust in business transactions (Williamson, 1993). In the resource-based view, the organizational actor is motivated primarily by a search for a competitive advantage and has been characterized as behaving instrumentally to that end (Ahuja, 2000.)

Much research, however, recognizes the role of well-developed social relationships, especially in entrepreneurial ventures. As previously discussed, because entrepreneurs often have limited resources, cooperative strategies are often employed (Larson, 1988; Stevenson and Jarillo, 1990). A key feature of these entrepreneurial cooperative strategies is the use of social transactions to acquire resources to achieve goals (Coleman, 1988). Social transactions are defined as social contracts where goods and services are obtained at the same time that social commitments are developed.

The concept that noneconomic characteristics of relationships affect economic exchange is recognized in a multitude of disciplines. In fact, the theoretical foundations for incorporating affective dimensions into economic exchange derive from social exchange theory (Gouldner, 1960, Blau, 1964 Homans 1950, 1974) and relational contracting (Macneil, 1978, 1980). Central to both perspectives is the idea that mere economic exchange becomes relational exchange in which personal, noneconomic goals are realized in conjunction with economic goals.

In other research, Ben-Porath (1980) incorporates ideas from anthropology, economics, and sociology to illustrate the effect of various forms of social organization (families, friends, and firms) on economic exchange. Granovetter (1985, 1992) relies primarily on sociology to argue that economic exchange is not purely a function of economic analysis but can be understood only in the context of social organization and social relations.

In earlier work, Granovetter (1973) describes strong relations between firms or individuals as strong ties. Ties may be examined between firms in pairs (dyads) or among several firms (a network); their strength ranges from strong to weak. Granovetter (1973) states that tie strength is a function of time, reciprocity, emotional intensity, and intimacy. Frequency of contact also contributes to strong ties (Aldrich and Zimmer, 1986). Further, tie strength is similar to the concept of friendship. Indeed, Granovetter (1973) suggests that strong ties represent social friends whereas weak ties are more akin to acquaintances. In a similar vein, Krackhardt (1992) characterizes strong ties as "philos," the Greek word for friend.

Strong ties create stability and facilitate cooperation between organizations. Strong interpersonal ties develop between firm members such that "continuing economic relations often become overlaid with social content that carries strong expectations of trust and abstention from opportunism" (Granovetter, 1985: 490). These themes are consistent with those found in the entrepreneurship literature.

Several authors have noted the importance of relationship strength to the success of the partnership. Dwyer et al. (1987) discuss the comparison between marriage and relational exchange. Like successful marriages, successful supplier partnerships have an element of "closeness." Strong relationships build trust, which reduces opportunism (Granovetter, 1985; Heide and Miner, 1992; Provan, 1993), and improve the efficiency of exchange and operations because firms share information in a detailed and timely manner (Larson, 1988, Hill, 1990; Hendrick and Ellram, 1993). Strong relationships may also create social capital that facilitates alliances with other firms by signaling reliability based on previous collaborative efforts (Gulati, 1999).

What has not been addressed, however, is whether the strength of the relationship also affects the strategic action a firm pursues with respect to a supplier in periods of change, specifically in periods of high growth. Although strength can be measured with a multitude of measures, for the purposes of this chapter, this "noneconomic" or relationship strength dimension consists of two components: behavior and attitude. Mohr and Spekman (1994) found that noneconomic factors or attributes of the partnership, such as the level of trust and commitment between the partners, as well as partnership behaviors, such as communication behavior, affect the partnership's success. Similarly, in defining the elements of relational exchange, Barringer (1997) focused on trust and open communications. Thus, the behavior that is proposed to have an impact on strategic action is the degree to which firms exchange quality information. An important attitude that is proposed to affect strategic action is interorganizational trust.

Quality information exchange: As indicated, value-chain partnerships develop over time and are reinforced through repeated interaction (Larson, 1988 1992; Ring and Van de Ven, 1992, 1994; Gulati, 1993). Although many types of interactions or behaviors may affect partnership development, the development of extensive and frequently used communication channels is critical in the development of value-chain partnerships (Dwyer et al., 1987; Larson, 1988; Ring and Van de Ven, 1994). An important indicator that reflects the development of communication channels and the strength of the relationship is the exchange of quality information between a value-chain partner and a focal firm (Mohr and Spekman, 1994). The quality of information is determined by such factors as accuracy, timeliness, adequacy and credibility (Daft and Lengel, 1986).

The exchange of quality information can contribute to the strength of the relationship in two ways. First, the exchange of quality information creates confidence in the continuity of the relationship and reduces dysfunctional conflict (Anderson and Weitz, 1989; Anderson and Narus, 1990). Second, the exchange of quality information is often cited as an antecedent of trust where trust reflects the strength of the relationship between firms. In studies of the development of interorganizational relations, well-developed channels of communication lay the foundation for the development of trust in value-chain partnerships (Anderson et al., 1988).

The procedural justice literature also supports the idea that communication quality leads to trust. Sapienza and Korsgaard (1996), for example, found that frequent and timely feedback increases trust between entrepreneurs and venture capital investors. Folger and Konovsky (1989) found that timely feedback in employee performance evaluations increases trust.

Research on groups provides a final basis of support for the positive relationship between the exchange of quality information and the strength of the relationship. Group research suggests that effective communication is related to social integration which reflects strong relationships between group members (cf. Smith et al., 1994). Thus, either directly through the exchange of quality information or indirectly via the development of trust, exchange quality suggests that a strong relationship exists between the value-chain partners.

Interorganizational trust.   As previously discussed, authors have different labels for the stages of partnership development but the processes of increasing interaction and interdependence are similar. Another aspect in common among different models is the behavioral attitudes that develop as a result of this process. For example, frequently mentioned relationship attitudes include loyalty, commitment, friendship, trust, and norms of reciprocity.

While some variance exists on which of these attitudes various authors recognize as developing in supplier relationships, virtually all authors agree that one attitude that develops as a result of repeated exchange is trust (cf. Lorenz, 1988; Larson, 1992; Ring and Van de Ven, 1994; Mariotti, 1996). Zucker (1986) refers to this as process-based trust. Although firms may not have trust at the beginning of a relationship and may initially rely on functional complements to trust such as contractual provisions that provide for monitoring, experience with a specific firm breeds trust (Barber, 1983). In relationships where strong form trust develops, trust may even become the source of a competitive advantage (Barney and Hansen, 1994). Consequently, trust reflects a strong relationship.

A problem with the use of the term trust is that, although it is used frequently, it is employed inconsistently. Much of this confusion may be attributed to the differences among disciplines in their approaches to trust. Zaheer et al. (1995) attempt to clarify this confusion by identifying three components of trust important in interorganizational relations. The three elements of trust include the "belief that an actor: 1) can be relied upon to fulfill obligations (reliability), 2) will behave in a predictable manner (predictability), and 3) will act and negotiate fairly when the possibility for opportunism exists (fairness)" (1995: 5, 6). In studying trust as it relates to interorganizational relations, trust can exist on two levels: (1) interorganizational trust, which describes the extent to which organizational members have a "collectively held trust orientation" (ibid.: 6) toward another firm; and (2) interpersonal trust, which encompasses trust between two individuals representing separate companies. In addition to the reliability, predictability, and fairness elements of interorganizational trust, interpersonal trust includes an emotional component that may result in a sense of betrayal if broken.

This research will look exclusively at interorganizational trust using the three components of reliability, predictability, and fairness (defined above). Several studies support this focus on interorganizational trust. For example, Zaheer et al. (1995) found that although interpersonal trust plays a role in relational exchange, interorganizational trust has a more profound effect on relations in a continuing relationship. Lorenz (1988) also found that interpersonal trust is possible but not necessary for interorganizational trust to develop. Thus, this study will focus on the effect of the level of interorganizational trust on strategic action.

Where partnerships are successful, firms likely want to preserve the relationship. Consequently, the exchange of quality information and a high level of trust may increase the likelihood of continuing a critical supplier relationship in periods of high growth. How important are noneconomic factors like high quality information exchange and a high level of trust? Does Hypothesis 1 imply that good working relationships are not important? No, but it does suggest that good working relationships are of a secondary concern to strategic factors such as costs, availability, and on-time delivery. Based on Larson's (1988) and Hendrick and Ellram's (1993) research, supplier relationships are continued or expanded not because of the strength of the working relationship but because partnerships are initially effective and were established with the future in mind.

Further, because these high-growth firms are by definition successful on some level, we would expect that the firms would be focused on continued success and profitability. Firms cannot expect to sustain profitability without carefully managing costs, such as costs of critical supplies. Thus, firms are not likely to continue relationships that are not effective in helping maintain costs regardless of the strength of their working relationship. Nevertheless, close working relationships do play an important, if secondary, role. Consequently, it is further proposed that a strong working relationship is a bonus that further strengthens the relationship between perceived effectiveness and the percentage purchased.

Hypothesis 2: The impact of effectiveness on the change in percentage purchased is moderated by the strength of the working relationship such that:

(a) when the quality of communication is high, the impact of effectiveness on the change in percentage purchased is stronger than when the quality of communication is low.

(b) when the level of interorganizational trust is high, the impact of effectiveness on the change in percentage purchased is stronger than when trust is low.

Methods

Sample

The sample consisted of small firms, high-growth firms in SIC 283. This included SICs 2833 (Medicinals and Botanicals), 2834 (Pharmaceutical Preparations), 2835 (Diagnostic Substances), and 2836 (Biological Products Except Diagnostics). Most of the firms in SIC 283 are pharmaceutical or pharmaceutical-related companies. Small is defined based on the SBA definition for these industries of less than 500 employees. This definition is also consistent with the definitions of small firms adopted in previous research (cf. Covin et al., 1990; Malekzedah and Nahavandi, 1985). High-growth firms are those companies where annual sales growth have averaged 15 percent or greater per year for a three-year period (Hambrick and Crozier, 1985; Dsouza, 1990).

The pharmaceutical industry was selected for two reasons. First, the industry was attractive because of the likelihood of firms in this industry to use partnerships. Recent editions of industry publications such as *Chemical and Engineering News* indicate that the use of partnering agreements between firms is on the rise throughout the chemical industry. The cost of raw materials for this industry has been increasing since mid-1994 and the use of partnerships to contain those costs and guarantee access to materials is helpful (Standard and Poor's *Industry Surveys*, 1995). Interviews with industry experts confirmed that partnering is a common practice in the chemical manufacturing industry in general and in the pharmaceutical industry specifically.

Second, the industry's above-average growth indicates that some high-growth firms exist. Based on the 1996 *U.S. Chemical Industry Statistical Handbook*, annual sales growth rates for SIC 283 averaged 10.6 percent from 1984 to 1994. For ten major drug companies, sales increases averaged 19 percent from 1994 to 1995. Although a few large firms are dominant players in the industry, a large number of small firms also compete. Both the sales growth figures and the existence of numerous small firms were confirmed by chemical industry experts, several of who were directly involved in the pharmaceutical industry.

Data collection

Potential respondents were identified through Dun and Bradsteet's (D&B) Dun's Market Identifiers database. Firms were selected based on three criteria: (1) the firm had to be in one of the four previously identified SICs; (2) sales growth must have averaged 15 percent or greater per year for the past three years; and (3) the company had to have less than 500 employees. D&B identified 211 US-based firms that had 500 or fewer 500 employees and fell into SIC 283. Through telephone calls to these 211 firms, 45 firms were screened out as potential respondents – mostly because the firm was a R&D facility only and had no sales. Consequently, 166 eligible firms were identified. The data for hypothesis testing were collected using surveys. Interviews on a small subset of these firms collected supplementary information. The survey format and measures will be discussed first.

Following survey procedures suggested by Dillman (1978), each of the 166 firms was contacted by telephone prior to mailing out the questionnaire. Either the purchasing manager or the manager in charge of operations was the targeted contact. In the screening call, the firm verified that it was a small manufacturing firm in SIC 2833, 2834, 2835, 2836 and that it had a relationship with a company as of 1994 that supplied a critical good essential to creating or assembling products that generate the firm's revenue and that this relationship could be characterized as continuing and having a long-term orientation. If the firm met these two criteria, it was asked to participate in the survey and given the opportunity to obtain a copy of the findings. It was stressed to the potential respondent that the company did not have to be doing business with the selected supplier now.

Although information on as many supply partnerships as possible would be interesting, each firm was asked about one relationship to limit the time and effort required to fill out surveys on the part of respondents as well as to facilitate analysis and interpretation of the data. In order to assess the reliability of the key informant's responses, both a primary and secondary respondent were sought (Phillips, 1981). The primary respondent was sent the full survey and the secondary respondent was sent an abbreviated version of that survey.

Assuming the primary respondent was suitable and agreed to participate, a cover letter explaining the nature of the study was sent out with the questionnaire. Further, respondents were assured confidentiality and the opportunity to obtain a copy of the results was reiterated. Approximately two to three weeks after the first mailing, respondents were sent a reminder postcard. Two to three weeks after the postcards were sent, respondents were again contacted by phone to ascertain their intention of responding. Three weeks after those calls, a final letter was sent to all potential respondents who indicated that they planned on returning the survey.

Based on the initial and follow-up mailings and calls, 91 firms responded to the survey for a response rate of 55 percent. Of these 91 firms, 78 firms responded that sales growth averaged 15 percent or higher for the last three years. This represents a 47 percent response rate from high growth firms. Secondary surveys were received from 54 firms (59 percent of responding firms). Of these, 46 firms (58 percent) had a secondary respondent.

Nonresponse bias was examined based on secondary data gathered for both responding and non-responding firms. Respondents did not differ significantly from nonrespondents on the following characteristics: year of incorporation, number of employees, aggregate sales levels, SIC, region within the USA, whether the company was public or private and whether the firm was a subsidiary.

For responding firms, the mean year of incorporation was 1980. These firms averaged $15,024,000 in sales and had on average 85 employees. Most of the responding firms (75 percent) were private and not subsidiaries of another firm (89 percent). The SIC most heavily represented was 2834 (52.7 percent), which was pharmaceutical preparations. All regions of the USA were represented in the sample but two areas of concentration were in the Pacific region (27.5 percent) and the Middle Atlantic region (26.4 percent).

The survey instrument

The survey instrument collected data on the relationship between sales growth in the percentage purchased and the effectiveness of the partnership in high-growth firms between 1994 and 1997. The survey incorporated previously validated measures as well as some developed expressly for this study. In order to increase the content validity of measures, pre-existing measures were used as much as possible. Specific measures are discussed in the next section.

Industry experts reviewed a preliminary draft of the questionnaire and had other members of their firms, usually in the purchasing department, pre-test the survey. The survey was subsequently revised to incorporate their suggestions and eliminate ambiguity in the instructions or in the questions. The review by senior managers of large chemical manufacturing firms provides further support of content and face validity. Two forms of the survey were developed, a five–page primary respondent questionnaire and a two–page secondary respondent version.

Measures

Sales growth.   Data were collected from the focal manufacturing firm, via self-report, on sales growth, the independent variable. Additionally, sales growth data were obtained from D&B. Data from both primary and secondary sources allowed an assessment of the convergence of the data (Venkatraman and Ramanujam, 1986). The self-report figures from 1993 to 1995 could be substantiated by the data provided by D&B, but the D&B sales figures did not incorporate 1996 performance. Further, because most the companies in the survey were small, privately held firms, other secondary data were not available. In cases like these, self-report data on 1996 financial performance are regarded as superior to other measures of performance such as subjective measures of satisfaction with performance or comparisons of firm performance with competitors (Chandler and Hanks, 1993).

Percentage purchased.   The dependent variable was the difference in the change in percentage purchased from this supplier from 1994 to 1997.

Effectiveness.   Based on Ellram and Cooper's (1990) study, supplier relationships have three broad categories of benefits to buyers/suppliers: economic, managerial, and strategic. Consequently, the survey collected information on the extent to which these three categories of benefits were realized by manufacturers. Focal firms were asked the extent to which they agree (strongly agree to strongly disagree) on a seven-point scale with the following statements: Because of our relationship with this supplier today, our firm has been able to: 1) transfer financial risk to the supplier, 2) lower production costs, 3) improve the quality of input materials, 4) routinize the supply function, 5) share development costs, 6) concentrate more on its core business, 7) reduce the number of supplier relationships to manage, 8) improve our manufacturing flexibility, 9) better meet deadlines and fulfill customer-service objectives, 10) achieve stability in pricing, 11) spend less time negotiating and renegotiating supplier contracts. The reliability analysis for effectiveness indicated that the reliability was enhanced when the first item in the scale, transfer financial risk, was eliminated from the scale. The coefficient alpha for the remaining 10 items was .83.

Information exchange quality.   This variable reflects the extent to which quality information is exchanged between the focal firm and the key supplier. The scale consisted of four items adapted from a scale developed by Mohr and Spekman (1994). Responses to the following questions were based on a four-item seven-point scale (strongly disagree to strongly agree): (1) this supplier typically provided us with any information we requested in a timely manner; (2) the information provided to us by this supplier was very accurate; (3) the level of communication between our firm and this supplier was adequate to effectively conduct business between our firms; and (4) this supplier usually provided us with complete information. The coefficient alpha for the quality of information exchanged scale was .88.

Interorganizational trust.   This variable evaluates the perceived degree of interorganizational trust between the focal firm and the critical supplier. Four items were adapted from a scale developed by Zaheer et al. (1995). Using a seven-point scale, respondents were asked the extent to which they agreed or disagreed (strongly agree to strongly disagree) with the following four statements: (1) this supplier was always evenhanded in its negotiations with us; (2) this supplier may have used opportunities that arose to profit at our expense (reverse scored); (3) based on our past experience, we could rely with complete confidence on this supplier to keep promises made to us; (4) this supplier was trustworthy. The interorganizational trust scale produced an alpha coefficient of .78.

Control variables

Industry differences.   The rate of change in an industry, the level of uncertainty, and the need for transaction-specific assets are just a few things that may affect strategic action. By focusing on one industry, the amount of variability can be controlled (McDougall and Robinson, 1990). Although this reduces the generalizability of the findings, this may increase the internal validity (Cook and Campbell, 1979).

Age of the firm.   The more established a firm, the more likely that the firm is subject to inertial pressures. Further, the older a firm is, the more likely that long-term, strong relationships exist, which may contribute to the tendency to continue or expand supplier relationships.

Sales.   Firms with high sales levels, as opposed to high sales growth rates, may be more likely to purchase more in periods of high growth because they just buy more in general and not because of a strong relationship with a supplier. Further, larger firms may be more likely to realize the benefits of a partnership than a smaller firm because they purchase a larger volume from a supplier.

Size of the supplier.   The decision to expand a relationship may be explained by the large size of the supplier. For example, large national companies like Westinghouse, Milliken, or Smith Kline Beecham, those suppliers may be more price competitive which explains why firms continue relationships. In the survey, respondents were asked: "What size company is the supplier about which you completed this survey relative to your company?" Responses were based on the following categories: 1 = "much larger," 2 = "larger," 3 = "about the same size," 4 = "a little smaller," 5 = "much smaller."

Secondary respondents

To evaluate the reliability of the primary respondent, multiple survey respondents were used for perceptual measures of the effectiveness of the supplier relationship and strategic action with regard to the actual amount purchased from the supplier in 1997 vs. 1994. The overall level of interrater agreement was assessed using within-group interrater reliability as proposed by James et al. (1984). Within-group interrater reliability is an appropriate estimate of the level of agreement between K judges on a single item or set of items that measure the same construct. The only criteria are that the items must have the same psychometric properties and the alternative responses must be based on an interval response scale. Since both of these requirements were met, an interrater reliability (IRR) estimate for each variable on which there were two or more responses was calculated.

As the secondary responses were gathered only to gauge the reliability of the primary respondent, secondary respondents were asked to respond to an abbreviated version of the questionnaire that contained a representative number of questions. The primary area where agreement was assessed was on the degree of supplier relationship effectiveness. Six of the ten items on the primary survey were included on the secondary survey. These items included: (1) lower production costs; (2) reduce the number of supplier relationships to manage; (3) improve our manufacturing flexibility; (4) better meet deadlines and fulfill customer-service objectives; (5) achieve stability in pricing; (6) spend less time negotiating and renegotiating supplier contracts. For the scale created with these items (alpha = .77), the IRR estimates ranged from .61 to 1.0. Again, the level of agreement was high, with 76 percent of the estimates at .90 or higher and the level of agreement in 89 percent of the firms at .80 or higher.

The second variable in which IRR was evaluated was in the respondent's estimate of the change in amount purchased from the supplier in 1997 compared with 1994. Although this variable was not used in testing the hypotheses (the *percentage* purchased from the supplier is used to test the hypotheses), agreement between raters on this variable is still an accurate reflection of whether the primary respondent is a reliable informant on this issue. Consequently, the fact that 89 percent of the responses were in perfect agreement (1.0) is a good indication the responses of the primary respondent represent the firm and not just the individual's opinion.

The interviews

This part of the study was designed to gather richer, anecdotal data on the motivations behind strategic action with the goal of evaluating the degree to which variance in the strategic action of high-growth firms is attributable to the strength of the relationship. In addition to providing anecdotes, the interview data were used to identify common themes in the relationships between firms and their critical suppliers. The data were not used to test hypotheses but were used only to better evaluate the results of the tests conducted with the survey data. The responses were organized on three dimensions: comments about the supplier referred to in the survey, comments about suppliers in general, and comments about potential suppliers.

Interviews were conducted with the primary informant of 12 focal firms. As the specific aim in the interviews was to develop a better understanding of how the relationship strength of relationships affected strategic action, firms were selected based on the strategic action pursued. Consequently, the interview sample consisted of four firms that expanded relationships with critical suppliers, four firms that continued relationships and four firms that decreased the percentage purchased or terminated relationships.

A second basis for firm selection was the sales growth rate. Six high-growth firms and six low-growth firms were selected. High growth was determined based on the sample criteria, firms with sales growth rates that averaged 15 percent or higher per year for the last three years. Lower-growth firms were those with average sales growth rates of 10 percent or less.

Results

Test of hypotheses

Both hypotheses were tested using regression analysis. The variables were entered in two steps. The control variables were entered first with the main effects entered in the second step. The zero-order correlation matrix and summary statistics for the variables in the hypotheses are presented in table 12.1.

Hypothesis 1 predicted that as the perceived effectiveness of the supplier relationship increased, the percentage purchased from a critical supplier will also increase. As indicated in table 12.2, the hypothesis is supported ($t = 2.192$, $p = .03$). The perceived effectiveness of the relationship is positively related to the percentage purchased from the key supplier.

Hypothesis 2 predicted that the relationship between the effectiveness of the supplier relationship and percentage purchased is moderated by the strength of the working relationship. That is, when the working relationship is stronger, the positive relationship between effectiveness and percentage purchased will be stronger. The strength of the relationship was measured and tested in terms of the quality of communication (Hypothesis 2a) and the level of interorganizational trust (Hypothesis 2b).

Table 12.1 Descriptive statistics and correlations

	Variables	Mean	s.d.	1	2	3	4	5
1.	Firm age	19.9	23.58					
2.	Supplier size	2.03	1.31.	.26^d				
3.	Sales	14079.59	21959.15	.15	.15			
4.	Effectiveness	4.44	1.0	.07	.05	.09		
5.	Change in % purchased	−5,43	31.04	.10	.15	.08	.26^b	
6.	Info exchange	5.88	1.07	.08	.05	−.15	.39^e	.16
7.	Trust	5.41	1.12	−.03	.09	−.20	.27^c	.09

$N = 91$; $^b p < .10$, $^c p < .05$, $^d p < .01$, $^e p < .001$

Table 12.2   Regression results for relationship between effectiveness and change in percentage purchased Hypothesis 1

Variables	B	SE	F	R^2	ΔR^2	F-test for ΔR^2
Firm age	8.00E	.15				
Sales	6.03E	.00				
Supplier size	2.79	2.66				
Constant	−13.60	6.59				
			0.69	.02		
Effectiveness	7.29	3.33				
Constant	−44.63	15.55				
			1.70	.08	.06	4.80[b]

[a] $p < .10$, [b] $p < .05$, [c] $p < .01$, [d] $p < .001$

Table 12.3   Moderated regression results for relationship between effectiveness and change in percentage purchased Hypothesis 2

Variables	B	SE	F	R^2	ΔR^2	F-test for ΔR^2
Firm age	8.00E	.15				
Sales	6.03E	.00				
Supplier size	2.79	2.66				
Constant	−13.60	6.59				
			0.69	.02		
Effectiveness	7.29	3.33				
Constant	−44.63	15.55				
			1.70	.08	.06	4.80[b]

[a] $p < .10$, [b] $p < .05$, [c] $p < .01$, [d] $p < .001$

As reflected in table 12.3, the overall model is supported ($F = 2.027, p = .05$). Looking at the individual hypothesis, Hypothesis 2a is supported ($t = 2.501, p = .015$) but Hypothesis 2b is not supported.

Conclusion

The rate of change and the speed with which business is conducted in the new entrepreneurial millennium have created critical strategic questions and challenges for the rapidly growing, entrepreneurial venture. This reality of a new era is causing traditional strategies to be re-examined and redesigned. One key strategic area for both large global companies and their small, high-growth customer or supplier firms is the supplier–buyer relationship. This strategic arena in the new, entrepreneurial global economy provided the central thesis of this chapter, that the perceived effectiveness of high-growth firms' relationship with their key supplier(s) is positively related to the emphasis on and expansion of that relationship during periods of high growth. Thus, a high-growth venture will buy more from a critical supplier with whom it has an effective relationship. For the purposes of this chapter, an effective relationship means that because of this supplier relationship, the focal firm can realize economic, managerial, and strategic benefits. For example, the focal firm can better manage costs, focus on core business issues, and meet customer deadlines.

The chapter also maintained and supported that even though these strategic factors may drive the purchasing decision, the nature and quality of the working relationship between the two firms also affect decision-making. The frequency and quality of information exchanged moderate the relationship between supplier effectiveness and the amount purchased such that when the quality of information is higher, the relationship between effectiveness and percentage purchased is stronger. Thus, strategic factors are the key consideration is purchasing decisions but a good working relationship plays an important secondary role.

The interview data strongly supported the survey data. Interviews with 12 firms – six high-growth organizations (sales averaged an increase of at least 15 percent for the last three years) and six lower-growth companies (sales averaged less than 15 percent a year for the last three years) – found that all 12 firms indicated that the strength of the relationship is an important but secondary component of the purchasing decision. The most common factors these companies cited as influencing purchasing decisions were price, quality, availability, and customer service. Six firms ranked price as the most important and six ranked quality as the key consideration. Whichever factors were ranked most important repeatedly dominated decisions regarding future purchasing patterns from a supplier. For example, one small company's most important purchasing factor was quality, and although they had several other rather serious problems with a supplier (the supplier was not meeting delivery deadlines), the company stayed with the supplier because the supplier represented the best alternative in terms of product quality. The firm has tried competing products but has not been as satisfied with the quality level. For this firm, the lack of a good working relationship was not reason enough for the firm to decrease or terminate business with a supplier. It is also interesting to note that this particular company had averaged sales growth increases of 20 percent per year for the last three years. Consequently, even if the delivery delays had caused some headaches for this firm, it does not appear to have decreased its customer base.

The consensus among all 12 firms interviewed was that once the top effectiveness criteria were met, then the strength of the relationship came into the decision process. That is, when alternative suppliers are equal on the key criteria, the strength of the relationship became the deciding factor of whether to expand the supplier relationship. One firm reported a big percentage increase in the amount purchased from a supplier (from 5 to 50 percent) because a sales representative with whom the purchasing manager had a good relationship transferred from a competing company to that supplier. Because the supplier to which the sales representative switched offered competitive prices (price was the top criterion), the strength of the relationship with that sales rep encouraged the company to increase its business with that supplier.

Two companies reported percentage decreases based on the lack of a strong relationship. In one situation, a company had two suppliers that were competitive with each other on quality and price. The company chose the supplier with which it had the stronger working relationship. Not only did the company reduce the amount it purchased from the other supplier (from 90 to 70 percent) but it also elected not to expand its business with that supplier in new areas when it could have. Because the company preferred the working relationship it had with a competing supplier, it elected to transfer and expand business with the new supplier.

Another point that emerged in the interviews is that the lack of a good working relationship can exaggerate a supplier's weakness in other areas and encourage the firm to reduce relations with a supplier. For example, one firm in the study had been with a supplier for about four years and the supplier had always been close to the prices and quality offered by competitors. Over time a poor working relationship developed primarily because the supplier did not respond to customer service requests and only contacted the firm twice a year. Consequently, the focal firm found another supplier that was only slightly better on price but displayed a willingness to work closely with the firm. Subsequently, the firm decreased the percentage purchased from the original supplier from 90 to 20 percent. So the absence of a good working relationship led this firm to scrutinize a supplier's weakness, leading in turn to a change to a new supplier for most purchases.

Overall, this study suggests a new way of looking at growth companies' partnerships in the new, entrepreneurial millennium that is a contingency theory. A strong relationship between a focal firm and a supply partner is important, but it is likely to explain the continuation or expansion of business between firms only when the firm's top purchasing criteria like price, quality, or availability have been satisfied. Once a supplier is competitive on the factors critical to a focal firm, a strong relationship can lead the focal firm to expand its business with the supplier. Similarly, a weak relationship alone is not sufficient cause for a firm to limit business with or terminate a supplier. A weak relationship may become a deciding factor if a supplier fails to be competitive on a factor of primary importance to the firm *or* a competing supplier can meet the primary factors and also offer a better working relationship *or* if sales performance is poor. Thus, both theoretical perspectives received support in this research. The results clearly support the economic perspective for explaining supplier relationships in high-growth firms. When high-growth firms perceived a supplier to be effective, they significantly expand their exchange (purchasing) from that supplier demonstrating that the supplier is an integral part of their high-growth strategy.

The social exchange approach also received support, albeit mixed. When the quality of communication is high – you understand what we need, take instructions well, etc. – high-growth firms will stick with a supplier but only if the perceived effectiveness of the relationship is also high. Trusting a supplier, on the other hand, does not seem to be enough to expand a relationship. A high-growth firm's choice to expand connections with an existing supplier appear to be driven much more by the quality of the communication – the ability to coordinate and integrate – than it is by simply trusting the supplier.

From a practical perspective, three important implications emerge. First, consistent with the management literature and futurist views (Naisbett, 1994) addressing the management of buyer–supplier relationships in the twenty-first century, the results of this study suggest that partnerships have significant benefits for high-growth firms. Some of these benefits include achieving stability in pricing, improving manufacturing flexibility, allowing the focal firm to better meet customer service objectives, and reducing the number of supplier relationships to manage. Further, the survey results indicate that these benefits increase as the percentage purchased increases. That is, the greater percentage a firm purchased from a supplier, the more effective the firm perceived the relationship.

This finding implies a second point of practical relevance: firms are establishing fewer, higher quality relationships with suppliers. If a company perceives a higher level of benefits from a supplier as the percentage purchased from that supplier increases, firms will seek to expand that relationship. As a company expands a relationship with one supplier, the percentage they purchase from another supplier of the same good will decrease. Following this pattern, the total number of suppliers with which the firm ultimately deals is reduced. While the survey did not directly address this issue, the survey results suggested it and the interviews sought to confirm the implication. The 12 firms interviewed unanimously stated a preference for establishing relationships with fewer long-term suppliers. Further, the companies in the sample provide some support for this. The proportion of sole source relationships increased from 18 percent to 23 percent in the three-year period covered in the survey. A key strategy in the entrepreneurial millennium is to identify, enact, and remain tied to fewer, quality supplier relationships or strategic alliances.

Third, strong relationships do matter. A supplier must be able to be competitive on other factors but a strong relationship may make the difference between a firm's increasing business with a supplier and switching to another supplier that offers a more compatible working relationship. Further, in light of the fact that interviewees uniformly reported that the trend in vendor relationship management is toward fewer long-term relationships, failure to establish a strong relationship when given the opportunity may preclude a supplier from securing a stable customer.

Two primary limitations of this research can be identified. First, the study of partnerships over a three-year period is a longitudinal study. For the purposes of this chapter, however, it was conducted in a cross-sectional manner. Respondents were asked to answer one set of questions about the strength of the relationships as of 1994. While recall can be a problem, two respondents were sought when the questions required information about perceptions from three years ago. The high level of correlations between the two respondents gives some reassurance of the reliability of the primary respondent.

A second limitation is that the survey asked only about a firm's relationship with one of its critical suppliers. Firms may have picked the best or the most unusual relationship about which to answer questions thereby obscuring the overall nature of relationships between focal firms and partner firms. The fact that so few firms reported about terminated relationships created some concern. The interviews helped to ascertain whether the survey results were skewed in such a fashion. Generally, they provided strong support that the survey responses were representative of the set of suppliers. Nevertheless, what was true for 12 firms may not represent all 91 firms in the sample.

Several promising directions for future research exist. First, the extent to which these findings apply to high-growth firms in other industries is a threshold question. Does the secondary nature of close working relationships hold in other industries? A second area of inquiry to explore would be to confirm the insights offered by the interviewees. Are the responses of 12 firms indicative of the pharmaceutical industry? Is the trend toward fewer, longer-term relationships present throughout the industry? Is the strength of the relationship a "swing vote" for other firms in the industry as well? This inquiry could be expanded to other industries as well. A more rigorous qualitative study or a larger survey study would shed some light on their representativeness.

A longitudinal study of supply partnerships represents a third avenue that would further develop this area of research. Because the data are cross-sectional, causal relationships cannot be inferred. Further, gathering data in year 1 on the strength of the relationship in year 1 would eliminate the need to rely on recollections. The dynamics of partnerships and how they change over time would be also interesting. For example, to what extent does a strong relationship in year 1 predict a strong relationship in year 3? What causes that strength to change? How does the shift in personnel impact the strength of the relationship, i.e., do firms have relationships or do individuals? Altering the measurement of strategic action may be a fourth fruitful area of inquiry. In this study strategic action was measured as the change in the proportion of a good purchased from a particular supplier. While this measure accurately gauges the purchases from a particular supplier as opposed to others, it does not tell whether the purchases from that supplier increased or decreased. For example, a focal firm may report that it purchased 100 percent of a particular item from a supplier in 1994 and 100 percent from that supplier in 1997. The difference between these percentages is zero which leads to the conclusion that the relationship has been stable. However, because these are high-growth firms, 100 percent in 1997 may be a much greater quantity in 1997 compared to 1994. So instead of merely continuing, the relationship has actually expanded. A gauge of the extent to which a change in this measure would affect the relationship between the strength of the relationship and strategic action and the relationship between strategic action and performance-related outcomes may be worth pursuing.

Another suggested direction for future research is to gather data from a more diverse sample. Of the 91 firms included in the study, 86 percent averaged sales growth increases of 15 percent or more and 96 percent averaged sales growth increases of 10 percent or more for the last three years. If data could be collected from a greater number of firms at the other end of the growth spectrum, insight into whether these factors vary in the decision-making process of higher vs. lower-growth firms would be given.

A final area of inquiry may be to investigate the extent to which strategy changes play a role in purchasing decisions. Perhaps actions regarding a supplier may be explained by whether the focal firm has experienced a change in strategy which affects the items provided by the supplier. For example, using Porter's (1980) framework, a firm may change from a low cost to differentiation strategy. In conjunction with this change in strategy, the quality and the price of the items required from the supplier may change. To the extent that the current supplier cannot provide these items, the focal firm will have to establish new supply relationships. Thus, the current supplier may be terminated or experience a decline in business because of changes in strategy and not due to the effectiveness or the strength of the relationship. By the same token, relationships may be expanded because the high-growth focal firm decides to expand into other market segments and the supplier can meet their increased demand in a speedy, high-quality manner that allows the high-growth focal firm to enhance its competitive advantage in a rapidly changing, challenging entrepreneurial millennium.

References

Ahuja, G. 2000: The duality of collaboration: inducements and opportunities in the formation of interfirm linkages. *Strategic Management Journal,* 21, 317–43.

Aldrich, H. E. and Auster, E. 1986: Even dwarfs started small: Liabilities of age and size and their strategic implications. In B. M. Staw, and L. L. Cummings (eds), *Research in Organizational Behavior,* 8, 165–98.

Aldrich, H. and Zimmer, C. 1986: Entrepreneurship through social networks. In D. L. Sexton, and R. W. Smilor (eds), *The Art and Science of Entrepreneurship.* Cambridge, MA: Ballinger Publishing Company, 3–23.

Anderson, E., Lodish, L., and Weitz, B. 1987: Resource allocation behavior in conventional channels. *Journal of Marketing Research,* 24, 85–97.

Anderson, E. and Weitz, B. 1989: Determinants of continuity in conventional industrial channel dyads. *Marketing Science,* 8, (Fall): 310–323.

Anderson, J. C. and Narus, J. A. 1990: A model of distributor firm and manufacturer firm working partnerships. *Journal of Marketing,* 54, 42–58.

Barber, B. 1983: *The Logic and Limits of Trust.* New Brunswick, NJ: Rutgers University Press.

Barney, J. 1991: Firm resources and sustained competitive advantage. *Journal of Management,* 17, 99–120.

Barney, J. B. 1995: Looking inside for competitive advantage. *Academy of Management Executive,* 9: 48–61.

Barney, J. B. and Hansen, M. H. 1994: Trustworthiness as a source of competitive advantage. *Strategic Management Journal,* 15: 175–90.

Barringer, B. R. 1997: The effects of relational channel exchange of the small firm: a conceptual framework. *Journal of Small Business Management,* 35, 65–79.

Baum, J. A. C., Calabrese, T., and Silverman, B. S. 2000: Don't go it alone: `lliance network composition and startup's performance in Canadian biotechnology. *Strategic Management Journal,* 21, 267–94.

Beekman, A. V. and Robinson, R. B. 1999: Supplier partnerships and the high-growth firm: Selecting for success. Paper presented at the 59th Annual Meeting of the Academy of Management, Chicago, IL, August.

Ben-Porath, Y. 1980: The f-connection: families, friends, and firms and the organization of exchange. *Population and Development Review,* 6, 1–30.

Blau, P. 1964: *Exchange and Power in Social Life.* New York: Wiley.

Bourgeois, L. J. and Eisenhardt, K. M. 1988: Strategic decision process and high velocity environments: four cases in the microcomputer industry. *Management Science,* 34, 816–35.

Carland, J. W., Hoy, F. and Carland, J. C. 1988: "Who is an entrepreneur?" is a question worth asking. *American Journal of Small Business,* Spring, 33–9.

Chandler, G. N., and Hanks, S. H. 1993: Measuring the performance of emerging businesses: a validation study. *Journal of Business Venturing,* 8, 391–408.

Chiles, T. H., and McMakin, J. F. 1996: Integrating variable risk preferences, trust and transaction cost economics. *Academy of Management Review,* 21, 73–99.

Chung, S., Singh, H., and Lee, K. 2000: Complementarity, status similarity and social capital as drivers of alliance formation. *Strategic Management Journal,* 21, 1–22.

Coleman, J. S. 1988: Social capital in the creation of human capital. *American Journal of Sociology,* 94, S95–S120.

Cook, T. C. and Campbell, D. T. 1979: *Quasi-Experimentation: Design and Analysis Issues for Field Settings.* Chicago: Rand-McNally.

Cooper, A. C., Willard, G. E., and Woo, C. Y. 1986: Strategies for high-performing new and small firms: a re-examination of the niche concept. *Journal of Business Venturing,* 1. 247–60.

Covin, J. G., Slevin, D. P., and Covin, T. J. 1990: The content and performance of growth-seeking strategies: A comparison of small firms in high- and low-technology industries. *Journal of Business Venturing,* 5, 391–412.

Dacin, M. T., Ventresca, M. J., and Beal, B. D. 1999: The embeddedness of organizations: dialogue and directions. *Journal of Management,* 25, 317–56.

Daft, R. and Lengel, R. 1986: Organizational information requirements, media richness, and structural design. *Management Science,* 32. 554–71.

Dillman, D. A. 1978: *Mail and Telephone Surveys: The Total Design Method.* New York: Wiley.

Dsouza, D. 1990: Strategy types and environmental correlates of strategy for high-growth firms: an exploratory study. Unpublished doctoral dissertation, Georgia State University.

Dwyer, F. R., Schurr, P. H., and Oh, S. 1987: Developing buyer-seller relationships. *Journal of Marketing,* 51, 11–27.

Dyer, J. H. and Singh, H. 1998: The relational view: Cooperative strategy and sources of interorganizational competitive advantage. *Academy of Management Review,* 23, 660–79.

Ellram, L. M. and Cooper, M. C. 1990: The supplier selection decision in strategic partnerships. *Journal of Purchasing and Materials Management,* 26, 8–14.

Folger, R. and Konovsky, M. K. 1989: Effects of procedural and distributive justice on reactions to pay raise decisions. *Academy of Management Journal,* 32, 115–30.

Gouldner, A. W. 1960: The norm of reciprocity. *American Sociological Review,* 25, 161–79.

Granovetter, M. S. 1973: The strength of weak ties. *American Journal of Sociology,* 78,1360 – 80.

Granovetter, M. S. 1985: Economic Action and social structure: The problem of embeddedness. *American Journal of Sociology,* 91, 481–510.

Granovetter, M. 1992: Economic institutions as social constructions: A framework for analysis. *Acta Sociologica,* 35, 3–11.

Grant, R. M., and Baden-Fuller, C. 1995: A knowledge-based theory of inter-firm collaboration. *Academy of Management Best Paper Proceedings,* 17–21.

Gulati, R. 1993: The dynamics of alliance formation. Unpublished doctoral dissertation, Harvard University.

Gulati, R. 1995: Social structure and alliance formation: A longitudinal analysis. *Administrative Science Quarterly,* 40, 619–52.

Gulati, R. 1998: Alliances and networks. *Strategic Management Journal,* Special Issues, 19, 293–317.

Gulati, R. 1999: Network location and learning: the influence of network resources and firm capabilities on alliance formation. *Strategic Management Journal,* 20, 397–420.

Hambrick, D. C. and Crozier, L. M. 1985: Stumblers and stars in the management of rapid growth. *Journal of Business Venturing,* 1: 31–45.

Hamel, G. 1991: Competition for competence and inter-partner learning within international strategic alliances. *Strategic Management Journal,* 12, 83–103.

Harrigan, K. R. 1988: Strategic alliances and partner asymmetries. In F. J. Contractor and P. Lorange (eds), *Cooperative Strategies in International Business:.* Lexington, MA: Lexington

Books, 205–26.

Heide, J. B. and Miner, A. S. 1992: The shadow of the future: effects of anticipated interaction and frequency of contact on buyer-seller cooperation. *Academy of Management Journal*, 35, 256–91.

Hendrick, T. E. and Ellram. L. M. 1993: *Strategic Supplier Partnering: An International Study*. Tempe, Arizona: Center for Advanced Purchasing Studies.

Hill, C. W. L. 1990: Cooperation, opportunism, and the invisible hand: implications for transaction cost theory. *Academy of Management Review*, 15, 500–13.

Hitt, M. A., Dacin, M. T., Levitas, E., Arregle, J., and Borza, A. 2000: Partner selection in emerging and developed market contexts: Resource-based and organizational learning perspectives. *Academy of Management Journal*, 43, 449–67.

Homans, G. C. 1950: *The Human Group*. New York: Harcourt, Brace and World.

Homans, G. C. 1974: *Social behavior: Its Elementary Forms*. New York: Harcourt, Brace, and World.

Hudson, R. L. and McArthur, A. W. 1994: Contracting strategies in entrepreneurial and established firms. *Entrepreneurship Theory and Practice*, Spring, 43–59.

James, L. R., Demaree, R. G., and Wolf, G. 1984: Estimating within-group interrater reliability with and without response bias. *Journal of Applied Psychology*, 69, 85–98.

Jarillo, J. C. 1989: Entrepreneurship and growth: the strategic use of external resources. *Journal of Business Venturing*, 4, 133–47.

Kanter, R. M. 1994: Collaborative advantage: the art of alliances. *Harvard Business Review*, July-August: 96–108.

Kirchhoff, B. A. and Phillips, B. D. 1987: Examining entrepreneurship's role in economic growth. In N. Churchill, J. Hornaday, B. Kirchhoff, and K. Vessper (eds) *Frontiers of Entrepreneurship Research:*. Wellesley, MA: Babson College, 57–71.

Krackhardt, D. 1992: The strength of strong ties: the importance of philos in organizations. In N. Nohria, and R. G. Eccles (eds), *Networks and Organizations:*. Boston, MA: Harvard Business School Press, 216–39.

Lane, P. J. and Lubatkin, M. 1998: Relative absorptive capacity and interorganizational learning. *Strategic Management Journal*, 19, 461–77.

Larson, A. 1988: Cooperative alliances: A study of entrepreneurship. Unpublished doctoral dissertation, Harvard University.

Larson, A. 1992: Network dyads in entrepreneurial settings: a study of the governance of exchange relationships. *Administrative Science Quarterly*, 37, 76–104.

Lorenz, E. H. 1988: Neither friends nor strangers: informal networks of subcontracting in french industry. In D. Gambetta (ed.), *Trust: Making and Breaking Cooperative Relations*. New York: Basil Blackwell, Inc., 194–210.

Macneil, I. R. 1978: Contracts: adjustments of long-term economic relations under classical, neoclassical, and relational contract law. *Northwestern University Law Review*, 72, 854–906.

Macneil, I. R. 1980: *The New Social Contract*. New Haven, CT: Yale University Press.

Malekzedah, A. R. and Nahavandi, A. 1985: Small business exporting: misconceptions are abundant. *American Journal of Small Business*, 9, 7–14.

Mariotti, J. L. 1996: *The Power of Partnerships*. Cambridge, MA: Blackwell Publishers.

McDougall, P. and Robinson, R. 1990: New venture strategies: An empirical identification of eight "archetypes" of competitive strategies for entry. *Strategic Management Journal*, 11, 447–567.

Mohr, J. and Spekman, R. 1994: Characteristics of partnership success: partnership attributes, communication behavior, and conflict resolution techniques. *Strategic Management Journal*, 15, 135–52.

Naisbett, J. 1994: *Global Paradox*. New York: Morrow.

Nielsen, R. P. 1988: Cooperative strategy. *Strategic Management Journal*, 9, 475–92.

Nohria, N. and Garcia-Pont, C. 1991: Global strategic linkages and industry structure. *Strategic Management Journal*, Summer Special Issue, 12, 105–24.

Phillips, L. W. 1981: Assessing measurement error in key informant reports: a methodological note on organizational analysis in marketing. *Journal of Marketing Research*, 18. 395–415.

Porter, M. E. 1980: *Competitive Strategy*. New York: The Free Press.

Provan, K. G. 1993: Embeddedness, interdependence, and opportunism in organizational supplier-buyer networks. *Journal of Management*, 19, 841–56.

Ring, P. S. and Van de Ven, A. H. 1992: Structuring cooperative relationships between organizations. *Strategic Management Journal*, 13, 483–98.

Ring, P. S. and Van de Ven, A. H. 1994: Developmental processes of cooperative interorganizational relationships. *Academy of Management Review*, 19, 90–118.

Sapienza, H. J. and Korsgaard, M. A. 1996: The role of procedural justice in entrepreneur-investor relations. *Academy of Management Journal*, 39, 544–74.

Shuman, J. C. and Seegar, J. A. 1986: The theory and practice of strategic management in smaller rapid growth firms. *American Journal of Small Business*, 3, 7–18.

Shuman, J. C., Shaw, J. J., and Sussman, G. 1985: Strategic planning in smaller rapid growth companies. *Long Range Planning*, 18, 48–53.

Smith, K. G., Carroll, S. J., and Ashford, S. J. 1995: Intra- and interorganizational cooperation: Toward a research agenda. *Academy of Management Journal*, 38, 7–23.

Smith, K. G., Smith, K. A., Olian, J. D., Sims, H. P., O'Bannon, D. P., and Scully, J. A. 1994: Top management team demography and process: the role of social integration and communication. *Administrative Science Quarterly*, 39, 412–38.

Standard and Poor's Corporation 1995: *Industry Surveys*. T. Nugent (ed.). Standard and Poor's Corporation: New York; C9–C66.

Stevenson, H. H. and Jarillo, C. 1990: A paradigm of entrepreneurship: Entrepreneurial management. *Strategic Management Journal*, 11: 17–27.

Stuart, T. E. 2000: Interorganizational alliances and the performance of firms: a study of growth and innovation rates in a high-technology industry. *Strategic Management Journal*, 21, 791–811.

Venkatraman, N. and Ramanujam, V. 1986: Measurement of business performance in strategy research: a comparison of approaches. *Academy of Management Review*, 11, 801–14.

Williamson, O. E. 1975: *Markets and Hierarchies: Analysis and Antitrust Implications*. New York: Free Press.

Williamson, O. E. 1985: *The Economic Institutions of Capitalism*. New York: Free Press.

Williamson, O. E. 1993: Calculativeness, trust, and economic organization. *Journal of Law and Economics*, 36, 453–86.

Zaheer, A., McEvily, B., and Perrone, V. 1995: Does trust matter? Exploring the effects of interorganizational and interpersonal trust on performance. Paper presented at the Annual Meeting of the Academy of Management, Dallas, TX, August.

Zucker, L. G. 1986: Production of trust: institutional sources of economic structure, 1840–1920. In B. M. Staw and L. L. Cummings (eds), *Research in Organizational Behavior*, 8, 53–111. Greenwich, CT: JAI Press.

Index